POWERFUL
PEOPLE

ALSO BY ROY ROWAN

The Intuitive Manager
The Four Days of Mayaguez
Co-editor of *A Day in the Life of Italy*

From Mao to now, a reporter's
fifty-year pursuit of

POWERFUL PEOPLE

Roy Rowan

Carroll & Graf Publishers, Inc.
New York

First edition 1996.

Carroll & Graf Publishers, Inc.
260 Fifth Avenue
New York, NY 10001

ISBN 0-7867-0312-1

Library of Congress Cataloging-in-Publication Data is available.

Manufactured in the United States of America.

For the Next Wave
Dana, Janice, Doug, Nick, and Marc

Contents

Introduction

THIS IS NOT A MEMOIR but an adventure story spanning fifty years of reporting on powerful people. Some of them left a permanent mark on the world and are vividly remembered. Others faded swiftly into obscurity despite the bright swath they briefly cut. Some sought fame and flaunted their power. Others preferred privacy and kept their power hidden. The only thing they all had in common was their ability to make important things happen—which is a pretty good definition of power.

As a correspondent, writer, and editor covering the United States, Europe, and Asia since 1946, my job was observing soldiers, politicians, artists, writers, athletes, scientists, business executives, labor leaders—even mobsters—who conquered their own worlds. *Job* conveys the wrong impression because pursuing those individuals to understand their victories and defeats was more than just an occupation for me. It became a quest.

All during this journalistic journey I kept looking for characteristics that separate the power-elite from everyone else. Rank, money, social status, fame, and the other trappings of power are often misleading. Is there some ingredient, I wanted to know, some chemistry that imbues an occasional man or woman with the strength to sway or even subjugate the rest of us? Does some mystical inner force enable certain leaders to turn events to their personal advantage? Or is it simply cunning or charisma? For a select few, roadblocks become shortcuts. Setbacks leapfrog them ahead. Even wars, depressions, and natural disasters can boost their careers.

My cast of characters begins with Mao Zedong and Chiang Kai-shek during their war for the control of China—a fight in which I was deeply immersed and believe changed our world more than any event of the past fifty years—and ends with Ross Perot, the blunt-speaking billionaire who emerged as a surprising force in American politics. Populating the pages between them are, among others, General Douglas MacArthur, Marshal Tito, Jimmy Hoffa, Henry Luce, Imelda Marcos, and the Hunt brothers, those two wealth-bloated, whippersnapper boys from Texas who tried to corner the world silver market.

Their selection was not made randomly. They were picked because of the interesting way each acquired and exercised power. Some had a clear vision, a strong sense of purpose, and an ability to motivate others—a rare combination of traits that gave them an inescapable aura. Then there were those who inherited or were accidentally thrust into a powerful position, unprepared to cope with the challenges it presented. Some tried to soft-pedal their own power, or use it instead to strengthen the standing of an ally or further a cause they passionately believed in. Others wielded theirs selfishly and ruthlessly. A few just frittered their power away in fruitless endeavors.

Getting close to these people was often difficult, sometimes even dangerous. But reporting and writing, first for *Life*, then *Time*, and finally *Fortune*—publications of immense power and influence themselves—gave me access I wouldn't otherwise have enjoyed. On occasion I was courted, purposely welcomed into the inner circle in the hope that my magazines might bolster a career or promote an idea. It's easy to fall for such flattery, or misconstrue it as a sign of one's own power. Maybe that's why many Americans speak angrily about the "arrogance of the press."

However they acted, the individuals included in this book produced widely varied results. Some are now revered for creating objects of beauty or establishing institutions. Others are still hated for wreaking havoc—which raises another question. To gain control, is it better to be loved or feared? "We should wish to be both," though the latter is "safer," proclaimed Niccolò Machiavelli in *The Prince*, his sixteenth-century primer on power. Is that still true? In today's permissive society, isn't clemency more effective than cruelty in keeping control?

The answers to these questions depend on the nature of those in power. Thomas Carlyle, the celebrated nineteenth-century English author, advocated strong governments run by powerful leaders. "The history of the world," he wrote, "is the biography of great men." But no attempt has been made here to present the main characters in a series of minibiographies. The book covers only one or two climactic events in each of their lives—defining moments that help to explain their capability. No claim is made, either, that those chronicled were *the* most powerful people in their field. Only that they were the ones I observed in action, and in many cases came to know personally.

While this is not a memoir, neither is it an analytical study of the elements and uses of power. It is a collection of narrative tales, related in roughly chronological order, about some of the people who have made a historic difference in the final fifty years of this millennium. I have tried to let them tell you by their own words and deeds what spurred them into action, kept them reaching ever higher, or, faced with calamity, forced them to retreat.

Because their lives still have currency, their stories raise a basic question relevant to us all. In today's world with so much emphasis on human values, how are we to view the pursuit of power? This book may help you decide.

"The desire of power in excess caused the angels to fall."
　　　　—Francis Bacon
　　　　1561–1626

"They who are in the highest places, and have the most power, have the least liberty, because they are most observed."
　　　　—John Tillotson
　　　　1630–1694

"The only prize much cared for by the powerful is power."
　　　　—Oliver Wendell Holmes, Jr.
　　　　1841–1935

"When power corrupts, poetry cleanses."
　　　　—John Fitzgerald Kennedy
　　　　1917–1963

"Power is the great aphrodisiac." *arousing sexual desire*
　　　　—Henry Alfred Kissinger
　　　　1923–

POWERFUL
PEOPLE

CHAPTER I

The Last Convoy

FOR THE FIRST FEW MONTHS I had driven cautiously, easing my jeep gingerly in and out of craters and over humps. Patience and care gradually gave way to masochism. Now I stomped the accelerator, holding tight to the steering wheel as the jeep smashed into holes or took off into the air. The windshield might crack, the springs might snap, and the radiator needed resoldering after every trip. Still, the engine kept whining angrily while I sucked in mouthfuls of red dust and cursed every jolt. Lurking in the back of my mind was the hope that with the next solid whack my battered jeep might finally lay down and die. Then I could walk, as was intended, on these ancient roads in China.

Following my jeep, a convoy of thirty-two surplus World War II army trucks banged along at a fifteen-mile-an-hour clip on a routine trip from Xuchang to Xihua. The year was 1947 and the run was considered routine only because a relief convoy like this one, laden with sacks of American flour, rice, or bales of old clothing, made this run every day through the middle of China's civil war.

From my viewpoint, no convoy starting out in Nationalist territory and threading its way across a bleak no-man's-land into Communist territory could be classified as routine. The trucks were painted with yellow and black tiger stripes to keep them from being shot at. But the clean bullet hole in the corner of my jeep's windshield was a constant reminder that a mere paint job offered little protection. Not that the Chinese drivers of the trucks trailing behind needed any re-

1

minding. They had a way of simply melting into the countryside at the first sound of gunfire, leaving the convoy stalled.

We were about thirty *li*, or twelve miles, past Xuchang in Henan Province. The road turned sharply and a gust of wind sent the red dust swirling over the wide barren fields. These roads were never intended for motor vehicles. Worn into existence by a 2000-year procession of oxcarts, mule carts, and wheelbarrows, the highway consisted of a deep groove ground into the loess of China's sprawling central plain. A six-inch blanket of silky dust covered the road's surface.

Over this route, UNRRA, as the United Nations Relief and Rehabilitation Administration was called, was attempting to run a fleet of 400 heavy-duty trucks. My job as operations chief was to see that the relief convoys made it to their rightful destinations without being looted by either Mao Zedong's or Chiang Kai-shek's soldiers. Sometimes it was hard to tell whose army the soldiers belonged to. This front just south of the Yellow River was so fluid, the little mud-walled towns often changed hands every week or two.

Further complicating my job was an UNRRA edict from Washington stipulating that seventy percent of all relief supplies shipped to China were to be distributed in Nationalist territory and thirty percent in Communist areas. Fair enough in theory, but in practice it was impossible to divvy up the food, clothing, fertilizer, farm tools, and other supplies that precisely. Just as it was impossible to jeep across this rough terrain without painfully jouncing your innards.

Xuchang to Xihua is sixty-three miles. With luck, our convoy would make it one way in six hours. Without luck it might take several days. If the convoy got bogged down by the war or weather, the trucks would pull in behind the protective mud walls of a town. But the small population centers of Henan had no hotels or even government guest houses, so the drivers would head for the local whorehouse—not for sex, just to sleep. Squatting on the dirt floor, they'd while away the evening sipping green tea, chewing watermelon seeds, and chatting with the girls before rolling up in the blankets they brought with them.

If there was a Jesuit mission in town, I would usually stay there, both for sanitary and social reasons. The fathers and brothers were always grateful for a Western visitor, and I returned their hospitality by dropping off magazines. If there was no mission, then I, too, would be stuck with the whores, though their nightlong nattering and spitting of watermelon seeds made it hard to sleep.

Leaving Xuchang an hour earlier, we had encountered long files of Nationalist soldiers marching through the streets. Equipped with tommy guns, light and heavy machine guns, and clad in new tan winter uniforms, they appeared to be a trim fighting outfit. One of the officers stopped our convoy. At first I thought he was out to commandeer one or two trucks, not an uncommon occurrence even though the trucks were clearly identified as UNRRA's. A yellow UNRRA flag flew from the front of each vehicle. The officer had seen these trucks every day for the past year. But it gave him face to hold up the convoy before a gawking crowd of civilian bystanders while he peppered my interpreter with questions.

"Where is this convoy headed? What does the cargo consist of? Who is it for?" Soldiers brandishing tommy guns broke ranks and covered the trucks menacingly during this grilling. It was a good show and obviously the civilian bystanders enjoyed it. But everyone knew the Nationalist army did this sort of bullying only inside the city's high wall.

In an age that already knew the destructive power of an atomic bomb, it was hard to appreciate the protection afforded by a mud wall. In China, however, a city wall forty feet high and twenty feet thick was still considered a formidable defense against infantry attack. Hiding behind it gave local commanders and their troops a sense of security.

Rarely did the troops venture outside, where they might encounter the enemy. In fact, there seemed to be a military understanding in Henan Province. The Nationalists could cling to the major cities and rail lines, while the Communists infiltrated the farmland and hacked away at the other lines of communication. Only when the Communists attempted to capture a city or threatened the rail lines did a skirmish ensue.

Xuchang, I discovered on an earlier trip, got its name from Emperor Cao in A. D. 200. He called it the Kingdom of Xu. Chairman Mao, whose troops now threatened to overrun the place, had already re-named it the Kingdom of Tobacco because of its cigarette factories. By any name, Xuchang's strategic location, fifty miles below China's key rail hub of Zhengzhou, made it a prime target. Mao had recently boasted that his armies would sweep south from the Yellow River to the Yangtze River, rip up both the north-south Ping-Han (Peking-Hankow) railway and the east-west Lunghai line, and thereby "nail the Nationalists to the Zhengzhou Cross," where the two lines intersected. If that happened, Xuchang would fall like a ripe melon into Mao's hands.

The first Communist forces had already crossed the Yellow River. A hit-and-run vanguard, 20,000 strong, commanded by General Chang Shao-hua, was pinning down Nationalist units here and there, while elements of the Eighth Route Army, or *Ba Lu*, commanded by the feared "One-eyed Dragon," General Liu Bocheng, probed all the way south to the Yangtze.

At the same time, General Chen Yi's Third Route Army had made good on half of Mao's boast by peeling away 140 miles of Lunghai track and cutting the rail connection with Shanghai. Every time the Nationalists rebuilt the trestles, replaced the wood ties, and relaid the old steel rails, the Communists would tear them up.

The Lunghai was central China's lifeline. But even when it was running, many of UNRRA's old boxcars, pulled by wheezing Japanese steam locomotives, were being used to transport Nationalist soldiers and their equipment instead of relief supplies. I had seen tanks, armored cars, and artillery rolling by on flat cars clearly marked UNRRA. The most pathetic sight of all were UNRRA's rickety old freight cars crowded with amputees—badly mutilated men whose leg and arm stumps oozed blood through their skimpy bandages.

Because rail service had become so unreliable, all the spare parts for our trucks were being flown in by CAT, as General Claire Chennault's Civil Air Transport was called. The famous World War II Flying Tiger commander had recruited many of his former P-40 pilots to fly a fleet of war surplus C-46s and C-47s. The old planes, with a newborn tiger kitten painted on their nose, were chartered most of the time by the Nationalists to transport guns and ammunition to isolated army units, or to rescue refugees fleeing the Communists. The pilots were a colorful, swashbuckling bunch: World War II heros like Joe Rosbert, a former Flying Tiger ace who had shot down seven Japanese Zeros; Lew Burridge, Bus Loane, and "Earthquake" McGoon, whose airline pilot's uniform consisted of khaki shorts, combat boots, and a T-shirt inflated by a huge beer belly. Earthquake became a legend in China after Milton Caniff, the creator of *Terry and the Pirates*, turned him into a comic strip character.

UNRRA had to settle for second call on CAT's planes. About once a week a C-46 laden with spare parts for our trucks would put down in Kaifeng, the provincial capital of Henan and UNRRA's headquarters in central China. CAT was our main contact with the outside world. The pilots could be counted on to bring our mail and newspapers, and always a fresh batch of rumors about the shifting tides of the civil war.

Xuchang's 200,000 residents needed no more rumors. Spreading rumors there was an offense punishable by death. Even facts were considered rumors until they were officially revealed. Everybody was acutely aware of how precarious the situation was as two Communist armies appeared to be converging on the city. Thousands of coolies, conscripted without pay, were out every day patching the stout forty-foot-high wall and widening the moat around it. All the gates except one were barricaded with huge timbers and strung with concertina rolls of barbed wire. At the open gate a squad of Nationalist soldiers frisked all travelers, poking their bundles and baskets with bayonets. Few of the sentries could read, but they scrutinized every traveler's identity card with exaggerated care.

Our convoy was now entering the disputed zone between Xuchang and Xihua. This was an area that both sides claimed, though neither controlled. Instead, they simply took turns taxing and looting it. It was not unusual to find on our return trip from Xihua that all the Nationalist sentries had been replaced by Communist sentries, or vice versa, this changing of the guard having been accomplished bloodlessly.

Once I asked a Nationalist sentry what he would do if a Communist column came marching down the road. He didn't answer, and my interpreter later reprimanded me for being impolite. Naturally, the sentry would run away, my interpreter explained.

Ahead appeared the arched gate of Wunudian, which translated literally means "five girls town." Legend had it that a retired warlord and his five daughters founded a thriving tea shop there some fifteen centuries ago. When it was discovered that the girls were selling more than tea to tired wayfarers, they were run out of town, and the place has been a provincial landmark ever since.

Few changes were wrought in Wunudian during the intervening millennium and a half. As in most Henan villages, the main street was a deep, sandy hollow running from gate to gate. Centuries of through traffic had worn the thoroughfare down ten feet below the level of the mud houses on each side. Chickens and pigs scooted out of the way of our oncoming convoy, while a mangy dog wearily roused itself from a sunbath in the center of the street and limped off. Most of the dogs in China were crippled. In the Communist areas, however, even the hale and hearty dogs were exterminated, and in some cases eaten because dog meat is considered a delicacy in certain areas. Food, in any case, was too precious to waste on pets.

The whine of the trucks coming up fast behind my jeep drowned out the shrieking and clapping of the kids racing excitedly along both sides of the street. They looked like miniature Buddhas, but with bare brown bottoms protruding from their split-tail rompers. The village children weren't accustomed to the roaring trucks. Every week, it seemed, a tot somewhere along our convoy route would become frightened by the noise and swirling dust and try to scamper between the trucks. Or worse yet, dart underneath between the front and rear wheels.

According to Chinese law, in all accidents involving a pedestrian and a motor vehicle, the driver was considered at fault. The law was simple enough, but sometimes its interpretation became knotty. A few weeks earlier a Nationalist soldier had been killed by one of our trucks. The driver was summarily carted off to jail, only to be released when it was discovered that the soldier had hitched a ride and had accidentally fallen off the truck. Three days later the driver was back in jail. It turned out the soldier had not really hitched a ride, but had forced the driver at gunpoint to pick him up. However, it was also confirmed that the soldier had fallen beneath the truck's wheels and had been crushed to death. Clearly, the driver had run over him. To avoid legal complications like that, UNRRA drivers were unofficially authorized to make a fifty-dollar roadside settlement with the victim's family.

Our convoy passed through the east gate of Wunudian and headed for Yanling. The Nationalist sentry offered a feeble salute, and then quickly cupped his hands over his face to ward off the clouds of dust. This stretch of road was good, and the jeep pounded along at thirty miles an hour. The windshield wipers ticked evenly back and forth, sending dry rivulets of dust streaming down the glass like rain. The sun was bright and the mid-November morning was beginning to warm.

On stretches of reasonably good road, where the driving wasn't so challenging, my thoughts tended to wander until they lit upon the question that had been hounding me for months: Why are you risking your rear end running a bunch of trucks through somebody else's civil war? What I wanted to do was write, to bear witness to the events and people changing China. Reporting had always been my ambition.

Winding up World War II as a twenty-six-year-old army major in the Philippines, I had accepted the offer from UNRRA only because I couldn't land a reporting job. The competition was fierce. Legions of returning war correspondents had come home hungering for assignments that would take them back abroad. My prewar professional experience had been limited to two low-paying college stringerships. During my senior year at Dartmouth the *Boston Post* had paid me twenty-five cents a column inch, and for carbon copies of the same stories, the *Springfield Republican* paid me another fifteen cents an inch.

Still in uniform, I spent two frustrating months making the rounds of all the wire services, newspapers, and magazines in New York City. My only offer was a fifty-dollar-a-week rewrite slot with the International News Service in Atlanta. Going to China for UNRRA, with all expenses paid, and for what was then a handsome $5,000-a-year salary, was much more enticing. Best of all, I'd be working in a part of the world that was only sparsely covered by the American press. And there would be nothing to stop me from trying to sell freelance pieces.

A typewriter and camera were always with me in my jeep. I had already taken hundreds of photographs. A few had been bought by the *National Geographic* for "stock," as the picture editor's letter explained, "to be kept on file for possible future use." He enclosed a check for fifty dollars.

I had also sold *Life* a macabre set of photographs that still hadn't been published, although the magazine informed me that they soon would be. They showed a grisly gallery of 5,000 skulls packed temple to temple on a hillside with 10,000 gaping eye sockets staring eerily into space. This "Stadium of Skulls," as I titled the photographs, had been erected by the citizens of Hengyang in Hunan Province as a memorial to their relatives massacred by the Japanese in 1944. Buried in shallow trenches, the fleshless skeletons were exhumed right after the war. Then the whitened skulls were arranged in tiers to simulate a grandstand of ghosts overlooking the scene of their slaughter. "It is much more eloquent than any man-made memorial," one of the *Life* editors had written, promising that a check for two hundred dollars would soon follow.

Taking pictures posed no problem. It was easy to stop my jeep and crank off a few shots. But the writing came much harder. It was difficult to settle down at a typewriter after being hammered all day by China's rutted highways.

Approaching our convoy in the distance I could see an antlike line of wheelbarrows. It was nothing for a man in China to push a 500-pound wheelbarrow a hundred miles in a week. If he heard shooting up ahead, he'd stop and wait for it to subside, just as he did for the rain when it washed out the road, or for the wind when it whipped the sand into blinding red clouds. As our convoy passed the wheelbarrow men, they covered their faces with rags to ward off the dust kicked up by our trucks. Several women without wheelbarrows, but with heavy bundles suspended from *biandan* shoulder poles, trudged by, their bundles jouncing rhythmically up and down.

Ahead, Yanling's sun-baked mud wall rose up out of the plain. As we reached the town, I saw that the main gate was locked and barricaded. Crudely painted Chinese characters above the sealed entryway exhorted passersby to "support Generalissimo Chiang Kai-shek's mobilization order and fight the Communist bandits." A poster tacked to the gate showed a Guomindang fist knocking Mao out of China, while Yen Wang, the king of hell, beckoned to him with death's claw.

Fortunately there was no longer any need to harangue the guards to open the gate and let our convoy pass. A freshly hacked-out detour skirted the city along Yanling's moat. A small creek emptied into the moat, and I parked beside it to wait for the convoy to catch up.

Two fishermen were skillfully dipping and raising their nets into the muddy creek. Tiny silvery minnows wriggled in the red water as their nets broke the surface. A crowd of old men soaking up the warm Indian summer sun watched the fishermen from a stone bridge. The easiest thing to get in China is an audience. Several young boys scrambled up from under the bridge to inspect my jeep. I tousled the hair of one and kidded with him in Chinese.

"You're my good friend," I said, whereupon his father suddenly appeared and asked if I wanted to take the boy with me. In rapid Chinese, not all of which I understood, the father explained that he had six other children and not enough food to feed them. It would be much better for the boy if I adopted him.

Clouds of dust puffed up on the horizon. Finally the trucks were catching up. This was a mongrel convoy—former U.S. Army and Navy ten-wheel GMC's and Internationals, smaller civilian Dodges, Studebakers, Chevys, and Fords. A couple of ugly, blunt-nosed Canadian Fords were last. "Yellow fish," as illegal passengers were called, perched dangerously atop some of the tarpaulin-covered loads.

After skirting the city, we entered the no-man's-land known as the Flooded Area. I decided to be a kind of rear guard to prod the stragglers. Trying to keep them from being picked off by either Communist or Nationalist soldiers was part of my job. The Nationalists were the real culprits. They had a nasty habit of grabbing two or three trucks at a time, stealing the cargo, and then turning the trucks into troop carriers until they ran out of gas and had to be abandoned.

Our trucks were especially vulnerable on this leg of the journey. Most of the Flooded Area had dried up, leaving only trickles here and there which our trucks could easily ford. However, there were still a few deep spots where we had to raft the trucks across one at a time, making us sitting ducks for any band of marauding soldiers.

This part of China had always been dangerous, but for an entirely different reason. Twenty-six times in Henan's history, the surging, silted Yellow River known as "China's sorrow" had wantonly changed course, flooding Yanling and hundreds of neighboring towns. Then, just when the armies of coolies manning the dikes found that they could keep pace with the silting that constantly raised the river bed and produced the floods, Chiang Kai-shek seized on the Yellow River as a tactical weapon. Employing a "scorched earth" policy to try to stop the Japanese invaders in 1938, he blew the dike 100 miles north of where our convoy was now traveling.

Surging south, the wide mustard-colored river found a new course spreading through the heart of Henan. Almost a million people perished, and as the alluvium continued to cover the central plain, many more millions were forced to seek higher ground in neighboring provinces. The remaining population hung on, almost starving to death on the fringes of the flood.

Then, in 1946, UNRRA flood-control specialists tackled the momentous task of sealing the dike's mile-long breach. In charge of this project was an American engineer, O. J. Todd, duly elevated to "Todd almighty" after he succeeded in repairing the dike and returning "China's sorrow" to its original riverbed.

The 5,000-square-mile Flooded Area, as it continued to be called, slowly dried up. Encouraged by UNRRA's promise to provide food, clothing, farming tools, seeds, and fertilizer, half a million families came back to reclaim their land. It was relief supplies for these people that our convoys were carrying.

The line of trucks, now churning the dust up ahead, were heading across the newly reclaimed farmland toward Fukou. Curly Chu, my interpreter, who had been riding shotgun in a truck at the rear of the convoy, joined me in my jeep. Fukou had been in Communist hands on our last trip, and Curly knew a couple of their officers. I wanted to find out if he thought they'd give us any trouble.

It may have been Curly's fluent English, or his tall, strong build and unusual hair, but I never thought of him as being Chinese. Only twenty-two, he had already acquired many American mannerisms working for UNRRA, including a consuming passion for pretty Western women. "A Shandong man is like a thermos bottle," he once told me. "Cold on the outside and hot inside." In any case, Curly's ardor hadn't stopped him from leaving his girlfriend behind in Shandong Province when he signed on with UNRRA. Even stronger, I suspected, was his desire for a ticket to the U.S., which he hoped UNRRA might eventually provide.

As our convoy snaked its way south, the sandy wasteland flanking the highway gave way to cultivated furrows. Scattered farming villages, all recently rebuilt, now dotted the landscape. Each village consisted of a collection of crude one-room structures. They were built out of dried sorghum stalks, the same *gaoliang* from which the Chinese brew *bai-gar*, their clear, throat-scorching liquor. Forced to suffer repeated *ganbeis* (toasts) with this white lightning at official banquets, we UNRRA employees always tried to empty our glasses under the table when our hosts weren't watching.

On a previous convoy Curly had led me inside a few farmhouses just to show me what they were like. "The people live very simply," he warned. But that was an understatement. The house interiors were almost identical. A straw bed occupied over half the floor space. In one corner a large iron pot rested on a brick stove. There was one porcelain bowl and a pair of chopsticks for each family member. A small mound of beans and a few dried bones constituted the customary larder. Winter was coming, so all the clothes a family owned were being worn, and slept in as well. But their poverty didn't stop the occupants from smiling as Curly rattled off an explanation of what this inquisitive American was doing in Henan Province. Most of them had never heard of America. "Does it rain there?" one of them asked.

Although their resuscitated land was being fiercely contested by the Nationalists and Communists, the farmers and their families seemed unpersuaded by the propaganda barrages from both sides. "If you're a soldier," one of the farmers explained to Curly, "you must fight with one army or the other. If you're a magistrate, you must be a Nationalist magistrate or a Communist magistrate. But if you're a farmer, that's what you are."

In an American magazine I had read a story about a nonpolitical Chinese farmer like this one, whose land had been overrun by both Nationalists and Communists. "Which side," he was asked, "is better?"

"They are both good," answered the peasant politely. "Only the people are bad."

When Curly and I reached Fukou, we found the trucks already strung out in a long line in front of the main gate, waiting for our jeep to lead them into the city. Food vendors and the usual horde of onlookers crowded around the convoy. A Nationalist sentry stood atop the high wall, silhouetted against the bright midday sky. There was no doubt who held Fukou today.

This was one of the few cities of the region that had been severely damaged by the opposing armies. Hit first by Communist artillery shells and then by Nationalist dive-bombers, a gaping hole had been blown in the outer wall, and many of buildings inside had been shorn of their tile roofs or completely gutted. But in Fukou, as in many of the neighboring towns, the sudden policy reversals implemented every time the city changed hands caused as much havoc as the fighting.

The first time the Communists captured Fukou, they published a roster of the richest families, whose houses could be ransacked by all comers in an informal wealth equalization program. Only removable items, it was expected, would be taken. But after hundreds of spirited looters had cleaned out all the porcelainware, furniture, and other valuables, they took to unhinging doors, prying out window frames, and peeling wood panels from the walls. So the Communists finally called a halt to the proceedings. When a few latecomers arrived and started chipping out bricks and removing roof tiles, they were hauled off to the dike and shot.

Four days later the Nationalists returned. Since when had looting been legalized? they wanted to know. An order was issued to immediately return all the stolen items. And to make sure everyone understood that the order was to be taken seriously, a dozen of the worst offenders were escorted out to the same dike and shot through the head. But the Nationalist authorities failed to mention where the loot was to be returned. When the sun came up the next morning, all the stolen stuff was scattered through the streets.

Our truck drivers didn't linger over lunch in Fukou. A bowl of noodles, a few pieces of steamed dough, and they were eager to leave. Their engines started with an angry roar and the crowd of onlookers backed away in a wave. The vendors hastily pulled in their rickety food stands so the trucks wouldn't knock them down. Once again I ran my jeep to the front of the convoy and headed south for Xihua, the final destination, where our trucks would be unloaded.

Two miles south of Fukou we overtook a Nationalist battalion bunched together in a plowed field. The troops were smartly dressed. Rifles and machine guns glinted ominously in the sun. Their commanding officer, mounted on a black pony, cantered over to the road to watch our convoy pass. For Nationalist officers like him, the army could be a profitable business. As the reigning local authority, he was free to shake down the wealthy merchants, or even sell some of his battalion's artillery and other weapons to the enemy. For his lowly foot soldiers, the army was at least a meal ticket. But from division commander to private, there was little will among the Nationalists to wage more than a mock war.

Communist militia units, on the other hand, looked ragtag but were capable of fighting hard. Local battalions in the Flooded Area were commonly clad in peasant garb, and it was possible to find squads in which no two rifles matched. Individual soldiers rarely carried more than four or five rounds of ammunition. Sometimes they were even forced to skimp on the powder charge in their homemade bullets. I once encountered a Nationalist private who'd been shot in the neck, but the bullet had bounced off, leaving only a bad bruise. Often the best weapons the Communists possessed had been captured or bought from the Nationalists. Nevertheless, the "Red Bandits," as the Nationalists called the Communists, were determined to wrest control of Henan Province, and all of China, from Chiang and his warlords.

Although the Communists' military strategy for engulfing Henan was carefully mapped out, coordination between local units in the field could be amazingly loose. Occasionally we met Communist sentries guarding a town, unaware that an entire Red division was camped a few miles down the road. Once a Communist battalion stormed Fukou only to discover it was trying to take the city from another Red battalion which had captured it the day before.

Our trucks were now running through deep sand, signaling the approach of Xihua. Even in four-wheel drive, my jeep labored hard to keep its forward momentum. When the tires gripped solid ground, the jeep sped ahead for a few yards, then slowed almost to a stop as the wheels spun freely in loose sand.

Two soldiers ambled across the road. Scanning the field on our right, I saw a hundred more. They looked like farmers except for their rifles which were slung muzzle down across their backs. A few wore telltale blue caps. We were in Communist territory.

I could hear the whine of the trucks pushing from behind. Instinctively the drivers speeded up when they first spotted Communist troops. It wasn't that the Communist soldiers were any more menacing than the Nationalists. But the Nationalists' propaganda posters effectively depicted bayonettings and beheadings, supposedly the work of the Red Bandits. The goriest poster of all showed a group of heads impaled on pungi sticks planted in the ground beside the road. Those bodyless heads made a lasting impression on the drivers now traveling over that same stretch.

At precisely three P.M. our convoy pulled up at the Xihua gate. The sentry sported a new blue quilted uniform, and with a quick flick of his bayonet waved us in. Although Xihua had been in Communist hands for five months, it still resembled any other small Chinese city. Hundreds of ramshackle shops, stalls, and food stands lined the narrow dirt streets. The proprietors feverishly pulled in their stands and lifted awnings so the convoy could squeeze by. Children ran in swarms beside the trucks, babbling greetings to the drivers. Anti-Guomindang and anti-American posters were plastered all over town. They pictured gluttonous American imperialists biting big chunks from the heart of China. Somehow the propaganda message had eluded the kids. "*Meiguoren dinghao*," ("Americans very good"), they shouted, spotting me at the wheel of the jeep.

The sight of an American bringing much-needed food and clothing to Xihua also contradicted what was being printed in the local Communist newspaper. "AGGRESSION IN THE NAME OF RELIEF" blared a recent headline. Repeated editorial tirades accused "traitor Chiang" of allowing "reactionary American relief representatives to travel freely throughout China, gathering military information and surveying economic resources." The fact that UNRRA was an international relief organization that included Canadians, Australians, and Europeans as well as Americans didn't matter. Some articles went so far as to charge the "sinful, bloody American UNRRA robbers with helping traitor Chiang to kill the Chinese people."

Xihua's older citizens also recognized the anti-American propaganda for what it was. Only when a Nationalist Air Force P-47 dropped an occasional bomb on Xihua did the accusations hit home. Everyone knew the planes and bombs were made in America.

Guomindang newspapers, on the other hand, spiced up their pages with a sprinkling of scandal. Curly had translated a couple of beauts. "YOUNG GIRL BRINGS FORTH BABY WITHOUT FATHER" proclaimed a headline in Kaifeng's *Great Eastern Evening News*. The article reported how eighteen-year-old Butterfly Wang slipped under her brother's bed to eavesdrop on his wedding night conversation, only to discover a young man was already there. "They had a happy meet under the bed" was the way Curly translated it. "But a few days ago Butterfly gave birth to a baby, and is now trying to locate the father."

As our convoy threaded its way along Xihua's cluttered main street, a company of soldiers blocked our way. The soldiers were young and high-spirited, although shabbily dressed and armed with old muskets. They had no machine guns or mortars. The commanding officer backed the company into a side alley to let our convoy pass.

Communist troops weren't always so obliging. Once, when control of Xihua was still seesawing back and forth, Communist soldiers broke into a nearby UNRRA truck compound, forced the drivers to take them to the city, captured it, hauled the defending Nationalist troops ten miles out of town, where they were stripped of their arms, ammunition, and uniforms, and then returned the trucks and drivers to the UNRRA compound.

Our convoy crept cautiously around a tight corner, knocking loose a few bricks from the buildings. Ahead, the green-tiled roof of a Buddhist temple reflected the afternoon sun. Although Buddhist idols still glowered down from high golden perches inside the temple, it now served as an UNRRA warehouse. A swarm of coolies quickly set about unloading our thirty-two trucks.

Unfortunately for Xihua, our convoy once again had brought more clothing than food. The people here needed clothing badly. But they needed food even more. So much of our cargo would end up being sold by its hungry recipients to buy rice or flour. As a result, a flourishing black market had sprung up in the city.

Thousands of sweaters, suits, and coats, distributed by UNRRA, hung from sales racks out on the street. Some of the clothing looked brand new: Hart Shaffner and Marx overcoats selling for the equivalent of $5, Magregor sweaters for $1, and stylish women's jackets bearing New York department store labels going for even less because they weren't very warm. Of course, the peasants who'd been given these items sold them for half of what the merchants were charging. Capitalism had not yet been expunged from newly conquered Communist towns like Xihua.

After the rough ride from Xuchang, the sight of all this supposedly free clothing being peddled by greedy merchants was pretty discouraging. A tremendous effort had also gone into getting it to central China. First, all the donated garments had to be collected at various volunteer centers around the U.S. before being baled and trucked to San Francisco for shipment to Shanghai. Unloaded there onto Huangpu River lighters, the individual bales were then borne on the sweating backs of coolies to the railway boxcars which carried them the last 600 miles to Kaifeng—provided the Lunghai line hadn't been cut.

The futility of being the last link in a tortuous supply chain leading to a black market was infuriating. Did I really want to spend another year escorting convoy after convoy through the middle of a civil war, only to have our cargoes end up in the hands of some petty profiteer?

Perhaps it was a combination of sun, dust, and the bone-rattling jeep ride that was getting me down. Certainly, the black-marketing of UNRRA clothing in one Communist town was a mere misdemeanor compared to the wholesale stealing our relief organization was encountering in Nationalist China. Only there the corruption was harder to detect. It usually emanated from polished, tea-laden conference tables, where the crooked deals were always camouflaged by the most polite conversation. Or, more precisely, where agreements were ironed out that the Nationalists had no intention of keeping.

CHAPTER II

Glimpsing the Generalissimo

DURING THE SUNG DYNASTY, 900 years ago, when Henan was known as the "Middle Province of the Middle Kingdom," Kaifeng served as the capital of all China. The city was then called Xiangfu, meaning "fortunate sign." But in the fall of 1947 the signs were far from fortuitous.

Hundreds of soldiers stood guard at the massive iron gates and atop the city wall. Thousands more roamed the muddy streets, doing everything they could to flaunt their authority and conceal their jitters. They had even erected pillboxes at the main intersections to prepare against the possibility of street fighting. Occasionally, they also sprang an air raid drill on the hapless citizenry, although the Communists had no planes.

With sirens blaring and Nationalist air force fighters swarming overhead, soldiers in the street would thrust their bayonets at the disoriented crowds, kick over wheelbarrows left in their way, and send the entire population scurrying for cover. When it was over, the people would shrug their shoulders and go about their business of buying and selling, eating and sleeping, procreating and dying. But for us Americans based there, it wasn't easy to pretend everything was normal.

Kaifeng had been selected by UNRRA and its Chinese counterpart, CNRRA (China National Relief and Rehabilitation Administration), as a field headquarters for their three most ambitious relief programs. The one with the highest priority was the so-called Gap Closure Project, the engineering feat that had sealed shut the nine-year-old mile-wide breach in the Yellow River dike. The other two subsidiary projects stemmed from the vast population shifts caused by rerouting "China's sorrow" back into its old riverbed.

The Yellow River Resettlement Program was designed to relocate the 600,000 peasants, who nine years earlier had moved into the dried-up old bed, only to be chased out again by the returning waters.

The Flooded Area Program, which my four hundred trucks were assigned to, was established to assist half a million other farmers and their families to reclaim the land that had been underwater before the Gap Closure Project was completed.

Although the Nationalist and Communist armies were already stalking each other around Kaifeng, UNRRA officials had plunged into this ambitious three-pronged effort, naively hoping that the immunity promised by both sides would permit them to proceed unmolested. That they quickly got sucked into the civil war was inevitable.

The Gap Closure Project had been the first to fall victim. Although the gap itself was in Nationalist territory, much of the old riverbed into which the torrential flow was being redirected was occupied by the Communists. This meant that Chiang Kai-shek controlled a giant spigot that could be turned on full force to flush out Mao's troops. Of course, thousands of peaceful peasants who were farming the old river-bed would be flushed out with them. To prevent this tragedy, Chiang's government had promised UNRRA that the dike wouldn't finally be sealed shut until all the riverbed people had been relocated.

Work on the gap had moved slowly at first. But then, as advance units of the one-eyed Communist general, Liu Bocheng, started filtering south, the Nationalist high command saw an opportunity to use the river to cut them off. Speeding up the gap closure could accomplish the work of thirty divisions, Chiang's generals figured. The calamity it would spell for the 600,000 farmers living in the riverbed—in fact the whole purpose of UNRRA's carefully planned Yellow River Resettle-ment program—was ignored.

One morning along the ruptured dike there appeared a new 50,000-man workforce. It was strung out for about half a mile in two parallel lines. The northbound line was pushing wheelbarrows heaped with red, sandy soil toward the gap, while the southbound line pushed their empty wheelbarrows back to the enormous gouged-out sandpits to pick up another load. From sunrise till sunset the opposing lines remained in perpetual motion as the breach in the dike visibly shrank. Trans-porting the thousands of acres of sandy soil surely took as much muscle and sweat as the building of an Egyptian pyramid. Except when this job was done, there was nothing to show for the prodigious human effort but a broad, muddy river flowing silently along in its old bed.

It was March 15, 1947, when the mile-wide breach in the dike was finally sealed. The last stage was completed secretly under the command of Nationalist military authorities while UNRRA's engineers were away attending a conference in Shanghai. The fact that UNRRA's relief mission had been sabotaged was of no concern to Chiang's generals, who assumed no responsibility for relocating the farmers who had been living in the riverbed for nine years. That was UNRRA's job.

Realizing what had happened and rushing into action, the agency dispatched relocation teams northeast from Kaifeng toward the river's mouth in the Gulf of Po Hai. At the same time, another UNRRA contingent, bringing food and other supplies from Shanghai, sailed up to the river's mouth aboard a flotilla of former U.S. Navy LSTs. The plan was for the two contingents to work their way toward each other along the river until they met. The Communists controlled the area around the river's mouth. But both they and the Nationalists had promised unimpeded passage for the two UNRRA teams.

As the first LST, the *Wan Ching*, arrived in the Gulf of Po Hai, a Nationalist plane plunked two bombs in the water beside it. Nobody was hurt and the pilots apologized for their mistake. But shortly after that, when the *Wan Ching* and another UNRRA LST, the *Wan Sze*, were discharging their Yellow River Resettlement Program supplies, Nationalist planes roared in for a repeat performance. The two vessels were raked with machine-gun fire from bow to stern. One Chinese crew member was killed, two more were injured, a barge was sunk, and much of the cargo destroyed.

This time Nationalist army chief of staff, General Chen Cheng, sent a written apology to Harlan Cleveland, chief of UNRRA's China mission in Shanghai. He promised there would be "no recurrence of these unfortunate accidents," which he attributed to "misidentification." But there was no mistaking the former U.S. Navy landing crafts for Communist vessels. Stripped of their antiaircraft guns, the LSTs displayed large UNRRA flags painted on their starboard and port sides.

Mao's propagandists played up the bombings as "more Guomindang outrages against the people of North China." But the Communists were hardly blameless. While the LSTs were being unloaded, they treated the crews to elaborate feasts. Brandy was plentiful in Shandong, and it flowed freely at these parties. Warmed by this unusual display of Communist hospitality, the crew members were then propositioned to smuggle guns and ammunition on future voyages. During one banquet, the skipper of the LST *Ching Ling* sold the Communists his reserve fuel supply, which was pumped ashore while the festivities were in full sway. But finding trustworthy skippers in China was almost impossible. Most of the LST officers were either unlicensed or derelicts plucked off the beach in Shanghai.

These shenanigans finally came to a halt after still another UNRRA LST, the *Wan Shen*, was bombed and strafed by two Nationalist P-47s. The bombs missed, but the planes darted back and forth over the vessel, stitching her down the middle and riddling the bridge with bullets. Both the British captain and Canadian chief officer were seriously wounded and had to be evacuated by an American destroyer summoned to the scene. From his hospital bed the wounded chief officer confessed that on the *Wan Shen*'s previous voyage, some one hundred unmanifested cases labeled "hardware" had actually contained thirty-caliber ammunition. How much contraband was smuggled on these ships from Shanghai, UNRRA never found out.

UNRRA's Kaifeng contingent fared no better. A Canadian doctor delivering medical supplies to one of the Yellow River towns died of what was officially termed "exposure," though nobody said to what. Gunfire, we guessed. Soon after the doctor's death, the field team director's truck was blown up by retreating Communists who mistook it for a Nationalist vehicle and rolled a couple of grenades under the rear wheels. Every attempt to supply the riverbed evacuees from either Kaifeng or Shanghai was countered with a combination of red tape, bombing, strafing, and sniping.

Eventually the Nationalists dropped all pretenses of safe passage for the Yellow River Resettlement crews. They slapped a blockade on all the Gulf of Po Hai ports. Even the right for UNRRA personnel to move freely around other parts of Henan was no longer assured.

At headquarters in Kaifeng we could only speculate about what had precipitated this policy reversal. It came right after General Hao Peng-chu, Chiang Kai-shek's senior military man in the area, had been taken prisoner. Possibly there was no connection, but we assumed there was, because the general's capture had panicked the Nationalists and made them lash out in all directions, including ours. And the way the Communist radio crowed about his capture only made matters worse.

Not only was General Hao the highest-ranking prisoner taken by the Communists up until this time, but he was also their most profitable catch—a cache of three hundred gold bars having been discovered in his possession. And since the general was notorious for shooting all prisoners, he had been sent before a firing squad to die as a war criminal. Then, to further humiliate the Nationalists, a couple of embarrassing postscripts were added to the news of his execution. It was only because of Hao's cowardly attempt to bribe his way to freedom that his gold hoard had been discovered. In the end, reported the Communists, Hao had tried to save his neck by offering them an additional million dollars in U.S. greenbacks, which he claimed to have stashed away in a safe deposit box in Shanghai.

Instead of ridiculing the story, the Nationalists in effect confirmed it by disclosing that they had opened General Hao's safe deposit box and confiscated the million dollars. But the Nationalists' embarrassment didn't end there. The U.S. promptly protested to Chiang's government that the general's gold cache had been stolen from a thirteen-ton emergency shipment sent from Fort Knox, Kentucky, to prop up China's sagging currency.

Tales like that didn't help morale at UNRRA headquarters in Kaifeng. By August our relief mission was ready to withdraw from the area. In fact, things had become so bad that Fiorello LaGuardia, the former mayor of New York City who headed UNRRA's worldwide operations in Washington, placed a temporary embargo on all future shipments to China.

That was the sad state of affairs when Harlan Cleveland, UNRRA's chief in China, and a group of officials from Washington flew to Kaifeng for an emergency conference on August 8, 1947. Only one project, they concluded, was still viable in the midst of the war—the mission my four hundred trucks and I were assigned to carry out—feeding and clothing the 500,000 families who had returned from neighboring provinces to the now-dry Flooded Area with the promise of UNRRA aid.

By November the provincial warehouses bulged with 30,000 tons of undistributed supplies. Thousands of tons more were due to arrive from Shanghai, all desperately needed to revive the area's agriculture and avoid another killer famine like the one in 1943. That year, *Time* magazine had published a harrowing account of human suffering in Henan. Reporter Theodore White told of seeing "dogs eating human bodies by the roads, peasants seeking dead human flesh under the cover of darkness, endless deserted villages, beggars swarming at every city gate and babies abandoned to cry and die on every highway." I had come across the old article in UNRRA's files, cited by the relief agency as "a damning indictment of Nationalist indifference."

Conditions in Henan hadn't reverted to that terrible state, but time was running out. Winter wheat, the main cash crop, had to be planted before the ground froze, while corn and millet, the secondary crops, didn't have to be sown until right after the wheat harvest in mid-May.

Yet, the whole planting cycle was destined to collapse if the relief supplies weren't distributed quickly, and there was little chance they could. The prospect of remaining in Henan under such dismal circumstances was dragging me down.

If my role had been to tell the story of a relief mission gone awry, that would have been different. The risks of running more convoys through a no-man's-land would have been worth taking. At least my reportorial urge would have been satisfied. But reporting was just a sideline for me. Besides, few people in the U.S. seemed to care a hoot about all the money and effort that was being wasted on China. White had ended his heartrending eyewitness account by admitting how Henan left him "mentally sick, depressed and filled with dire forebodings." Now it was having the same effect on me. My frustration had reached a climax when without warning one Saturday morning, the generalissimo himself suddenly appeared in Kaifeng.

The day began like any other. A long line of men, women, children, oxen, mules, dogs, chickens, pigs, and sheep stood quietly outside the city wall, waiting for daybreak, when the soldiers normally opened the heavy spiked iron gate so they could proceed inside to sell their goods. Waiting was no trick for them. The Chinese are a patient people, and the war had made them more so. But on this particular morning they grumbled to the soldiers because the gate remained closed.

At the railroad station inside the city, the waiting scene was repeated. Streaks of light were beginning to show in the sky above the sea of weary travelers sprawled out on the platform beside their belongings. As they commenced to stir, young girls carrying kettles of warm water and cakes of soap in brass basins circulated through the crowd, charging 500 Chinese dollars (one cent) a wash. But the rail yard behind the station stayed quiet except for the shouts of a few naked, soot-smeared children picking through the stones and ashes for pieces of coal for their mothers to sell. The eastbound express arriving from Xian and proceeding on to Xuzhou, Nanjing, and Shanghai, hadn't appeared for two days. And it wouldn't again today, the stationmaster announced, although nobody knew why.

The city center, too, was just coming awake. The clock atop the thousand-year-old drum tower, where men once thumped out the hours on huge brass drums, struck six. That signaled the official lifting of the all-night curfew, not that it was very carefully observed. Those people who had business after dark that couldn't be postponed would walk through the ink-black streets listening for the click of a rifle bolt, or the bellowed cry of "Halt" coming from an unseen sentry. Everyone knew the sentries had orders not to shoot.

At the sound of the drum tower clock, shopkeepers on *Sheng Fu Lu* (Provincial Government Street) began to peel the protective board panels from their display windows. The "honey cart" men were already out collecting wheelbarrows full of pungent human excrement for delivery to the outlying farms. A few rickshaw boys padded noiselessly up and down the street pulling early morning fares. Others stood in the shafts of their empty rickshaws slurping noodles from crockery bowls. An oxcart creaked by, the sharp crack of the driver's whip shattering the morning air.

A boy suddenly raced down the street, chattering excitedly to the baffled rickshaw boys and shopkeepers: "The soldiers are coming, the soldiers are coming." Soon soldiers swarmed down *Sheng Fu Lu* and the traffic stopped. Shopkeepers hurriedly put back the boards on their windows, and the pedestrians, rickshaws, carts, and animals were herded into the alleys and side streets.

Rumors flew. "The one-eyed Liu Bocheng and his Red Bandits were attacking from the north." "General Chang Shao-hua had broken out of the Flooded Area and was attacking from the south." "The dikes had burst and Kaifeng would soon be flooded."

Scare headlines, mobilization orders, and emergency proclamations were always accepted in Kaifeng with stoic calm. But when the gates remained shut, when the trains stopped running, when the people were herded off the streets and all work came to a halt, something truly bad must be happening. Then a strange sight dispelled everyone's worst fears.

Platoons of coolies carrying shovels over their shoulders trudged down *Sheng Fu Lu.* They quickly dispersed and set to work leveling off bumps and filling deep ruts and holes in the dirt street.

Amazing! The streets hadn't been repaired for years. Then more coolies with shovels arrived and the tempo of the work increased. Soon all the way down *Sheng Fu Lu* the clank and scrape of shovels could be heard as the coolies labored with unusual vigor.

The bamboo telegraph works fast in Kaifeng and a fresh rumor swept the city. "The generalissimo is coming. What else would move the municipal authorities to repair *Sheng Fu Lu?*"

This rumor caught hold. Shopkeepers quickly splashed whitewash over their storefronts and swept their walks. Women hurriedly dressed their children ordinarily allowed to run naked through the streets. Overhead the air suddenly droned with the sound of P-51 fighter planes circling the city.

An olive-colored C-47 hovered over Kaifeng and then quickly set down on the concrete airstrip left by the Japanese. A few minutes later a motorcade of armed trucks and dilapidated official cars roared down the freshly smoothed out *Sheng Fu Lu*. In the middle of this procession appeared a shiny black limousine, and while it sped by I glimpsed the bald-headed generalissimo sitting erect in the backseat.

This was no comic-opera general like the one the Communists cartooned. This was one of the world's "Big Five," the leader who had dared challenge the Asian military strategy of Winston Churchill and Franklin Roosevelt, passing right in front of me. I had read about their World War II summit meeting in Cairo at which the American president and British prime minister finally placated the stubborn generalissimo by promising to restore to China all of the territory it had lost in half a century of struggles with Japan. Still vivid in my mind was the famous picture of the three men sitting side by side in front of the Nile: Chiang posing confidently in his crisp uniform; next to him FDR; then the prime minister in a white suit with a gray homburg resting in his lap. On the extreme right, chic as ever in a Chinese gown that looked like it came from Bergdorf Goodman, sat the smiling Madame Chiang.

Now, here he was in the flesh, in Kaifeng, and without a reporter within 500 miles to record this historic moment. If only I could interview him, what a scoop that would be.

Suddenly I envisioned myself conducting a Q and A with the generalissimo. My imagination had catapulted me into the backseat of that black limo, where I was peppering him with questions: "Mr. President, how can your armies keep control of the central plain when your generals are selling their weapons to the enemy?" Good question, but too insulting, I realized. Better be polite. The generalissimo is known for his temper. Every American in China had heard the apocryphal story of how he'd shot his wife's dog in a fit of rage.

"Mr. President, do you expect President Truman to provide you with more military aid?" From what I'd read, I knew Truman opposed the U.S. becoming bogged down in China's civil war. Yet there was a powerful lobby at work in Washington agitating for more aid to Chiang. And I suspected the generalissimo was counting on it.

"Mr. President, many Americans consider Mao and his followers agrarian reformers, not hard-line Communists. Do you agree? And if so, is there any chance of you and Mao sharing power in a coalition government?" That, I realized, was a loaded question, or, rather, two loaded questions. First, I knew Chiang didn't care whether Mao was a true-blue Communist or not. He was the enemy. And second, despite General George Marshall's best efforts to create a coalition, the Chinese all knew Mao and Chiang would never join forces.

"Mr. President, do you believe a relief agency like UNRRA can operate effectively in the middle of a civil war?" Of course, I already knew the answer to that one. And because I did, I suppose it was already clear in my mind that the time had come for me to quit and go home.

Before my imaginary interview was over, the motorcade had pulled up at the provincial government headquarters. The generalissimo quickly disappeared inside and a cordon of guards sprang into position around the building.

For five hours the city hung in suspense. The fighter planes kept on droning overhead, but on the street the soldiers relaxed their vigil, permitting the people to come out. They crept cautiously from shops and houses to gape at the array of vehicles parked at the end of *Sheng Fu Lu*. Mothers nudged their children, pointing to the well-guarded provincial headquarters, while the men speculated on the reasons for the generalissimo's visit. On one thing they agreed. It was a bad sign. The war was too close to Kaifeng. Chiang was probably there to prod his generals to stand and fight.

At three P.M. the guards surrounding the government headquarters sprang to attention. The soldiers posted in the street sent the crowds scurrying back inside. The armed trucks and cars, including the shiny black limo, sped back up *Sheng Fu Lu*. Once again I caught a fleeting glimpse of the shiny bald head and the erect figure propped up in the backseat. Then, as suddenly as he had come, the generalissimo was gone.

What intrigued me most about this man was the way he had dominated China for twenty years and yet remained an enigma to Americans. General Joseph Stilwell, the World War II commander of the China Burma India Theater, was completely baffled by Chiang. He didn't understand why this convert to Christianity would preach the principles of Confucianism to his troops, or waste men and ammunition trying to contain the Communists before the Japanese were defeated. Stilwell called Chiang the "Peanut." But could a peanut have skillfully played off one warlord against another, or won the backing of China's commercial class, traditionally distrustful of the military? No, and neither could a mere peanut still be moving vast armies, evacuating whole cities, and, as we UNRRA people knew, changing the course of a mighty river. A tyrant, perhaps, could do all of those things, but not a peanut.

Glimpsing this remarkable leader again triggered my yearning to bear witness, to decipher confusing world figures such as Chiang, and to analyze the intangible chemistry of their power. Powerful leaders, those with the tactical ingenuity, the jugular timing, and, above all, the ability to make things happen had always fascinated me. No matter how bleak the job prospects in journalism, I knew that I had to pursue a reporting career.

Right after Chiang's surprise visit to Kaifeng, I applied to the Columbia University Graduate School of Journalism, hoping to go on the G.I. Bill. My grades at Dartmouth had been only fair. However, having risen through the ranks from private to major in four years in the army, most of it overseas, followed by two years' work with UNRRA in the midst of China's civil war, I assumed made me a likely candidate. But I was turned down. No explanation. Just a form letter of rejection. "To hell with Columbia," I thought. "Somebody back home will hire me."

CHAPTER III

Slow Boat to Shanghai

THE BARREN, HIGH-CEILINGED RESTAURANT was almost empty. Sucking noises came from the back, where two elderly Chinese gentlemen bent low over their soup, their chins almost touching the rims of the bowls. Three Russians in soiled serge uniforms were settling a bill at the only other occupied table.

As the Russians rose to leave, a white woman emerged from behind the bar and brushed past me to bid them farewell. The four were talking near the door when I noticed what a brute of a woman she was. Her massive square shoulders, heavy chest, and stocky, pillarlike legs gave her the husky look of a linebacker. She wore her short-clipped black hair matted down tight against her head like a skullcap. But her head was turned so I couldn't see her face.

The Russians left and the woman walked back toward my table. "Hullo, Toots, where you from?" she boomed.

She knew I was a stranger. There were few foreigners left in Wuhan, or Hankow, as it was then called. The civil war hadn't hit this once-booming Yangtze River city very hard, but its business had dried up. "Kaifeng," I answered.

"How long it take come from Kaifeng?" she asked, thudding down into an empty chair at my table.

"Four days," I replied. "One day by truck along the dike to Zhengzhou. And three days and three nights on the train." The Communists had torn up the rails on the Lunghai again. So I was taking the easiest detour—the Ping-Han down to Hankow, and a river steamer from there to Shanghai.

"Terrible train, the Ping-Han," she said. "Stop every town."

True, my train had dawdled along. But only because I'd hitched a ride on the Ping-Han director's private car. At every station all the railway workers and their families were waiting in formation to greet the director. And at the main stops the private car was left on a siding so the local bigwigs could fete him with a twenty- or thirty-course feast—squab, sharks' fins, duck, lobster, doves' eggs, bird's nest soup, and tiny live freshwater shrimp that were served and swallowed while they were still wriggling. The most memorable dish was a Henan specialty called "living fish." While the guests clapped appreciatively, a Yellow River carp was dipped tail-first into hot oil and then smothered with sweet and sour sauce, before being delivered to the table with its gills and mouth still opening and closing. But I didn't want to go through all that with her. "Yes, the Ping-Han just crawls along," I agreed.

"You must be tired, Toots. Better have bottle UB before eat," she said, motioning to the waiter. "Eh, boy, one bottle beer and bring extra glass."

The birdlike old waiter sauntered back to the bar and returned with a cold, dripping quart of UB. "Only four thousand CN, one dollar gold," she said, filling the two glasses. "Very cheap for Hankow. How much in Kaifeng?"

"Maybe five thousand," I answered. "But that was before the exchange rate went up again. Probably six thousand now."

She eased forward in her chair to rest her mammoth bosom on the table. "They call me Mama," she said, smiling and glancing down at the curve of her breast. "What you think of my place?"

I turned and surveyed the room carefully for the first time. Four bare lightbulbs hung on long cords from the ceiling. A large overhead fan revolved slowly, hardly moving the air. The faded tan wallpaper was streaked and torn. In the rear right corner was a small bar with a heavy brass rail running along the top instead of the bottom. Only a few bottles rested on the shelf behind the bar: six or seven bottles of Chinese whiskey and the familiar tall blue gallon jug of vodka. But the fresh flowers and clean tablecloths indicated an effort had been made to brighten the place.

"Terrible," she snapped before I could answer. "But soon I fix up. Have paint, nice chairs, and hundred cases of American whiskey in Shanghai. My friend just leave when you come is captain. Next trip upriver to Hankow he will bring. Good fellow. Never charge."

My Yangtze River steamer was leaving for Shanghai in the morning. I wondered if her friend could be the skipper. Might let me have a cabin, I thought. Otherwise I'd have to sleep out on deck during the five-day trip. "What's the captain's name?" I asked.

But Mama was intent on telling me more about her plans for refurbishing. "Toots, you know nightclub, DD's in Shanghai?" she asked, ignoring my question.

I nodded. DD's was a popular cabaret, best known for its dozen or so Russian hostesses strategically perched on high stools inside the mahogany bar. Some were probably French and German, but they were always referred to as "DD's Russian girls." I remember the first time I ordered a drink and faced that solid wall of women.

"Well, you know Jenny? Nice girl. No gold digger. Never ask for drink, but everybody buys for her anyway, and every night she makes fifteen or twenty dollars gold," Mama added, meaning U.S. dollars.

"That's what she makes just behind bar. Soon as I fix up, Jenny come to Hankow and work here. How long you stay, Toots?" Mama asked.

"Only tonight," I said, and she looked disappointed that I wouldn't be around to witness all the improvements, especially Jenny's arrival. "I'm headed home. Back to New York to look for a job."

A scraggly spitz raced across the room and angrily pawed the screen door. Mama called sharply to the dog in Russian, but it kept on snarling and pawing. Wearily she rose from the table, walked over, and flung open the door to shoo away the rickshaw boys who were taunting the dog from out in the street. The door banged shut and the dog scampered under a table.

The waiter handed me a menu. But when Mama returned to the table, she snatched it away. "I'll order for you, Toots. You better have borscht and after that a nice fillet. No water buffalo like in Kaifeng. Good cow steak."

I watched Mama squirm, trying to fit her huge, blunt body back into the chair. She had a handsome face, her features softened by a wistful look, as if she were trying to smile through invisible tears. Her thick Russian accent was magnified by the loudness of her voice. But when she lowered it, a guttural growl crept into her speech. "What's your name, Mama?" I asked.

"Olga. Olga Kosloff," she answered. "As little girl I go from Tomsk to Harbin. Three times I am rich and lose everything. The last time with the B-29s in Hankow," she blurted rapidly, as if to keep me from prying further. "Better have another UB before the borscht," she said, waving the empty bottle at the old waiter.

These White Russians are survivors, I thought. Thousands of them had fled to China during the Revolution, most of them on the Trans-Siberian Railway to Vladivostok, then by ship to Manchuria. When the Japanese captured Manchuria, they moved south. Somehow the White Russians seemed to make out much better than the German and Austrian refugees who escaped to China two decades later.

The birdlike waiter returned with another quart bottle of UB, wrestled with the cap, and then poured the beer too quickly so the collars rose up over the rims of the glasses and spilled down the sides, making two large wet rings on the tablecloth. Mama scowled at him and grunted something in Chinese before he ambled back to the bar, where two younger waiters were laughing at him.

"Always they forget the foam," Mama groaned.

"Listen, Toots, I tell you," she said, suddenly growing nostalgic. "It will make me cry, but I tell you anyhow. I noticed her eyes were slightly swollen, as if she might have told the story earlier that evening.

"In Qingdao they called me the Queen of Diamonds. I have big club called Starlight Cabaret. Maybe you heard. Mine is the biggest place because I am the biggest woman. I have thirty girls, twelve-people orchestra, beautiful garden, and tremendous business. Afternoon at four o'clock I open for navy. Eight o'clock all sailors must leave." Mama gestured as if she might have personally bounced a few. "We close for one hour to straighten out, and then open at nine o'clock for all high officials and wealthy peoples."

Mama sniffed. The second session was obviously her favorite. "Every night I am dressed like queen," she continued. "I wear big curved band of diamonds on top my head like halo, around my wrists diamond bracelets, and on all fingers diamond rings. One ring, six carats, was beautiful like a dream. One night navy Captain Brown stares at me breathless for five minutes, and then he says, 'Olga, you are the Queen of Diamonds.' After that everyone in Qingdao calls me Queen of Diamonds."

It was easy to picture her twenty years ago. Like the girls at DD's today, heavy-framed, voluptuous, slightly bovine, but attractive. Only this one not teasing for drinks from behind the bar, but the glittering centerpiece of her own cabaret. I assumed the Japanese had closed her down.

"Sometimes old captains come here and recognize me," she added. "Call me Queen of Diamonds, though I don't look the same today. Just to make me feel good."

It was growing dark outside. The oil lamps on passing rickshaws were lit. I could hear the muffled clicking and squeaking of their springs, the whirring of their wheels, and the light scuffing of bare feet on the pavement as the rickshaw boys jogged by. The wailing chant of a distant vendor echoed up the street.

The scraggly spitz edged toward the door. "Beauty," shrieked Mama, rapping sharply on the table so the glasses jumped. The dog turned slowly and trotted back to her side. She reached down and patted a bald spot on its rear end. "She's spoiled. Knows she lives in restaurant. Every day must change menu. Beef Stroganoff she likes best."

"Beauty and the beef Stroganoff," I said. But Mama didn't get it.

"How my little dog came downstairs through fire, I never know," Mama continued. "For three days disappeared. Then came back all burned black. I don't know who looked worse, me or Beauty."

"What happened, Mama?" I asked, though by this time I was more concerned about what happened to the waiter with the borscht.

"When I move from Qingdao, I lose everything. But I get new place in Hankow called the Cottage. Not big cabaret, but cute. Three years ago, eighteen December exact, I will always remember, beautiful clear day. My Chinese cook Willie says he must go away for two days to visit family. He brought over old man to cook, so I said okay, though old men are dirty and all the time spitting. You know, Toots, sometimes I think the Chinese can tell when something's going to happen. After fire I found old man burned crisp like bacon."

I still didn't understand what had happened. But I was concentrating on the old waiter while he delivered the soup under Mama's fierce gaze, making certain not to spill anything on the tablecloth this time. I assumed that there had been some kind of grease fire in the kitchen of her former cabaret. "Were you hurt, Mama?" I asked, spooning into the thick beet soup.

"Very lucky, Toots. At noon number-one boy carry warm water upstairs for my bath. Every day he bring ten buckets before *tiffin* [lunch]. When the B-29s come, I am all undressed. No alarm, Toots, but there is terrible explosion. It looks like whole city is on fire. I don't remember anything except I'm in flower garden all scraped and bruised. Have nice garden under my window and the earth was just dug fresh the day before. Everything is lost. Everything except Beauty," she added, nudging the dog with her heel.

"Later, when American GIs come, I always ask which is B-29 pilot because I must charge triple. They were nice boys and I only kid," she explained.

I finished the borscht. The waiter removed the empty bowl and returned with a steak, still sizzling. Mama beamed. "See, Toots, good cow steak," she exclaimed proudly.

She shook a cigarette from the pack I had placed on the table. The old waiter lit it, and she took long, thoughtful drags, allowing me to eat the steak in peace. A few foreigners and several Chinese men had come in. At the next table two ruddy-faced British merchant sailors were sharing a quart bottle of beer.

"You know, Toots," Mama finally said, "I always think when war is over will be good times like before. Maybe not so good as Qingdao, but nice." She shrugged her heavy shoulders. "But it's terrible. No chance in Hankow now. Just a few foreigners. Only the Chinese come back. Very few ships come upriver anymore."

She was right. Compared to Shanghai or Nanjing, Hankow's broad boulevards were practically deserted. "Maybe the foreigners will come back," I said, trying to strike an optimistic note.

"Even if many people, what good is business with this money? One day two thousand, the next day four thousand for one dollar gold."

She hiked her chair nearer the table and leaned over close to me. "It's not only Hankow," she whispered. "My friends write it's same everywhere. It's the Chinese. These people think they won the war and they won't listen anymore. Before the war they come into my place and they don't get served. Now they want everything. And the Communists say, 'Go ahead, take it.' We know Communists in Russia. Very bad peoples."

"But, Mama, it's their country," I said. "The Chinese will do what they want with it. Anyway, didn't the Russian government offer you all a chance to go back?"

"I speak Russian, that's all," she snapped.

The conversation was unraveling fast, and I decided to beat a strategic retreat to my room at the YMCA, though she tried to coax me into staying with a brandy. "My ship's sailing early in the morning," I said. "What's the name of your captain friend, Mama?"

"Major," she said, smiling again. "Easy to remember. He's both captain and major."

Unfortunately, Captain Major wasn't skippering my ship to Shanghai. And my river steamer, I soon discovered, was going to meander slowly down the Yangtze, running only during daylight hours as a precaution against a Communist attack. However, I was able to secure a cabin, a small box of a stateroom with double-decker bunks.

My cabinmate in the lower bunk was a Chinese merchant of some means, who I gathered was giving up his business in Hankow and moving to Shanghai. But he wasn't very communicative, except for perfunctory *ninzaos* ("good mornings") and *wan'ans* ("good evenings").

That was fine with me. Needing time to think, I welcomed the silence. I had to work things out in my own mind about how to proceed in my quest for a reporting job.

But my head was still too full of China to focus hard on my career. An inspiration of some kind, I hoped, might strike during the slow ride down the river. After all, as Buddha preached to his disciples, "Enlightenment originates within the mind, just as different things appear from the sleeve of a magician." The enforced isolation, I hoped, might provide the necessary magic.

In any case, the solitude of the ship would be conducive to a little soul-searching. It was that aspect of shipboard life that had always drawn me to the sea. During college I spent two summers in the merchant marine. Back then jobs on ships were hard to get, and I had to sweat out weeks in the Marine Firemen & Engineers' Union hall before signing on as a wiper aboard the *Edward L. Shea*. That tired old Tidewater Associated Oil Company tanker was spending its dying days plying between such unglamorous ports as Bayonne, New Jersey, and Beaumont, Texas. Not exactly the kind of voyages that inspired Joseph Conrad. Rather, trips so monotonous, and with such brief stops in port, it took extra pay and extra good food to keep the crew from jumping ship. However, the ship's destination never mattered to me. The sea's lonely beauty and limitless horizons always stirred my imagination.

I liked to stand on the forecastle head at night and peer down at a school of porpoises frolicking in the phosphorescent bow wake. Or lean against the stern rail under a skyful of stars and feel the whole ship shudder as the propeller churned out a frothy white path in the sea behind me.

During my second summer at sea, the union put me on a freighter named the *Floridian*, an old America Hawaii Line rust pot running intercoastal between Portland, Maine, and Portland, Oregon. Entering the Panama Canal on July 4, 1941, I remember seeing a small fleet of Japanese cargo vessels twirling idly on their anchor chains. The "Fuck-you Marus," as our crew called all Japanese freighters, had been banned from using the canal as of that date. It was still five months before Japan bombed Pearl Harbor. But the tension between our two countries was already high.

As we sailed past the "Fuckyou Marus" into the canal, the Japanese deckhands shook their fists. Five years later, I was surprised to see the old *Floridian*, all spruced up in a fresh coat of paint, discharging UNRRA cargo in Shanghai.

Those summer months on merchant ships led to an unusual seafaring assignment in the army. In the spring of 1942, a few months after I'd graduated as a second lieutenant from Engineer Officers Candidate School at Fort Belvoir, Virginia, I was assigned to the Hampton Roads Port of Embarkation. From there the army sent me to North Africa aboard the liberty ship *John Harvard*, one of the brand-new floating boxes slapped together in World War II. By coincidence, the ship's captain was the former third mate of the *Floridian*.

In addition to its merchant crew, the *John Harvard* carried a navy armed guard unit to man the antiaircraft guns, as well as an army detachment which I commanded. Our duty was to oversee the military cargo being transported to North Africa. On the return voyage we would be responsible for guarding several hundred Italian POWs packed into the empty cargo holds.

Our seventy-eight-ship convoy, escorted by eight or nine sub chasers and a small aircraft carrier, crossed the Atlantic without serious incident, even though the ocean swarmed with German submarines. On several occasions the convoy's commodore hoisted the William Fox flag, signaling the proximity of a U-boat. All the cargo ships would then maneuver evasively while the sub chasers raced around the convoy's perimeter dropping "ashcans," as the depth charges were called. "Stunning geysers are erupting out of the sea that is flat as an ice rink," I noted in a diary that I kept to relieve the monotony of the voyage.

On our sixteenth night we slid past the hulking black Rock of Gibraltar and entered the Mediterranean. What had been an almost blissful Atlantic cruise suddenly became a hectic series of war exercises. Sirens sounded general quarters. Barrage balloons blossomed over the convoy, and our captain ordered everyone aboard the *John Harvard* to wear life jackets and to sleep in their clothes.

We awoke to see British and American bombers circling over the convoy. A couple of pursuit planes swooped beneath the barrage balloons, barely missing the steel cables. Once, when our ship lurched violently, I was sure we'd been hit, but it was the liberty ship off our starboard beam that had taken the torpedo. She sent up a red distress flare, then, listing to port, slowly disappeared as the convoy plodded on.

After three days of zigzagging across the Med, we peeled off from the convoy and entered a pale blue harbor surrounded by a gleaming white city. "Algiers," we were finally informed.

Allied ships of all shapes and sizes lay at anchor, and it quickly became clear we were engaged in that old army game of "hurry up and wait." For the next three weeks, while Algiers beckoned temptingly in the distance, we twirled idly on our anchor chain, unable to go ashore. The forty-five Sherman tanks, howitzers, and crates of ammo stowed in our cargo holds might just as well have remained warehoused back in Hampton Roads.

The only Algerians we encountered were the bum boat boys who paddled out to trade bottles of "dago red" for cartons of Camels and Chesterfields. Wine, naturally, wasn't permitted aboard, so the bottles were hoisted up over the rail wrapped in souvenir scarves and shirts. A few bottles were reeled in on fishing lines rigged by a couple of the merchant sailors who had spotted schools of bonito chasing sardines around the harbor.

Unfortunately, our nights at anchor were not so idyllic. Often we were awakened by the wail of air-raid sirens, followed by the distant drone of the British interceptor planes taking off. Then a smoke screen would settle over the harbor. Sometimes through the smoke we could see the orange bursts of antiaircraft shells exploding high over the city. Then, the 40mm Bofors and "Chicago pianos" would join in, scorching the blackness with thousands of red tracers. The distant chugging of pompoms added to the din.

Usually this protective screen of antiaircraft fire chased the Italian bombers away from the city, though occasionally we glimpsed the white flashes of bombs bursting on the docks where we would unload. Searchlight beams would quickly sweep the sky directly overhead, seeking out the culprits. If the beams converged, we strained to see the tiny speck of a plane before antiaircraft shells peppered the sky all around it—at first a little above or below, then right where the light beams intersected. We never did see any of the shells find their mark.

One night our sky watch was diverted by an orange flare drifting silently down into the water about five hundred feet off our port bow. All at once the air around our ship exploded with bursting shells. Shrapnel zinged into our wire rigging and rained down on the superstructure and hatch covers as a half-dozen Italian planes roared in over the anchored ships. A plume of smoke billowed from the tail of one, looking for all the world like a wounded plane in a war movie.

The *John Harvard* lurched violently, then rolled gently as a bomb exploded in the water just off our stern. More bombs exploded, causing more lurches, followed each time by the same gentle rocking and gurgling, until the ship stabilized. Our own antiaircraft guns barked into action. Several neighboring ships joined in the free-for-all, firing a barrage of 20mm tracers that looked and sounded puny against the heavy thudding and bright flashes of the shore batteries.

Just as unexpectedly as they came, the Italian bombers flew back out to sea. One swooped low over the *John Harvard*, giving us a farewell buzz that made everybody freeze. But the plane soared harmlessly away.

A pall of acrid smoke still hung over the harbor like an early morning mist when Sparks, our radio operator and the ship's only source of news, announced that Allied troops had landed at Messina and started up the boot of Italy. We guessed the air raid had been a retaliatory gesture, although Algiers no longer really figured in the war.

That didn't seem to faze the Italians. Their bombers returned several more nights before we pulled the hook and headed east for Bizerte, a Tunisian port known to Americans back home by the hit song "Dirty Gertie from Bizerte."

In Bizerte we finally did get ashore. But by then everybody aboard had a bad case of cabin fever, adding to the friction between the navy armed guards and merchant sailors, who bragged about the $150 bonus they were being paid for every air raid. The bad feeling had finally boiled over into a fistfight during one of the daily poker games atop the forward hatch.

It took the four hundred "wop POWs," as we called them, to break the tension. Deliriously happy to be out of the war, they jammed into the cargo holds, broke out their accordions and guitars, and serenaded our ship with Italian love songs all the way back to Hampton Roads. There they were deloused and sent off, still singing, to detention camps in the Midwest, where they remained until the end of the war.

Sometimes, when one of my UNRRA truck convoys in Henan passed a Nationalist battalion slogging along, I was reminded of those Italian soldiers, who were just as downtrodden and despirited until they were taken prisoner. Chiang's soldiers had no more stomach for war than Mussolini's. No wonder the Communists found them so eager to surrender.

Before being mustered out of the army, I was treated to two more sea voyages. As a first lieutenant on the way to a replacement depot in New Guinea in early 1944, I spent eighteen days on the *Marine Swallow*, a jam-packed troop transport. Most all of my shipmates were members of the Mississippi National Guard with nicknames like "Possum," "Gray Squirrel," and "Woodchuck." There didn't seem to be a Tom, Dick, or Harry among them.

Then, at the end of the war, just after my promotion from captain to major, I shipped home from Manila on another army transport, the *Marine Adder*. To celebrate my birthday, which occurred at sea, I had smuggled aboard a case of Old Crow bourbon. The drinking bout lasted two days. During the first night's festivities we crossed the International Date Line. And as the sun's first rays peeked through the porthole, one of my cabinmates pointed out that another birthday of mine was just dawning, which also had to be celebrated. So we partied right through the second day until the Old Crow gave out.

The rest of that voyage, like this one down the Yangtze, provided plenty of quiet time to consider my prospects as an aspiring foreign correspondent. Before landing in San Francisco I had mapped out a head-on assault on the various news organizations, which failed to yield a single overseas job offer.

On this trip down the Yangtze, I took a more creative approach. I outlined several possible magazine articles about China, which I might first write to help sell myself as journalist. I also made a list of publications, including Life, National Geographic, and The Nation, which had shown interest in the articles and pictures I had already submitted. But I knew converting some editor's flickering enthusiasm, expressed in a one-paragraph letter, into a solid, full-time job offer wouldn't be easy.

Aside from all this soul-searching about my future, the five-day river ride was relaxing. Sliding downstream past tile-roofed pagodas and fertile paddies that descended in pale green steps to the riverbank, I was seeing a picturebook China that bore little resemblance to the one I'd just left behind in Henan.

Sometimes our steamer would steer a course close to the shore. From the deck I could hear the banging hammers, barking dogs, and distant ai-ho, ai-ho chant of a group of coolies unloading a sampan. Most of the shoreline villages had no docks. So the sampan noses were simply shoved up onto the mud bank. I asked a woman passenger who hailed from one of these villages what she would do if the Communists came to her place. "I'll stay," she said. "When the Japanese came I fled. But the Communists are Chinese. Fleeing once in a lifetime is enough."

During the day, these village scenes plus the peaceful parade of junks revealed no signs of the armed struggle going on for control of China. Only at night was there any evidence that precautions were being taken. With their faded orange and purple sails lowered, the high-sterned junks could be seen silhouetted by the shore in protective clusters—reminicent of the way our westward-bound pioneers circled their wagons to ward off the Indians.

The river craft came in an eye-catching assortment of sizes and shapes. Smallest and fastest were the sampans, propelled by the jerky wagging of a short stern oar. Hundreds of these little water bugs ferried passengers back and forth across the river. Between fares the sampan men would sidle up to passenger steamers like ours to catch any salvageable refuse.

In greatest profusion, especially around big ports like Wuhan and

Nanjing, were the lighters. Ranging from forty to fifty feet long, these cigar-shaped vessels were used in place of barges to unload the steel rails, sugar, flour, rice, cattle, and other cargoes from the big freighters venturing upriver from Shanghai. A few of the lighters had throbbing diesels. Most, however, were powered by a long, heavy oar, worked slowly back and forth by everybody aboard, from the tiny tots to the old grannies.

The most beautiful vessels of all were the large cargo junks, seaworthy enough to continue on down the South China coast to Fuzhou and Xiamen, or Amoy as it was called then. They were easy to identify by the big fish eye protruding from each side of their curled bow, and by the colorful mural splashed across their high stern.

A Chinese missionary on our steamer told me that he'd given up trying to convert these junk people to Christianity. "They rarely go ashore," he explained. "Births, marriages, and deaths all take place afloat." So it didn't seem likely that these fiercely independent people, who stayed on their boats right through the Japanese occupation, would ever succumb to Communism. Mao's teachings didn't fit their free lifestyle. Yet Communism was creeping steadily south toward the Yangtze. Several river towns had recently been given a taste of the Eighth Route Army's hit-and-run tactics.

By the time our steamer reached Shanghai, I was rested and ready to go through the bureaucratic ordeal of resigning from UNRRA. But somehow I'd forgotten the culture shock foreigners always feel upon entering that seething city, no matter how many times they'd been there before. It wasn't just the stunning clash of East and West, or rich and poor—barefoot rickshaw boys padding down Nanjing Road alongside sleek Rolls Royces; starving beggars sprawled on the pavement outside elegant restaurants; the Bund's marble banks and modern offices towering over the ramshackle shanties of the Huangpu waterfront. It was the inbred violence and rampant corruption that set Shanghai apart.

This was the place that prided itself on having a street named Blood Alley and on the variety of vices it offered, from the gambling halls and opium dens in the old city of Nantao, to the Broadway bars of Honkew lined with smiling Chinese singsong girls and White Russian "hostesses." This was where an exasperated missionary once cried out, "If God lets Shanghai endure, He owes an apology to Sodom and Gomorrah." This was also the place that inspired Marlene Dietrich to rasp, "It took more than one man to change my name to Shanghai Lily." And it's where sailors still got shanghaied.

Yes, all of that was true. But it was great to be there again after more than a year in Kaifeng.

CHAPTER IV

Coming to *Life*

SHANGHAI WAS ACTUALLY SEVERAL CITIES crammed into one. French Town accommodated Gallic transplants who gathered in the afternoon for an aperitif and tennis at the *Cercle Sportif*. The International Settlement was populated by Brits, whose favorite sport after a few pink gins followed by *tiffin* [lunch] was a game of lawn bowls on the manicured greensward of their Sporting Club, and by a few Yank businessmen, who tirelessly threw Yahtzee dice from a leather cup on the long mahogany bar at the American Club. An army of Austrian and Russian refugees rounded out the ranks of resident *yangquizis*, as all of us foreign devils were called.

I checked into the Park Hotel, a sleekly modern UNRRA billet located in the heart of the International Settlement's shopping district. UNRRA maintained rooms in several Shanghai hotels. The Park, overlooking the racecourse, was considered the best. From my tenth-floor window I looked straight down on the nine-hole golf course covering the racetrack's infield. The players there used two caddies—one to carry the bag, the other posted at the far end of the fairway to follow the ball. I'm sure it was cheaper to hire a second Chinese caddy than to lose a ball.

In Shanghai, I quickly discovered that I had to keep my own eye on the ball so as not to be sandbagged into signing up with UNRRA for another year, even though the relief program wasn't likely to last that long. It had become hopelessly bogged down in scandal as well as the war. At the center of the scandal was Chiang Kai-shek's financier brother-in-law. T. V. Soong, one of the most powerful men in China.

37

Early on, Soong stipulated that "in order to preserve the dignity of the Chinese people" all UNRRA supplies had to be placed under China's control as soon as they landed in Shanghai. That didn't make much sense since the relief programs themselves were being run by Americans and the other foreign nationals employed by UNRRA.

But Soong persisted. And that's how CNRRA, the China National Relief and Rehabilitation Administration, came into being. Soon there was no telling how much of the $685 million worth of food, clothing, and equipment turned over to CNRRA was going directly into the black market before it ever left Shanghai.

Only occasionally did UNRRA take any action against this wholesale plundering. Once when it was discovered that blood plasma donated by the American Red Cross was being sold in Shanghai drugstores for $25 a pint, UNRRA ordered the U.S. Navy shore patrol to seize the rest of the 3,500 cases which were still stored in a CNRRA *godown* [warehouse].

Another time it was a shipload of war-surplus jeeps that had to be recovered. But in this case the jeeps all had traceable serial numbers, preventing CNRRA from peddling them through local car dealers. Miffed at missing out on a hefty piece of black market business, the dealers got their good friend T. V. Soong to lodge an official protest. He accused the U.S. of "dumping free vehicles on the local market," and requested that henceforth UNRRA buy all of its jeeps in China before turning them over to CNRRA. The stench of that proposal carried all the way to Washington, where it was rejected. Most of the time, however, UNRRA simply refused to act, claiming corruption was too deeply rooted in the Nationalist regime to do anything about it.

What finally brought the scandal to a head was a bill for $190 million submitted by Soong for storing and transporting all the supplies that CNRRA had supposedly shipped to the hinterlands. A good portion of the $190 million, it was assumed, would go directly into Soong's pocket. But by this time Chiang had named his brother-in-law premier, so the outrageous bill couldn't be challenged without causing a diplomatic ruckus.

By handing over the $190 million, UNRRA erased what little morale was left among its American staff members in Shanghai. However, Soong's bogus storage and transportation bill didn't seem to faze the British staffers, who, feigning heavy cockney accents, humorously referred to Chiang as "Generalissimo Cash-my-check," and to his brother-in-law as "Shake-me-down Soong." But then, the Brits had a long history of doing business in China and were used to paying cumshaw.

The Americans were so shocked by Soong's theft from a relief agency dedicated to salvaging the lives of his own countrymen that many of the officers quit. As a result, pressure was being put on everyone else to stay to prevent the whole China program from collapsing prematurely. I could tell how desperate things were by the way I was being sweet-talked into going back to Kaifeng.

No sooner had I turned in my resignation than the personnel director whisked me upstairs for a friendly pat on the back from Harlan Cleveland, the dynamic young chief of UNRRA's China mission. The grandson of President Grover Cleveland began by reciting the importance of my job to the suffering hordes in Henan. You would have thought my leaving was undermining UNRRA's whole China effort. About all his enthusiasm did was to keep me from explaining how frustrating it was escorting one truck convoy after another through an active war zone, only to discover that half the cargo had been stolen, sold, or was sitting undistributed in some crooked warlord's warehouse. So I just sat there and listened. Finally, to end the session, I made my return to Kaifeng contingent upon UNRRA assigning armed guards to our convoys, which I knew was impossible.

A few months earlier, the veteran *New York Post* correspondent Robert Martin, or "Pepper" Martin, as he was known throughout China, had written an article about an incident another UNRRA officer and I had when our jeep was hit by three supposedly stray bullets on one of those "routine" runs down to Xihua. I thought that story, which Harlan Cleveland surely must have read, provided enough reason for my wanting to quit. But he never mentioned it. Instead, he kept playing up the need for us Americans to complete the task of helping China recover from so many years of flood, famine, pestilence, and war.

After that unsettling session, I headed straight for the Palace Hotel bar. The Palace was one of several Shanghai watering holes that boasted of having the "longest bar in the world." Its polished Philippine mahogany surface stretched about 100 feet from the front of the hotel, facing the Huangpu River, all the way back to the dark wood-paneled lobby. It was the perfect place to reinforce my resolve to quit and go home.

The bar itself was for men only. Or, at least, that was the closely observed protocol. A cadre of White Russian prostitutes, who also frequented the Palace, sat in pairs at tiny tables by the windows, but never at the bar. However, it was to their professional advantage, because they could smile through the windows at prospective male customers passing by on Nanjing Road.

Perhaps it was fate, or just a remarkable piece of luck, but the American standing next to me at the Palace bar on that Pearl Harbor Day in 1947 would forever change my life.

He was sipping chilled vodka that the bartender poured from a tall blue bottle sheathed in ice. "Will you have one?" he offered, motioning to the blue bottle. "I'm Bill Gray, Time-Life bureau chief in Shanghai."

I would not have guessed it. Short and bespectacled, his mien was more that of your friendly corner druggist than dashing foreign correspondent. But when he spoke, the words came crisply, accompanied by a wide smile that would have thawed the coldest interview subject.

During the course of our conversation I discovered that *Life* had just published my pictures of the "Stadium of Skulls," the hillside war memorial I'd stumbled upon in Hunan Province. I had mailed the negatives and story directly to the magazine's editorial office in New York City several months earlier, so nobody in the Shanghai bureau knew where they came from.

After we'd cleared up that little mystery and downed another vodka, Bill suggested that I drop in at the Time-Life bureau the next morning, where he already had an air-expressed copy of the magazine with my pictures. "Our office is on the Bund," he said. "Just around the corner from here."

The Time-Life bureau didn't fit my idea of the office of a powerful, worldwide news-gathering organization any more than Bill's almost mousy appearance fit my preconceived notion of a glamorous journalist. The old iron cage that served as an elevator at No. 17 the Bund wheezed its way up to the third floor, where the smudged walls sorely needed a fresh coat of paint, and the frayed furniture looked like it had been bought secondhand at an office-closing sale.

The view was nice. Out the window, as far as the eye could see, the Huangpu was filled with freighters, ferries, junks, sampans, and strings of ancient barges being pulled by decrepit tugs. Anchored off in the distance, and towering over the swarm of small craft like a great gray ghost, was the U.S. Navy cruiser *St. Paul*. It was there to show the flag. To let Americans in Shanghai know that they had a floating fortress to fall back on should the civil war suddenly engulf the city. Separating the teeming river from the teeming street below, clogged with rickshaws, pedicabs, trolley cars, and automobiles, was Shanghai's famous waterfront esplanade, the Bund.

I soon surmised that Bill hadn't invited me there simply to give me a copy of *Life* with my pictures. He got right to the point. Could I write a "situationer," as he called it, about the fighting in Henan Province? "We haven't had a reporter there in years," he said. "Not since Teddy White covered the Henan famine of 1943."

A situationer, Bill explained, was different from a news story about a specific event. It was a more general report about a developing crisis that hadn't yet come to a head.

At the Palace bar I'd told him about the new Communist threat to immobilize Chiang Kai-shek's armies in Henan. Everybody there knew that Zhengzhou's capture would be a crucial victory for Mao. But somehow word hadn't seeped down to Shanghai about the possible loss of this strategic rail hub where the east-west and north-south lines crossed. What Bill wanted me to write was an on-the-scene assessment of whether Mao might actually make good on his threat.

"If Chiang's armies are cut off at Zhengzhou," Bill continued, "and are then bottled up on the central plain, that will leave Nanjing and Shanghai virtually unprotected."

I hadn't carried my own civil war scenario that far. "Don't know about Nanjing and Shanghai," I said. "But if the Communist strategy succeeds, Kaifeng won't last a week."

The view from Kaifeng, about fifty miles east of Zhengzhou, didn't provide much perspective. But even up there we'd all heard about the top secret China white paper submitted to President Truman by General Charles Wedemeyer. Leaks about it had appeared in the American-owned *Shanghai Evening Post and Mercury*, copies of which eventually found their way to Kaifeng. The newspaper quoted Wedemeyer as warning Truman that the "military scales are now tipped in Mao's favor." It labeled his report as "the bluntest appraisal of Chiang's declining fortunes made so far by any U.S. official."

"Put in plenty of local color," Bill advised, assuming that I had accepted his assignment. "Give me an eyewitness account with so much detail and color that it's irrefutable. I don't want *Time*'s editors coming back at me, saying, 'Well, what does that relief worker up in Kaifeng know about covering a war.' "

He then explained how another *Time* correspondent stationed in Nanjing had been filing glowing accounts of Chiang's military victories along the Yellow River. "Sheer fantasy," Bill added. "But that's what the proprietor wants to hear."

The *proprietor*, he explained, was Henry Luce, or "Harry," as Bill called him, whose unswerving support of Generalissimo and Madame Chiang was known throughout China. *Time*'s man in Nanjing, I guessed, was probably pandering to Luce, but Bill didn't go into the internal politics of the magazine's China coverage. "Put in plenty of local color," he repeated. "But be sure you've got your facts straight," he cautioned as I stepped back into the wheezing old elevator.

Three days later I returned to the Time-Life bureau with my report. In eight double-spaced typewritten pages I described the sham battles being fought by the Nationalists, the stealing, the starving, the black-marketeering, and all the other rotten stuff I'd witnessed running my trucks through the Flooded Area south of the Yellow River. I even threw in Napoleon's old war maxim: "Nothing will disorganize an army more completely than pillage." It was hardly an unbiased account. But its conclusion was right: "Mao's armies are indeed going to nail the Nationalists to the Zhengzhou cross."

I left the eight-page report with the bureau secretary. The next morning Bill called and asked me to come back. "Oh, shit," I thought. "Too much detail. It wasn't colorful enough."

"Precisely what I wanted" were the words he greeted me with. The reason for my return summons, he explained, was to talk about the possibility of my going to work for *Time*.

"When are you flying to New York?" he asked.

"I hope in time for Christmas," I told him.

"Okay," he said. "I'll set up some interviews for you between Christmas and New Year's. That's a good time to see our people," he added. "Nobody gets any work done then."

I could hardly believe this conversation was taking place. Not after being flatly rejected by the Columbia School of Journalism and racking my brain all the way down the Yangtze River trying to figure a way to get a foot in some publisher's door.

A week later Bill called to say that my appointments at *Time* were all set. But I didn't get to the States until two days after Christmas. My island-hopping Pacific Overseas Airline plane had developed engine trouble in Guam. Then a blizzard dumped two feet of snow on New York, further delaying my arrival there until right after New Year's.

For some reason I suddenly felt apprehensive about those interviews. Bill had given me his copy of a new book called *The Great Ones* to read on the plane. "It's a hatchet job," he warned. "But it'll teach you a little about Time Inc."

The Great Ones was a thinly disguised novel about Henry Robinson Luce and Clare Boothe Luce. The author, Ralph Ingersoll, was a former *Time* editor, and supposedly a friend and protégé of Luce's. While the book's subtitle—*The Love Story of Two Very Important People*—sounded harmless enough, I found Ingersoll's description of the vicious power struggle going on between them pretty scary.

In the book, Sturges Strong, unmistakably Henry Luce, leaps straight from Yale to founding editor of *Facts*, "the knowing weekly." Stuck in Albuquerque overnight because of an airplane breakdown, he falls in love with a fellow passenger, the multitalented and recently divorced Letia Long, who bears a strong resemblance to Clare Boothe Luce.

Thrown together by chance, the fusion of their dynamic personalities is near nuclear. As Letia explains: "He was a male who could impose his will on the world." Yet in the novel's most dramatic chapter, titled "The Big Touch," Sturges is down on his knees in their bedroom, tearfully begging Letia to lend him $5 million to keep Facts, Inc., from being bankrupted by the unexpected success of its new picture magazine, *Fantasy*. Just as happened in the early days of *Life* magazine, *Fantasy* couldn't raise advertising rates fast enough to keep pace with its exploding circulation, thereby threatening the financial foundations of the company.

"I'll have to touch you for a small loan, my little blond kitten," Sturges pleads.

But the kitten turns out to be a tough cat. "Do you know what you're asking, Sturges," she replies. "You're asking for practically every cent I have."

Finally she adds, baring her true self, "It's too much a part of me, all that money, for me to risk."

Like *Life*, *Fantasy* not only survived without the loan, but became so successful that its only problem was finding sufficient advertisers with mass markets profitable enough to justify the high space rates charged by the wildly popular picture magazine.

Corny as it was, the novel made me worry that my interviewers at *Time* might be as intimidating as the Luces were portrayed in the book. I was wrong.

Manfred Gottfried, or "Gott," as everybody called the fatherly chief of correspondents, was assigned to shepherd me through a quick succession of informal chats with Max Ways, the foreign news editor of *Time*, Wilson Hicks, the picture editor of *Life*, Eleanor Welch, the assignment editor of *Life*, and finally with Edward K. Thompson, then the assistant managing editor of *Life*. Those conversations, surprisingly, were about China, not about my qualifications. Nobody even asked me to fill out an employment application.

Three days later I was on the payroll. But only after agreeing to go right back to Shanghai. The *Life* correspondent there apparently was being fired, though nobody explained why, and I was to be his replacement. "You've been away a long time," said Gott. "Spend a little time exploring the U.S. on your way back to China. Get a feel for America again."

Those were my only instructions. The idea of traveling around America visiting friends at *Life*'s expense seemed a little crazy. But who could object.

CHAPTER V

Suddenly, It's Mao's Manchuria

ONLY THREE WEEKS HAD ELAPSED since my departure from Shanghai. Yet the China I returned to in January 1948 seemed far different from the one I'd left. As a regional trucking supervisor for UNRRA, I'd been sucked into the civil war as a semiparticipant, stymied often by Guomindang corruption and stalled occasionally by Nationalist or Communist gunfire. Coming back as a correspondent, I was now essentially a spectator.

There was another important difference. *Life*, my new employer, was at that time the world's greatest visual communicator. From its inaugural issue in 1936, with an aerial view of Fort Knox and a picture of the first moment of a baby's life, the magazine offered both dazzling spectacles and revealing intimacies—coronations, weddings, wars, and death—such as had not been seen before. Its power and influence then far exceeded television's. Even though the magazine was already printing and selling more than five million copies a week (circulation eventually peaked at eight million), it considered itself as much a family as a business—full of hard-driving, exciting, and sometimes difficult people. So I was now backed by an organization with an almost magical aura. It was a heady feeling.

Working for a picture magazine, however, precluded covering the war from the sidelines in Shanghai as quite a few of the newspaper and wire service correspondents did. It meant being at the front—that is, if you could find out where the fighting was going on.

Long-distance phone service in China was still pretty primitive. With luck, patience, and shouting you might get through to Beijing or Nanjing. But calling any other city, particularly those under siege, was like trying to telephone Mars. Relying on the government's Central News Agency to follow the war's progress was just as dicey. Threatened attacks were purposely unreported for fear of alarming the public. And the actual battles were always heralded as Nationalist victories, sometimes even after Chiang's soldiers had abandoned their weapons and fled. There was only one way to find out where the fighting was going on. That was by hitching rides with CAT—the Civil Air Transport planes operated by General Claire Chennault.

They were the same war-surplus C-46s and C-47s, flown by the same soldier-of-fortune pilots that had been ferrying UNRRA supplies from Guangzhou and Shanghai to Kaifeng and various other remote cities. Having come to know many of these former army, navy, and marine corps flyers from their weekly trips with spare parts for my trucks made it easy for me to bum rides with them now. But it was a hit-and-miss proposition. Their destinations and cargoes depended entirely on the vicissitudes of the war. On one flight it was sixty-three Trappist monks, accompanied by eight cows, being moved to a safer locale. On another, it was two-hundred orphans being flown out of harm's way.

Most of the flights, however, were routine supply shuttles delivering everything from hog bristles and goatskins to sacks of flour, wheat, and millet. Because so many cities were already cut off from their surrounding farmlands, they depended on daily airlifts. And with only three airlines operating in China, CAT's fifteen planes and fifty pilots were being pushed to the limits of their respective maintenance and endurance.

Flying from 150 to 200 hours a month, Chennault's romantic World War II veterans would frequently switch on the automatic pilot, put their cowboy boots up on the dashboard, and catnap at the controls, which wasn't so reassuring if you happened to be occupying the jump seat in the cockpit right behind them. Yet even semicomatose, they seemed to cope all right with the most unusual midair emergencies.

Once Robert Rousselot was jolted awake when an engine conked out at 11,000 feet. Jumping into action, he kept the plane aloft by jettisoning $48 billion ($1.5 million U.S.) worth of Chinese currency that he was transporting for the Central Bank of China. The money fluttered down into the unbelieving hands of peasants working in the fields below.

Another unexpected emergency arose while CAT was evacuating 625 prize New Zealand sheep from a northern grazing area that had come under Communist attack. Most of the passengers were ewes. They were a well-behaved flock, leaning forward on takeoff like seasoned sailors into a stiff wind, relaxing again when the plane leveled off. But a few rams accidentally got mixed in with one load. The ensuing stampede almost caused the plane to crash when a pair of hotly pursued ewes charged into the cockpit. Nobody had warned pilot Bill Gaddie that it was mating season.

Landings and takeoffs under enemy fire were another matter. They required total concentration, particularly during the airlifting of artillery shells and hand grenades. On these ammo runs the Chinese copilots were routinely ordered to "assume the position," which meant clasping their hands atop their heads during takeoff so they couldn't throw any switches which might cause the plane to crash. But landing on the hacked-out dirt runways with the fat-bellied C-46s loaded to the ceiling with high explosives required the copilots' close cooperation. It was their responsibility to scour the surrounding hills for camouflaged Communist batteries that might start taking potshots at the runway.

To cover the civil war, *Life* had teamed me up with Jack Birns, a burly, high-spirited photographer from California. Some mornings we would drop in at the CAT operations center (called the CAT house, naturally) at Longhua Airport in Shanghai with no special destination in mind. Then for three or four days we'd hopscotch to remote airstrips all over China, looking for action. Sometimes we'd hear of heavy skirmishing, only to come upon a peaceful pastoral scene. Other times we'd discover the leftover desolation of a battle already finished. As a result, most of our trips turned out to be wild-goose chases.

You might expect that accompanying airlifts of guns and ammunition would frequently lead to some action. That wasn't the case. In the best-fortified bastions like Shenyang, Beijing, Tianjin, and Qingdao— the cities Chiang Kai-shek was determined to hang on to—the Nationalists and Communists seemed to be perpetually maneuvering for position instead of fighting.

What happened at my old UNRRA headquarters town of Kaifeng was typical. Six months after I left, the "One-eyed Dragon," General Liu Bocheng, and General Chen Yi amassed 200,000 Communist troops in western Henan. Then, just as Mao had threatened, they nailed the Nationalists to the Zhengzhou cross, overrunning Kaifeng as well as the vital Zhengzhou rail hub. But having demonstrated their military superiority, the Communists then pulled back, leaving the two cities to stew in the realization that they could be recaptured anytime Mao wanted. That, of course, was the Communist leader's strategy, letting the main population centers hang precariously on the Nationalist vine until they fell by their own weight.

Occasionally, our aerial barnstorming paid off. By the last week of October 1948 Chiang Kai-shek had personally taken command of the so-called Northeast Bandit Suppression Headquarters in Beijing. From there he was deploying what was left of his 700,000 troops defending Manchuria. With Henry Luce's help we had been granted a rare appointment to interview and photograph the generalissimo. Madame Chiang, whom Luce had recently escorted around the U.S. on a highly lucrative aid-to-China fund-raising tour, served as her husband's interpreter.

From the moment we entered the generalissimo's reception room it was clear that the interview and picture-taking were going to be a bust. He was dressed as usual in a plain olive green uniform devoid of decorations or insignia. But on this day, at least, the man appeared just as empty of energy and emotion, although once the interview commenced, he became terribly fidgety. Either he was uncomfortable at being subjected to my questions and Jack's stage directions for the pictures, or he resented giving up precious time he needed to spend with his generals.

"The gimo," I jotted in my notebook, "keeps hopping nervously around the room like a sparrow, as if he thought we were trying to trap him. Each time the shutter clicks he takes another hop. Asked a question, he hops again, impatient, it seems, to end the whole unpleasant encounter with the two *Life* interlopers."

Not once did he wait for his wife to finish translating a question before spouting in his choppy Ningbo accent what sounded like a testy retort. Obviously, his staccato replies were being softened by the smiling Madame as she turned them into her best Wellesley English. "Perhaps the war is eroding his equilibrium" was the last comment in my notebook.

Five months earlier in Nanjing, I had watched this same man coolly preside over the National Assembly. It was the first time in China's long history that delegates from all the far-flung provinces and border regions had come together under one roof to try to resolve their differences and adopt a new constitution. There were Lolo tribesmen, Turkis, and the Grand Pan Chun Lama from Tibet, a so-called "living Buddha." Ma Huang-kwei, the Moslem warlord of Ningxia, was also there, as was his hard-riding cavalryman cousin, Ma Pu-fang, governor of Qinghai. They came dressed in colorful costumes, and spoke in strange tongues and dialects. Women delegates, surprisingly, were present, including a stunning representative from Manchuria, who, at the closing ceremony, was crowned "queen of the National Assembly." In all, more than 2,600 delegates showed up. Adding to the democratic spirit of the event was a group of self-proclaimed hunger strikers who confused the foreign press by gnawing on bananas and oranges while loudly protesting the proceedings. Fasting, they explained, simply meant not eating rice.

Not even these hecklers rattled Chiang, whose commanding presence kept the proceedings moving along at a nice clip. More than that, the usually autocratic Guomindang leader actually urged the delegates to air their grievances. And some of them hotly responded by demanding that he shoot Army Chief of Staff General Chen Cheng for letting the Nationalist forces fall into such a precarious position in Manchuria. But throughout the conclave the generalissimo managed the disputes skillfully. "His performance," I reported at the time, "was most impressive."

At our private interview in Beijing, the commanding presence had given way to edginess and impatience. Chiang kept glancing at his wife as if to say, "Who let these guys in?" His only message for our magazine was one he had delivered many times before: "Our fight against the Communist rebels is a continuation of the war of resistance against the Japanese." Chiang had a habit of mentioning the Reds and Japs in one breath. Even when he and Mao were jointly arrayed against Japan, he'd say: "The Japanese are like a terrible skin disease, but Communism is a cancer."

After fifteen minutes of this charade he summoned two of his generals from an adjoining room. One was Fu Zuoyi, the heavyset, bemedaled defender of Beijing, the other Wei Li-huang, the balding, mustachioed commander of the Nationalist forces in Manchuria. Their entrance signaled our interview's abrupt end, but as Madame Chiang politely explained: "The generalissimo has asked his field commanders to brief you."

With wooden pointers and war maps, the two generals proceeded to explain the gimo's "pocket strategy" for holding on to Shengyang, or Mukden, as Manchuria's capital was then called, and the name it is still better known by today. This threatened coal, iron, and arms-manufacturing center, they indicated, was the linchpin of Chiang's whole northern defense plan.

On a couple of flights to Mukden we had already observed the generalissimo's pocket strategy in action, and it didn't seem to be working. We had photographed CAT's round-the-clock airlift bringing in thousands of tons of supplies for the army, but also carrying out thousands of fleeing civilians, an indication of the city's nervousness. More than 200,000 Nationalist soldiers supposedly were dug in solidly around the city. Yet a few army units, we knew, had already mutinied or defected.

Some of their officers, meanwhile, had turned carpetbagger, selling truckloads of military rations in Mukden's black market. We heard about one general who signed for a planeload of currency, and then instead of paying his troops had the money flown back to his bank in Shanghai. But we never could verify that story. Despite its many festering problems, Mukden and its million residents continued grimly to hang on.

Before finishing our briefing, General Fu Zuoyi launched into an account of Mukden's embattled history. Back in the seventeenth century, he explained, the city flourished as the throne of the Manchu Dynasty. However, once the Manchus moved to Beijing, greedy foreign powers began to eye the whole resource-rich region. He then recapped the bitter Japanese occupation: how in 1931 they renamed Manchuria Manchukuo, installed puppet Henry Pu Yi as regent, and used Chinese slave labor to build Mukden's heavy industry.

Chiang Kai-shek, said General Fu, had vowed that China would regain Manchuria as soon as Japan was defeated. But three days after the atom bomb destroyed Hiroshima in 1945, the Russians marched into Mukden, disarmed the Japanese, handed their weapons to the Communists, and then proceeded to strip the steel mills and factories, carting off all the machinery to Siberia.

"That," concluded General Fu dramatically, "was the most recent rape of Mukden. Now," he warned, "Mao's soldiers are trying to do it again. But they won't succeed."

He was wrong. Landing in Mukden a few days later, we discovered the situation had suddenly become desperate. "This is a ghost city," I cabled Life's editors in New York. "No preparation has been made for a last-stand defense. Most of the government troops are encamped near rail sidings awaiting evacuation. In the heart of the metropolis, freezing blasts of wind whistle down the broad, empty thoroughfares. Shopfronts and army pillboxes at main street intersections are boarded up. Jagged walls in factory areas built by the Japanese, blasted by American bombers during World War II, and later pillaged by Russian occupation forces stand silhouetted against a steel-gray sky. Mukden, the capital of China's richest industrial area, looks as desolate as the ragged, half-frozen refugees picking their way through debris on the few streets where people can still be found."

No other reporters or photographers were there, a situation hard to imagine with today's media saturation of even the smallest war. Photographer Birns and I figured we probably had no more than seven or eight hours to grab what pictures we could before the city fell.

We started up the road to Tieling, thirty-five miles north of Mukden, only to discover that the Communist troops of General Lin Biao, once Chiang Kai-shek's star student at Whampoa Military Academy, were coming down the other way. Surplus U.S. Army tanks and howitzers, abandoned by retreating Nationalists, littered the fields. A freight train chuffed by packed with fleeing soldiers. Those that couldn't squeeze inside sat shivering atop the train in their padded yellow uniforms. In my notebook I scribbled: "From a distance they made the long string of boxcars look like sausage links smothered with mustard." Another clump of yellow-clad soldiers covered the coal pile in the old steam locomotive's tender.

On our way back to town we passed members of the highly touted 207th Infantry Division holding a close-order drill as if they were practicing for a peacetime parade. Their commanding officer had just received word that Chiang's 100,000-man Blue Force was locked in battle below Mukden, trying to open an escape corridor for them and the other Nationalist units attempting to run the gauntlet south. "We drill to keep warm and to keep our spirits up," the officer explained.

By the time we returned to the city, business and traffic had come to a halt. We stopped at Tschurin Co, Ltd., the Soviet subsidized department store. Still fully staffed, its display counters were filled with canned delicacies, chinaware, boots, furs, jewelry, and other luxuries. But not one customer appeared.

Most of the city's activities centered around the railway station and airports. An enormous crowd of would-be ticket buyers had wedged themselves between the train depot and the one-hundred-foot-high Russian victory obelisk, topped with a Soviet tank. Some of the people were selling their belongings to raise money for a ticket, though all of the departing trains were already filled with soldiers.

At Pai Ling Field, Mukden's military airport, a succession of Chinese air force C-46s and C-47s were evacuating one army company after another. We were told that during this mass exodus, General Wei Li-huang, the Nationalist commander who had briefed us in Beijing, had managed to slip away.

At South Field, the civilian airport, CAT and the two other cargo carriers were running a hundred shuttles a day to Tianjin, Qingdao, and Beijing. Thousands of civilians, awaiting their turn to board a plane, swarmed over the frozen field. They stood in the wan sunlight shaking the chill from their limbs as C-46s droned monotonously in and out. For those lucky people, however, the slip of white paper that entitled them to board one of the departing cargo planes had suddenly become the most precious possession in the world. But it took more than just a ticket to get on one of the planes.

As soon as the crew of an arriving C-46 finished tossing out its cargo of rice or flour, a wild human phalanx would surge toward the open hatch. Kicking, punching, and clawing, men, women, and children would then try to fight their way aboard. The pilots had to stamp their cowboy boots on the outstretched fingers of those still desperately trying to climb in, to finally close the hatch.

At the U.S. Consulate we found everything moving in reverse. Instead of preparing to evacuate, Consul General Angus Ward and his staff were busy barricading themselves in behind a year's supply of flour and canned goods. All their files and records had already been flown down to Qingdao for safekeeping. But the State Department had ordered the consular personnel to stay put.

As we entered the consulate compound, Major John Singlaub, head of the External Survey Detachment (a forerunner of the CIA) was chopping up a shortwave radio transmitter with an ax. He hadn't gone bonkers, the young, crew-cut major said. He was simply following emergency orders from Shanghai to prevent the consulate's intelligence equipment from falling into Communist hands. (Twenty-nine years later, as a major general in South Korea, Singlaub was dismissed by President Jimmy Carter for publicly criticizing the administration's national security policy.)

Consul General Ward, who had served in Vladivostok and come to know the Russian Communists intimately, claimed to welcome the chance to stay behind in Mukden—"an usual opportunity," he said, "to make contact with China's Communists as well." He certainly looked the part of an international go-between. Fluent in both Russian and Chinese, this large, imposing man with a white goatee could have stepped right out of a Hollywood spy thriller. But behind that façade was a tough old foreign service coot, perfectly cast for the role he was about to play.

Ward, nevertheless, realized that reestablishing a dialogue with Mao's hardliners wouldn't be easy. Contact with them had been broken off almost two years earlier, when an exasperated General George Marshall finally gave up trying to mediate a peace agreement between Mao and Chiang. But if any American could get a conversation going again with the Chinese Communists, Angus Ward was the man to try.

His attempts, it turned out, failed abysmally. At first the Communists kept Ward under virtual house arrest. Later they denounced him as a spy, but refused to let him close the consulate and go home. Finally they clapped him in jail, concocting a story that he'd beaten up a Chinese employee. After a month of solitary confinement in a filthy, unheated cell, he was deported. However, the humiliation suffered by

Ward and his staff during their fifteen months under the Communists wasn't fully revealed until 1993, when an interview with a surviving member of the Mukden consulate appeared in the State Department's *Foreign Service Journal.*

"Yes, Angus was trying to make contact with the Communists, but he couldn't," former consular officer Eldon Erickson recalled. "They said they didn't recognize America or its consul general."

Erickson also described how the Communist guards treated the Americans like prisoners of war. "Just to go to the office from the official residence, they would come and march us with pistols in our backs." But Erickson claimed their most terrifying moments in Mukden came during the nightly attacks by the Nationalist air force. "Here we were, being bombed by our own planes," he said. "We had to put water in the bathtubs and open the windows because of the concussion. But one evening when we were hit, quite a few of the windows blew out anyway." Two of Erickson's colleagues were injured. "I remember," he said, "picking slivers of glass out of their lips with a pair of tweezers."

Birns was still photographing Ward behind the mountain of canned goods collected in the consulate when word came that Lin Biao's forward units had already reached Mukden's outskirts. "Get your asses out to the airport, or you'll be stuck with us," ordered the diplomat rather undiplomatically.

Racing back to South Field, we found CAT had already stopped flying the refugee shuttles. Fortunately for us, the airline had made it a rule to keep one plane on the field at all times to evacuate its own ground crew. We clambered aboard.

En route to Qingdao, pilot Neese Hicks was warned by radio to steer clear of Dairen [now called Luta] and Port Arthur [Lushun] Soviet fighters apparently had buzzed a couple of CAT shuttles earlier that day after they strayed too close to those two Chinese ports still controlled by Russia. Instead, Hicks flew us over Yingkou so Birns could shoot aerials of the evacuation port which we thought might become Manchuria's Dunkirk. Riding at anchor below was the cruiser *Chongqing,* formerly the *Aurora* when it belonged to the British Royal Navy, plus a flotilla of Chinese destroyers and LSTs. But only a few thousand Nationalist soldiers ever reached Yingkou, before it, along with Mukden, fell the next day.

Twenty-four hours later we were back in Shanghai. The Central News Agency still hadn't announced the fall of Mukden, and with it the loss of all Manchuria. None of our reporter friends at the Foreign Correspondents' Club was aware of what had happened. A chunk of China bigger than California, Oregon, and Washington combined had just been wrested from Chiang Kai-shek's control. More than 400,000 of his troops had died or been captured. Yet the Nationalist government was still trying to keep this Armageddon a secret.

The problem now was to get our pictures and exclusive eyewitness account into the issue of *Life* scheduled to be put to bed the next night in New York. The words, which went by cable, weren't a problem. But the dozen or so rolls of undeveloped film had to be sent by plane. And the trans-Pacific flight to San Francisco on Pan Am's lumbering DC-4s took forty hours, minus the thirteen hours of clock time gained crossing the International Date Line. Today's instantaneous satellite feeds make logistical obstacles like that hard to imagine. But back in 1948, clearing film packets through customs, sweating out weather delays, and all the mechanical breakdowns that plagued those old prop planes provided a suspenseful climax to covering every overseas story.

Fortunately, our editors in New York refused to let the difficult logistics deny us a scoop, even if it meant holding the presses for a day. They ordered a portable photo lab set up at the San Francisco airport. Processed between planes, the undried negatives were then couriered in jars of water to Chicago, where *Life*'s printing plant was located. But Chicago was socked in and the plane landed in Cleveland. A charter pilot was persuaded to fly the courier to fogbound Chicago. Holding the now-dry negatives against the window of a taxi, the managing editor, who had flown out from New York, selected five pages of pictures on the way to the printing plant.

People who picked up a copy of *Life* the next day had no idea of the extraordinary effort made to get that story into the pages of their magazine—and probably couldn't have cared less. But knowing that millions of Americans were looking at those pictures and reading that article made Birns and me feel pretty good. The thought, too, that Generalissimo Chiang Kai-shek could no longer hide the truth that control of a vast industrial province had just slipped from his grasp made us feel that we were helping to set the record straight on China's civil war. For the first time I appreciated the enormous power invested in me as the representative of a worldwide news organization.

CHAPTER VI

The Mad Assault on Amnyi Machen

TWICE A MONTH tribes living in the foothills of the Amnyi Machen range in wild and remote western China sing an ode to the icy peaks above. They sing that Amnyi Machen is a sacred mountain holding untold stores of gold, and that travelers who tamper with its treasures or mysteries will provoke divine wrath.

Yet it was Mao Zedong's adherents, not any mountain dieties, whose wrath was provoked by an American aerial expedition that had come to measure the height of Amnyi Machen. Arriving at the climax of the civil war in 1948, the single-minded planners of the expedition were oblivious of the life-and-death struggle going on between the Nationalists and the Communists. Their sole interest was to end, once and for all, the long-simmering argument of whether this unexplored peak was taller than Mount Everest.

"They have really come to hunt uranium for the manufacture of atomic weapons," screeched the Red radio, which accused the Nationalist government of "trading Amnyi Machen's aerial survey rights for millions of dollars of American military aid."

Another Communist broadcast denounced the expedition as a military adventure. "A death sentence," the Red radio insisted, "should be given at once to any of the imperialist traitors aboard the plane if by chance they fall into our hands."

There was little chance of that happening. Whatever political control existed over the region was still in the hands of warlord Ma Pufang. Spiritually, the region was controlled by the Panchen Lama, the ten-year-old "living Buddha" whom some ten million followers honored as the incarnate god of Tibet.

For the American survey party, Amnyi Machen represented one of the last great natural challenges—a mountain few civilized men had seen and none had accurately measured. In 1922, a British Army officer, General George Pereira, traveling through Tibet, reported sighting a tremendous mountain. "It towers above everything around," he wrote. But the following year Pereira died trying to lead another expedition to the mountain.

In 1930, *National Geographic* published the journals of an American botanist, Dr. Joseph Rock, stating that the frozen peak "towers more than 30,000 feet." Several other explorers then set out to reach Amnyi Machen. After a few more died in vain attempts, the legend grew that the mountain's god had jinxed them.

During World War II, U.S. fliers who strayed north of the regular "Hump" route between India and China came back with fresh tales of an incredible mountain. One pilot, Rowan Neff, was flying at 22,000 feet and snapped a picture of an icy rampart that he said reached "much higher." From all of these reports grew excited speculation that Amnyi Machen might indeed be taller than the 29,141-foot Everest.

The aerial survey party consisted of three principals, each an imposing figure in his own field and each a dissimiliar personality with diverse objectives.

Milton Reynolds, a multimillionaire ballpoint-pen manufacturer from Chicago, had financed the expedition and come along hoping to bask in the glory of proving conclusively that this mountain was indeed higher than Everest. He egotistically expected that a grateful China might rename Amnyi Machen Mt. Reynolds.

Bradford Washburn, director of the Boston Museum of Science and the world's foremost mapper of mountains, provided the expertise and equipment required to accurately measure Amnyi Machen. He wanted to use this opportunity also to study the glaciers and geology of this isolated area protected on the north and west by the Qinghai and Tibetan plateaus, and on the east by the dramatic gorges of the upper Yellow River. (In Tibetan, Amnyi Machen means "father of the Yellow River.")

The third member of the team was Bill Odom, a World War II Hump pilot who had recently broken Howard Hughes's round-the-world speed record of 91 hours and 14 minutes by circling the globe in 78 hours and 55 minutes. He accomplished that feat in a stripped-down, souped-up Douglas A-26 attack bomber christened the *Reynolds Bombshell*. Reynolds had also provided the financial backing on that adventure, and had gone along, purportedly as "navigator," to share in the glory and promote his ballpoint pens.

For the aerial survey flight, Odom converted a B-24 bomber into a long-range, high-altitude survey plane that he redesignated a C-87 and christened *Explorer*. He claimed it was capable of probing China's most remote mountains and returning to its base with fuel to spare. "I want nothing more," he said, "than to swoop and soar round those forbidding peaks where few pilots have ventured before."

Life's editors in New York had obtained the exclusive rights to cover the expedition, which is how I got involved. But from the day this powerhouse triumvirate blew into Shanghai, things started going awry. When the team finally fled China in their converted bomber, a squadron of Nationalist air force fighters chased after them—or so Milton Reynolds claimed. The fumes of ill will left behind by their expedition forced a full-fledged State Department investigation.

First to arrive in Shanghai was museum director Washburn. An impecunious scientist, he decided to save hotel expenses by spending the nights in a sleeping bag on my office floor. In addition to his mountain-measuring equipment, he brought with him the journals of Dr. Rock.

Dr. Rock's journals recited hairbreadth escapes from death in this wild frontier region controlled by demon-fearing local chiefs. He reported fighting blizzards, trudging over 16,000-foot passes, and crossing rivers on inflated goatskin rafts or by creeping over precarious rope-and-vine bridges. He told of being trapped by bandits in the funeral chamber of an old temple. Holding a .45-caliber pistol in each hand, he said he hid between the coffins, all the while protecting his precious plant collection. By morning the bandits were gone, though he noticed the heads of several of them hanging from poles outside the village.

The closest Dr. Rock came to Amnyi Machen was about fifty miles. It was by rough triangulation that he estimated the icy peak to be at least 30,000 feet, lending credence to General Pereira's belief that it might truly be taller than Everest.

With Rock's journals in hand, Washburn's first task was to secure the assistance of the Academia Sinica, the government-sponsored scientific institute, and through it the cooperation of the China Institute of Geography and the Chinese Geological Survey. By pooling all of their previous findings, those three research organizations created a new map for Washburn that he claimed was the "most complete combination of all known information on the Amnyi Machen area." Grateful for their help, he promised each group a seat on the *Explorer* during the survey flights.

Next, Washburn set about obtaining the all-important logistical support for the expedition, a task severely complicated by the war. After meeting with the Standard-Vacuum Oil Company and with the China National Aviation Corporation, he was able to arrange for Explorer's refueling at the expedition's jump-off base in Lanzhou, which despite its remoteness had come under sporadic Communist attack.

Washburn also had to fend off continuing verbal attacks by the Communists. "Their assertion of American military aggression is a ridiculous distortion of the truth," he replied in a press conference. "This expedition is wholly scientific in nature." He also announced that a Chinese army officer would be on every flight to prevent photographing anything of military importance.

The boss of the expedition, Milton Reynolds, burst upon the scene in China unconcerned about the war, and seemingly more intent on promoting his so-called "atomic pens" than in measuring Amnyi Machen. At that time, ballpoint pens were a brand-new invention, and Reynolds had built a quick fortune by retailing for $12.50 what cost him 33 cents to manufacture. At one New York City department store alone, Time reported that "thousands of customers all but trampled one another to buy what was advertised as the fantastic, atomic era, miraculous pen that needs refilling only once every two years, and can write underwater on paper, cloth, or plastic."

On his first day in Shanghai, Reynolds almost started a riot by giving away fifty pens on a busy street corner. Emerging from his car with yellow pen cartons sprouting from every pocket, he stopped a passing pedestrian and offered him a free pen. In a few seconds Reynolds was ringed in, and a minute later was cowering in a doorway while hands clawed at every pocket. Urchins climbed on their parents' backs or burrowed between their legs. Rickshaw boys put down their shafts to join in the treasure hunt. Even two policemen, who came to investigate, were soon scrambling for pens. Picked clean, Reynolds finally pried himself free of the mob and escaped in his car. Of course, he had hired a photographer to record for posterity that tumultuous scene.

Reynolds quickly called a series of press conferences at which he proved no less bashful. Plans were already afoot, he claimed, to manufacture his pens in China. He promised to retain only a modest royalty for himself, passing on most of the profits to the Nationalists' New Life Movement. His first "gift of friendship," he announced, would be 10,000 pens which he had brought with him for Madame Chiang Kaishek to sell and then donate the proceeds to charity.

Initially, Reynolds's whirlwind appearances and pronouncements provided a pleasant diversion from the war. Dressed in a gaudy safari suit with gold and green insignias on each shoulder and shiny brass buzzers on both breast pockets, the pen manufacturer became instantly recognizable wherever he went. He claimed to have had the uniform made so he could send his only other suit out for dry cleaning. Cynics suggested he was trying on for size and effect the costume he intended to be photographed in upon his triumphant return from Amnyi Machen.

As Reynolds's fame in China spread, he started referring to himself as "a modern Magellan," an explorer "eternally seeking new frontiers." Although he didn't come right out and suggest that Amnyi Machen be renamed Mt. Reynolds, he reminded reporters that Everest had been called Chomo-Lungma (Mother Goddess of the Land) until the Welch surveyor, Sir George Everest, had taken the trigonometric measurements that established it as the world's tallest mountain.

Newspapers in China got the hint all right, and tweaked Reynolds in a flurry of ego-deflating editorials. "Our mountains are named after famous men," Beijing's *Xinminbao* pointed out. "Thus we have Tai Shan named after Confucius and Wu Tai named after Buddha. But here is Mr. Reynolds, holding an atomic pen in hand, coming to seek his fame from a Chinese mountain."

Shen Bao, in a more serious vein, cited other differences between the Chinese and American view of mountains. "The Chinese think of mountains as refuges for hermits and disappointed politicians, or as inspiration for poets and painters," the newspaper explained. Unhappily, it concluded: "Mountains are also famous for the coal and iron in them. But the mining rights have usually fallen into the hands of powerful foreign businessmen like Mr. Reynolds, who then spoil their natural beauty."

Shanghai's *Ta Kung Pao* took a different tack and hung its editorial head in shame, because Chinese scientists hadn't already answered the riddle of Amnyi Machen. "When American scientists come to China they look upon us as backward," *Ta Kung Pao* lamented. "Naturally, we should be ashamed of our backwardness. But their arrogance is also embarrassing."

All this needling didn't faze Reynolds, who reveled in the bad publicity as well as the good. "This may be called the lousiest, most disorganized expedition in history," he announced when one delay after another kept the survey group from getting off the ground. "But when it's over, it will be said: 'They made it.' "

Washburn, on the other hand, was becoming increasingly embarrassed by Reynolds's antics and pronouncements. Privately to me, he said he regretted having lent both his own and his museum's name to an expedition sponsored by a publicity seeking tycoon. In front of the Chinese, however, he praised Reynolds's generosity. "Mr. Reynolds's personal keenness for exploration and adventure," he said, "is making possible the first genuine collaboration of Chinese and American scientists."

Finally, ace pilot Bill Odom, together with his copilot and radio operator T. Carroll Sallee, arrived in the C-87, newly outfitted with auxiliary gas tanks and with the name *Explorer* freshly painted on its nose. The moment had come at last for all the press briefings to end and for the expedition to set forth in search of Amnyi Machen. But taxiing out to the runway in Beijing, the *Explorer's* right wheel sank into the mud, the plane tilted sharply, causing the right outboard propeller to hit the ground. The nose wheel then collapsed and the big transport embarrassingly settled down on its belly.

"The expedition is over," announced Reynolds abruptly. "Captain Everest has won again." No apologies were offered to the Chinese scientists who had given their full cooperation to the expedition.

After making emergency repairs, Reynolds ordered Odom to file a phony flight plan to Calcutta, the first leg of the plane's purported return trip to the U.S. Fourteen hours of flying later, the *Explorer* mysteriously returned to Shanghai, triggering a furious exchange between Reynolds and Dr. Sah Pen-tung, director general of Academia Sinica, whose organization had been promised a seat on the plane during the search for Amnyi Machen.

"We were on our way to India," contended Reynolds lamely, "when we discovered we didn't have the necessary visas. So we came back." He didn't mention that they had really gone to look for the mountain.

Dr. Sah demanded Reynolds's arrest and that the *Explorer* be impounded, charging the Chicago pen manufacturer with "freezing out the Chinese scientists and trying to find the mountain himself."

Washburn unfortunately was trapped in Reynolds's lie. "Well, I'll curl up and die," he admitted to the Chinese press. "We must have flown over Amnyi Machin." But the Boston Museum of Science director didn't reveal whether the mountain presented a challenge to Everest. In fact, he refused to give any description of what they had observed on their long flight.

This brouhaha erupted at a crucial moment in Sino-American relations. The cold reception given Chiang Kai-shek's repeated requests for stepped-up military assistance had caused serious diplomatic friction between the two countries. Now the corrupted attempt to find Amnyi Machen was another blow to Nationalist China's pride. At Dr. Sah's urging, government authorities picked up Reynolds's, Washburn's, and Odom's passports and impounded the *Explorer*, placing it under round-the-clock armed guard.

Reynolds raced up to Nanjing and tried to cajole the government into releasing the plane. He apologized for his "negligence and discourtesy" and promised to take eight Chinese scientists on another flight to Amnyi Machen. The Academia Sinica haughtily refused. Dr. Sah claimed that his scientific colleagues were still stranded in Lanzhou after Reynolds's abrupt cancellation of the expedition.

Finally, Reynolds convinced the government to allow him to refuel the *Explorer*, which he claimed was necessary "to protect the gas tanks from corrosion." In return, he promised to remain in China until his quarrel with Dr. Sah was settled.

All of this wrangling, which was extensively reported, aroused the curiosity of one of China's ace airmen, Moon Chin. Raised and trained in Baltimore, he, like Odom, was among the original Hump flyers before being picked by Generalissimo Chiang Kai-shek to be his personal pilot. Now, as vice president of operations for the Central Air Transport Corporation, he announced plans for what ostensibly was to be a routine inspection flight of his company's West China installations.

"I think we might detour a bit and have a look at this mountain that's causing so much commotion," drawled Moon in his Baltimore accent. "I don't think it's as high as Mr. Reynolds claims," he added with the assurance of a man who knows what he's talking about.

Rigging one of his airline's C-46s with auxiliary oxygen equipment, but doing little else in the way of preparation, pilot Chin took off on the thirteen-hour first leg to Lanzhou. His crew consisted of a copilot, navigator, and two technical reps from the Shell Oil Company and Pratt & Whitney aircraft engine company. Also aboard were fourteen newsmen, including *Life* photographer Jack Birns and myself, invited along to record all the details of the flight. Everyone carried a portable oxygen cylinder and was fitted with a parachute, though God knows for what. If the twin engines conked out over the frozen wilderness surrounding Amnyi Machen, we might just as well have jumped without one.

Taking off from Lanzhou, the C-46 gained altitude as the neatly terraced mountains of Gansu faded behind us. After an hour the headwaters of the Yellow River appeared far below, snaking through its deep upper gorge. Here and there a desolate Golok village nestled along the riverbank. A thread-line trail wound along the steep south side of the gorge connecting the villages. Using that barely discernible trail as a reference, Moon Chin turned the plane southwest on a course headed for Amnyi Machen.

Looking down on those rocky spines and deep abysses, I marveled at the raw courage and rugged independence of General Pereira and Dr. Rock for having ventured on foot into that hostile region.

The rear door of the C-46 had been removed so Birns and the four other photographers could take unobstructed aim at the soaring peaks with their K-20 aerial cameras. Lugging their portable oxygen cylinders behind, and harnessed with safety straps hooked to their belts, they were able to work precariously close to the open door.

It took another thirty minutes before the first snow-covered peaks started poking up at our plane. Moon flew straight into this mountain range, almost scratching some of the icy escarpments, it seemed, with with his port wing tip.

By this time we were flying at 18,000 feet. The three Chinese reporters, including Susan Hung Hsu-tsai of *Shun Pao*, the only woman aboard, became giddy from the altitude and conked out on the canvas litter seats. They never saw any of the jagged peaks that were soon jutting up menacingly all around us. But not one of these pinnacles came close to the height of the towering mountain described by explorers Pereira or Rock.

Visibility was excellent. A dome-shaped peak loomed ahead in the precise spot where the map showed Amnyi Machen. Moon Chin climbed to 19,000 feet, the same height as the mountain, and did a lazy 360-degree turn around its frozen white summit. Clearly, this was the highest peak in the whole Amnyi Machen range. "Two myths ballyhooed to the skies by Milton Reynolds are hereby exploded," I wrote in my notebook. "Mighty Amnyi Machen contains neither gods to repel its trespassers, nor a peak to rival Everest."

On the off chance that the Everest-topping peak had been misplaced on the map, Moon Chin then flew one hundred miles due south, where we circled an unnamed 22,000-foot mountain in the neighboring Kuo-Lo Shan range. After that he doubled back to a point sixty miles north of Amnyi Machen, where we spotted another unnamed 20,400-foot peak in the Ugutu Shan range. These were the two tallest mountains we found during the entire 1,000-mile aerial survey.

The next day, on the way from Lanzhou back to Chengdu, Moon Chin detoured past the 24,900-foot, pyramidal-shaped Minya Konka (or Gongga Shan, as it's now called), the tallest known mountain in China. Even it presented no challenge to Everest.

Meanwhile, Milton Reynolds was up to his old tricks. He promised the armed sentries guarding his plane a box of ballpoint pens if he and the *Explorer*'s crew were permitted to go aboard. Then, as Reynolds described their escape from China to reporters in Tokyo: "We climbed in and I threw out fifty pens and slammed the door. Pilot Bill Odom gunned the plane. As more Tommy-gun-toting guards came running, Odom turned on one wheel and roared down the runway, scattering the guards."

Reynolds also claimed that on the plane's radio they heard the Shanghai airport alerting a fighter squadron to chase the *Explorer*. "So for the first three hundred fifty miles we flew about twenty feet above the water," he told the reporters, further embellishing his account of their wild retreat from China.

"Good riddance," sang the Nationalist press, which facetiously thanked Reynolds for providing "some comic relief from the war against the Communists."

The newspapers also congratulated Chinese pilot Moon Chin. "When Moon came over the mountain," wrote *Shun Pao* reporter Susan Hung Hsu-tsai, who had collapsed from the high altitude during the flight and never saw Amnyi Machen, "he put the millionaire Magellan from Chicago to shame."

But the confusion and mystery enshrouding Amnyi Machen was not that easily dispelled. Believing that Moon Chin had missed the mountain, a daring American explorer, Leonard Francis Clark, mounted a month-long overland trek the following year to find it. His exploration party consisted of eighty yaks, seventy saddle horses, numerous sure-footed pack mules and camels, as well as fifty hand-picked guerrilla calvarymen, all of whom he said "bore wounds from fighting the Communists."

In a long article published by *Life*, Clark wrote: "By the calculations I made, the peak stands 29,661 feet above sea level, 520 feet higher than Mt. Everest." However, it quickly became evident that he should have taken more precise measurements. The U.S. Coast and Geodetic Survey reported that Clark's computations could have been off by sixteen percent. And Brad Washburn, after studying the snow formations in Clark's pictures, said the mountain could not have exceeded 24,000 feet. Washburn was right. In 1960 Amnyi Machen was finally scaled on foot by a Chinese expedition. It was determined to be 23,491 feet high.

Even though Amnyi Machen did not prove to be the king of all mountains, it did appear to unleash its divine wrath on the men who tampered with its mysteries. Shortly after returning from his arduous trek, Clark was shot during a barroom brawl that took two lives. A few weeks later Bill Odom was killed competing in the Thompson Trophy air race in Cleveland. Reynolds then tried to redeem himself by funding a number of aeronautical fellowships at Stanford University in Odom's name. But the wealthy ballpoint king's credibility as both explorer and businessman had already been ruined—not by any mountain diety, but by his own publicity-driven antics.

Moon Chin also had difficulties. But his misfortunes were caused by the sweeping military advances made by the Communists, which sharply curtailed his airline's routes and brought the civil war to its final phase.

CHAPTER VII

Tale of Two Warlords

THE AMNYI MACHEN ESCAPADE didn't keep me away from the war for long. With Mukden lost, *Life* wanted a profile on General Fu Zuoyi, the former warlord from Dinner Mongolia who was now Chiang's trusted defender of Beijing.

Politically, Fu was considered progressive, at least compared to the other Nationalist commanders. Militarily, he enjoyed an outstanding reputation for his successful hit-and-run tactics against the Japanese. In the civil war he had also scored an early victory against the Communists, capturing Zhangiakou, or Kalgan, as Westerners call this camel caravan center on the edge of the Mongolian plateau. For that victory Fu won even the begrudging praise of Mao Zedong. "We know we can beat him in battle," the Communist leader reportedly said. "But we'd rather not try."

When General Fu had briefed Jack Birns and me on Manchuria following our interview with Chiang Kai-shek, he promised to personally escort us on an inspection tour of Beijing's defenses. The time was at hand to take up his offer. However, Fu was either too busy, or with Chiang no longer present to prod him, didn't want to bother.

A couple of other things had occurred that may have made Fu less eager to cooperate. His own crack troops from Inner Mongolia had been cut off by the Communists on their way to Beijing. Also, supplies from the Central Government had slowed, suggesting that the generalissimo had given up trying to save the Northeast provinces.

Then there was the disappointing U.S. presidential election. Fu and

Chiang's other generals had counted on Governor Thomas Dewey replacing Harry Truman in the White House. Dewey had advocated stepping up military aid to China, while Truman, the stubborn "show-me" Missourian, claimed the U.S. had already squandered $2 billion in arms for the Nationalists since V-J Day, and opposed giving Chiang one more plane or tank. "His armies couldn't fight their way out of a brothel," the pithy American president had been reported to remark.

Three days after Mukden fell, Dewey was defeated. And immediately after that rumors began circulating that Fu was secretly negotiating Beijing's surrender. For almost a year Beijing had been a Nationalist island, as life there continued serenely in spite of the war. Finally, the two million inhabitants seemed to be waking up to the fact that the Communists were closing in. General Lin Biao's soldiers were pouring south through the Shanhaiguan corridor, rearmed with the American equipment captured in Mukden. They were moving fast, spreading like a blood stain over north China. Yet, Beijing's citizens could not believe that any modern army would sweep in like Genghis Khan's Mongol legions had centuries before. Not even the Communist Bandits, they thought, would dare desecrate the architectural triumphs of China's ancient capital.

"Fu Zuoyi holds a beautifully delicate and priceless vase in his fingers" is the way the people put it. "If the Communists try to take it, it will be smashed."

This feeling about the city's fragility probably helped spread more surrender rumors. So Jack Birns and I decided to relax and hang around Beijing for a few days to see what happened. There was still a chance that General Fu would relent and permit us to photograph and interview him.

It's not easy to decompress after covering a war. Our exclusive story on the fall of Mukden, and the lauditory cables it elicited from our editors in New York, made us eager for another challenge. There is also something addictive about living with danger. The adrenaline shooting through your veins produces a habit-forming high, a false sense of well-being, even invulnerability, that propels some correspondents and photographers to take greater and greater risks until they get killed.

Even so, the peaceful sights and sounds of Beijing came as a relief. It was reassuring seeing the city acting and looking so normal—watching large groups of spry ladies and gentlemen performing their early morning *tai chi* routines around the Temple of Heaven, or wizened old men flying birds on a string as if they were kites, or children tickling caged crickets with a horsehair to make them sing. The streets were full of food vendors, jugglers, and beggars. To record these scenes, *Life* had flown in the acclaimed French photographer Henri Cartier-Bresson, figuring it was perhaps the last time the magazine would have access to the Forbidden City. "Relax and be tourists for a couple of days," the assignment editor in New York cabled Jack and me.

We got bored relaxing while waiting for General Fu Zuoyi. To kill time, we started shooting a short, unsolicited color story for the magazine on a famous old painter known to Americans in Beijing as the "Grandpa Moses of China."

This deaf, eighty-eight-year-old artist called himself by many strange names: "Old Man of the Apricot Orchard," "Hut on Chieh Shan Mountain," "The Man Long Separated from the Studio of Eight Ink Stones." But to the Chinese, any of those names signed with slender brush strokes upon pieces of thin bamboo paper were immediately recognized as belonging to Qi Baishi.

That, however, was not the name he started with. Many years before, he was plain Chih Huang, a carpenter's apprentice from Hunan Province. Coming home from work one day, he collected some shrimps, crabs, crickets, and tiny bugs, and put them in a bottle. "I observed these little animals with my eye," he said, explaining the unusual assortment of creatures populating the scrolls on the walls of his studio. "Then I put them into my heart."

One by one he painted their portraits. And one by one, to his great surprise, he sold what he painted. "Only the rich have seen beautiful landscapes," claimed Qi. "But every rickshaw boy recognizes a shrimp or a crab." Apparently, he wanted his work to be appreciated by the poor, though it was the rich who had raised the price of his paintings from $1 to $15 a square foot. Back then, art in China was frequently priced according to its size. Today, those same paintings sell in the U.S. for $15,000 to $20,000 each.

At first Qi flatly refused to be photographed. "I'm very sad," he moaned. "Because of my success, the rest of my family won't go out and work." Thirty relatives, he claimed, were living with him in the rambling house, and that didn't appear to be an exaggeration. While we were there, ducks and relatives alike either waddled or wandered in. And he complained of paying for twenty more relatives back in Hunan.

"To support everyone, I must work fast," said Qi, whose whispy white beard and high, reedy voice belied the sure, swift strokes with which he painted. The slightest error in wetting or pressing the brush would have made a smear and meant starting over. But while we were there, he never missed. His nimble fingers could finish a masterful scroll in less than twenty minutes. But after each one he would hobble over to a chair to relax while his nurse took his pulse on both wrists. She also stood behind him while he painted, patiently handing him his brushes, or his "chop" (Chinese signature printed with a carved ivory stamp) to sign a finished scroll.

I asked Qi if he would keep on painting if the Communists captured Beijing. He didn't fear the Communists, he said. His only worry was that somebody might steal his paints. So he kept them locked up, carrying the keys on a rope around his waist. "I'm too old for the Communists to convert," he said as we were leaving. "If they try, I'll take them for a drive into the country outside Beijing to a quiet place where there is already a stone on which are carved the words 'The grave of Qi Baishi.' "

Though Beijing appeared to have been spared temporarily, the region around it was caught in a combination of local sieges and pitched battles, accompanied by political and economic disintegration. The most crucial of these local fights was taking place in Taiyuan, 240 miles southwest.

Taiyuan was an important Nationalist stronghold because its arsenal was one of the last sources of munitions for Chiang Kai-shek's armies. But it was completely surrounded. The craggy peaks enclosing the parched Fen River valley, where the walled city stood, were honeycombed with Communist gun emplacements. From those positions the Reds could lob shells onto all roads leading into the city and blanket its three airstrips with mortars.

Holed up in this redoubt, Taiyuan's durable old warlord, Marshal Yan Xishan, had vowed never to surrender. His tenacity was understandable. Shanxi Province, of which Taiyuan was the capital, had been his personal fiefdom for thirty-one years. At the same time, he was recognized as China's most progressive governor, having built roads and bridges, and laid miles of irrigation ditches. He also had encouraged reforestation, promoted literacy and public health, and published a manual for citizenship, which all of Shanxi's ten million people were supposed to learn.

Before the rise of Mao, Yan had even attracted worldwide attention as the feudal country's most likely savior. "Has China found a Moses?" queried an American magazine. "Will he lead his people out of the wilderness?" Many foreign observers who came to visit Taiyuan were duly impressed. His Oxford-educated Chinese secretary at his side, Yan was reported by author-historian Barbara Tuchman and others to have "presided over a dinner table set with damask, silver, garnet-colored crystal wineglasses, and napkins intricately folded into roses, birds, and pagodas." But the civil war had long since ended all of those niceties as well as his forward-looking projects.

All that Yan now retained of his old domain was its walled capital. He still had 90,000 troops under his command, including 400 vagabond Japanese soldiers left over from World War II. And he suffered no shortage of weapons. He could manufacture all the machine guns he needed, as well as quite a few 75mm cannon, which were delivered directly from the factory to the front. But food and ammunition were running dangerously low. Tons of rice and ammo had to be flown to Taiyuan every day to keep it alive.

The airlift was daunting. Most of the Nationalist air force pilots would spiral down to 200 feet over the city before their "cargo kickers" started tossing out the sacks of rice and flour. If their aim was good, the sacks landed in a puff of dust inside the high-walled warehouse compound. If it wasn't, they'd smack down in a cabbage patch or on the roof of a building. Double sacking kept the flour bags from bursting. But the wooden ammo crates had to be gently parachuted down to keep them from splintering open. If a stiff wind was blowing, the boxes of shells would sometimes drift over into the Communists' welcoming arms.

CAT's seat-of-the-pants pilots followed a different procedure. After dropping half their load from the air, they'd usually try to bring the lightened-up C-46 in for a hot landing. The trick was to zoom in fast, jam on the brakes, dump the cargo out onto the runway, and take off again before Communist mortars could bracket the plane. The CAT planes rarely got away without an enemy shell or two kicking up a cloud of dust somewhere on the airstrip, and without Marshal Yan's artillery responding. At dusk his big guns could be seen flashing like firecrackers all around the field.

Birns and I had visited Taiyuan several times. We'd stay only four or five hours, always making certain there was at least one more CAT plane coming back before nightfall. The foot race to and from the airstrip was the hairiest part of each visit. Running and ducking through a forest of pillboxes and rabbit warren of trenches, we were spurred on by the deafening cacophony of mortars and machine guns. No matter how far away a shell exploded, it would send us sprawling into the nearest ditch.

In the comparative calm behind the city's high walls we had photographed just about everything of interest: the steel mill, the arsenal, the cotton mill, the machine tool factory, and the improvised hospital set up in the former middle school, where more than 1,000 crudely bandaged soldiers hobbled in and out. Yet, we had never photographed Marshal Yan Xishan. It wasn't until our last trip to his besieged stronghold that we were finally invited into his headquarters compound.

He greeted us in one of the small visiting rooms. It was furnished with overstuffed chairs and handsomely carved tables. Several cloisonné boxes containing Philip Morris cigarettes were left open for his guests. Suffering from diabetes as well as from the Communists' gradual encroachment, the sixty-six-year-old marshal looked exhausted. His green uniform, decorated with five rows of campaign ribbons, hung from a body that he complained had recently lost twenty-five pounds. But when he spoke of his determination to hold Taiyuan at all costs, his expression changed. His eyes lighted and his sagging jowls and scraggly gray mustache became mobile.

He told us how he was prepared to defend more than just Taiyuan. He'd concocted a desperate recipe, he explained, for saving the rest of China. Its main ingredients were a volunteer American air force commanded by his friend, General Claire Chennault, and a volunteer army of 100,000 Japanese foot soldiers. He realized it would take U.S. funds to pay for these volunteers, and he knew that was contrary to American policy. Yet he wanted *Life*'s readers to understand that given the right kind of military personnel, he was sure Chiang Kai-shek's forces could keep on fighting. "The trouble with the Nationalist pilots," he complained, "is they bomb and strafe from too high. One low-flying U.S. plane with napalm," he said, "could clean out all the Communists around Taiyuan in three days."

We didn't let the wild impracticality of Marshal Yan's plan disrupt his running commentary during Jack's picture-taking. He next led us into his office. On his desk was a cardboard shoebox filled with five hundred white potassium cyanide capsules. "See these," he continued, pointing to the pills. "A German doctor prepared them. They are for my five hundred commanders to swallow if the Communist Bandits capture Taiyuan." Before closing the box, he pointed to a single black capsule amid all the white ones. "That one's for me."

This vow of suicide coming from a warlord known to have collaborated extensively with the Japanese sounded hollow indeed. But Marshal Yan swore that he meant it. Not only would he keep the Communists from taking him alive, he said, he would not even let them find his body. He opened a closet containing several cans of gasoline. "After I swallow the poison," he explained, "I will set fire to this room."

As we took off from Taiyuan that evening, I looked down on the spiderweb of trenches and bunkers radiating out from the walled city and wondered if potassium cyanide worked fast enough so the marshal would already be dead before the gasoline flames consumed his body. As might be expected, he and his officers never put their poison pills to the test. After holding out in his isolated bastion for ten more months, the old warlord finally took flight for the island of Taiwan, where he lived out the rest of his days.

General Fu Zuoyi, who began his military career as a protégé of Marshal Yan's, and then, following his mentor's example, turned one of the provinces of Inner Mongolia into his own fiefdom, never did flee from Beijing. But he didn't stand and fight either. Fu realized the only way to save Beijing was with political weapons. His soldiers seemed to understand that too, and started fading away from the city's perimeter after the first flurry of fighting. Rapidly, they retreated through the massive gates leading into the city, as the Communists closed in around them.

Once the lines were drawn, the fighting almost stopped. The so-called "40-day siege of Beijing" consisted only of sporadic sorties. And the few heavy rounds that the Communist did pump into the city turned out to be duds. Later, Mao's troop commanders claimed the duds had been used intentionally so as not to do any damage. They knew Mao wanted Beijing taken intact so he could make it his capital. As a result, the soldiers on both sides simply stood their watch and cursed the cold wind sweeping down from Inner Mongolia.

Wandering out to the front, Birns and I were surprised to see farmers strolling idly through their fields, or even gathering winter cabbages in the no-man's-land just ahead of the Communist trenches. A dire food shortage gripped Beijing, and the cabbages were gold in the city, even though the airdrop continued. But most of the sacks were dropped from so high, they exploded when they hit the ground. One of the few civilian casualties during the "siege" was a passerby killed by a falling bag of flour.

We were supposed to be covering the siege, but there was no fighting to photograph. So, still hoping to catch up with General Fu, we again busied ourselves shooting another offbeat little feature—this one on James Wong Howe, the famous Hollywood cameraman who showed up unexpectedly in Beijing to film *Rickshaw Boy*.

The movie was based on novelist Lu Shaw's 1947 best seller. Howe, a Chinese-American, had bought the motion picture rights and had formed his own company to make it. John Garfield was slated to come to Beijing to play the lead. But before bringing over the cast, Howe wanted to do some preliminary filming, or, as he said in his best Beverly Hills slang: "First we gotta get somethin' in the can."

Sometimes I think the denizens of Hollywood view the whole world as a movie set. They don't care what real-life dramas may be unfolding in a place as long as the local atmosphere and background scenery fit their needs. In any case, Jimmy, as everybody called him, appeared, script in hand, in Beijing after the city was already doomed. He somehow didn't realize there was no chance of finishing the movie before the city fell.

Another problem with trying to shoot the movie at this late hour in Bejing was the fact that most of rickshaws had already been replaced by bicycle-powered pedicabs. Added to all this was another minor difficulty. The celebrated cameraman, known for filming such hits as *Kings Row* and *Abe Lincoln in Illinois*, didn't speak Mandarin, or any other Chinese dialect. He had been born in China. But his father, having been hired to work as a coolie on the Northern Pacific Railway, brought Jimmy to the United States when he was only five years old.

For one scene Jimmy had recruited more than fifty rickshaw boys still using the old human-drawn conveyances. He ordered them to line up in front of the Wagon Lits Hotel, where they were supposed to be waiting for fares. That was fine for the still pictures we needed for our *Life* story about the making of this movie, but Jimmy wanted to film the rickshaw boys in action. "Chop chop! Run run!" he kept shouting to his army of extras standing motionless in front of the hotel. "I'm paying you sonsabitches by the hour. Chop chop! Run run!"

Well, the fifty rickshaw boys stood their ground. They couldn't understand why this Chinese man didn't address them in their own tongue. But they weren't stupid. "No run with empty rickshaw," explained the hotel doorman, who was decked out for the movie in a uniform with more gold braid than a Chinese admiral's.

Communication breakdowns, Jimmy admitted, were not a new experience for him. He told us how back home in Hollywood, where he owned a restaurant, the manager had hired a photographer to take a postcard picture of the place. Jimmy happened to be there that day and noticed the photographer, who was using a camera mounted on a tripod, backing farther and farther out into the busy street as he tried to squeeze the entire building into the picture. "Why don't you use a wide-angle lens before you get hit in the ass by a car," Jimmy shouted.

The photographer's head popped out from under the black cloth draped over his camera. He spotted this little Chinese guy kibitzing from the doorway. "Hey, you," he hollered. "Go back in and tend to your noodles. I'll take the picture."

Before John Garfield and the rest of the cast ever got to Beijing, General Fu Zuoyi decided to sue for peace. His ambivalence had been well known. Sitting in his Winter Palace headquarters, he was said to have changed his mind nine times. As one of Chiang's most trusted military commanders, he still felt a strong loyalty to the generalissimo.

"I will defend this city to the last," he had repeatedly proclaimed. And for a brief time he made it look as if he intended to do so.

Eventually, the Communists became impatient and started putting on the squeeze. They branded Fu a major war criminal, but at the same time offered him a pardon if he agreed to surrender. The Red propagandists also astutely began broadcasting promises directly to the people, describing how they and their property would be protected under Mao's regime.

On January 6, 1949, General Fu sent a university professor to meet secretly with his chief adversary, General Lin Biao. But Fu never publicly revealed his intentions. Without warning, two weeks later his headquarters simply announced the signing of an agreement designed "to shorten the civil war, to satisfy public desires for peace . . . and prevent the vitality of the country from sinking any further." The agreement made no mention of "surrender."

Beijing thereby became the first city in the civil war to come under Communist control by peaceful negotiations. It was also a face-saving solution for Fu Zuoyi, who simply disappeared. A few years later, in a stunning postwar resurrection, he returned to Beijing as Mao Zedong's Minister of Water Conservancy. His skillful maneuvering had not only prevented the "delicate, priceless vase" of Beijing from being smashed, but resulted in his being given a token position in the Red regime. Frustratingly for Birns and me, we never got to do the profile *Life* wanted on this warlord who cast his lot with the Communists.

CHAPTER VIII

Waterloo At Huai-Hai

THE FATE OF CHIANG'S CHINA was not in the hands of warlords Yan Xishan or Fu Zuoyi. Nor did it hinge on the Nationalists holding on to Mukden, Beijing, or Taiyuan. It was being decided in the dusty city of Xuzhou, where the Grand Canal bisects the Yellow River plain.

As one Nationalist minister put it: "Manchuria is a limb that has been amputated. The body can live despite amputation. North China is another limb, and even that may be sacrificed. But central China is the Nationalist heart, and if the heart is pierced, the body dies."

Mao Zedong was now trying to pierce that heart. To deliver the fatal blow he had amassed two powerful Communist columns pointing like twin daggers at the rail hub of Xuzhou. Pronounced "shoe Joe," the nondescript little city of 300,000 straddled railroad lines running north and west, and in this pivotal position was the gateway to Nanjing and Shanghai.

Sweeping in from my old UNRRA stomping grounds two hundred miles to the west came the One-eyed Dragon, Liu Bocheng, with 400,000 troops. From neighboring Shandong Province came the hard-bitten poet-general Chen Yi, commander-in-chief of the Communists' east China theater, with another 200,000 men. A third Communist force commanded by General Chen Keng provided support. The whole area seethed with Red soldiers on the move.

Chiang held nothing back. He committed 55 divisions, totaling 600,000 men, a force exactly matching the Communists. Among them was his treasured tank corps, commanded by his second son, Chiang Wego.

73

Gambling on fall floods to defend the swampy plain to the north and northwest, the generalissimo concentrated his armies east of the city. He guessed right. The Communists attacked from the east and the Nationalists were there to meet the assault in the greatest battle in China's history.

After two weeks of bitter fighting, both sides were in precarious positions. Cloudless days and nights with a bright moon had helped the Nationalist air force disrupt the Communist supply lines, as Generals Liu Bocheng and Chen Yi tried to reinforce their badly mauled forces. At the same time, Chiang's 7th Army Group, commanded by General Huang Botao, had been cut off and was being pummeled by Red mortars and artillery.

At this crucial moment, *Life* photographer Birns, *Time* correspondent Robert Doyle, and I decided to fly to Xuzhou to cover what Chinese historians later were to call the Battle of the Huai-Hai (named after the muddy Huai River to the south and first syllable of Haichou, a town to the east).

Landing in a Chinese air force transport, we found Xuzhou overwhelmed with refugees and soldiers. Fortunately, though, it had not been hit with the panic of a mass exodus that had paralyzed Mukden. The city was packed, but calm. Thousands of coolies, collected at random from the teeming streets, were digging trenches and patching the city's thick protective wall.

Trucks and ambulances filled with wounded soldiers rumbled in from the front twenty-five miles to the east. More wounded arrived heaped high in mule carts, while the most seriously injured followed in rickshaws or suspended from bamboo poles shouldered by sweating bearers.

The Nationalists' 13th Army Group was still grimly protecting Xuzhou. Word had gotten through to Lieutenant General Li Mi that the *Time* and *Life* team was coming, and he'd sent his adjutant to meet us at the airstrip. The red-cheeked adjutant spotted us watching a couple of P-51s being loaded with bombs for their next sortie. "We go see general," he said, proudly demonstrating his English. "She very busy today," he added, also demonstrating that he had a gender problem with our language, like so many Chinese did.

Heading east out of Xuzhou in the adjutant's jeep, we were escorted by a truck mounted with Bren guns. The two vehicles churned the fine dust into a long brown cloud that clung to the road behind us. It was slow going. Stretching ahead to the horizon tramped some 25,000 men of the 72nd Army. "Help-out soldiers," the adjutant called them. Evidently they were heading to the front to reinforce Li Mi's 13th Army Group.

In addition to their rifles and backpacks, the soldiers carried huge cooking pots and coils of telephone wire as they marched doggedly toward the thump of artillery and crunch of bombs. Far ahead to the east, and in some of the rocky hills to the south, we could see puffs of white billowing from where the shells and bombs found their targets.

We passed through a village which the adjutant explained had been retaken the day before. About all the Communists had left behind were slogans splashed in white paint across the mud walls of the burned-out houses: "Fight on to Nanjing!" "Capture the liar Chiang alive!"

An old woman squatted in front of one of the gutted houses, whacking at her laundry with a wooden paddle, oblivious of these exhortations or to the shelling that was getting louder.

A procession of mules hauling captured Communist rifles and machine guns passed through the village. Among the war booty, I spotted some old American Enfields and a few newer Japanese rifles that I couldn't identify. "Belong Ba Lu," explained the adjutant, indicating that the weapons had been lost on the battlefield by Liu Bocheng's Eighth Route Army.

The adjutant pointed toward a hill where General Li Mi was directing artillery fire. Our jeep veered off the road, following a telephone line stretched across the parched, lumpy land already sown with winter wheat. On top of the hill we shook hands with the handsome general. About a hundred soldiers sprawled over the steep, craggy slope, eating their evening bowl of rice. Tommy guns and rifles rested across their laps or on the slope behind them. Some read old newspapers while they ate. Others gazed absently over the rich brown furrowed plain presently held by the 50,000 troops of their 13th Army Group.

"Come sit on my sofa," said the general, motioning to a rock ledge. Li Mi, we knew, had learned English while serving under General Joseph Stilwell in Burma. There he had also earned the reputation for being a good leader and a hard fighter. A deep scar creased his left cheek. "My Burma decoration," he called it.

An orderly brought yellow pears that were big as grapefruits. As we munched the pears, Li traced the battle lines on the palm of his hand. Twelve miles to the east, his old comrade, Lieutenant General Huang Botao, and his 7th Army Group, were encircled. They were trapped in the railway town of Nienchuang, Li explained, an area three miles in diameter. Huang, he claimed, had already lost 40,000 men in eleven days defending that shrinking perimeter.

Li, from his position above the rail line, was driving south and east, attempting to relieve Huang. At the same time, the Nationalists' 2nd Army Group, commanded by General Chiu Ching-chuan, was pushing up from the other side of the rail line. "We have orders from the generalissimo to advance at any cost," said Li. "In eight days we have gone eight miles. But this is the worst fighting I have ever experienced. I've lost two hundred officers and more than eight thousand soldiers."

As Li continued to brief us, a Chinese air force Mustang hummed along in the fading twilight and then swooped down on a village about three miles to the east. We could hear the sharp chatter of machine guns. "That village is Makutze," said Li. "It's my objective tonight. After the sun sets, my artillery will open up and then the infantry will move in."

The glowing red sun dropped below the horizon and a white ground mist crawled slowly up the valley floor, covering the black line of the Lunghai railroad. Li's adjutant cranked the field phone and shouted curt commands to the forward gun positions. Suddenly the war was on.

Huge muzzle flashes from 105mm howitzers ballooned from the plain, hung for an instant, and then blinked out. Ahead of the artillery, the 37mm guns on Li's tanks cut red streaks through the blackness. Occasional flares and signal lights lit up the sky. Between the thundering blasts came the incongruous creak and groan of an oxcart bumping its way across the field below. After an hour the barrage slowed and flames licked the dark sky over Makutze. "Now the infantry," said Li, who indicated it was also time for dinner.

Our jeep trailed behind the general's as we ground in low gear across the rough fields toward his headquarters in Chouchuang village near the front. The two drivers kept flicking their lights on and off, trying to skirt the deeper holes. The bumpy ride reminded me that it was just a year since I had stopped making those bone-rattling runs over Henan's rutted roads for UNRRA. There my truck convoys had faced threats from the same two Communist generals, Liu Bocheng and Chen Yi.

As we neared General Li's headquarters, we passed an artillery position. The hulking forms of tanks also loomed up against the night sky. A 105mm gun directly in front of the tanks cut loose, its red flash silhouetting for an instant the crouched figures of the gun crew. The acrid smell of gunpowder wafted over our jeeps. Li leaned out and said in Chinese, "Careful, careful, we are passing under your muzzle."

The 13th Army Group headquarters was located in a small compound ringed by freshly dug trenches. Mud pillboxes bristled with machine guns, and sentries lurked in every doorway. Outside the door of the general's hut, a soldier squatted beside a twig fire, drying his cotton shoes. Inside the hut, one of Li's officers was bent over a map. Two candles stuck upright in their own wax drippings on the table provided the only light. In the corner of the room was a cot and a couple of benches.

Li motioned for us to pull up the benches and sit down as he called for food. Orderlies quickly appeared with steaming dishes of chicken, beef, bean sprouts—remarkably, ten courses in all. Nevertheless, with typical Chinese politeness, he apologized for not serving wine.

The periodic booming of artillery punctuated the meal. Once Li was called to the phone. He talked for a moment in a low voice and returned to the table. In the candlelight the lines of his youthful face sagged. He stared at his rice bowl and then explained that he had just received a radio message from his friend General Huang Botao. "The Communist trap is closing," said Li. "We must reach him in two days."

After dinner he led us across the compound to another hut, where we were to spend the night. Through the bright moonlight, Chinese air force planes droned overhead, some dropping bombs that shook the ground, others, as Li explained, silently parachuting supplies to the encircled General Huang.

Again Li apologized—this time for our crude quarters and for the straw-covered boards that were our beds. But sleep was out of the question. The howitzers, dug in behind the village, kept up their intermittent fire. First came the muzzle blast, then the scream of the shell overhead, finally the distant crunch as the shell exploded. Added to those sounds was the throbbing pulse beating in my ears. For a couple of days I had felt sick with a low-grade fever coming on late each afternoon. Now I could feel the fever rising. My forehead was wet with sweat.

Shortly after midnight, the crackle of small-arms fire seemed to be drawing closer. Li Mi had shown us a pillbox just outside the door of our hut, where we were to take cover if the Communists counterattacked. "Don't try to leave the compound," he had warned us. "You'll run right into our own machine-gun fire."

When we first met Li, I noticed that he was wearing a private's uniform. At dinner he told us that he also wore fake dog tags bearing the name Li Wen-hua, the Chinese equivalent of John Smith, in case he was captured. Very smart, I thought. But with the rifle fire now sounding dangerously close, those precautions didn't exactly bolster my confidence that his troops would be able to hold. So I reached over and woke the adjutant, who was bedded down next to me in the hut, and asked if the time had come to seek refuge in the pillbox. He roared with laughter. "*Buyaojin, buyaojin*" ("no matter, no matter"), he said in Chinese. Then, remembering that I was an American, he added: "No worry. Same thing every night. Communists attack. But we stop."

He was right. Glancing outside at first light, everything looked the same. Soldiers carrying bowls of steaming rice ambled along the narrow streets of the village. I could now see that the streets had been carved into a network of trenches and foxholes. Li's troops were dug in everywhere. Mortar and machine-gun emplacements occupied the heart of the village, while tanks and howitzers were parked on the fringes just beyond the dilapidated village wall. But amid all this modern equipment were signs of China's ancient past. A donkey hitched to a centuries-old wooden-wheeled cart loaded with shining 105mm shell cases slowly munched on hay outside our hut.

In just twenty-four hours Li's troops had transformed this peaceful village into a bristling fortress. Most of the residents had fled. Those remaining puttered dazedly around their huts. A few timidly crept up to the soldiers knotted around the army's steaming rice cauldrons in the hope of getting some food. Fresh Nationalist slogans splashed over the mud walls exhorted: SOLDIERS AND CIVILIANS COOPERATE TO EXTERMINATE THE RED BANDITS.

Inside Li's headquarters hut we found the general splashing water on his face from a basin. His adjutant reported that Li had had a good night. He had been able to sleep from midnight until three A.M. But over breakfast the general explained that his troops had been unable to take Makutze. Although a thousand shells had been poured into the village, the Communists held their line and mustered enough strength to send a counterattack within half a mile of Li's headquarters. "We will take Makutze today," he said confidently. "We must. We attack at ten."

I wanted to go back with Li to his hilltop artillery observation post to watch the battle as it progressed. The odds didn't seem very good for rescuing General Huang Botao. Yet, Li's courage and determination were convincing. The compassion he showed for his cornered comrade-in-arms was touching. Li Mi was certainly different from any Nationalist general I had met before. From the moment we arrived, I noticed the deep concern he showed for his soldiers.

By nine o'clock my fever was still rising. According to Birns, the whites of my eyes were also turning yellow. A number of the CAT pilots we'd flown with recently had come down with jaundice, and I suspected that might be my problem.

"I'm afraid I must to return to Shanghai," I told the general. He had enough worries, so I didn't mention my fever. When Birns and Doyle announced they were going too, Li seemed genuinely disappointed that none of us would be there to watch the artillery bombardment, and following it, the infantry assault on Makutze.

Returning to Xuzhou, we boarded a Chinese air force C-46 that was taking off to parachute ammnition into Nienchuang, where General Huang's 7th Army Group was surrounded. After that the plane would fly straight to Nanjing, and from there we could hitch another ride to Shanghai.

As the C-46 spiraled down to 2,000 feet over Nienchuang, we saw the crumpled parachutes from previous drops covering the brown ground all around Huang's headquarters. From the air we also got a good view of the town's heart-shaped double wall and double moat, nestled up against the smashed Lunghai railway. Trenches webbed out from the outer wall like some scabrous disease infecting the good earth. The southern section of the town was burning, and pillars of smoke rose from all the nearby villages as well.

Our C-46 began to drop its cargo. Communist guns surrounding Nienchuang opened up on our plane and puffs of black smoke blossomed all around us in the sky. Fortunately, the antiaircraft gunners were firing short of their mark.

The day after we returned to Shanghai, word came that Nienchuang's moated walls had been pierced. General Huang Botao was reported by the Communists to have committed suicide while his segmented army was being chewed to pieces by poet-strategist Chen Yi. After the war, when Chen became China's foreign minister, he summed up his victory with a verse:

When old friends meet you and inquire about me,
Tell them to look closely at the desolation in the enemy's rear.

Of course, that wasn't the way the government reported the situation. "The enemy offensive suffered a complete collapse," the Central News Agency claimed. "Because of the continued pressure of the Nationalist forces, the Communists are having to fight like cornered animals to avoid annihilation." But it was really Li Mi's troops who were fighting like cornered animals. Having seriously overextended their lines trying to rescue Huang, they had left themselves open to a calamitous pincer attack.

The initial report on my physical condition wasn't much cheerier, though unfortunately it proved to be accurate. I was diagnosed as having typhoid fever and yellow jaundice, a combination that kept me hospitalized for the next four weeks.

During my confinement the battle at Xuzhou raged on, but with no reprieve for Chiang's troops. Stuck in bed, I reflected on the generalissimo's rapidly failing leadership. Even *Time*, consistently pro–Chiang

Kai-shek, reported that his "prestige has sunk lower than the Yangtze." The magazine quoted an American observer as saying: "The generalissimo's name is mud among all classes."

Yet, at sixty-one, the besieged president remained uncompromising. He continued to portray himself as China's salvation. And as heir to Sun Yat-sen, the republic's founder, he kept on proclaiming Sun's "three principles": Min Tsu ("national unity"), Min Chuan ("political democracy"), and Min Sheng ("people's livelihood"). Chiang also bade his field commanders to remember Sun's dying words: "You shall never yield to the enemy."

Nevertheless, Chiang failed to see that the feudalism which Sun had fought to eradicate still flourished, just as he seemed blind to the fact that by outlawing even the most innocuous liberal movements, he was driving their members over to the Communists. On the battlefield, defections were jeopardizing his key defensive maneuvers. Yet, when the Communists switched from guerrilla warfare to fighting conventional battles with massed armies, as they did at Mukden and Xuzhou, Chiang welcomed the change in tactics. His air force and armored corps, he declared, would at last give him the edge. Buoyantly, he popped in and out of his private map room, masterminding his troop commanders' movements by long-distance telephone. But as Li Mi had hinted, the generalissimo was interfering too much. His daily calls from Nanjing failed to take into account developments at the front.

In desperation, Chiang formed a new war cabinet, persuading Sun Fo, the liberal son of Sun Yat-sen, to become premier. Still, the Communist armies kept spreading south like hot lava. Not that this could be discerned from the Central News Agency's "frontline" dispatches. The reports simply repeated the generalissimo's favorite pronouncement: "The Bandits are fleeing in disorder."

Mao's propagandists reciprocated by broadcasting a list of forty-five war criminals that placed Chiang and his wife right at the top. Their being branded "running dogs of American imperialism," infuriated the generalissimo. "After all I've done for China," he fumed. "How can we talk to such people?" However, Vice President Li Zongren and most of his cabinet said they were ready to talk peace.

Furious with them as well, Chiang drove out to Purple Mountain to visit the mausoleum of Sun Yat-sen. He would draw strength, he said, from being in the presence of his former mentor. Observers watched the slim, uniformed figure, wearing a military cape and leaning on a cane, mount the white stone stairway. Before entering the tomb, Chiang took off his cape and handed it to his aide. Then, going inside, he bowed three times before Sun Yat-sen's white marble statue. When he emerged, he walked slowly down the steps, saluting to the thousands of soldiers standing in formation around the mausoleum.

That was Chiang Kai-shek's last troop review as president. After sixty-five days of fierce fighting at Xuzhou, his forces were defeated. Fifty-five Nationalists divisions, totaling 550,000 men, had been lost. More than 300,000 of them were captured, including most of his son's vaunted armored corps. The rest either died or defected. General Tu Yu-ming, Chiang's deputy field commander, tried to slip away, pretending to be a prisoner of his own aide-de-camp, who had changed into a dead Communist soldier's uniform. But the ruse failed, and Tu also was captured.

Li Mi, I was glad to learn, managed to elude the enemy. Two years later he showed up in northern Burma, and from there continued to lead armed forays against Chinese Communist garrisons in the border province of Yunnan.

How he escaped from the Xuzhou battlefield was widely disputed. Some said he flew away with the generalissimo's son. Others claim he was taken prisoner but broke out of a Communist jail. Still others reported that he disguised himself as a merchant and was hauled through Communist lines in a wheelbarrow. The most likely story, though, was that he and his 13th Army Group remnants trudged all the way to a base in Burma's mountainous Shan States that Li remembered from his World War II days with Stilwell.

What happened to his anti-Communist fighters after that has been well documented. Soon unmarked C-46s were flying in weapons purchased by wealthy Chinese merchants in Bangkok. For a while, even the U.S. was secretly airlifting arms to Li's strike force. Burma was too busy combating its own rebels to pester Li. But after he built his original ragtag group of 1,700 into the 10,000-man National Salvation Army, as he named it, the Burmese government complained to the U.N.

A heart attack finally forced Li to leave in 1953. But by then many of his soldiers had married Burmese girls and switched to farming. That made it easier for William "Wild Bill" Donovan, the former U.S. spy chief, who was then ambassador to Thailand, to negotiate a deal to fly the National Salvation Army's remaining 2,000 die-hards to Taiwan, where Li had retired.

For the rest of Chiang's troops who fought at Xuzhou, the battle ended horribly. Horses were slaughtered for food. The surrounded soldiers even tried peeling bark off the trees and scrounging for roots in the fields. Women and children froze to death in crowded huts. On the edge of the city, Communist loudspeakers offered food and safety if the Nationalists would surrender. "There is no escape," the loud-speakers boomed before the final artillery barrage began on January 6.

Years later, the Communists gave much of the credit for their great victory to a party organizer whom they cited for mobilizing two million peasants to provide logistical support for their soldiers. "His pick-and-shovel crews," the Communists claimed, "also neutralized Chiang's armored corps by digging a ring of tank traps around Xuzhou." This belatedly acclaimed hero, Deng Xiaoping, eventually succeeded Mao Zedong as China's paramount leader.

Just before the Nationalists surrendered on January 10, Chiang Kai-shek sent another desperate appeal for help to President Truman. But Major General David Barr, head of the Joint U.S. Military Advisory Group in China, had already convinced Truman of the futility of sending more military aid. "No battle has been lost since my arrival due to lack of ammunition or equipment," Barr cabled. "The Nationalists' military debacles, in my opinion, can all be attributed to the world's worst leadership and other morale-destroying factors that led to a complete loss of will to fight."

Truman himself wrote in a letter to a friend: "Chiang Kai-shek's downfall was his own doing. His field generals surrendered the equipment we gave him to the Commies, who then used the arms and ammunition to overthrow him." To those scolding remarks Truman added: "Only an American army of two million men could have saved him, and that would have been World War III."

In a final plea, Chiang asked the U.S., Britain, France, and the Soviet Union to intervene with Mao. Each country separately refused. Physically drained and psychologically beaten, Chiang then summoned Nationalist leaders to a meeting in Nanjing. The small reception room at the Ministry of Defense on that afternoon of January 21, 1949, was jammed with Guomindang officials. As usual, the generalissimo wore a simple khaki uniform without insignia. "With the hope that hostilities may be brought to an end, and the people's suffering relieved," he said slowly and with no show of emotion, "I have decided to retire."

An hour later I watched this beaten man leave the ministry wearing a long blue gown and black jacket, the traditional dress of a Chinese gentleman. It was a clear and unusually warm winter day as he stepped into his black Cadillac bearing "No. 1" on its license plates. At Nanjing's military airport he boarded the twin-engined *Mei-Ling*, named after Madame Chiang, who at that moment was in Washington, still fruitlessly trying to muster support for her husband. Chiang said quick good-byes to the officials gathered to see him off, headed for retirement in his hometown of Ningbo, not yet threatened by the Communists. Then he climbed aboard and pulled the door shut himself.

The *Mei-Ling* thundered down the runway, climbed and circled Purple Mountain, where the white stone of Dr. Sun Yat-sen's mausoleum reflected the fading daylight. It was only thirty-seven years since that rebellious little physician had overthrown the Manchus and established the Chinese Republic. It was also just ten days since Xuzhou fell and the epic Battle of the Huai-Hai ended.

CHAPTER IX
The Flight of Gold

"IRON," IT HAS BEEN SAID, "weighs at least as much as gold on the military scale." Yet, as the Nationalist armies reeled back toward Nanjing and Shanghai, it was not just the tanks, cannon, and all the rest of the iron lost on the battlefield that hastened Chiang Kai-shek's resignation. The flight of gold from China and the financial chaos that followed further undermined his authority. "The seriousness of the situation has seeped up to the highest levels," said Cyril Rogers, a British adviser to the Central Bank of China. "Near panic reigns on Olympus."

Beginning in August 1948, Chiang had tried to staunch the gold drain by imposing stringent currency reforms. Everybody was ordered to surrender their gold, silver, and American greenbacks. In an unprecedented act of faith, coins and pieces of precious metal were pulled from iron pots all over China and handed over to the government. New gold-backed banknotes called GY (for "gold yuan") were then issued in exchange. But this time the government promised to keep its paper money convertible at the official rate of four GY to one U.S. dollar.

With the new currency came a fascinating new political figure. The generalissimo appointed his Russian-educated elder son, Chiang Chingkuo, to be economic czar of Shanghai. If the chubby thirty-nine-year-old major general could make the reforms stick in Shanghai, where hoarding and speculation were rampant, he just might set an example for what was left of Nationalist China. First, however, he had to capture the city's attention, and he did this with a combination of scare tactics and humor.

Hauled through the streets in an open coffin appeared a grimacing corpse clutching a carton of cigarettes, two boxes of laundry soap, and a roll of cloth. Every block or so the corpse would climb out of its coffin to harangue the crowd on the evils of hoarding and speculating. Signs painted on the coffin's two sides warned: THOSE WHO HOARD ARE PUBLIC ENEMIES. HE WHO DAMAGES THE GOLD YUAN WILL HAVE HIS HEAD CHOPPED OFF.

At the same time, Chiang's son attacked Shanghai's wealthy businessmen by branding them "armed robbers." He didn't care whether they had given financial support to his father. "Their wealth and foreign-style homes," he railed, "are built on the skeletons of the people who live in crude sheds and cubbyholes, or writhe in the streets and ditches."

He also declared war on what he termed the city's "traitorous merchants" by establishing price ceilings. "If you don't scare these people," he said, "they will scare you." Ching-kuo, as the press corps affectionately called him, was suddenly being hailed as the Robin Hood of Shanghai. "Automobiles, refrigerators, and nylon hosiery imported from abroad are the opium destroying our national economy," he shouted to his youthful followers. "I'm launching a social revolution."

But then, Chiang Ching-kuo never did have much sympathy for *Dahu*, or "wealthy families." After graduating from the Moscow Military Academy, he worked on construction jobs in the Caucasus. "I had numberless hard days and did the lowest sort of work," he told me. "But I survived thanks to my father's teaching that man's spirit, not his money, is omnipotent."

Returning to China with a blond Russian wife, he proved himself both tough and incorruptible in several apprentice posts in Jiangxi Province. He also demonstrated a strong antielitist philosophy and deep concern for the common man not shown by his father. So in Shanghai it was not surprising when he shed his major general's uniform for an open-necked short-sleeve shirt, and listened like a good ward boss to people's complaints.

I went to one of those sessions. A laborer in black cloth coolie pants was bewailing his boss's decision to close down his well-stocked rubber factory rather than sell his products at the new ceiling prices. Ching-kuo promised to investigate. He did, and the factory stayed open. He also met with the city's financiers, whom he complained are "friendly toward me in person. But behind my back there is no evil they won't commit."

At first, these get-tough tactics seemed to be working. The banks closed for three days to convert their accounts into gold yuan. When they reopened they began exchanging the almost worthless old *fabi* dollars into GY at the rate of three million to one. The public cooperated with surprising good grace. I watched men and women stand in line for hours waiting to turn in whole suitcases and basketloads full of the crumpled old currency for crisp yellow and brown GY banknotes.

The new money, naturally, took getting used to. We Americans had become accustomed to arriving at a restaurant with a shopping bag full of cash to pay for dinner, or having an airline ticket invalidated right after buying it because the price of aviation fuel had just doubled.

A few months earlier I had written an article for *Life* on the Shanghai Telephone Company's hopelessly inflated six-billion-yuan fortnightly payroll. The story didn't run right away. By the time it was published, the company's payroll had shot up to $385 billion.

With the gold yuan, everything changed. A trolley ticket cost only ten cents instead of 300,000 yuan, a copy of the *Shanghai Evening Post and Mercury* twenty-five cents instead of 800,000 yuan. Factory workers no longer had to sprint to the nearest rice shop each payday to beat the hourly price hikes. And a farmer could now buy a water buffalo for fewer yuan than it would have cost him before to feed the beast for a week.

To keep the value of the new currency from eroding, Ching-kuo enlisted hundreds of young volunteers from the Bandit Suppression National Reconstruction Corps. They posted ceiling prices at all markets, raided warehouses looking for hoarded goods, and placed "secret report" boxes in the streets so consumers could squeal on the cheaters. During the first few weeks, several hundred merchants were arrested for overpricing.

"It doesn't matter if pork and perfume disappear from the markets," Chiang's son declared, "so long as the people aren't starving." However, he was only marginally concerned with the small shopkeepers who added a few cents to the price of a catty of pork or pack of cigarettes. It was the *Dalaohu*, or "big tigers," who were causing the commodity shortages and manipulating the markets. He soon acquired the reputation for being the fearless "big tiger hunter."

While most citizens had obediently turned in their gold and American greenbacks, many of the wealthy families converted just enough to demonstrate compliance. So Ching-kuo sent loudspeaker trucks out cruising the streets. They stopped in front of homes of the rich, booming out orders to turn in their gold. He even issued a list of the worst hoarders.

The next day a number of "big tigers," including some of the most famous names in Shanghai, were arrested. The story of Ching-kuo's crackdown was now moving so fast, it was difficult to keep up with. First, Tu Wei-ping, son of the local gangster boss known as "Big Ears" was charged with illegal stock transactions after the Shanghai Stock Exchange had been shut down. Next, Aw Haw, son of the Tiger Balm patent medicine king, was arrested for gold and foreign currency smuggling. Then Jung Hung-yuan, a cotton mill operator and former member of the National Assembly, was charged with making illegal overseas remittances. But the story that drew worldwide attention, including Life's, was the execution of millionaire merchant and currency speculator Wang Chun-cheh.

Shot to death by a police executioner, the event caused a sensation in Shanghai. "In Wang's fine home," as I reported to the magazine, "his family cried, but their tears made no impression on the man responsible for Wang's death. 'I would rather see one family cry than to see a whole street weeping,' said Chiang Ching-kuo."

One other well-publicized case, however, put a momentary brake on Ching-kuo's "big tiger" hunt. When word reached Madame Chiang that her nephew, David Kung, general manager of the Yangtze Development Corporation, was about to be arrested for hoarding, she stormed down to Shanghai to confront her stepson.

Right afterward, I tried to track down David and his sister Jeannette, only to learn they had slipped away to Hong Kong. Their company subsequently moved its head office to Florida. But very few other "big tigers" escaped Ching-kuo's clutches. As Indian ambassador K. M. Panikkar remarked: "For four weeks Shanghai was practically terror-stricken into good behavior." During that time prices held steady, although customers complained that "meat sold at official prices has more bone," and that "hens are apparently laying smaller eggs."

Meanwhile, prices elsewhere in China kept right on rising. Shanghai was said to be "a tiny island of controlled prices in a raging sea of inflation." So Ching-kuo's jurisdiction was expanded to include Nanjing and three provinces—Zhejiang, Jiangsu, and Anhui. But that move backfired. Goods vanished from the shelves, forcing the government to revoke price controls altogether.

Reacting with Confucian humility, Chiang Ching-kuo resigned and publicly apologized for "increasing the suffering of the people." He took all the blame for the failed economic reforms. "To make clear my responsibility," he said, "I am petitioning the government for punishment."

By now, however, the whole economy was disintegrating. Food prices doubled almost every day, setting off rice riots in Shanghai as the people demanded the return of price ceilings. Instead, government banks began selling gold again, but for ten times what they paid for it when the new currency was issued. Even at that price, crowds stormed the banks to buy the precious metal. Seven people were trampled to death in one Shanghai gold rush. Compared to the mountain of gold converted into the now virtually worthless GY, only a molehill was changed back. The rest was secretly loaded into sturdy wooden boxes in the vaults of three local banks.

One night, strolling along the Bund, I found myself facing a detour. Several blocks had been cordoned off without explanation. Soldiers roamed the area with cocked pistols, guarding a fleet of trucks parked in front of the Central Bank of China. For the next five hours, a bucket brigade of coolies wearing special white armbands transferred hundreds of small, heavy crates from the bank to the trucks. At dawn the trucks roared off to Jetty No. 12, where the crates were quickly stowed aboard the lighthouse tender *Hai Hsing*. Later I learned that those wooden boxes contained seventy-five tons of gold. Another night, twenty-five more tons were removed from the Charter Bank and Bank of China and placed aboard a Chinese navy LST.

"The banks are moving their archives south," claimed the Central News Agency. No mention was made of gold. But by February 1, ten days after Chiang Kai-shek resigned as president, a $300 million hoard was safely tucked away in Taiwan—the "golden nest egg," I called it in my report to *Life*, that eventually financed his transplanted Nationalist government. More than half the loot, I found, had come from Shanghai.

Grasping for whatever gold they could still find, Shanghai's speculators turned to the pirates and smugglers of Macao. Every night, from the tiny Portuguese colony appended to the South China coast, a string of armed junks called the "golden chain" slipped into Shanghai. Hidden in crevices under their teak deck planks were chunks of gold, ranging in size from $22,000 ingots down to $50 slivers.

As Shanghai's demand multiplied, so did the junks in the golden chain. Jack Birns and I decided to take a holiday from the war and fly down to Macao. It would be a nice scoop for *Life* if we could trace these illegal shipments back to their source and find out who was behind the smuggling.

We arrived on a Catalina flying boat operated by Macao Air Transport, the same charter company that was hauling one planeload of gold after another into the Portuguese colony. Skimming across the green water of the Porto Exterior, our plane pulled up alongside another flying boat bobbing gently on the waves. We could see coolies wrestling wooden cases out through its open hatch onto a launch. A police boat, bristling with fifty-caliber machine guns, patrolled back and forth. The boxes were smaller than beer cases but extremely heavy. Each was plastered with more airline stickers than decorated a movie star's suitcase. Labels marked LIMA, RIO, DAKAR, AMSTERDAM and PARIS, CALCUTTA and SAIGON, traced the precious cargo's path around the globe.

There was nothing illegal about bringing gold into Macao. Portugal hadn't signed the Bretton Woods monetary agreement, which tied most nations to a fixed price of $35 an ounce. The crates entering Macao contained free-market gold, sold to the highest bidder. And with the Chinese clamoring for more and more, a large portion of the world's free-market supply was being collected at this minute six-square-mile Portuguese enclave—the spot where Europeans got their first foothold in Asia four hundred years ago.

Macao's ruler, or dictator, as we soon discovered, was not the Portuguese governor, but Pedro Jose Lobo, a wiry little Malay-Chinese born in East Timor. His father had been a cook for a Dr. Lobo, who adoped the bright young boy and sent him off to boarding school in Macao. He never left. During World War II he kept the colony alive by organizing a ring that smuggled food across the border from Japanese-occupied China. Eventually, he became chief of the colony's Administrative Service Department, in charge of all imports. In that position he levied two taxes on each ounce of gold arriving on the flying boats: an official tax of 35 cents for the Macao treasury, and another of $2.10 for himself.

Lobo claimed to know nothing about Macao's "invisible export," as the gold smuggled to China was called. That $330-million-a-year business, we learned, was being handled by his silent partner, Ho Yin, owner of Macao's Tai Fong Bank.

It was easy enough locating Lobo, or "P.J." as everybody called him. When he heard that a team from *Life* magazine was in Macao, he latched on to us. His hobby was composing, writing, staging, and conducting operettas, and he insisted on our photographing the opening night of his newest musical creation, *Cruel Separation*. But just finding Ho Yin, much less wangling our way into the bowels of his bank, where the gold bricks were secretly melted down, was another matter. Some people said the mercurial thirty-nine-year-old banker was in South Africa, others said South America. "Mr. Ho visits many countries buying gold," his secretary told us.

Jack and I were about to give up and fly back to Shanghai, when a little man wearing black pajamas knocked on our hotel room door.

"You would like to meet Mr. Ho Yin?" he inquired in impeccable English. "Then, please come with me."

I noticed a holster bulging from beneath his pajama top as we followed him a few blocks along the banyan-shaded waterfront promenade to the Bela Vista Hotel. The Bela Vista was a Mediterranean-style villa with a large marble patio overlooking the harbor. Cocktail-hour dancers filled the patio, swaying to the muted playing of a Filipino band.

The little man motioned to a table where we were to wait for Ho Yin. Despite his fluent English, our escort obviously wasn't strong on conversation. He then disappeared into the hotel.

We sat for an hour sipping Madeira and watching the dancers. It was a beautiful evening. Junks, tied bow to stern, jammed the harbor, which seemed to reach all the way to China, just a mile away. Kerosene lanterns flickered from a thousand masts. Slowly, the moon rose over the whole scene, turning it into what could have been a travel poster for a tropical paradise. But Ho Yin never appeared.

Finally, our escort returned. There had been a mix-up, he explained. It was the Central Hotel where Ho Yin was waiting for us.

The Central was Macao's glittering gambling casino, packed every night with Portuguese prostutes, high rollers from Hong Kong, and hundreds of Chinese fantan players. Flanking the brightly lit casino entrance was a pair of Mozambique sentries. Half of Macao's 4,000-man security force was made up of these black soldiers from Portuguese Africa. They saluted us smartly, perhaps recognizing our escort as one of Ho Yin's minions.

The ground floor of the casino was lined with slot machines, or "coin-eating tigers," as the one-armed bandits were called in Macao. As we entered, an angry woman practically yanked the iron arm off one machine. Apparently it had eaten her last coin. At the same time, whistles, bells, and sirens were sounding farther down the line, signaling a jackpot.

Our pajama-clad guide pushed through the dense crowd, opening the way for us to a heavily carpeted back room furnished with overstuffed chairs. Again he motioned for us to sit down. A white-coated waiter appeared, deposited two glasses and two bottles of orange soda on the polished blackwood table, and then vanished. "What kind of cat-and-mouse game is this?" Jack asked as we continued to wait.

At last the door opened a crack. A fat Chinese face, half hidden behind tinted eyeglasses, peeked in. Then the door closed again. He's sizing us up, I thought. Can't decide if he really wants to meet us. But I was wrong. A few moments later, in strode Ho Yin, full of apologies for the mix-up in hotels and for making us wait. More important, he seemed amenable to our photographing his gold operation—or "factory," as he called it.

The next day, in the steamy basement of the Tai Fong Bank, among the furnaces and crucibles and sweating, half-naked workers, we received an education in how 400-troy-ounce, 99.6-percent-pure gold bricks were smelted into small, 99-percent-pure gold bars for the smugglers to transport to China. Actually, the smuggling syndicate trafficked in gold of all shapes and sizes, from whole bricks down to tiny gold beads that could be flown across the border strapped to the legs of carrier pigeons. But the syndicate's biggest trade was in ten-tael (13.333-ounce) bars. Turning out almost a million dollars worth of these every day was the main business of Ho Yin's bank.

We were permitted to photograph the entire process step-by-step, starting with the arrival of the bricks by armored truck from the Catalina flying boats. We shot the gold being weighed, then being melted, five bricks at a time, in ancient furnaces that looked like they came from some medieval alchemist's laboratory. We even recorded how the silver was added to the glowing molten metal, reducing its purity to 99 percent before it was poured into long, thin molds. The final stages were less dramatic photographically, but we documented them anyway—the cooled strips being cut into ten-tael pieces, checked on a finely calibrated scale, and then remelted and recast into the small, cigarette-size ten-tael bars, ready for sale to the smugglers.

That was merely one part of the smuggling operation. We still had to find out from other sources how the gold was sneaked into China. So we hung around the harbor, talking to the coolies who stowed the gold aboard the junks. For a wad of pataccas (the Macao currency) they showed us the hiding places deep in the bilges where even an honest Chinese customs inspector probably wouldn't think to look. The coolie stevedores also led us to two former U.S. Navy PT boats, camouflaged to look like fishing launches. Outfitted with twin-Packard engines, they could outrun any Chinese customs vessel.

We were informed that the syndicate rarely used planes. A few months earlier, two men boarded a flying boat bound for Hong Kong, tried to hijack the plane in midflight, and succeeded in killing all twenty-two passengers aboard, including themselves.

The sea route was dangerous enough, often ending in gun battles with Chinese customs agents or with ruthlessly enterprising pirates. We were told how one pirate crew, disappointed with its gold haul, had pulled a section of the Hong Kong–Singapore telephone cable up from the bottom of the ocean and sold the copper for scrap in Macao.

Our editors in New York loved the story. Smugglers and pirates plus the feisty little operetta-writing dictator made for a nice change of editorial fare from our usual grim civil war coverage. But the story wasn't a hit in Macao.

The headline was harmless enough: A DREAMY OLD COLONY WHOSE SMUGGLERS PLY THE CHINA COAST FLOURISHES AS RICHEST TRAFFIC CENTER OF WORLD GOLD TRADE. And so was the moody double-truck (as a two-page picture is called in magazine jargon) opener picturing an armed smuggler's junk setting sail for China. It looked for all the world like a nineteenth-century man-of-war, only, as the caption explained, "with a hidden cargo of gold stashed beneath its cannons." However, the sequence of shots on the fourth and fifth pages showing in detail how the purity of the gold was reduced before it was recast into small smuggling-size bars caused a terrible ruckus.

When the magazine went on sale in Macao, Lobo took one look and ordered his flunkies to buy up all three thousand copies. He also declared Birns and me persona non grata in the Portuguese colony. Even though the magazine pictured him animatedly conducting his operetta, *Cruel Separation*, before a large, fawning crowd, he couldn't abide being called "Macao's real ruler, who writes music to get his mind off gold."

Lobo's fury taught me two lessons I wouldn't forget. It demonstrated the effect *Life* had on even the most remote flyspeck of a place. More important, it illustrated how thin-skinned local tyrants can be when light is shined directly on them. Lobo's gold syndicate [which he ran until he died in 1965] was an open secret in Macao. Yet, laying out the illicit smuggling operation in pictures and words for the rest of the world to see was another matter.

Of course, *Life*'s article didn't slow the gold entering China. The publicity may have forced a few of Lobo's junks to land their precious cargoes in remote coves and bays along the lacy South China coast instead of sailing straight to Shanghai, which had developed an insatiable appetite for every ounce the smugglers could bring in. Besides, in Shanghai the members of the Macao syndicate could count on the cooperation of corrupt customs agents to keep from being caught.

Before Ching-kuo resigned, he had fought the syndicate as best he could. He enlisted members of the Greater Shanghai Youth Service Corps to hang around the Huangpu River docks and spy on the customs agents. He offered rewards to the sampan dwellers, packed into Shanghai's Suzhou Creek, to squeal on the smugglers. Nothing worked. The city's growing instability was simply too powerful a magnet. The yellow metal kept pouring in until Shanghai's whole economy became a raging black market pegged to gold. Then suddenly in April 1949, as Mao's troops started prying the Nationalists from their footholds on the north bank of the Yangtze River, it was the Communists' iron, not the smugglers' gold, that threatened Shanghai's survival.

The battle for Shanghai began in the most unexpected way. Steaming slowly up the Yangtze, the Royal Navy sloop *Amethyst* was headed for Nanjing to protect British subjects. A Union jack was painted on each side of her gray steel hull as she plowed the brown, silted waters. Sixty miles below the Nationalist capital, two Communist artillery shells smashed into the *Amethyst*'s bridge and wheelhouse. Her rudder controls jammed, and the sloop twisted helplessly with the current until she ran aground. Although her forward guns were pointed in the wrong direction, her stern guns began shelling the Communist positions. The Communist shore batteries cut loose again. Within a few minutes the captain was mortally wounded, and many of the crew members, including the ship's doctor and pharmacist's mate, were dead.

At the *Amethyst*'s first SOS, the British destroyer *Consort* started downriver from Nanjing. She, too, was fired on and retaliated with her four-inch guns. The 10,000-ton cruiser *London* also raced up from Hong Kong. But she never got within sight of the *Amethyst*. The Communists riddled the *London*'s vulnerable superstructure. Built to fight in open water, the heavily armed cruiser proved even more helpless in the Yangtze than the smaller ships. Before the *London* got back to Shanghai, shells tore some twenty-five holes in her hull. One shell exploded in an ammunition locker, killing fifteen crew members. Altogether, forty-four Britons died in these river battles.

Seeing the battered *London* limp into Shanghai made a deep impression on the city. Years later, after Chiang Ching-kuo succeeded his father as head of the Taiwan government, and had built the island into the economic powerhouse it is today, he told me how shocked he'd been by *Life*'s pictures of stretcher bearers carrying the wounded British sailors off the *London*. "I realized," he said, "the Communists had done something no Chinese army ever dared do before. They blew the warships of a Western power out of one of our rivers."

CHAPTER X

Lunch with Luce

THE VIEW FROM THE SIXTY-FOURTH-FLOOR dining room was magnificent. Straight ahead, standing as a sentinel over the skyscrapers of lower Manhattan, the Empire State Building glistened in the midday sun. Beyond it, in shadow, the stunted dwellings of Greenwich Village formed a dark valley that ended abruptly with another wall of sun-drenched skyscrapers rising from the southern tip of the island. Dissolving into the distant haze, the shimmering water of New York harbor spread out for miles, punctuated only by the tiny green Statue of Liberty.

It was my first time in one of these private dining aeries atop the RCA Building. Arriving ten minutes early for my lunch with Harry Luce, I savored this spectacular scene half a world away from Shanghai. The wait also was a chance to consider how the conversation might go.

China, obviously, was the topic. There were many questions about the Nationalists' crumbling defenses and what might happen to his old friends Chiang Kai-shek and the Madame that Luce would want to discuss. Not having met him, I was both flattered and surprised that my views were being sought, however drastically they might differ from his.

Many of my correspondent friends in Shanghai assumed that Luce simply dictated the China policy of his magazines. His birth and boyhood in China were well known. He often publicly admitted being "hopelessly sentimental" about the place. But while *Time*, his flagship publication, might have been obliged to reflect his personal opinions about Chiang, Mao, and the civil war, *Life* had been allowed to print stories pretty much as we reported them.

"Sure, pictures don't lie" is how my friends at the Foreign Correspondents' Club in Shanghai dismissed the fact that *Life* had accurately published Birns's and my coverage. These friends seemed to forget, however, that our stories also included sharply critical words about Chiang's military incompetence and Guomindang corruption—words that must have been repugnant to Luce. It wasn't that as editor in chief he brooked any dissent about who controlled his magazines. But he applied different measuring sticks to his two weeklies.

Time spoke for him and his company. And because it did, the magazine's editors were expected to rework the raw stuff that came in from the field. And not simply to insert Luce's sharply etched views of the world. But to forge an intellectual link between Luce and the magazine's readers. Once he'd even used that link to send a personal letter to all of *Time*'s subscribers asking them to contribute to the United China Relief Fund.

Life, because of its emotional appeal, was given a lot more latitude. Its basic fare was the world as seen through the camera's viewfinder, and quite often than view didn't conform to Luce's. As a result, there were weeks when the two magazines presented divergent views of the civil war. But then, as Luce once told the staff, "It is the business of *Time* to make enemies, and *Life* to make friends." We reporters and photographers on *Life* appreciated our less confrontational role.

When I started working for *Life* in Shanghai, bureau chief Bill Gray showed me a cable signed "HRL" (for Henry Robinson Luce) that he received when he first arrived there. Bill thought it might be helpful for me to read it as I set forth on my new career in China.

"A brief statement of our journalistic and editorial policy toward Chinese affairs" is the way the cable began.

Luce then laid down certain "boundaries," as he called them, for what he considered *Time*'s accurate, nonpartisan coverage. He made it clear that he accepted Chiang as "a loyal American ally," that *Time* wouldn't support "any propagandistic efforts to overthrow him," and that "U.S. interests would be best served by an independent China free of foreign domination of any sort."

Luce ended the cable saying: "This is not sent to you for your guidance in reporting the news. It is sent to you simply as a sort of first-aid kit to help you in the fierce partisan and propagandistic battle which you may encounter in Asia."

Afterward, when I was in Mukden or Taiyuan or some other besieged Chinese city, I sometimes wondered why Luce would disguise his guidelines as a first-aid kit. Were they intended as bandages to bind any future wounds that Bill, or any other reporter working for the company, might incur during ideological clashes with the editor in chief? After all, two of Bill's predecessors, John Hersey and Teddy White, had fought hard with Luce over China, and quit. Both men were stars whom Luce hated to lose. Perhaps, the first-aid kit was offered more as preventive medicine to keep Bill in a healthy frame of mind, and thus avoid the loss to the magazine of another talented reporter.

Those thoughts were still flashing through my head when Luce walked into the private dining room. The large head with its receding hairline, the bushy eyebrows partially hiding piercing blue eyes, the corners of a mouth creased into a half smile, all matched the portrait shot by his favorite *Life* photographer, Margaret Bourke-White.

I had glimpsed him only once before, stepping quickly into an elevator. But the elevator operators in the Time & Life Building had orders to close the door right behind him, whisking Luce on a solo ride to his thirty-third-floor office. That way he wasn't forced to make small talk, which he hated.

Now, up close, he was shorter than I remembered. Perhaps my previous impression was thrown off by his known predisposition for hiring very tall editors and publishers. In any case, here he was, greeting me with a paternal pat on the shoulder, as if to confirm that I had done all right in my first year on *Life*, and that he was glad to have me in his Time Inc. family.

To my surprise, Ed Thompson, then *Life*'s assistant managing editor, entered the room right behind him. Bringing Ed along must have been a last-minute decision because only two places had been set at the table. A tuxedo-clad waiter quickly appeared with the cutlery and napkin for another setting. He also asked for drink orders, which Thompson eagerly responded to by ordering a straight-up double martini. Luce declined, and I followed his lead. Ed, I decided, had invited himself to lunch to jump in as my protector should I lock horns with Luce on China. The double martini would fortify him for such an emergency.

Luce seemed oblivious of the magnificent view. The private sixty-fourth-floor dining room might just as well have been windowless. Without glancing out at the whole southern end of Manhattan displayed magnificently before him, he pointed to the chairs. The three of us sat, and got right down to discussing China.

"God and country and China," one of his biographers wrote, "is the passionate core of the Luce heritage." The author should have added the Republican Party, as Luce made it clear immediately that as a staunch Republican he bridled at President Truman's obvious contempt for Chiang Kai-shek. There was nothing inconsistent about the combination of those four elements in his background.

As the lunch progressed, Luce showed himself to be a man of contra-
dictions. He was shy yet candid. He was very opinionated, but he was
also consumed with curiosity. At one moment he sounded cold and
controlled, the next moment he was full of boyish enthusiasms. He
was bright, all right. But as his mind darted and jumped, several ideas
seemed to be trying to escape from his mouth at once, causing a
slight stammer.

I was amazed to hear that he no longer held any illusions about
saving Chiang's crumbling regime. Oh, yes, he had expected Mao's
"Godless revolution" to fail. Right up until the Nationalists lost Manchuria he admitted he still retained hope that Chiang would prevail.
He had put pressure on Truman, he said, to send more military and
economic aid. He'd also searched for splits within the Guomindang
Party that might have spawned a more popular movement in China to
resist the fast-running Red tide. But none appeared.

"Now," lamented Luce, "it's too late for outside aid or for internal
political repairs." Even Ed Thompson was taken aback by Luce's recognition of Chiang Kai-shek's total defeat.

But there was nothing defeatest about Luce. He struck me as being
too bright and upbeat for that. After delivering his dismal appraisal of
the war, he dwelled on happier days, when he was a "mishkid," as the
sons and daughters of American missionaries in China were called.
He described the avid fund-raising his father had done for Yenching
University. He mentioned that at Hotchkiss, where he waited on tables,
he'd even thought of becoming a businessman in China because of
"the big economic opportunities in a country where everybody had
their nose to the grindstone." But after starting *Time*, his determination
to participate in China's economic development, he said, was confined
to supporting Chiang's modernization efforts.

Suddenly ending this philosophical soliloquy, the editor in chief
started firing questions at me. "Would Mao's troops have to regroup
before sweeping on south?" "How long could Nanjing and Shanghai
hold out?" "Would a wave of panic hit those cities before the Communists marched in?" "When did I expect Chiang, still living in supposed
retirement in Ningbo, to flee to Formosa [Taiwan]?"

Luce's reputation for being a relentless questioner was legendary
among his foreign staff. Once on the way in from the airport in Co-
logne, he discombobulated *Time*'s bureau chief in Germany by asking
him to identify every structure along the way. Passing an excavation
for a new building, Luce said, "And what's that?"

"It's a hole in the ground, Harry," blurted the exasperated bureau
chief.

As Luce continued to pepper me with questions about the National-ists' impending collapse, I noticed how he cocked his head slightly to the left, carefully weighing each answer. He was a good listener. I wondered whether William Randolph Hearst, or Colonel Robert McCormick, or any of the other publishing giants with immense power and influence would have been so receptive to the ideas of a lowly reporter.

Luce, I discovered, was not always that way. Three years later, when I was assigned to the Bonn bureau and busy planning a *Life* special issue on Germany, Luce dropped in for a visit. Clare Luce was then ambassador to Italy, and Harry would sometimes busy himself bureau-hopping around Europe.

He arrived full of ideas for the German issue. And over lunch at the Adler Hotel in Bad Godesberg, he kept reciting them without pause, stopping only to go to the men's room. So I followed along, hoping finally to get a word in. "Harry," I started to say as he stood with his back to me at the urinal relieving himself. Before I could utter another word, he raised his right arm for silence.

After I'd answered his last query about China, he lapsed into descrip-tions of his most recent visits there. He'd met Mao in Chongqing in 1945, he said, but confessed to being appalled by the Communist lead-er's "sloppy dress and peasantlike look." At the same time, he said he'd enjoyed "a wonderfully relaxed and frank chat" with Zhou Enlai, even though Zhou complained that *Time* hadn't been very nice to him re-cently. The fact that these two Chinese leaders were Communists hadn't lessened Luce's eagerness to meet them. As a magazine pub-lisher, he clearly enjoyed mingling with the power-elite whose lives he chronicled. In the original prospectus for *Life*, before its birth, when it was still being called *Show-Book of the World*, Luce had defined its purpose: "To see life; to see the world; to eyewitness great events; to watch the faces of the poor and the gestures of the proud." And he was still a spirited enough reporter to relish doing those things himself.

Luce described how on that trip he had also visited Qingdao, where he said he'd spent many happy vacations with his family. "It's the most beautiful place on earth," he recalled, describing how the mountains come down to the sea. He then explained that Kaiser Wilhelm II, after grabbing Qingdao for Germany, referred to it as "the fairest jewel in his crown." But added Luce: "All I wanted to do was swim on the beaches of the bay as I did when I was a boy."

Some years later, after Mao was firmly in control of China, Luce was telling a group of us about that same visit to Qingdao. Again he mentioned going swimming and how he was accompanied by Major General Lemuel Shepherd, whom he described as "the finest swimmer in the United States Marine Corps." Added Luce: "If American affairs had been entrusted to General Shepherd and me, China would not now be Communist."

Reminiscing some more for Ed Thompson and me, Luce told us about another visit to China in 1946. He was there, he said, for the generalissimo's birthday, and recalled going on a "beautiful and memorable outing" arranged by Madame Chiang.

"We traveled for about two hours on a private train," said Luce, "to a large lake, where we boarded a houseboat and were served a delicious lunch. After lunch we came upon an island with an ancient temple." There were steamer chairs in front of the temple, and Luce described how he and the generalissimo both "stretched out for a nap in the warm November sunshine."

During this same trip to China, Luce said he had also spent several evenings in Nanjing dining with the American ambassador, John Leighton Stuart, whom he called "an old missionary friend of my father's."

"I was briefed extensively," Luce explained, "by both the ambassador and by General Marshall, who was then still trying to mediate peace between the Nationalists and Communists." But Stuart, according to Luce, had come to the opposite conclusion from Marshall. He believed the only solution was American support of Chiang, including use of American troops if necessary. "So we had the ironic situation," recalled Luce, "of the man of God favoring military action and the soldier unwilling to use the sword." In the years that followed, I heard Luce repeat that wonderful line.

It was almost three o'clock when he interrupted those reminiscenses with the reminder: "Time to get back to work."

Before we broke up, he confided that just a few months ago, while Birns and I were with General Li Mi covering the battle of Xuzhou, he had fired off an angry letter to Republican Senator Arthur Vandenburg about the U.S. government's shabby treatment of the generalissimo. Luce didn't say much else about the content of the letter. But after Luce died, I read that in it he complained bitterly of being perceived as "a guy peddling America's vital interest in China as if it were some sort of bottled chop suey that I was trying to sneak through the Pure Food Laws"—another wonderfully funny line from this serious man not known for his wit.

As we headed for the elevator, Luce mentioned that he'd also written a personal letter to Chiang Kai-shek. "It was," he said, "my final plea for the generalissimo to defend the Yangtze, and to broaden his government so that it represented all the non-Communist elements in China."

He ended the letter, Luce added, by suggesting to Chiang that he move his capital from besieged Nanjing to the temporary safety of Canton.

"And that reminds me," said the editor in chief as we shook hands, "when and where should we move the Shanghai bureau?"

"Hong Kong," I answered. "From there we'll be able to keep a close watch on China. And it's the best transportation hub in Asia."

I could see the disappointment spread across Luce's face. The idea of his magazines finally having to abandon the country of his birth was clearly painful.

"Could we stay on in Shanghai under the Communists?" he asked, and then answered the question himself.

"No, Time Inc. couldn't do that."

CHAPTER XI

Shanghai, Good-bye

"TO CONVERT HOSTILITIES INTO PEACE and to save the people, I will accept without evasion the severest punishment, even to the extent of being boiled in oil or having my physical self dismembered into many parts as a so-called war criminal."

No victor in China's millennial history ever received a more humble plea for mercy or a more complete admission of defeat than this telegram sent to Mao Zedong by Li Zongren, the man picked to replace Chiang Kai-shek as president.

"Your message has been received," Mao wired back. "Our party is willing to adopt lenient terms."

For a week the Nationalists and Communists bargained and bickered over what *lenient* meant. The Nationalists petitioned for an "equal and honorable peace." The Communists shouted back: "Mad and erroneous. There is only one way to peace, and that is by complete surrender." Mao finally drafted an ultimatum and sent it south to Nanjing by special messenger. He demanded that in four days all Nationalist troops be put under Communist command.

Mao's heart was clearly with his soldiers, not in negotiations. When Li Zongren failed to hand over his armies, Mao followed his own famous axiom that "power flows from the barrel of a gun." He ordered his forces to "advance boldly, resolutely, thoroughly, cleanly, and completely annihilate all who dare to resist."

Seven hours before the ultimatum's deadline, Mao's shock troops jammed onto river craft and struck across the Yangtze in a vast envelopment on both sides of Nanjing. "The river rang with silvery notes of bugles and martial music," exulted the Communist radio. "Boats by the thousands shuttled between the northern and southern banks as 1,000 guns belched fire and smoke, lighting the Yangtze waters in a lurid glare."

Life had sent photographer Carl Mydans from Tokyo to help me cover the hurried evacuation of the Nationalist capital. Called "Stump" because of his short, stocky build, Carl was one of the magazine's original photographers. He and his reporter wife, Shelley, had been captured by the Japanese and held prisoner in Shanghai during World War II. "I'll never surrender again," he said as we watched the long lines of frightened Nationalist soldiers fleeing the city. "Next time I'll run and risk getting shot in the back."

Most of the American wives and children had already left, ferried down the river to Shanghai aboard U.S. Navy landing craft. So had the Joint U.S. Military Advisory Group, sent to China by President Truman to teach the Nationalists modern warfare.

Major General David Barr and his officers were forced to make quick decisions about what to take and what to leave. Documents were burned "with an odor of red tape," I noted. Destroyed, also, but for reasons we didn't understand, were some 14,000 Armed Forces Radio transcriptions, used to bombard Nanjing with just about every kind of entertainment from Bob Hope to Spike Jones. "Those tapes would have confused the shit out of the Commies," commented the sergeant, who hated having to destroy them. But he proudly declared the supreme achievement of the whole hurried American evacuation was his rescue of some 30,000 cases of beer.

Chinese civilians left just about all their possessions behind. Cursing, bribing, and fighting, they surged aboard any train or boat that would carry them away from the Nationalist capital.

Finally, Nanjing lay quiet. Streetlights still flickered wanly until the eleven P.M. curfew, then blinked out. After that the streets were deserted except for rifle-toting municipal gendarmes wearing shabby black uniforms and yellow armbands.

Daylight did nothing to lift the funereal mood of the city. At Sun Yat-sen Circle, in midtown, the loudspeaker that used to blare out Strauss waltzes was silent. The throngs of shouting, arm-waving money changers had dwindled to a few individuals. The price of their clinking stacks of silver dollars kept on climbing dizzily, although there was no shortage of these coins because the Nationalist soldiers were now being paid in silver to keep them from defecting.

At the Old Ming Palace Airport inside the city wall, salvage crews belonging to the Da Hwa Hardware Company were busy cutting up the last aluminum wings and fuselages of wrecked Chinese air force planes. Melted down in furnaces right on the field, the molten aluminum was then poured into ingots to be used for making kitchen utensils.

"Instead of turning swords into plowshares," I said to Carl, "the Chinese are converting American war surplus planes into pots and pans. Wouldn't that piss off our taxpayers."

It was 3:30 in the morning on April 22, 1949, when the Communist attack on the city began. Nationalist artillery fired a few perfunctory shots at the Communist positions. Government leaders promised: "We will fight to the bitter end. Nanjing will hold out for six months." But at dawn, President Li Zongren, together with Premier Ho Yinching and Nanjing's garrison commander, sped to the airport. Soldiers put them aboard waiting planes, hastily jumped in after them, and slammed the doors.

Most of the gendarmes changed quickly into civilian clothes. The rest disappeared as a wave of looting swept the city. At President Li's abandoned gray brick home, I watched a mob swarm up the long tree-lined driveway. A boy shoved a porcelain sink through a smashed door to his friends outside. "The sooner they clean out the place, the better," explained Li's housekeeper, who helped the looters remove scrolls and furniture.

The flower beds of the mayor's gardens were littered with broken glass and pieces of plaster. There, I saw a man wrestle with a steam radiator, trying to lift it onto his shoulder. "I didn't like the mayor anyway," he said.

At a food shop, coolies shoved their way through the crowd to confiscate the few remaining sacks of flour. A man who was empty-handed jumped onto the back of a little fellow lugging away a sack. They rolled together into the gutter. When Mydans started to take their picture, a young Chinese woman cried out: "No, no, you must not. This is a disgrace."

Before dawn the next day, 20,000 troops of Chen Yi's Third Field Army marched into the capital. Country boys from Shandong stared in wonder at Nanjing's modern government buildings, while university students gathered to sing patriotic songs of welcome. The foreign community, surprisingly, was almost ignored. American ambassador J. Leighton Stuart was roused from his sleep by three soldiers tramping into his bedroom. But after looking around, they left.

Shanghai was too boisterous, too unruly, too much of a throbbing, freebooting metropolis to die the quick death of Nanjing. As the warm

May evenings brought big crowds back to the riverfront park behind the Bund, the people tried hard to hide their panic. Shopkeepers pretended it was business as usual, even though inflation had soared into the stratosphere. I saw a rickshaw boy dive headlong for a cigarette butt, but ignore a one hundred GY note lying in the street. Still, the virtually worthless currency didn't stop the buying and selling that was the heartbeat of Shanghai. Deals continued in U.S. dollars, gold bars, or by barter.

Our editors in New York kept badgering us for information on Shanghai's fate. "For planning purposes need best guess when city will fall," queried assignment editor Bill Churchill. "State Department warns Shanghai garrison planning last-ditch defense. Do you expect street-by-street fight or fast surrender?"

Only the "double-domers," as I called the crystal-ball-gazing political analysts, could answer questions like that.

"Whatever happens, want stark, gutsy 'Last Days of Shanghai' essay," wired Wilson Hicks, the picture editor.

"Need stirring eyewitness account," chimed in foreign editor Filmore Calhoun with yet another cabled request.

Nobody in New York had a clue about what was going to happen. But they all knew precisely what kind of pictures and words they wanted.

The problem was the sights and sounds of Shanghai hadn't changed much with the approach of Mao's armies. Dice still rattled atop the mahogany bar of the American Club. Only now these noontime dice players called themselves the "Die-hards." The Brits likewise continued their beloved afternoon lawn bowls, fueled by the usual number of pink gins—but with one slight alteration. Rolls of concertina wire enclosed their manicured greenswards to keep out potential rioters. And the ping of tennis balls could still be heard all day long at the Cercle Sportif Française. Residents of the French Concession remained unperturbed. As far as they were concerned, Shanghai would continue as the "Paris of the East."

Shanghai was known to others as the "Whore of Asia," and it was still living up to that name too. Business was now slow in the honkytonks of Hongkew. But a sailor on the prowl could still find hookers aplenty perched on the barstools at Duke Lear's, or Bo Brown's Diamond Bar, or the Tango or Rainbow, though not at ex-Navy Chief Frank Yenalevicz's New Ritz Bar in Blood Alley. "Yen" never did allow "hostesses" in his place, and he still didn't.

"You wanna buy this joint?" he asked me facetiously. "Some dope offered me forty thousand last year. I couldn't give it away today."

For the fifty foreign correspondents living in Broadway Mansions, life there too was little changed. The lower floors had already been vacated by departing American military personnel, so we now had the whole building to ourselves. The only sign of an impending battle was the shouted commands of troops holding close-order drills on the garage roof directly below my fifteenth-floor bedroom window.

"You stay Shanghai?" my room boy inquired hopefully. "Stay Shanghai long as I can," I replied. But he saw through my feigned optimism and shook his head.

My morning walk to the Time-Life office remained routine. "Push boys" still chased pedicabs across the Garden Bridge, offering a helping shove going up the steep incline, and then hanging on going down the other side of the bridge until the rider produced a tip.

The wide waterfront promenade along the Bund pulsated as always with those practicing the ancient art of *tai chi chuan*. A pair of blind beggars who were there every morning staring out of empty eye sockets greeted me as usual with palms outstretched. They seemed able to tell the sound of my footsteps from all the rest, and, being on my daily payroll, so to speak, showed no sign of giving up their profitable positions.

Unlike in Nanjing, the big Shanghai companies belonged to foreigners. The Brits ran the waterworks, wharves, shipping, banks, and trolley cars, while the power plants, telephone, and gas companies were owned and operated by Yanks. Most of these Old China Hands had weathered wars and uprisings before, and had no plans to leave. Their only immediate problem was protecting their posh homes in Hongqiao. That western suburb had been picked by the Shanghai garrison for its last stand against the Communists.

When Birns began photographing the army's defense preparations there, a colonel tried to wrest his camera away. *"Buhao, buhao"* ("very bad, very bad"), shouted the colonel, assuming that every foreigner understood that Chinese word. But he quickly disappeared and Birns resumed his picture-taking.

Here, at least, was some photographable action for the "Last Days of Shanghai" essay requested by our editors. We found one squad of soldiers ripping up headstones from the Hongqiao cemetery to form protective shields around their machine-gun positions. Another squad was dynamiting trees, leveling hedges, and burning down houses to open an unobstructed field of fire. Even the Hongqiao golf club was being torn down, although we noticed that its ceramic roof tiles had been carefully removed and set aside for future use.

The razing and burning was being carried out almost in a carnival spirit. "These soldiers are having a wonderful time destroying what their foreign masters spent decades building," observed Randall Gould, the American editor of the *Shanghai Evening Post and Mercury*.

Jack and I moved on to the lavish twenty-acre Jardine, Matheson & Company estate. The British firm's imposing managing director, John Keswick, and his wife, Clare, had just had their breakfast interrupted by a fresh-faced young officer. Behind the officer we saw several soldiers holding baskets of wood shavings. Obviously, they had come to burn down the Keswicks' house.

"Young man, I was living in this house before you were born," roared Sir John. "This is our home and we intend to stay here."

Keswick was the biggest taipan in town. His company owned the EWO textile mill, Holt's Wharf, the Shanghai-Hongkew Wharf, and numerous other buildings and enterprises. The giant conglomerate had grown out of a little opium-trading company founded in 1932 by Keswick's great-great-uncle, Dr. William Jardine. A shrewd scotsman, Jardine had written: "If the opium trade is ever legalized, our business will cease to be profitable." But family continuity and tenacity, not opium, resulted in the firm's survival and prosperity.

"Three times," bellowed Sir John, "I was forced to evacuate Shanghai, and I'm not going to let you people or the Communists drive me out again."

The young officer stared at the glowering figure, not knowing how to respond. Then he grinned. On a map that showed all the houses to be demolished, he drew a circle around the Keswicks' estate, indicating that this one spot would be spared, at least for the moment.

As Birns and I were leaving, Sir John handed us a copy of a book by him titled *What I Know About China*. "I had this published in England," he said. "It's been quite popular. This is the third edition." It was an unusual book all right. Beautifully bound, it consisted of one hundred blank pages, a stunning admission from an Old China Hand with Keswick's experience.

Several families besides the Keswicks were holding out in Hongqiao. Nearby, at an estate called "The Limit" (because it was the last house on the city's southwest boundary), *Time* correspondent Bob Doyle looked in on Mrs. Gladys Hawkings. By the time he arrived, soldiers had already pulled down fences on neighboring properties, dug trenches through the gardens, and started chopping down trees. When one group of soldiers began chopping down Mrs. Hawkings's trees, she flew out of the house and started scolding them in Chinese. The soldiers were overwhelmed by her bearing and perfect Chinese. Obediently they put away their hatchets.

Mrs. Hawkings then took Doyle into the pantry, where she and her husband planned to hole up if fighting erupted around their house. "The bathroom is overhead," she explained, "and that has a thick cement floor. Between the outside walls of the house and the pantry are two thick inner walls." She had already moved a mattress and four gunnysacks of rice into the hallway by the pantry. Doyle also noticed that the living room windows were barricaded with piles of logs and a six-foot Union jack was draped over a bookcase. "I know the Communists don't like a display of flags," she told him, "but we just wanted to look at it."

Before Doyle left, she summoned her two servants, a smiling, white-jacketed No. 1 boy and a graying, gold-toothed *amah*. "Here," she explained, "are Lao Wu and Amah. Lao Wu has been in the family for forty-five years, Amah for thirty-four. What would they do if we ran away and left them?"

White Russians were the only people who were running away en masse. As part of our "Last Days of Shanghai" essay, we photographed some 6,000 of them milling around the International Refugee Organization's headquarters, seeking help. They had become an important part of the Shanghai community, building churches, schools, and clubs. Yet, they feared the Chinese Communists would send them back to Russia. At first the IRO couldn't get any country to accept them. Finally, the Philippine government granted all who wanted to come temporary refuge on Samar Island. Birns and I ended up spending several days down at the docks photographing the crowds of Russians as they waited for Chinese freighters to ferry them to safety.

By mid-May the anti-Communist propaganda had been turned up full blast. Paraders marched up and down the streets waving Nationalist flags, while sinister-looking pictures of Mao blossomed on storefronts. "Shanghai will be his graveyard" was printed in Chinese under the pictures. "Sacrifice everything to defend this great city."

Outside Shanghai the defense perimeter rapidly shrank. "We will fight to the last drop of blood," promised garrison commander General Tang En-po, a sure sign that the situation was becoming desperate. Few Shanghailanders, however, hoped this promise would actually be kept. They knew the Nationalist cause was hopeless, and feared that a prolonged defense would bring nothing but pillage and destruction.

In the absence of any observable fighting, Birns and I continued to seek out the "stark" and "gutsy" pictures our editors had requested. We didn't have to look very hard. As Shanghai went through its dying convulsions, the populace was being given a gruesome show every morning, and sometimes a matinee.

The show commenced with a mock trial in the courtyard of the central police station on Fuzhou Road. Three or four accused looters, gold smugglers, or suspected Communist agents were herded in to face the tribunal. Beneath a large Nationalist flag sewn to a somber black cloth, they stood and listened as a policeman recited their crimes, which were also spelled out in large Chinese characters painted on long-handled wooden paddles. Nobody, it appeared, was ever declared innocent.

Quickly convicted, the doomed men (women were spared from this ordeal) were handed pen and paper to scratch out a will. Then, with their arms bound behind them, and with the paddles proclaiming their crimes wedged between their rope bindings, they were loaded into an open truck for a slow ride around Shanghai. Thousands of silent onlookers lined every block to watch them pass. Of course, that was the purpose of their grisly parade, to make a spectacle of a few scapegoats and keep the rest of the citizenry in check. "The looting that wrecked Nanjing will not be tolerated here," announced Acting Mayor Chen Liang after the elected mayor, K. C. Wu had fled.

Arriving at Zhabei Park behind the railway station, the condemned men were shoved out of the truck, stood up against a bamboo fence, and shot point-blank through the back of the head. At least that's the way the executions had been described by Chinese reporters taken along as witnesses.

After documenting several mock trials, Birns and I felt obliged to ask permission to complete the photographic sequence by following one group of victims to their gruesome end. Surprisingly, the police chief said okay.

On this particular day, three purported Communist agents were loaded into the back of an old-style "black mariah" instead of a truck. The cops told us to climb in with them. With the siren wailing and the doomed men screaming for mercy, we circled Shanghai. Peering out through the police van's wire grille at the huge, gawking crowds, I felt like a caged animal going to my own slaughter.

At Zhabei Park, Jack handed me a Rolleiflex. "You shoot with this, and I'll use the Contax," he said. "Shoot" was the wrong word. I was verging on nausea.

The cops wasted no time. They lined the men up a few feet apart. One cop held a revolver in his outstretched hand, leveling the barrel at the back of the first victim's head. As I peered down at the ground glass of the Rollei and adjusted the focusing knob, the executioner and his victim appeared as small images even though they were standing but a few feet away. Suddenly I was grateful for the camera. Better than seeing this through naked eyes, I thought.

Click! The victim froze at the sound of the trigger as the revolver failed to fire. So did I. Terrible moment for the cop too, it suddenly occurred to me. At least with a whole firing squad doing the dirty work, nobody knows who fired the fatal shot.

Another policeman jumped forward and fired a quick burst with his tommy gun. Blood spurted from the man's mouth as he crumpled onto the ground. The first cop then leaned down and delivered the coup de grâce. This time there was no chilling click. The revolver fired. But it didn't matter. The man was already dead.

For a second, while I cranked the handle of the camera to advance the film, I thought I'd forgotten to press the shutter button. So what if I missed the picture. *Life*'s audience wouldn't be any poorer. And as the reporter I wouldn't have to grope for words to describe this butchery.

By the time I'd refocused the Rollei, it was the second victim's turn. Another executioner stepped forward, pointing a carbine at the man's back. The macabre notion that the cops were using different weapons to give our pictures a little variety crossed my mind. I watched the executioner switch the gun onto automatic. Then the rapid-fire crack of his carbine rang in my ears.

Through the camera's ground glass I saw the victim pitch forward and fall. No spurting blood. Studying the contact prints after they'd been air-expressed to us back from New York, I realized that the Rollei's fast shutter had caught the speeding bullet precisely as it was exiting from the victim's body. I could tell because his sweater was stretched to a sharp point out in front of his chest just before the bullet pierced the threads.

All this time the third victim stood perfectly still, stoically waiting for the searing explosion that would be his last conscious moment. He was neatly dressed in black trousers and a white short-sleeve shirt. He never flinched. The tall wooden paddle proclaiming his crimes that was stuck between his two tightly bound hands never even quivered. The man either had no nerves or he'd been drugged.

Another cop, much younger than his comrades, came forward like a batter stepping up to the plate, but brandishing a snub-nosed grease gun. He planted his feet firmly in an open stance behind his target. Slowly he raised the weapon and sighted down the short barrel, aiming between the shoulders of the white shirt.

I held my breath to steady the camera, expecting to hear the gun chatter. What's he waiting for? I wondered. Scared to pull the trigger?

A shouted order came from behind me and the chattering erupted— ten, twelve, fourteen shots, before it finally stopped. The white-shirted figure toppled backward, falling on the wooden paddle still wedged behind his hands. Slowly, the clean white shirt turned crimson.

On our way back to the bureau, Birns and I stopped in at the Palace Bar for a couple of slugs of whiskey. I felt both sick and angry that we had given those cops the satisfaction of photographing their wanton cruelty, even if they were carrying out orders. Slightly drunk, I felt like sounding off when we finally reached the office.

"Bearing witness to these killings," I cabled Life's managing editor, "is not the work of a reporter, but of a sacrificial priest."

Actually, I think I was mad at myself for having felt compelled to cover the executions. A secondhand report would have sufficed. And feeling that way, I wanted to express my thoughts to the person who would soon be deciding whether or not to inflict these pictures on the public.

"It took about one minute at today's executions to make me forget I'd ever had that breather with you folks back in New York," my cable continued. "The reason will be clear, I believe, after you've developed these rolls of film. The scenes of incomprehensible savagery that you will see were committed by a regime that has already been stripped of its power. In a few days Shanghai will be lost. Since the killings were pointless, doesn't that make publishing these pictures pointless too?"

I ended the cable by saying: "I'll be curious to learn of your decision." The managing editor didn't reply. But he opted not to run the pictures.

The daily executions were still being carried out when apartment dwellers in the French Concession reported hearing the first sharp bursts of machine-gun fire coming from the south. The next day every road into Shanghai was clogged with retreating Nationalist soldiers. Some marched almost in parade formation. Others, caked with mud from the battlefield, streaked through the city in terror and confusion. Soldiers who were walking yanked civilians from their bicycles and pedicabs. Others grabbed everything they could carry or roll.

The few remaining government officials made a last-minute getaway from Kiangwan Airport. Among them was Acting Mayor Chen Liang, who had just announced the beginning of "Health Week" in Shanghai. Commented the Shanghai Evening Post and Mercury: "The mayor certainly was sincere. He found out what seemed best for his health and promptly did it."

At midnight on May 24, Communist infantrymen commanded by General Chen Yi began filtering into the city through the French Concession. They moved as quietly as they could. In small groups they advanced slowly down the sidewalks of Avenue Joffre, sidling close to the buildings for protection against fire from isolated Nationalist snipers.

The Communists' mustard-colored uniforms were clean and the men well armed with Bren guns and tommy guns. Hand grenades hung from their belts, bandoleers of cartridges from their shoulders. At every halt, they slumped on the sidewalk to rest.

Along Nanjing Road, Shanghai's main business street, the Communists herded captured Nationalists into gas stations and stores. When an angry crowd of civilians turned on a frightened Nationalist soldier, Red troops dispersed them. At one busy corner, a Communist noncom stood guard over a lone Nationalist squatting in a doorway. "What about him?" asked a passerby. "He's very happy now," replied the noncom. The soldier, puffing a cigarette, grinned sheepishly.

Most of the Communists were peasant boys, clearly more amazed at Shanghai than Shanghai was at them. They gawked at the fancy hotels and movie palaces. "What day is it?" asked one. "We've been walking and fighting for a week."

Finally, by nine A.M. the conquering troops reached the business district along the Bund. "Have the Communists really come?" asked a civilian onlooker. *"Balu laile"* ("the Communists have come"), replied an officer.

Within an hour Shanghai turned out to celebrate. A hastily thrown-up banner near the American Club proclaimed: WELCOME TO THE PEOPLE'S LIBERATION ARMY. Red flags were draped over shop doorways, and truckloads of students careened through the streets jubilantly waving pennants.

From loudspeakers all over town, Communist songs rasped out above the distant rattle of machine guns. The Nationalists were still putting up rear-guard resistance around the Suzhou Creek, while the remnants of their armies headed for the scores of ships waiting farther down the Huangpu River.

Not until November did Mao Zedong appear in Shanghai. A month earlier, riding through Beijing's Tiananmen Square in a captured American jeep, he had proclaimed the founding of the People's Republic. But his arrival in Shanghai marked for most people in China the true beginning of the new order. Always a hive of colliding ideas, Shanghai was, after all, the birthplace of China's Communist Party.

Its plenary session there in July 1921 had been held secretly on the top floor of a girls' school in the French Concession. Mao, who had been drifting around Shanghai discussing the *Communist Manifesto* and other Marxist books which had just been translated into Chinese, represented his home province of Hunan at this meeting.

When he returned victorious to Shanghai twenty-eight years later, the people were still uncertain what to expect. This home-grown poet-philosopher from China's heartland had brought with him the myth of an unending class struggle. His speeches quoted everyone from Friedrich Engels to Sun Yat-sen. Yet, despite his strong ideology, he remained a genuine romantic with an ability to arouse fervent popular devotion.

Once, while flying over a civil war battlefield, Mao had written a poem that ended with these lines:

The emperors Shih Huang and Wu Ti were barely cultured,
The emperors Tai Tsung and Tai Tsu were lacking in feeling,
Genghis Khan knew only how to bend his bow at the eagles,
These all belong to the past,
Only today are there men of feeling.

Mao was a man of feeling all right. But as tough and tyrannical as any emperor who had preceded him. Not only would he revolutionize China. He would change the world more than any man of this century.

CHAPTER XII

Dominoes That Didn't Fall

As Mao swept to power in China, the winds of insurrection blew down over Southeast Asia. My time was now spent accompanying French foreign legionaires on fruitless jungle raids against the followers of Ho Chi Minh in Indochina, and covering the three so-called "dominoes"—Siam, Burma, and Malaya—that were expected to swiftly fall to the Communists. But in each domino a leader emerged who helped stave off Red domination.

Siam's savvy, soft-spoken Field Marshal Pibul Songgram (pronounced "Pee-boon San-grum") kept a moist finger in those winds of insurrection. A devout Buddhist and a staunch believer in the stars, he relied on an astrologer to pick the date for the coup that catapulted him to power. Then, after further consulting his horoscope as the newly installed premier, he quickly changed the country's name from Siam—the Sanskrit word for "brown," which he considered insulting—to Thailand, meaning "free." And *free* is the way he vowed to keep it when I first met him in 1949.

Conflicting with this pledge was the new legal status of the Communists. The ban on communism had been lifted in 1946 to win Soviet support for Thailand's entry into the U.N. Although the party was assumed to be only 30,000 strong, it had been busily recruiting new members, using Chinese night schools—like the School for Marching Young Orators—and Chinese sports clubs as a front. Most of the new recruits were students and laborers, whose announced mission it was, to "dig quietly with shovels from within."

113

During my first interview with Pibul (Thais traditionally call each other, as well as their leaders, by their first names), he pretended not to be concerned about the Communists. "Internally," he told me, "we can combat communism by economic means. Our economy is good. We have neither beggars nor roadblocks."

The next time I saw him, portraits of Mao had already started blossoming on the walls of Chinese-owned shops. "Before Mao conquered Shanghai," he said, "the Chinese came here with the idea of becoming citizens. Now they are suddenly proclaiming themselves Chinese. They want to be with the victors."

I got the impression that the former field marshal now viewed practically all of Thailand's three million Chinese as potential subversives. "Over half of them," he told me, "are China-born with strong economic and family ties back home." He revealed, though not for publication, that when he caught any known Chinese Communist leader, he secretly deported him. But what he feared most, he admitted, was the possibility of armed Maoists flooding across Thailand's unprotected borders and overpowering the rest of his fifteen million cheerful countrymen. "Our people are too gentle to resist outside aggressors," he explained.

Pibul was right. Dubbed "toyland," Thailand was still a place where kite flying was the national sport, where boxers fought with their feet, and governments traditionally came and went in overnight coup d'états. During one attempted coup against Pibul, a British resident of Bangkok told me that he slipped behind a sailor crouched by a machine gun in the street. "What's it all about?" asked the Brit. "Navy fight army. Bloody good!" snapped the sailor. Coups, I noticed, rarely disrupted the happy mood of the capital.

Alighting in glittering, jingling Bangkok was like landing in the middle of Shangri-La. Shops bulged with niello silverware, hand-woven silks, carved teak figures, and snakeskin bags—all offered at bargain prices. Tourists could breakfast at the Floating Market, visit cobra-raising farms, or simply stand and gawk at the magnificent Emerald Buddha. By night they could watch graceful Siamese dance exhibitions or sip a drink or two under the fake banana trees of the Silver Palm Club. The more adventurous had no trouble finding fleet-footed *samlor* ("pedicab") boys to wheel them off to the Cathay Night Club, where they were expected to jitterbug the night away with wriggly taxi dancers. But lest they got any improper ideas, signs at their hotel informed them that "it is forbidden to entertain lady guests in the bedroom without permission of the management."

Thailand's incredible cheerfulness, I found, didn't stop at Bangkok.

It spread across the whole funnel-shaped land—to the rice farmers slogging knee-deep in the paddies behind lumbering carabao; to the tappers working their way down long, slanting rows of rubber trees; or even to the tin miners swinging picks far underground. They had reason to be happy. Thailand was comparatively rich and not overcrowded. More important, its citizens bore no smoldering resentment against any former colonial masters. Since the middle of the eighteenth century they had been free from foreign rule, except for the Japanese occupation during World War II.

Ironically, it was as puppet premier under the Japanese that Pibul first gained political prominence. Although he insisted to me that he had collaborated simply to save lives, he was jailed right after Japan's surrender and was awaiting trial in 1947 as a war criminal, when an astrologer predicted that he would once again rise to power. Almost immediately, by a surprise ruling of Thailand's supreme court (whose members Pibul had picked), he was freed.

That same year, after consulting still another astrologer—the famous one-eyed Tong Kam—Pibul plotted his political resurrection. Yet, there was some doubt whether he really put any faith in the stars. During the Japanese occupation he had banned both the chewing of betel nut and the hiring of astrologers. "Belief in astrology," he proclaimed, "is not a characteristic of a civilized people."

The betel nut part of his proclamation wasn't so bad. Everybody knew that chewing the nuts turned their teeth black as watermelon seeds. But astrology had a stronger hold on the people than any science or religion. There were, indeed, four occasions, called the "Four Crises of Life," when an astrologer's services were considered absolutely mandatory. When a child was born an astrologer was immediately summoned to cast its horoscope—a lifetime prediction covering all major events until death. The transition from childhood to adult life was marked by a traditional haircutting ceremony called *Kone Chuk*. On a date set by an astrologer, the child's topknot was snipped off, indicating entry into adulthood. For marriage astrologers performed varied functions besides picking the propitious wedding day. They frequently doubled as matchmakers, introducing couples with "harmonious horoscopes." Since the final "crisis"—cremation—could have considerable effect on both the spirit of the departed and on the surviving members of the family, astrologers were always summoned to set the date and hour of that ritual.

Publicly, Pibul still pooh-poohed such reliance on astrology. "I believe in myself, not in the stars," he tried to convince me during an interview I had requested because of an assignment for a *Life* Special

Report titled "Siam and the Stars." Nevertheless, he admitted waiting until November 8, 1947, the date selected by the one-eyed Tong Kam, before ordering tanks to rumble through the streets of Bangkok signifying his return to power.

It was then that he first came under Communist fire. The Reds called him "Mr. Strange," the literal translation of "Nai Plaik," the name he was born with. (Pibul Songgram, meaning "war victor," was the name bestowed on him by the king.) "Mr. Strange," charged the Communists, "is not only parading falsely under a hero's name, but is a two-faced dictator more interested in his own power than in making democracy work."

At the same time the Communists were pillorying Pibul, they were appealing to the Thais' Oriental sense of inevitability. "They want my countrymen to believe they are riding a crest in Asia," said the premier, veering off the subject of astrology and back into politics. "They say they will do what Mao did, liberate the lower class and kick out the foreign imperialists. How ridiculous. There is no threadbare lower class here. And the British, and particularly the Americans, are more popular than the Chinese."

I decided the Communists had not only misread the mood of the Thai people. They also vastly underestimated Pibul's determination to throttle them.

But there were also several inherent factors working in Pibul's favor that made the Thais less susceptible to communism. As devout Buddhists, they feared religious persecution from the Reds. They also venerated their twenty-one-year-old, clarinet-playing King Bhumibol (pronounced "Poo-mee-pone") Adulyadej, whom they hoped would return from voluntary exile in Switzerland, where he was spending his time writing songs. His " 'Tis Sundown" and "Rainfall" were sung by Thai students everywhere and played frequently in Bangkok nightclubs. At the movies, whenever a picture of the skinny, cowlicked king appeared on the screen, everyone stood respectfully.

Pibul never achieved that kind of popularity himself. Not even out on the hustings, where he traveled without pomp or fanfare listening to people's problems. Several times when I saw him in action he seemed to exude the toughness of an old warlord, not the pull of a winsome politician.

At a moment when the rest of Southeast Asia was seething, resilient little Pibul Songgram maintained strong Western ties and maintained enough internal stability to keep Thailand from being crushed by the Communists. Some of his Occidental leanings might have looked a little foolish. Once he told me he was going to order all Thai men to

kiss their wives good-bye before leaving for work in the morning because that's what Americans did. But under his leadership the national
budget stayed in the black, and the balance of trade remained favorable
because the production of rice, rubber, tin, and teak kept on rising. In
that economic environment, Thai-style democracy gained its first foot-
hold. For those accomplishments Columbia University awarded him an
honorary doctor of law degree.

Pibul was finally booted from power in 1957. He turned up in India
a few years later, where he was ordained a Buddhist monk, before dying
of a heart attack in Tokyo in 1964. But he left his mark on Thailand.
Even opposition party leader, Seni Pramoj, admitted that during Pibul
Songgram's ten-year rule, "There was nothing wrong with Thailand.
We just happen to have had contentment instead of refrigerators."

In Burma (now called Myanmar), contentment was just as scarce as
refrigerators. When I first landed there in 1948, five months after it
had broken away from the British Commonwealth, the country was
falling apart. A battle royal of rebellion, mutiny, and murder surged
around Rangoon. The government could not govern. The army scarcely
knew whom to fight. And the amiable, ascetic premier, U Nu, had
moved into a thatched hut behind the official residence, taking a vow
of chastity (after siring eight children) "in the hope of becoming a
Buddha," he said, "nine hundred ninety-nine worlds from now."

But then U Nu had always been a rabid cultist and a man of ex-
tremes. Graduating from Rangoon University in 1929, where he was a
champion swimmer, he joined the Thakin (Master) Party composed of
young intellectuals determined to throw off the British yoke. He became a student of Marx, a yogi, and a disciple of Dale Carnegie's,
translating Carnegie's self-improvement bible, *How to Win Friends and
Influence People*, into Burmese. When the country gained its independence, he became its first premier, combining Buddhist, socialist, and
democratic ideals in an attempt to create a sense of national unity.

The first time I met U Nu, he complained that his political power
was being badly eroded by the rebellions going on around him. "The
trouble," he said, "is that we in Burma have a two thousand-year-
tradition that he who can kill a king becomes a king." Yet, U Nu
exuded enough good-natured confidence to make me feel that this
gentle forty-two-year-old *king*, and his rather whimsical administration,
was somehow going to survive. He might lack the toughness of Pibul
Songgram, but he was an ardent and unwavering nationalist fired with
desire to see Burma's seventeen million citizens elevated from their
position of servitude. "I must keep my sights high," he said, "no matter
how mixed up the military situation is."

It was, indeed, confusing. Four different enemies were at war with his government. And trying to follow their ideological and tactical maneuverings was like trying to understand Abbott and Costello's "Who's on first, What's on second" description of a baseball game. Most of the confusion was caused by the rival Marxists—the so-called Red Flag (Trotskyite) Communists, and their more radical bretheren, the White Flag (Stalinist) Communists. Closer to the government but cooperating with the Communists were veterans of the People's Anti-Japanese Army, organized by Burma's magnetic young leader, Aung San, who was assassinated in 1947 shortly before independence.

But the Communists were not the only ones rebelling against the government. Karen tribesmen, mostly Baptists, held much of Burma's richest land. They threatened the ancient capital of Mandalay, and were in control of the lush lower Irrawaddy valley stretching southward below it. Their guns also ringed Rangoon.

Two months earlier, regiments of Karens had risen in open rebellion against the government. The tough hill tribesmen, led by the army's former chief of staff who had defected, had grown tired of waiting for the infant Burma Union to grant their demand for a separate state.

Arrayed against all of these rebel elements, U Nu had an army of only 20,000 men, including three British Spitfires, but only two pilots to fly them. Fortunately for his outnumbered government forces, personal animosities and a wide gap in principles separating the four rebel factions had prevented any lasting military mergers. Each group maintained its own base of resistance from which it struck sporadically.

Trying to cover this mad, five-sided, multifront war for both *Time* and *Life* required a journalistic juggling act. Battles flared and fizzled faster than photographer Jack Birns (my *Life* teammate from China) and I could get to them. We'd fly off to one beleaguered city, only to learn that more serious fighting had erupted in another. Finally, the fighting came so close to Rangoon that excursion buses were bringing sightseers out from the capital to view the battle as if it were some championship sporting event. A few of these spectators even had rifles thrust in their hands and joined the fray.

In one twenty-four-hour period Birns and I found ourselves on four different fronts. That hectic day began at Insein, just ten miles north of Rangoon. Stepping out of a taxi, we were soon crawling on our stomachs along a scorched road littered with charred automobiles. The deep whoomp of mortars firing from behind us, punctuated the splatter of machine guns. Ducking in and out of a web of trenches, we encountered several companies composed of Burma Rifles, Kachins, and Gurkha mercenaries, all fighting together under the government banner against the Karens, who were dug in just two hundred yards down the road. Suddenly, a battalion runner rushed forward, shouting: "Stop shooting! Stop shooting!" The government soldiers, apparently, were shooting at their own men, dressed in the same uniforms as the Karens.

On our way back to Rangoon that night, we spotted the hulking silhouettes of three Catalina flying boats parked on the apron of Mingaladon Airport. A spotlight quickly caught our taxi, and two soldiers jumped out of the thicket with sten guns leveled at the driver. They searched the taxi and then let us proceed, assuming that we had come to board one of the planes. So before proceeding on to Rangoon, we decided to find out where the three Catalinas were headed.

As we approached the planes, government soldiers wearing red-checkered *longyis* (skirts) to hide their uniforms were already shuffling aboard, while ground crews loaded heavy cases of ammunition and tommy guns concealed in blankets. One of the pilots poked his head out of an open hatch. "What d'you guys want?" he yelled.

We told him we were from *Life*. "Hell, I'm Bruce Olsen," he said apologetically. "From Inglewood, California," he added, just in case we didn't realize he was a fellow American. "You guys want a ride up to Mandalay?"

Olsen then explained that the three chartered Catalinas were ferrying reinforcements to Mandalay to bolster the government garrison. "Come on," he urged, "we'll be back this afternoon."

Bucking a stiff early morning headwind, our Catalina lumbered north over low hills covered by tiny farms and dotted with pristine white pagodas. The fields and network of narrow dirt roads veining the verdant countryside were empty. Charred smudges marked villages burned by one rebel force or another.

Three hours later, golden temple spires and gleaming palace towers soared skyward beneath our wings. "There she is," announced Olsen, "the city Kipling made famous." And as he eased the stick forward for a closer look, he began humming "On the Road to Mandalay."

While we circled, the soldiers unwrapped their weapons. Some peered uneasily out the Catalina's Plexiglas gun blisters, trying to detect any signs of fighting. Olsen finally swooped low over the airport, scanning the ground for signals to land. But the field looked deserted and the radio was dead. "Everybody's gone," he said, swinging the Catalina northwest. "Let's see how things look in Shwebo." Shwebo, he explained, was a government stronghold only thirty miles away.

The sun-baked strip there looked just as deserted, but Olsen decided to land anyway. As we bounded down the pitted runway, the cockpit became an oven, acrid with the smell of the sweating soldiers behind us. The other two Catalinas followed us in, their wheels kicking up thick trails of dust.

Olsen shoved open the hatch. Ringing the little airfield we could now see clusters of soldiers peering from behind piles of rocks, their tommy guns trained in our direction. An officer trotted across the field to our plane. In crisp British English he presented Olsen with a crazy-quilt picture of the military situation. The Karens had already captured Mandalay. Red Flag Communists had reached the outskirts of Shwebo, while Monywa, seat of the government treasury, was now threatened by bands of White Flag Communists moving up both banks of the Chindwin River. "You must hurry and evacuate the treasury," said the officer, at the same time waving to the soldiers to get out of our plane. From the hot tarmac, the troops glanced forlornly at the Catalina as we taxied back for takeoff without them.

Twenty minutes later our empty flying boat was skimming over the shining Chindwin. The plane hissed along the river's green surface, plunging to a stop in a deep swell. Thousands of natives, in a mass of bright red, green, and blue longyis, packed the high-sloping riverbank like a Sunday bleacher crowd at Yankee Stadium. Hundreds more came paddling and swimming toward our plane. In the flotilla were several canoeloads of orange-robed monks holding black umbrellas over their shaved heads. Soon giggling children clambered over the Catalina's nose, fuselage, and floats. A few tried to wriggle through the open hatch into the cabin.

A fishing boat edged through the crowd of splashing spectators, its deck stacked high with sealed wooden crates. Armed guards hoisted the crates aboard our plane. Then the guards jumped in, closing the hatch behind them. First one, then the other of the plane's twin engines started with a roar, scattering the canoes and swimmers.

That same afternoon, as Olsen promised, we were back in Rangoon. "Sorry we missed Mandalay," he said. "But at least we kept the government from going broke for a few more days." Those wooden crates, he informed us, contained 4.5 million rupees.

When I visited Premier U Nu in his thatched hut and described the airborne rescue of his government's funds, he seemed delighted. Apparently, the White Flag Communists had called off their attack on Monywa once they discovered its coffers were empty. What distressed him, though, was the way the warring factions, which had struggled in closest harmony to win Burma's freedom, were now gunning for his government. "The rebels," he said, "remind me of an actor playing the tiger in the famous Burmese drama Mai U. While waiting for his cue to chase the villain, the tiger fell asleep, only to wake in the middle of the next play, where Gautama Buddha was setting out to seek the life of an ascetic. Thinking he was still in the previous play, the sleepy actor pounced on Buddha."

Although U Nu saw himself as the savagely pursued Buddha, he and his government survived. I went back to Burma a few times. On each return visit to see U Nu, the almost-magical political powers of this Gandhi-like premier kept Burma from disintegrating internally, and his country neutral externally. In 1958 he voluntarily stepped aside to give Ne Win, his tough army chief, a chance to clean out all the dissidents. But U Nu returned to power two years later in a landslide election victory. Finally, in 1962 Ne Win threw him out in a lightning coup and put the country under martial law, which still exists today.

Right up until he died in 1995, the popular U Nu remained a force for reestablishing democracy in Burma. As premier he may have appeared weak and disorganized. He once told me: "I am a dreamer, slow to go from thought to deed." But throughout the cold war he probably did more than any other Burmese leader to keep his country from slipping into Red China's orbit.

The third Southeast Asian domino in danger of falling to the Communists was British-controlled Malaya (now called Malaysia). Hanging like a five hundred-mile-long pendant from Thailand, its jade-green jungle was alive with elephants, tigers, bears, and deer. Flying foxes, monkeys, and parrots chattered and screeched from its trees, while 130 varieties of snakes slithered across its dank ground.

Also slithering through its jungle was an army of 5,000 Red guerrillas. Divided into eight regiments, they had been quietly gathering strength ever since the Japanese occupation. Suddenly, in 1948 they went on a rampage. Killing and burning, they launched an all-out war aimed at driving out the British. It was to cover this anticolonial campaign of terror that Life ordered Jack Birns and me to drop the story we were shooting in French Indochina and fly straight to Kuala Lumpur.

The military leader of the insurgents, we soon learned, was Lau Yew, a thirty-four-year-old Malay Chinese who ironically had been feted in London as a World War II hero. As a young anti-Japanese volunteer with Force 136 (Britain's O.S.S,), he had proved himself a brave and brilliant guerrilla tactician. But after the war, his highway and railway ambushes, his hit-and-run raids on rubber plantations and tin mines, and his arson attacks on wealthy estates had created a countrywide state of emergency. Whole companies of Gurkha troops combed the jungles for Lau Yew. The police did corner him once during a surprise raid on his underground Communist newspaper in Kuala Lumpur. But he jumped out of a second-story window and escaped.

Captain Bill Stafford, the police superintendent in Kuala Lumpur, decided the only way to fight Lau Yew's kind of terror was by employing similar terror tactics himself. The stocky, barrel-chested Stafford had the reputation of always spoiling for a fight. He carried a pair of submachine guns, one slung over each shoulder, and a revolver tucked in his belt. He slept with a pistol under his pillow in a bedroom lined with mirrors to spot any intruders.

I had heard stories about Stafford in Shanghai, where as a young detective back in the 1930s he was known as the International Settlement's "most feared crime-buster." The word was, he had come to China as stoker with the Royal Navy, and quickly gained fame by rescuing Charles Lindbergh and his wife when their Lockheed seaplane almost sank in the Yangtze River near Hankow. When World War II broke out, he, like Lau Yew, joined Force 136, parachuting fifteen times behind Japanese lines in Burma.

The emergency in Malaya had further enhanced the Stafford legend. To chase Lau Yew and his so-called "assassination gangs," Stafford created his own "killer squads." They wore black suits, packed automatic weapons, and crept like cats under the jungle canopy, stalking the Communists. Before we arrived, they had already bagged more terrorists than any other police or army outfit on the peninsula, earning Stafford the nickname "Iron Broom" for his successful jungle sweeps.

We first met Stafford at his police headquarters. But we were told the only way you could appreciate the Iron Broom's raw courage was to follow him into the jungle. Not that all of his sweeps bagged terrorists. In fact, we spent several nights tagging along on futile raids that got us nothing more than badly barked shins and a rash of insect bites. Then one morning we were sitting around his headquarters, drinking coffee and reminiscing about Shanghai, when a frightened Communist informer was led into the room by one of Stafford's sergeants. The informer said he knew where Lau Yew was hiding.

"I don't trust the bastard," Stafford whispered to me. The bounty on any terrorist killed or captured was $400, so he had good reason to be suspicious.

Several hours of interrogation finally convinced Stafford to risk it. "Probably a wild-goose chase," he warned. "But if you want to, come along."

The surprise attack was set for dawn the next day. We left Kuala Lumpur at two A.M. with the nervous little informer hidden in the back of Stafford's weapons carrier. About a mile out of Kajang the line of red taillights in our convoy of jeeps and several more weapons carriers blinked off. Tires crunched the gravel as the vehicles pulled onto the road's shoulder and stopped. There was no moon. The jungle rose thick and black on both sides of the road.

Carbines and tommy guns scraped lightly against the vehicles as Stafford assembled his killer squad in the dark beside the parked convoy. At first he recommended that Birns and I remain with the vehicles. But he quickly relented and let us go along.

The squad moved down the road. Occasional flashes of heat lightning caught the black-suited men and held them silhouetted against the sky for an instant and then let them slip back into the night.

Stafford motioned to the informer up ahead and whispered to his Chinese sergeant, "If you think he's pulling a fast one, shoot him." Those were Stafford's standing orders for dealing with informers.

The squad stopped. Coconut oil torches carried by a group of tappers on their way to work in the rubber plantation where the informer claimed Lau Yew was hiding flickered dimly in the road ahead. Stafford signaled the squad to move off the road and into the jungle.

For an hour we waded through the dense thicket. Moist ferns brushed our faces. As we pushed on toward the high ground, I could hear carbines catching on vines and feet tripping over roots. A cock crowed in the distance. "You've got to be crazy to do this," muttered Stafford. He pointed to the informer. "I think the bloody bloke's lost. We'll wait here until dawn." The men squatted down to rest.

When the stars faded and pink streaks lit the morning sky, I could see that we were huddled on a ridge about half a mile in from the road. A thick mist rose from the hollow below. The men grabbed their guns and followed Stafford and the informer down the steep slope into the mist.

We picked up a narrow path that opened into long, slanting rows of rubber trees. The trees were freshly tapped and white driblets of latex lined the spiral cuts in their bark. Stafford speeded up the pace. "These bloody assassination-gang blokes never stick around much after dawn," he said. "They may already be back in the jungle or on a raid of their own."

The rows of rubber trees ended abruptly on the rim of a deep basin blanketed with yellow kunai grass. At the bottom were three flimsy shacks beside a little brook. The informer pointed to the center shack, where a woman puttered over her morning chores. It was a peaceful scene.

The squad fanned out as Stafford led them cautiously out of the rubber plantation, down into the basin. Creeping through the deep kunai grass, they moved toward the shacks.

As they approached, the woman glanced up and shrieked. Three men burst from the house brandishing revolvers. They wheeled and fled. The crack of carbines firing in rapid succession rang through the ravine. There was a scream followed by more shots. Then it was quiet. Two terrorists were dead. Six women and two other men were in custody.

Stafford hurried up the hill to where one body lay in the grass. It looked like Lau Yew. Blood dripped from his neck and trickled into the grass. A Luger lay on the ground beside him. Two of Stafford's men came up and dragged the body down toward the now-handcuffed prisoners, while other members of the killer squad hauled maps, rifles, uniforms, and a burlap sack of ammunition from the shack.

One of the squad members recognized Lau Yew's wife among the prisoners. "See if that's her old man," Stafford said. They forced the woman close to the corpse. She stared blankly at it and nodded.

"All right," Stafford yelled. "Let's burn this place and get out. There may be more of them around." A squad member sweating in his black uniform lit a torch and touched it to the thatched roof. In a moment the shack was in flames. Thick yellow clouds of smoke rose in a column from the ravine. Elated by their catch, the squad herded their handcuffed prisoners together and packed up to leave.

I was about to zip up my leather shoulder bag containing the exposed rolls of film Birns had shot, when the whole hollow suddenly exploded in a blast of Bren guns and rifles firing in rapid bursts. A band of some thirty guerrillas had been hiding in the jungle and were counterattacking. Bullets spat in the dirt. Two hand grenades exploded. A third bounced harmlessly on the ground.

Stafford and his men sprawled on the ground and crawled with their faces pressed hard against the turf toward a brook. They wriggled through the water and then burrowed into the coarse kunai grass on the opposite bank.

I clutched the shoulder bag and dove headlong over the embankment, shattering my glasses on the ground and rolling into the brook. About six feet away, two squad members poked their tommy guns through the deep kunai grass and fired ear-splitting bursts directly over my head. I crawled from the creek into the grass behind them.

In the grass I noticed that my film bag was open—and empty. Somewhere in my wild dive for cover I had dropped the whole photographic record of the raid. I shouted for Birns, but there was no answer. For ten minutes I groped around, calling his name, expecting any moment to stumble on his body. When I finally found him he was crawling around, waving one of the cop's revolvers looking for me. "I thought you were dead," he said.

The house still burned fiercely, and more Communist guerrillas were slipping downhill into a position behind it. Birns and I lay flat, afraid to raise our heads to take pictures. One of Stafford's weapons carriers suddenly appeared in the narrow cart tracks near our position. As we found out later, he had sent six of his men to get the squad's vehicles just after Lau Yew was shot.

"Here come the Gurkhas! Here comes the army!" shouted Stafford, hoping the sight of the weapons carriers would fool the Communist guerrillas. His men took up the cry and moved forward in a fake charge.

The firing gradually subsided until only the sharp report of single shots echoed in the hollow. Then it was quiet. The Communists had gone as suddenly as they had come. "That was bloody promiscuous shooting," growled Stafford. "Now let's really get out of here."

One of his men raced back to the smoking house and found our film lying in the mud. Nearby were the bodies of the eight prisoners, crumpled on the ground with their arms still handcuffed behind them. Stafford claimed later they'd been killed in the crossfire. But I believe his men intentionally sprayed them with bullets during the guerrilla counterattack. The killer squad, after all, was not trained to show mercy.

Lau Yew's death marked a turning point in the terrorists' assault on Malaya. The *Life* picture of the dead Communist leader's blood-smeared faced was plastered everywhere in the country, and with the desired effect. Newspapers, and then books like *The War of the Running Dogs* by Noel Barber (which also used *Life*'s pictures for illustrations) described that raid as "the climactic event in a brutal anti-Communist campaign." Although the terrorists kept up their attacks for four more years, and even killed one British high commissioner, the loss of Lau Yew was a crippling blow from which the Communists never recovered.

Unlike Thailand and Burma, where the political cunning of their two premiers prevented the Communists from winning control, in Malaya it was the raw courage of "Iron Broom" Stafford, and a few other cops like him, that kept the country from becoming a domino.

For several years I received a Christmas card mailed from England from Bill Stafford. Then about 1955 the cards stopped coming. I never did find out what happened to this brave man.

CHAPTER XIII

The Richest Man in the World

OF ALL THE EXOTIC RULERS IN INDIA, His Exalted Highness, the seventh Nizam of Hyderabad, was surely the most bizarre. A shriveled little figure, five foot three and weighing barely ninety pounds, he was the wealthiest man of his day with $6 billion in precious stones, coins, and gold bullion. The legends of his riches were surpassed only by his eccentricities. Shunning the leisure and luxury he could so well afford, he was known to work a twelve-hour day, wear rumpled cotton pajamas and a soiled fez, and favor a sputtering 1934 Ford touring car over the Rolls Royces, Humbers, and Cadillacs filling the palace garage. He was also said to live in constant dread of being poisoned, and therefore was followed everywhere by a food taster, who sampled his daily diet of cream, sweets, fruits, and his nightly bowl of opium.

When *Life* sent me to Hyderabad to interview the nizam, the assignment came with an added request to "please try for pictures of his nibs wriggling his dried-up little toes in great mounds of pearls." My editors back in New York City seemed unaware that this regal personage, whose full title was Asaf Jah VII, His Exalted Highness, Lieutenant General Nawab Sir Mir Osman Ali Khan Bahadur, Grand Commander of the British Empire, the Nizam of Hyderabad and Berar and Faithful Ally of the British Government, might not want to pose barefoot on a pile of pearls. In fact, I had barely arrived in Hyderabad in August 1948, when one of his palace functionaries informed me that "His Exalted Highness never grants interviews or poses for pictures." *The Saturday Evening Post*, the last publication to have been extended the

126

privilege of an exclusive interview five years earlier, had described how the nizam sat picking his nose throughout the question-and-answer session.

There was a more urgent reason why His Exalted Highness might not want to talk to a *Life* reporter or pose for a *Life* photographer at this particular juncture. His landlocked dominions in the heart of India—bigger than England and Scotland combined—were about to come under siege. Jawaharlal Nehru, Gandhi's heir and the first prime minister of newly independent India, was ready to depose the nizam—the last remaining holdout among India's 562 princely rulers. His Exalted Highness in turn was stubbornly determined to convert his state into a wholly independent sovereign nation. In reprisal, Nehru had imposed a blockade on Hyderabad. Nobody was allowed in or out.

That made my presence there technically illegal. But legal or not, I arrived in Hyderabad grossly uninformed to cover a power struggle of such magnitude. The first order of business, therefore, was to familiarize myself with the historical background of the confrontation.

The sixty-two-year-old nizam, I discovered, claimed direct descent from the prophet Mohammed and from Abu Bakr, the first caliph of Islam. His state was the most populous in the subcontinent. It contained fifteen million Hindus and three million Muslims, whom he had ruled with British backing since 1911. There had never been any foolish talk of democracy in Hyderabad, inspired by Gandhi's preachings, as there was in the rest of India. The Muslims owned most of the fortunes and held the best jobs. Assisted by this powerful minority, the nizam ran the state like a private game preserve.

I had never seen such a dazzling display of fancy palaces. Hyderabad City alone boasted thirty-two palaces, including the Grecian-style Falaknuma, used to house state visitors, and the ornate Chow Mahalla, a copy of the ornate residence of the shah of Persia. Earlier nizams had made full use of these properties. But the present nizam elected to live in the more modest, unpretentious King Koti Palace.

The truth is, as I soon found out, this nizam was a miser. His servants claimed he smoked the cigarette butts that his guests left behind. And he kept the palace voltage so low that a visiting physician who came to give the nizam a cardiogram reported that his EKG machine wouldn't work.

A vast fortune was known to be stashed in the corners and crevices of King Koti Palace. I was told that in one drawer of the nizam's desk, wrapped in an old newspaper, was the famous Jacob diamond—a 280-carat bauble the size of a lime that he occasionally used for a paperweight. Sapphires, emeralds, rubies, and diamonds were said to be piled like coal in scuttles in the palace basement, where rats reportedly chewed their way through three million pounds in British banknotes. Parked in the overgrown garden were trucks weighted down with gold ingots that had never been unloaded. And although the nizam owned a gold dinner service for one hundred, the servants claimed he ate off a tin plate, squatting on a mat in his bedroom. "Someday my gold will save Hyderabad," he had once proclaimed, explaining his frugality. Now, finally, he was attempting to make that prediction come true. In the past year he had spent $60 million on new weapons to preserve Hyderabad's independence. His small, well-equipped army was outfitted with heavy artillery, tanks, and planes.

In the midst of his defiance, tales of the nizam's eccentricities took a kinky turn. He was known to have an insatiable interest in pornography. But lately it was said he started combining that hobby with a passion for photography. Stories circulated that he had hidden automatic cameras in the ceilings of the guest bedrooms at Falaknuma Palace to spice up his picture collection. Apparently, that rumor didn't faze the dashing young British viceroy, Lord Louis Mountbatten, who visited with his wife, Edwina, to make a last-minute appeal to the nizam to lay down his arms.

By the time I arrived, Mountbatten had left, having failed to convince the nizam that his military position was hopeless. His meager forces consisted only of 22,000 Arab mercenaries, plus another 150,000 Muslim irregulars called *razakars* (volunteers), who were led by the wild-eyed firebrand Kasim Razvi. But they were pitted against the whole Indian army, which was poised to invade.

One of the nizam's privy councilors confessed to me that it wasn't simply a matter of his not being able to grasp the overwhelmingly unfavorable military odds. His Exalted Highness was so blinded by his enormous wealth that he failed to comprehend the momentous events that had been reshaping India. The partitioning in 1947 of the religiously divided subcontinent into Hindu India and Muslim Pakistan had left the Muslim nizam on the wrong side of the fence. Now, without Britain's support, it was obvious that he was going to be swallowed up.

With a full-scale war imminent, I heightened my efforts to interview the nizam. I began by presenting a formal request to Claude Scott, the imported British information officer. Next I approached the figurehead prime minister, Mir Laik Ali. Then I went to see Major General Syed Ahmed El Edros, the army commander, who was known to confer daily with His Exalted Highness about troop deployment. Each request required several days for an answer, during which I was treated to the full hospitality of the state. Bearers at the Greenland Guest House kept stepping out of doorways, asking sonorously, "Would Sahib like anything?" Government guides trundled me off to Hyderabad's tourist attractions, including the ancient Golconda Fort, captured by the great Moghul emperor Aurangzeb in 1687, and the famous Ajanta and Ellora caves, filled with primitive stone carvings. But in the end, all my requests to see the nizam came back with the same flat refusal: "His Exalted Highness thinks it would appear to the world that he had solicited the publicity in his critical hour of need."

As a last resort, I went to see Deen Yar Jung, the chief of police. Besides keeping a close watch on the nizam's two hundred concubines, he was reputed to be his closest adviser. The police chief produced the first glimmer of hope. "*Life* will be allowed," he said, "to photograph His Exalted Highness on Friday as he walks from his car to the Public Gardens Mosque." At least photographer Jack Birns was being handed a few crumbs in return for the three weeks we had squandered together in Hyderabad.

Shortly before the appointed time to shoot the pictures, Deen Yar Jung showed up at the guest house bursting with more good news. "His Exalted Highness," he announced, "has consented to a private audience." However, the police chief went on to explain that the nizam was preoccupied with the military situation and would be dressed in working attire.

Arriving at King Koti Palace, Birns and I were met by a platoon of special police, plus an assortment of army colonels—and, of course, by Deen Yar Jung, who seemed very pleased with himself for having wrung this concession from the nizam. A Persian carpet, table, and high-backed chair had been placed in the center of the palace courtyard. Before Birns could even open his tripod, out sauntered the nizam, covered head to toe in his official finery—from his high yellow crown-like Dastar to a robin's-egg-blue sash, festooned with oversized gold medals, draped diagonally across the front of his pigeon-gray uniform. The blue sash kept slipping down over the shriveled little man's right shoulder as he tried to strike a distinguished pose for Jack's camera.

"I welcome you to Hyderabad," said the nizam in flawless English. "What is it you would like to know?"

What I really wanted to know was whether he believed that his inherited wealth and authority could stem the tide of history in India. And if not, was he prepared to die for Hyderabad as he had publicly vowed? But I knew those questions would be considered impolite.

"Your Exalted Highness, are your armies ready for war?" I asked.

The nizam nodded, the tall yellow Dastar sliding to a rakish angle on one side of his head. "My soldiers are well trained and well armed," he said. "They man all of our borders." Then he paused, impatient for my next question.

"Does His Exalted Highness expect the United Nations to intervene in Hyderabad's behalf?" I asked.

"We have appealed to the U.N.," he said without further elaboration.

"Have you spoken to Prime Minister Nehru about the possibility of a peaceful solution?"

This time the nizam merely shook his head, sending the yellow Dastar wobbling precariously to the other side of his head. Then he rose unsteadily from the chair and disappeared back into the palace. The private audience had lasted less than five minutes. Clearly, His Exalted Highness, who had never had to answer to anyone during his thirty-eight-year reign, felt no need to suffer the questions of a foreign reporter, particularly one who had entered Hyderabad illegally.

The war with India, which began a few days later, lasted exactly four days and thirteen hours. It ended before the U.N. could even consider Hyderabad's case. No casualty reports were issued. But by best estimates only twelve Indian soldiers were killed, and not many more of the nizam's mercenaries died in the futile defense of his dominions.

At Hyderabad's border the Indian troops had been welcomed by Hindu peasants. All along the invasion route it was hard to tell that a war was going on. Here and there an overturned truck could be seen at the side of the road. But peasants tilled their lands and animals grazed peacefully. Few prisoners were taken, though at one village jubilant Indian soldiers were seen parading around a crazed razakar colonel, captured with a sword clenched between his teeth.

In Hyderabad City the streets were quiet. The Muslims, who made up half the capital's population, were frightened. Some barred and shuttered their homes. They had been fed ridiculous rumors that the Indian Army was putting gunpowder in the mouths of captured razakar boys and setting it off. Actually, the Indian Army had been told to treat the invasion as a mission of mercy. "It is not our job to hurt anybody," announced Lieutenant General Sir Maharaj Rajendrasinjghji, the Indian chief of staff.

Just the same, eager Indian war correspondents, who arrived with the invading troops, sent back dramatic eyewitness accounts that ran under banner headlines. NIZAM'S FORTRESS TOWNS FALL LIKE NINEPINS declared one headline. The story under it failed to mention that the fortresses had been built in the fifteenth century.

Before the Indian Army reached the capital, the nizam's army surrendered. A shiny Buick brought the black-mustached Major General El Edroos, who had told me he would "fight to the end," to a village outside the city. There he met the commander of India's 1st Armored Division, which had spearheaded the invasion. They shook hands, lit cigarettes, and talked quietly while spellbound villagers looked on. "It's the game of life," sighed the surrendering El Edroos. "We did our best."

The game for *Life* magazine didn't end so smoothly. After flying back to New Delhi, all of Birns's film and my notebooks were confiscated by Indian customs officers, who charged us with being agents of the nizam. "We were his guests, not spies," we protested.

"But you violated the Indian blockade," insisted the customs men, locking up the film and notebooks.

Several days of dickering with the Indian customs bureaucracy proved futile. The film and notebooks would be returned only on direct orders from the prime minister, I was informed.

It seemed inconceivable that Jawaharlal Nehru, India's busy new chief of state, would concern himself with the impounding of a few rolls of film and notebooks. But he did, and very graciously received me in his office.

I was instantly struck by the contrast between Nehru's forceful persona and the nizam's skittish manner. Perhaps the difference was caused by the way each man acquired his power—the nizam by birth, Nehru by helping to lead Gandhi's struggle for Indian independence. "You have been naughty," he said. "You weren't supposed to be in Hyderabad." Then, like a stern principal scolding an errant schoolboy, he lectured me on the reasons for the blockade, and why the nizam had to be made to heel to the will of the Indian government.

"You see this flower," he said, removing the rose that traditionally decorated the third buttonhole of his tunic. "This flower bloomed in my garden. Hyderabad is rightfully a part of India's garden. Only there will it bloom in the future."

Our film and notebooks were then immediately returned to us with the full apologies of the customs officials. The nizam was almost as quickly divested of his authority. He was allowed to retain much of his vast riches, although his dominions were absorbed into the Indian state of Andhra Pradesh. There he remained in seclusion. In 1967 he died, perplexed to the end how a man with his huge personal fortune and long ruling heritage could be so suddenly shorn of his power.

But the battle for his inheritance sputtered on for another twenty-eight years. Wary of his family's extravagance, the nizam had tied up his fortune in a web of trusts. One of those held the glittering jewel collection, under terms that forbade its sale until after the death of his oldest son, Azam Jah Bahadur.

When that son finally died in 1970, his heirs moved to sell the treasures abroad. However, by that time Nehru's daughter, Indira Gandhi, had become prime minister, and she annulled the old agreement made by her father under which the nizam and his heirs would continue to receive generous state pensions and other privileges for having ceded their dominions to India. The government contended that Hyderabad's crown jewels were now rightfully state property and should be handed over without compensation. It took until 1995 for the Indian Supreme Court to work out a compromise according to which the heirs were paid $71 million for the jewels appraised at between $250 and $300 million.

The armored car that carried four steel trunks of treasure from a Bombay bank vault to a government strongroom in New Delhi was the final punctuation mark in the life of His Exalted Highness, the seventh and last nizam of Hyderabad, whose fabled wealth and authority once extended across much of southern India.

CHAPTER XIV

"God's Right-Hand Man"

MY TRANSFER TO ROME IN 1950 was supposed to be a plum assignment that involved nothing more hazardous than reporting on Ingrid Bergman's torrid romance with Italian movie producer Roberto Rossellini, or covering Francis Cardinal Spellman's Holy Year pilgrimage to the Vatican. Then suddenly the Korean War erupted, and by Thanksgiving Day I found myself attached to a 7th Division reconnaissance unit called Task Force Cooper. We were inching our way westward through the steep Yalu River gorge that separates North Korea from Manchuria. The temperature was minus 25 and the terrain just as hostile.

A few days earlier we had spotted a few Chinese sentries in yellow quilted uniforms patrolling peacefully atop the snowy cliff on the opposite side of the gorge. China had not yet entered the war, although at this crucial moment General Douglas MacArthur was pressuring President Truman to let American units cross the Yalu in "hot pursuit" of the Chinese, who were secretly supplying Kim Il Sung's North Korean forces.

Commanding the 7th Division task force, and providing its name, was Carroll Cooper, an aggressive thirty-five-year-old major from Los Angeles. He had with him a reinforced company of 360 men, bolstered by tanks, light artillery, and heavy mortars. His mission was to "feel out the enemy" in that bitter cold canyon, and for three days and three nights we had been pushing back a stubborn band of "gooks," as we called them, about two hundred strong. "I want to get some of those bastards," said Cooper. "And I don't mean dead. If they're Chinese, I want to know how many more there are ahead of us."

Turkey, naturally, was on the menu that Thursday, November 23, scheduled to be dished into all 360 mess kits with at least some of the trimmings. But this was not the place or the time to pause for a Thanksgiving feast.

As the enemy troops retreated slowly through the gorge, they had burned all the bridges and blasted gaping holes in the cliffside road, forcing Cooper to park the kitchen truck, along with his tanks and self-propelled 75mm guns, three miles back. His exhausted infantrymen, bundled in their clumsy winter clothing, were now trying to pick their way along the exposed southern face of the canyon without their big guns' protection. A sheer rock wall towered 500 feet above. Far below, the emerald water of the ice-clogged Yalu slithered like a cold green snake through the bottom of the gorge.

Cooper's immediate objective was a tunnel that would offer protection, and a vantage point from which to view Posong-ni village, where the Communists were dug in. The tunnel was about 1,000 yards ahead. But to reach it, we had to duck through a barrage of burp gun bullets ricocheting off the cliff. I was crouched behind a boulder with *Life* photographer Hank Walker, waiting for the firing to subside, when two medics dove in behind the boulder next to us.

"Look, dearie," said one of the stretcher bearers, "we better stop here and catch a smoke."

"Okay, honey," agreed the other. From their conversation, I gathered they had just rescued a soldier who'd been shot in the stomach. Unfortunately, the wounded man had been shot again in the hip as they carried him to safety.

The medic called Honey studied Hank's two cameras dangling from neck straps down the front of his parka. "Wish I had your job," he finally said. His breath billowed clouds of steam as he spoke.

"How come?" I replied. "Here we are on Thanksgiving Day, freezing our asses off together behind the same boulder, hoping we don't get shot."

Honey looked at me like I was crazy. "Yeah," he said. "But if I had your job, I'd quit."

Just then somebody yelled, "Medic," and Honey and Dearie scurried on toward the tunnel without their smoke.

Hank and I dashed after them, stopping behind another boulder, from where Major Cooper was shouting orders to a mortar crew. They were trying to knock out a brick tower sticking up behind a sharp bend in the Yalu. Only the top of the tower, where the Communists had a machine-gun position, was visible. A little knoll jutting into the river from the Manchurian side concealed the tower's base.

"I think that tower's in Korea," yelled Cooper. "Tell the 81's to nail it."

A loud blast, then another, rocked the tower. When the first shells exploded, a man and a woman ran out of a house perched atop the knoll and burrowed into a haystack. "I guess that old geezer and his missus figure we've just declared war on China," laughed Major Cooper. "Seriously," he added, "to fight a war up here on the border you need a squad of lawyers traveling with the infantry."

Cooper was right. A courageous and skillful battlefield commander, he'd nevertheless been given an impossible assignment—chasing a well-armed enemy around the hairpin turns of a frozen frontier without violating Chinese territory. In retrospect, it was a reckless mission ordered by MacArthur himself. The order had then been bucked down through the entire chain of command—from the supreme commander to Lieutenant General "Sick 'Em" Ned Almond's X Corps, to Major General Dave Barr's 7th Division, to Colonel Herb Powell's 17th Regimental Combat Team—before it finally reached Major Carroll Cooper's little task force to carry out. In the three days since this order was received, Cooper's reinforced company had eeked out only fifteen hard-won miles from the city of Hyesan, where the 7th Division had set up its command post on a high plateau overlooking the Yalu.

Cooper was responsible for making only the initial reconnaissance probe. But that was a risky maneuver after widespread intelligence reports of an imminent Chinese attack.

A month earlier, Hanson Baldwin, military analyst for the *New York Times*, had reported the massing of 250,000 Chinese soldiers on the Manchurian side of the Yalu. Another 200,000, he claimed, were probably already on North Korean soil. Yet the whereabouts of these Chinese armies was a mystery. Cooper's reconnaissance was expected to provide the answer, though MacArthur had stated publicly that he was still convinced the Chinese would stay out of the war.

Evidence was already mounting that he was wrong. Just a week earlier, another *Life* correspondent, Hugh Moffett, had interrogated one of the first Chinese infiltrators captured in Korea. Private Li Tsu was a peasant from Hopeh Province. He'd been conscripted, he said, as a messenger and ammunition carrier, and sent to Antung on China's side of the border. From there, he and 1,000 other conscripts had slipped into Korea during a week of night marches. But again MacArthur assumed the mission of these Chinese infiltrators was strictly defensive. They had entered Korea, he believed, to protect the Yalu River power dams that supplied Manchuria with electricity.

Cooper, however, harbored serious doubts about China's intentions.

In one place where the Yalu was frozen solid, he studied a path of fresh footprints in the new-fallen snow and said to photographer Walker: "Better snap a picture of this. Looks like the 'Chicoms' (as he called the Chinese Reds) may be trying to cut us off. When you get back to Tokyo, show that picture to Mac and see what he says." Walker took the picture. But for the magazine, not for MacArthur.

The 81's finally silenced the troublesome tower and we made a dash for the tunnel. Seated in a ditch inside the tunnel sat the two medics, Honey and Dearie, finally enjoying their smoke. They were waiting for the assault platoon to cross a small tributary below. The bridge was burned, and the platoon members were forced to crawl on their hands and knees over the charred timbers imbedded in the ice. A sergeant, positioned at the tunnel's mouth, squinted down the long black barrel of his 50-caliber machine gun, covering the assault troops as they crept toward the smoking village.

The village was still. Only a few of the buildings were ablaze, but even they seemed to be burning silently. "I hope that old woman goes back inside," said the machine-gunner pointing to a lone figure standing in front of the first house.

"Watch her," cautioned Major Cooper. "Sometimes old ladies throw hand grenades."

Just then the whole gorge exploded with machine guns, burp guns, and carbines firing in unison. Most of the assault platoon had already crossed the tributary. The men were now running, crouched low, up the snow-covered field toward the first row of houses. A herd of startled pigs scurried past them in the opposite direction. The pigs were the only sign of life left in Posong-ni. The woman had disappeared and no enemy troops were visible. But watching from the tunnel, we saw two members of the assault platoon suddenly pitch face-forward into the snow, picked off by snipers hiding somewhere in the village.

"Medics," yelled Cooper. "Go get those two guys." Honey and Dearie slipped out of the tunnel and crawled across the charred timbers spanning the little tributary. But they came back empty-handed. The two men, they reported, were dead.

As quickly as it had flared, the fight for Posong-ni ended. The town was once again eerily quiet. All the inhabitants, including its Communist defenders, had fled. So Cooper still didn't know if they were Chinese or North Koreans. Two Koreans had been captured laying land mines on the road leading out of the town. But they were civilians.

"We'll stay here tonight," Cooper announced, surveying the rows of empty houses. This was welcome news. His men had spent three sleepless nights lying in the snow, zipped up tight in their mummylike mountain bags. That was against regulations because of the risk of being bayonetted while snugly zipped up. But it was too cold to worry about regulations.

November 24, the day after Thanksgiving, dawned just as cold and blustery. By first light the assault platoon had already moved down the undefended road past Posong-ni, reporting back to Cooper by walkie-talkie. "All them gooks disappeared, Major," crackled the platoon leader's voice. "Looks like they crossed the river."

It was the enemy's use of Manchuria as a sanctuary that had prompted MacArthur to seek permission from Truman to chase them. But his request had been quickly turned down. "We have never at any time entertained the intention to carry hostilities into China," announced the president, seeking to calm world fears that MacArthur was intent on widening the war.

On the same morning that our little task force lost contact with the enemy, we learned that MacArthur was on his way to Eighth Army headquarters in Korea to launch what he announced to his generals would be a "massive compression envelopment." That pincer operation, he promised, was going to "close the vise" around the enemy. "If successful," he added, "this should for all practical purposes end the war."

You can imagine what a heady moment this must have been for the Supreme Commander of the Allied Powers. In barely ten weeks his United Nations forces had broken out of their defensive Pusan perimeter at the southern tip of Korea, and raced 450 miles to Hyesan on the northern frontier. Hank Walker and I had traveled the last hundred miles with them.

MacArthur, I heard later, was in high spirits. Chatting with his field commanders, he predicted the struggle would end "very shortly." And within earshot of several of my correspondent friends, he said, "I hope we can get the boys home by Christmas." Later that day these same correspondents heard him repeat his optimism to the 24th Division. "I have already promised your wives and mothers that you'll be back by Christmas," he said. "Don't make me a liar."

Before heading back to Tokyo that afternoon, MacArthur decided, unannounced to the reporters traveling with him, to fly the length of the Yalu to see if he could spot any concentrations of Chinese troops. In retrospect, it was a harebrained stunt since his unarmed plane was in range of Chinese antiaircraft batteries on the river's north bank. American fighter pilots had already tangled with Yaks and MIG-15s high over the river. In fact, two weeks earlier I had ghosted a short article for Life by F-80 pilot Russell Brown, who downed the first MIG in one of those dogfights.

Luckily, MacArthur's reconnaissance flight encountered neither flak nor enemy aircraft. He reported seeing only the empty, ice-glazed landscape. "When we reached the mouth of the Yalu," he wrote in his diary, "I told Story [his personal pilot, Anthony Story] to turn east and follow the river at an altitude of 5,000 feet. At this height we could observe in detail the entire international no-man's-land all the way to the Siberian border. All that spread before our eyes was an endless expanse of utterly barren countryside, jagged hills, yawning crevices, and the black waters of the Yalu."

Of course, Cooper and his men had no idea that the supreme commander was passing directly overhead. And MacArthur had not glimpsed them below, dug in at Posong-ni, although he was aware of their reconnaissance mission. His previous day's communiqué had noted that an unnamed unit of the 7th Division had swept forward fifteen miles from Hyesan "against almost no resistance." That was us.

On November 26, two days after his observation flight, MacArthur's communiqué again reported only "moderate resistance" along the Manchurian border. Then just one day later, his communiqué described "strong enemy counterattacks. Countless thousands of Chinese," the supreme commander claimed, were suddenly howling down from the Yalu and attacking along a 300-mile front. Disaster had struck.

Of course, Hank Walker and I didn't need MacArthur's daily communiqué to tell us that. We knew right away we'd been cut off, though we had no idea that our magazines, previously staunch supporters of MacArthur, would jump on him so hard. *Time* claimed he was responsible for one of the greatest military catastrophes of all time—"the worst the U.S. ever suffered." *Life* compared the rout of the U.S. troops and their U.N. allies to the humiliating defeat suffered in Burma in 1942 when General Joseph Stilwell admitted, "We got a hell of a beating." But as the magazine pointed out: "General Douglas MacArthur, no longer a victorious commander, but a deeply harassed one, used loftier words" to escape the blame.

"This situation," he announced to the press, "repugnant as it may be, poses issues beyond my command—issues which must find their resolution within the councils of the U.N. and chancelleries of the world."

MacArthur also claimed it was "an entirely new war." And indeed it was for Task Force Cooper and the rest of the 7th Division. Fighting furiously to break out of the Chinese trap, Cooper's men cursed MacArthur, calling him "Bugout Doug" (a play on his World War II nickname "Dugout Doug") because of the massive, helter-skelter U.S. retreat.

"He'd promised the troops they'd be home for Christmas," I reported to Life in my story. "Now some of them would never get home, victims of this military hero's hubris."

From my World War II days in the Philippines, I remembered that MacArthur had not been popular with his troops. We never thought of him as a soldier's soldier, the way the troops in Europe thought of Dwight Eisenhower or Omar Bradley. Rather, we pictured him as a remote and imperious tactician, rarely seen by his troops, except when striking a victorious pose as he did for the famous wading-ashore photograph in Luzon, shot by Carl Mydans and run as a full page in Life. I also recalled that a commemorative bronze plaque had been quickly put up by grateful Filipinos to mark this spot where the general had waded ashore. It was where my battalion was bivouacked. One night, a group of resentful GIs bared their feelings for the general by prying the plaque off its wooden base and tossing it down a latrine.

Fortunately, the soldiers we were with on the Yalu didn't know that MacArthur had ignored widespread reports of the Chinese buildup, so intent was he on total victory. Even India's prime minister, Jawaharlal Nehru, had warned that Mao meant business. Too late now. Chinese mortars were already exploding in Task Force Cooper's front, on its flanks, even in its rear.

Hank Walker and I were lucky. We hiked fifteen miles back to Hyesan and then hitched a ride on an L–17 courier plane to Hungnam. A week later, at the Fourth Field Hospital near Seoul, I visited several survivors from Task Force Cooper and from some other 7th Division units, who had fought their way down from the Yalu. They described a chaotic, ragtag retreat.

James "Red" Cagle, from Quinton, Oklahoma, a private first class and a mortarman, had been shot in the stomach (though "not in the appetite," as one of my colleagues reported). He had a light bandage over his belly. Between efforts to catch up on his eating from a three-day fast, he told a group of us the story of his escape:

"I was a forward observer the night the Chinese struck. About nine o'clock the bugle played and they were on us. A captain killed the bugler and that stopped the music. The Chinese swept down on us from the hills and we started pouring mortar shells into them. One mortar fired 142 rounds in ten minutes. The tubes got red hot and burned out. We held the Chinese off until ten-thirty the next morning. Then we destroyed all our equipment except for enough trucks to carry the wounded and set out east to try to join the marines. The wounded were piled six deep in the trucks.

"Four miles down the road we hit a roadblock. We had about five hundred able men left. Half of the group started over a hill to try to clear out the Chinese firing at the road. But I stayed with the trucks and got hit in the belly. It felt like somebody slugged me. It didn't hurt at first, but a half hour later it began to burn. Then the Chinese came in on us again. We were out of ammunition and had to scatter. I lay in the woods and saw Chinese throw phosphorous grenades into our trucks of wounded. I could hear the screams. It's an awful thing to hear men dying and not be able to do anything.

"Another fellow who wasn't wounded finally helped me. The next day we must have walked eight or ten miles. I had my carbine and three rounds. He had a .45 with two rounds. We saw plenty of Chinese to shoot at, but couldn't because they would have run us down. We had to walk across the corner of the Changjin Reservoir and I broke through the ice and got wet up to my knees, but for some reason I didn't get any frostbite. We finally reached the marines, who helped get us to the airstrip from where we were evacuated."

It was obvious that Red Cagle and the other wounded men at the hospital doubted MacArthur's ability to halt the Chinese onslaught. They expected to be routed out of their beds at any moment. So they kept their pile-lined jackets on over their hospital gowns. "When we bug out of here," explained one, "I don't want to run in nothing but pajamas." They referred to the escape road running east from the hospital as the "haul asbestos route."

Some members of MacArthur's staff claimed the 7th Division troops panicked. But that talk came from officers who hadn't faced the Chinese legions. MacArthur himself referred to the retreat as a "fluid situation," which Truman acidly noted in his diary "is a public relations man's way of saying that he can't figure out what's going on."

On November 30, just one week after Thanksgiving, we learned that MacArthur had determined that holding the line against the Chinese was "quite impractical." Truman then declared a national emergency. Even the Joint Chiefs, it was later revealed, were reconciled to the prospect of the general evacuating his entire army to Japan. They radioed MacArthur: "We consider that the preservation of your forces is now the primary consideration."

During the desperate days that followed, Truman reversed the administration's Korean policy. MacArthur's mission, he announced, was no longer the unification of the peninsula. But the general himself was unwilling to settle for anything less, having become, as his critics said, "a victim of his own legend of invincibility." Instead, he recommended dropping thirty to fifty atomic bombs on China's industrial centers and blockading the coast. He also sought permission to use Chiang Kai-shek's 800,000 troops on Taiwan to invade the mainland. Turned down flatly by Truman, MacArthur then suggested severing Korea from Manchuria by laying down a field of radioactive waste—"the by-products of atomic manufacture"—all along the Yalu River.

As I learned many years later reading Truman's memoirs, he couldn't stomach the way this "supreme egotist," as he called MacArthur, was trying to take U.S. policy into his own hands. Even back then, we correspondents in Korea couldn't understand why Truman didn't reprimand MacArthur or bare his anger publicly. I was delighted that Truman in his memoirs also revealed having written a letter to a friend that referred to the general as "God's right-hand man" and "Mr. Prima Donna Brass Hat Five Star MacArthur."

I was still in Korea when General Matthew Ridgway took command of the American forces and reestablished a stable front along the old 38th parallel dividing line between North and South Korea. But I had just come back home when Truman decided it was time to seek a cease-fire agreement with China. It didn't surprise me that when MacArthur received an advance copy of the cease-fire proposal, he tried to sabotage the president's offer. As historians have now reported, without warning MacArthur then issued an insulting ultimatum to China, threatening to expand the war.

"A decision of the U.S. to depart from its tolerant effort to contain the war," MacArthur announced, "would doom China to the risk of imminent military collapse." In conclusion, he said that he personally "stood ready at any time" to meet with the Chinese commander to reach a settlement.

Furious that MacArthur had effectively cut the negotiating ground out from him, Truman decided to relieve the supreme commander. This time the Joint Chiefs also agreed the general had gone too far. MacArthur's feeling of infallibility had ruined his credibility with his staunchest backers in the Pentagon. But they warned Truman that MacArthur would probably prefer to quit than be shorn of his command. "The son of a bitch isn't going to resign on me!" sputtered the president. "I want him fired!"

MAC IS SACKED screamed an April 11, 1951, headline, just a few weeks after I had returned to the U.S. I was getting ready for my new assignment in Germany. But it suddenly struck me that less than five months earlier I had peered through Major Cooper's binoculars at Chinese sentries in their padded yellow uniforms, patrolling peacefully up and down the north bank of the Yalu. "We're gambling that those guys will stay on their side of the river," grimaced Cooper. I sensed then that the major had deep misgivings. But he was too disciplined a soldier to cast doubts on orders that came from the supreme commander. It might have been better for MacArthur if Cooper and the other field officers up on the Yalu had voiced their dissent.

go along the edge of

ROY ROWAN

above: A convoy of United Nations Relief and Rehabilitation Administration (UNRRA) trucks skirts the walled Chinese town of Yanling in Henan Province in 1947. Trucks were painted with yellow and black tiger stripes supposedly to keep them from being fired on by Communist or Nationalist soldiers in this civil war battle zone.

below: Refugees returning to the former flooded area south of the Yellow River in Henan Province. These heavily-silted, centuries-old roads were intended for mule carts and wheelbarrows, not for trucks.

ROY ROWAN

above: Part of the flooded area in Henan was still under water in 1947 as the refugees slogged their way back. During World War II, Chiang Kai-shek ordered the Yellow River dikes dynamited to inundate the area and slow the Japanese invasion.

below: A well-equipped Nationalist battalion passes through Xuchang in a show of strength. Chiang's soldiers were better marching in formation than in fighting the Communists.

ROY ROWAN

A rag-tag Red militia unit enters Xihua, one of the Communist-held towns supplied by Rowan's UNRRA convoys in Henan.

ROY ROWAN

The author, then 27, poses with a Communist sentry in Xihua.

above: Truck operations chief Rowan (driving) and maintenance chief Claude Lievsay in their mud-spattered jeep. Bullet hole is visible in lower left corner of windshield.

below: Weatherbeaten old women line up for food provided by UNRRA in town of Fukou after it was retaken by the Nationalists.

above: Stadium of skulls, assembled on a hillside as a memorial to Chinese victims of the Japanese occupation. Rowan sent this photograph to *Life,* which ran it for a two-page spread in its December 8, 1947 issue and led to his being hired by the magazine.

below: *Life* photographer Jack Birns, (left), pilot Moon Chin and the author before takeoff
(left) from Lanzhou in 1948 in search of Amnyi Machen, a mountain which was rumored to be higher than Everest.

below: Warlord Yan Xishan, the Nationalist defender of Taiyuan, displays his box of poison
(right) capsules. Yan vowed in 1948 that he and his 500 officers would commit suicide before surrendering to the Communists. Picture of former Flying Tiger commander, General Claire Chennault, is on the desk.

Rowan (left) and Birns hefting 400-Troy-ounce gold bricks in smuggling syndicate's steamy basement foundry in Macao in 1949. Smelted into ten-ounce bars, the gold was then hidden aboard junks destined for black markets in Shanghai and other China ports where the Nationalist currency had become virtually worthless.

Smiling White Russian "hostesses," as prostitutes in Shanghai were politely called, found business slack as Communists approached the once-raucous metropolis in May 1949.

above (left): Daily public executions like this in Shanghai in May 1949 were intended to discourage looters, gold smugglers and suspected Communist agents from further disrupting the city's already collapsing economy. The victims were convicted at a mock trial, and then paraded through the streets before being shot.

above (right): On May 21, 1949, a seemingly endless column of Nationalist troops pass through Shanghai, supposedly to halt the Communist forces approaching the city. The well-equipped soldiers, however, put up only token resistance.

left: Barbed-wire barricades and sand-bagged defense positions were erected in Shanghai's deserted streets just before Mao's forces marched into the city on May 24, 1949.

Ascetic Premier U Nu of Burma (now called Myanmar), offers prayers to Buddha in Rangoon's 2,000-year-old Shwe Dagon Pagoda. He combined Buddhist, socialist and democratic ideals to create a sense of national unity that staved off rebellious Communist factions and held the newly-independent nation together.

The "Iron Broom," as tough British police superintendent Bill Stafford was called, kicks in door of a jungle hideout belonging to Communist terrorists near Kuala Lumpur. This raid by Stafford and his black-suited "Killer Squad" in July 1948, resulted in the death of terrorist leader Lau Yew and nine of his followers. It was a crippling blow from which the 5,000 armed Communists in Malaya (now Malaysia) never recovered.

A sweating Rowan poses for photographer Birns in front of captured Communist shack which had just been torched. Moments later, some 50 more terrorists, who had slipped undetected into the jungle hollow, opened fire. Rowan dove into a nearby creek smashing his eyeglasses and scattering the rolls of exposed film from his unzipped shoulder bag. The film was later retrieved after the attackers were driven off.

"Iron Broom" Bill Stafford relaxes back at headquarters after the raid. Always spoiling for a fight, he carried a submachine gun slung over each shoulder and a revolver tucked into his belt. He also slept with a pistol under his pillow in a bedroom lined with mirrors to spot any intruders.

above left: Italian film producer Roberto Rossellini is about to take a swing at photographer Jack Birns (pointing finger) in front of a hospital in Rome, where Swedish movie star Ingrid Bergman has just given birth to Rossellini's illegimate son. Rowan (right foreground) jumped in and separated the two men. The picture made the front page of the *New York Daily News* and other U.S. dailies on February 5, 1950 because of the scandal created by Bergman, who was still married to Swedish doctor, Peter Lindstrom.

above right On Thanksgiving Day, 1950, a cold and exhausted Major Carroll Cooper led a 360-man task force on a risky chase of retreating Communist troops through the ice-clogged Yalu River gorge separating North Korea from Manchuria. Two days later, Mao's armies slipped across the frozen river and cut off Cooper's men and other Army and U.S. Marine units nearby. President Truman eventually fired General Douglas MacArthur for his tactics of "hot pursuit" which precipitated China's entry into the war.

left: Cooper's men fire a 60-millimeter mortar at a smoking tower held by North Korean troops in village of Posong-ni. Because of the winding course of the river, the mortarmen had to fire across Chinese territory to hit their target. "You need a squad of lawyers travelling right with the infantry to fight a war up here," Cooper claimed.

Marshal Tito before delivering a fiery speech in 1952 to 250,000 former Partisans filling a field in Slovenia to celebrate the 10th anniversary of the formation of their anti-German brigades during World War II. After the rally, Tito urged Rowan to write a story about the widow of a Partisan who was trying to retrieve her kidnapped son from the Storm Trooper's family, which had raised him in Germany.

A dramatic moment in "A Tale of Two Mothers," a story that Marshal Tito suggested Rowan cover for *Life* in 1952. Pavla Pirecnik (center), the Yugoslav mother whose son (left) was kidnapped by the Germans during World War II, is finally reunited with the boy as the foster mother, Josefine Sirsch (right) who raised him looks on. The emotional meeting took place during the custody battle in a U.S. occupation court in Frankfurt, which eventually awarded the boy to his "blood Mother." The British movie "Divided Heart," produced by J. Arthur Rank, was based on Rowan's story.

Disgruntled workers in East Berlin go on a rampage and set fire to buildings on June 17, 1953, during Europe's first anti-Soviet uprising. Puppet Premier Walter Ulbricht was forced to call in Russian tanks to finally quell the rioters.

Rowan virtually lived with Hoffa for three weeks in 1959, while he and Photographer Hank Walker worked on *Life*'s three-part series on the teamsters. At his Woodner Hotel apartment in Washington, Jimmy even cooked breakfast for the author.

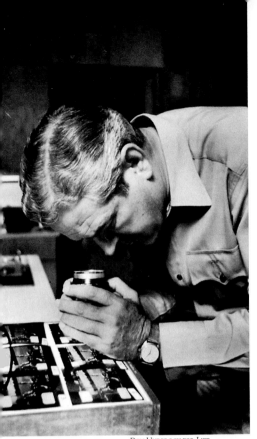

Governor John Connally of Texas peers though a magnifying glass at blown-up frames of Abraham Zapruder's assassination film. Connally claimed the movie showed clearly that the first bullet which pierced President Kennedy's neck did not hit him. "You can see the grimace in the President's face," he said. "You can't see it in mine. There's no question I haven't been hit yet." The Warren Commission's conclusion that Lee Harvey Oswald was the lone gunman hinged on this so-called "single bullet theory." Connally's insistence that he was hit by a second bullet led *Life* to publish a 14-page article in 1966 urging that a new investigative body be appointed and the case be re-opened because there was "reasonable and disturbing doubt that Oswald acted alone."

DON UHRBROCK FOR *LIFE*

Abraham Zapruder, the Dallas dressmaker, whose amateur movie of JFK's assassination became the Warren Commission's prime piece of evidence in concluding that Oswald was the lone gunman.

above: China's Deputy Foreign Minister Qiao Guanhua (right) bawls out Rowan (left) for his breach of protocol in presenting Premier Zhou Enlai with an album of old civil war pictures during reception for Princess Ida of Ethiopia at the Great hall of the People in Beijing in 1973.

right: In the White House Oval Office, Rowan tape-records President Ford's blow-by-blow account of the military action he took to secure release of the *Mayaguez*, the American cargo ship in 1975. Rowan, who wrote a book about the incident, flew back from Hong Kong for the taping session.

OFFICIAL WHITE HOUSE PHOTOGRAPH BY DAVID HUME KEN

below: State dinner in 1975 given by then-Deputy Premier Deng Xiaoping for President Ford in Beijing's Great Hall of the People. At the banquet, Deng criticized the U.S. for trying to seek peace with Russia. The tension was broken when the People's Liberation Army band (foreground) broke into the "Yellow Rose of Texas."

above: The "Iron Butterfly," Imelda Marcos, lunching in Manila with Rowan at the peak of her power in 1979. He had flown out to Manila from New York to write a pair of articles about her for *Life* and *Fortune*. The next time he dined with her was in 1986, just before she and her husband were deposed.

below: Herbert (left) and Bunker Hunt with the author in Dallas during his three-day series of interviews with them for *Fortune* during the 1980 silver crisis.

In January 1990, the author spent two weeks on the streets of New York City disguised as a homeless man for an article in *People*. As he stated in the book's "Conclusions," Rowan wanted to find out "how drifters who had once experienced success could completely lose their resiliency and succumb to such squalor."

Rowan returned to Dallas in October 1995 to interview Ross Perot and find out if the billionaire business man intends to run for president in 1996.

CHAPTER XV

Tito and a Tale of Two Mothers

By eight a.m. the hills around Toplice were black with invading armies of old soldiers. They sat in the woods, built fires, sang, danced, and got drunk. Then they poured down the still-green Slovenian slopes into a half-mile-long open field to greet their former commander and now chief of state, Marshal Josip Broz Tito.

Exactly ten years earlier, in September 1942, Tito had formed the original four Partisan brigades to resist the German and Italian divisions sweeping into eastern Yugoslavia. This was the Partisans' first reunion since the war. Planes droned overhead and swooped low to buzz the crowd of 250,000 men, women, and children filling the field. A parachutist floated from the sky, his chute painted with a bright red star. He sailed over the scrambling people and landed in a tree. Band music blared from the woods on both sides of the field, then suddenly stopped as the crowd took up its chant: "Tito, Tito, Tito."

I had been *Life*'s Bonn bureau chief for more than a year. But I had never encountered the Yugoslav leader, though I knew quite a bit about him. Just a few months earlier *Life* had excerpted his autobiography. In four installments it described how courage and charisma had catapulted this son of a Croatian blacksmith over one obstacle after another on his way to creating a federated Yugoslavia. Remarkably, each setback seemed to propel him further ahead. The First World War taught him to fight, and then took him to Russia as a prisoner, where he became steeped in revolutionary thought. Back home again, he was arrested for spreading radical ideas. He used the five years in jail to educate himself.

143

After Stalin's purges wiped out many of his comrades, he became secretary of the Yugoslav Communist Party. He eventually turned that underground organization into the Partisan resistance movement, using it first to fight the *Wehrmacht* in World War II, and then to stave off Stalin's postwar attempt to make Yugoslavia a Soviet satellite.

Life, I remembered, had run the series with a disclaimer acknowledging that the editors were aware of many Americans' dislike of Tito's communism and his anticlericalism. "But the fact remains," stated this preamble, "he is an important ally. Moreover, we believe that a man so feared by the Kremlin is one who should be heard by the world."

My purpose in joining the mammoth Partisan celebration was to try to make contact with Tito. That wasn't easy. His anti-Soviet remonstrances made him an assassination target and almost inaccessible to foreign journalists. But since my beat after leaving Korea was reporting on tensions along Europe's Iron Curtain, the Yugoslav dictator figured prominently in my plans for future coverage.

For the first year in Europe, it seemed that almost all my stories had come from hair-raising Iron Curtain escapes rather than cold war politics. One of the most tragic tales involved an eight-year-old Hungarian boy who was so traumatized by the sight of a Russian soldier shooting his mother and father that he could no longer hear or speak. For four years he had wandered from house to house. Finally, he fled alone on foot to Austria, where I found him huddled in the corner of a refugee camp, ignored by the other inmates as deaf and dumb. Not even the camp authorities knew much about him. But when I showed him a little attention, the boy perked up. Then with considerable coaxing he drew some line sketches of his parents' execution, followed by more penciled drawings of his adventure-filled flight. His crude drawings provided *Life* with a poignant story that needed few words.

There was also the story of a Czech railroad engineer who became so intent on fleeing the Communists that he drove his steam locomotive through the steel barricades at the West German border, hauling three cars of flabbergasted passengers to freedom with him. When I arrived, each passenger was still faced with the dilemma of whether or not to stay and seek political asylum. In the end about a third remained in Germany, while the rest returned to Czechoslovakia, including the panic-stricken conductor, whose decision I couldn't comprehend after he told me he might be shot for failing to stop the train.

Covering the Iron Curtain often failed to produce anything publishable. Once, my editors in New York dreamed up a cockamamie scheme to try to liberate Associated Press correspondent Bill Otis from a high-security Communist prison in Prague. Otis had become a cold war cause célèbre after being arrested on trumped-up charges of espionage. *Life* desperately wanted his exclusive story, even though he worked for the AP. The magazine located a former FBI agent who claimed that for $10,000 he could bribe Otis's guards and spirit the AP reporter to a hideout in Austria, where I would be waiting to interview him. Instead of springing Otis, the FBI man vanished with *Life*'s money, but only after leading me on a three-week-long chase up and down the Czech frontier.

The trip to Toplice for the Partisan rally was also a gamble. There was no guarantee that I could penetrate the phalanx of security guards to get to Tito. Just getting to Toplice was a problem. All the buses in Slovenia had been requisitioned to transport the Partisans. For twenty-four hours preceding the reunion, the roads winding through the Kocevski Hribi Mountains were clogged with buses, trucks, and bicycles—with a few private cars, including mine, wedged in between them.

By the time Tito appeared, I was standing next to the podium. Back in Ljubljana I had wangled a press pass from Borba, the official Yugoslav news service. The security guards apparently mistook me for a member of the dictator's press party.

A mighty cheer rose from the huge field as Tito mounted the podium. Deeply tanned and resplendent in the pearl-gray marshal's uniform which he had designed for himself, the magnetic leader treated his former Partisans to the fighting speech they had come to hear. "Never in history," he cried, "has such a small country been bullied by such political, economic, and military threats."

He was referring to Russia, of course. Recently, Stalin had denounced him as a "malicious deserter" and ordered menacing troop movements along Yugoslavia's borders. "When I protested," Tito told the Partisans, "the Kremlin ridiculed us. They said we were like poodles barking at an elephant."

The crowd roared its approval. During the war Stalin had publicly belittled the Partisans' fighting ability. Now Tito was giving it back to him, and the Partisans loved it. And they loved Tito too. Stubborn, proud, and irrepressible, he was ready, they knew, to die or kill for an idea. The external threat from Russia had enabled him to unite Serbs, Croats, and Slovenes in a confederation that has disintegrated into warring states today. Before winding up his fiery speech, Tito accused the Russians of betraying socialism. "They have degenerated into the worst sort of imperialists," he shouted. "But they will never intimidate us."

Yet another anti-Stalin tirade from Tito wouldn't make a story for *Life*. What I needed was an exclusive interview. I wanted him to tell of his recent contacts with Burma's U Nu, India's Nehru, and Egypt's Nassar, while attempting to coordinate the world's nonaligned powers. But when I finally reached Tito and introduced myself, he was already being led away from the podium by his new young wife, Jovanka. "Come with us," he said in halting English. "We will go visit Baza 20."

Baza 20, I was informed, was the secret mountain headquarters 6,000 feet above Toplice, from where the Partisans had directed all guerrilla operations in Slovenia. When we got there, Tito spurned my attempts at an interview. But he did have a story in mind that he hoped *Life* would cover. It involved the custody battle for a kidnapped boy whose Partisan father had been executed by the Germans. "Very sad, very sad," said Tito. But not trusting his English any further, he let an interpreter fill in the details.

After a Gestapo firing squad had killed the father, his twenty-month-old son was sent to Germany, where he was adopted by a Nazi storm trooper and his wife. That happened in 1942. Now, ten years later, the interpreter explained, the boy's Slovenian mother succeeded in tracing his whereabouts through the International Refugee Organization and petitioned to get him back. But the U.S. occupation court in Germany ruled that the boy should remain with the German family. "Justice! We must have justice!" interjected Tito, jabbing his fist in the air.

What caught my interest was not the story itself, but the fact that the Yugoslav strongman who had bravely resisted the Germans during the war, and was now brazenly defying the Kremlin, would have such tender feelings for the widow of a former follower whom he didn't even know.

The next day I drove to Sostanj, where the boy's mother lived. Bordered by steep green hills planted with apple orchards, the town straddled the Pava River north of Ljubljana. It consisted of 2,000 inhabitants, three Catholic churches, two inns, and about thirty small shops. Except for one prize possession, a bright red Skoda fire engine imported from Czechoslovakia, the town had nothing to distinguish it from all the neighboring Yugoslav communities. My hopes for culling a *Life* article out of this nondescript place were not high.

A record of the boy was easy enough to find. His name, Ivan Pirecnik, appeared as the first entry for 1941 in the town's book of births, deaths, and marriages. Born on New Year's Day, he was listed as the son of Pavla Pirecnik.

With the help of a local schoolgirl who spoke some English, I finally located Pavla. She was still living in the same dingy, one-bedroom apartment where Ivan was born. When I mentioned Marshal Tito's interest in her plight, she produced a certificate signed by the Yugoslav leader hailing her murdered husband as a "fallen fighter for liberty."

Pavla's own war saga was much more involved than Tito's interpreter had indicated. After her husband had been picked up and shot by the Gestapo for smuggling guns to the Partisans, she fled with Ivan and his eleven-year-old sister, Marija. It took the German *Feldpolizei* eight months to catch them. They sent Marija away. Then Pavla, also about to be sent away, said she looked back in the dawn light and saw little Ivan asleep on the straw-covered floor of the detention camp. She told me how she carried that image with her and cherished it with prayer through three bitter years of concentration camp.

In 1945 she returned to Sostanj. What Auschwitz could not do, her empty apartment apparently did. Pavla said she lay on the floor and cried out for her vanished children. Two months later, miraculously, an almost-adult Marija came running up the street. She had been raised by a German lieutenant and his wife in Vienna. Heartened by Marija's reappearance, Pavla described how she doggedly kept after the International Refugee Organization for news of Ivan. But there was none.

Then in 1950 a letter came. Another miracle. Ivan was alive. But it took a year, Pavla claimed, before she learned he had a new name and new parents—"German parents," she said spitting out the two words venomously. She appealed to the I.R.O. to get him back and once believed he was actually on his way. But the U.S. occupation court in Germany ruled that Ivan should remain with his foster mother. Unbelieving, Pavla cried, "But I am his blood mother! She is only his bread mother!"

Newspapers in Yugoslavia echoed her cry. Even the German papers sided with Pavla.

As the young student continued translating Pavla's sad story, I found myself becoming caught up in her plight. Tito's sympathetic account hadn't prepared me for this heartrending tug-of-war between two mothers. Soon I was on my way to Lohfelden, a small German town near Kassel, to hear foster mother Josefine Sirsch tell her side of the story.

To my great surprise, her claim on Ivan was as plausible and impassioned as Pavla's. Only the boy was no longer Ivan. In 1943, after ten childless years of marriage, Josefine told me, she had returned from an orphanage near Leipzig with a two-and-a-half-year-old boy—"A son finally to call my own." She named him Dieter. "We had what we always wanted!" she exclaimed. She said her husband Gustav, an SS man and a loyal Nazi, felt extra pride in making a home for this child after the orphanage told them he was the son of a *Volksdeutsche* woman murdered by Yugoslav Partisans.

When the war ended, Josefine said Gustav was sent to a Soviet prison camp. He finally came home thin and sick from Russia in 1948. But gradually he worked back into his painting trade, and things got better for their family.

It wasn't until 1951 that the blow fell. From the I.R.O. came word that Dieter's real mother was not a murdered German but a living Yugoslav. And she wanted her son to come home. Shaken and fearful, Josefine described how she and Gustav endured the suspense of the first court hearing before the judge ruled that Dieter was theirs to keep.

Through all this, the Sirsches had somehow protected Dieter's belief that they were his real parents. But when another appeal by Pavla was entered, Josefine knew that she had to "burden her eleven-year-old boy with an adult's load of heartbreak," as she put it. Taking Dieter to a movie with a problem similar to her own, *You Should Not Ask My Heart*, she asked whether he approved of the ending of the film in which the small-boy hero chose his real mother over his foster mother. Dieter nodded yes. Appalled, Josefine blurted out the truth.

For the first time since she began telling me her story, Josefine broke down and began to weep. But she quickly pulled herself together and explained how Dieter, after a long silence, had changed his mind. "Mother, I want to stay with you," he said. Thus the boy's choice was made.

My own choice, predisposed partly by Tito's angry account of the case, was no longer so clear-cut. No question, the boy would be better off in Germany, even though its secret police had executed his father and wrested him from his mother before sending her to Auschwitz.

Hurrying back to Yugoslavia, I found Pavla nervously preparing to leave for Lohfelden to see her son and attend the final court hearing. The whole town of Sostanj was helping to speed her on her way. The local beauty parlor provided a free finger wave. The Women's Antifascist League, whose president boasted of killing nine Germans as a Partisan and threatened to kill me too if Ivan wasn't returned, held a farewell lunch for Pavla. Her train fare to Germany was paid for by Tito's government.

The case again went to court. At the start, it seemed to be weighted in favor of the Sirsches. As Chief Justice William Clark and Justice Marc Robinson had held earlier, "to place Ivan among strangers, of whom his mother is one, seems cruel." Justice Carl Fulghum, however, had dissented, protesting that "a former storm trooper is being considered a more suitable parent than she who suffered so much at the hands of the Nazis."

I was surprised how impressed the court was by Pavla's coming in person. But I feared the hearing was becoming an international incident that might be resolved on political grounds. There was Tito, the powerful anti-Soviet renegade, and his rubber-stamp press demanding the boy's return. At the same time, there was the caustic American judge William Clark, declaring: "I would not want to live in the Communist dictatorship of Yugoslavia. So why should I condemn a helpless child to do so?"

The boy was spared this courtroom ordeal. But in chambers he sobbed to the judges, "I want to stay here."

In the end, the three judges found the issue was bigger than a young boy's heart. They announced a decision. Justice Robinson had changed his mind and Ivan would go home with his blood mother.

At the final scene of this saga, Lohfelden was awash in tears. Four hundred weeping townspeople turned out to bid the eleven-year-old boy good-bye. His schoolmates sobbed while they sang him a farewell song. Josefine managed to keep her composure as she clutched his hand reaching out from the mobbed car as it drove away. But after the car had gone she cried out in despair, "I will never see him again."

For me, a hardened journalist, it was still one of those indelible scenes that will never fade from memory—a whole town crying as if some natural disaster had struck.

But neither will the image of the Yugoslav dictator raising a clenched fist at Baza 20, his old mountaintop command post, and demanding justice for the widow of a fallen Partisan. That moment also remains firmly fixed in my memory, though I purposely never mentioned Tito's role in the eight-page picture essay that I wrote for *Life*, titled simply: "The Tale of Two Mothers."

One aspect of this story never came clear. Why did the American court in Germany change its mind? Did Tito work his wiles on the U.S. government which was then wooing him hard with armaments and money? I also omitted that possibility from my *Life* article. There was no purpose, I finally decided, in interjecting cold war politics into a heartrending human drama.

Two years later, J. Arthur Rank, the British film producer, turned *Life*'s story into a powerful movie called *Divided Heart*. It, too, was a tearjerker that barely touched on Tito's role. But in 1980, when Tito died, I was reminded of the tenderness displayed by the Yugoslav strongman, whose name in America was always preceded by the word "dictator." It was a side of Josip Broz Tito that the world never saw.

CHAPTER XVI

Stalin's Boy

THE STREETS OF EAST BERLIN swarmed with workers who would not work. They wore the uniforms of their trades—masons in white overalls, carpenters in traditional black smocks, day laborers and factory hands in hobnailed boots. In chanting, snaking columns they streamed from all directions on that drizzly afternoon of June 16, 1953. Merging finally into one matching phalanx, they moved on to the headquarters where the Communist proconsuls rule. "We want free elections! We want more butter! Lower the workers' norms!" they shouted. Then they yelled for party boss Walter Ulbricht to come out.

At that moment three surly, zoot-suited *Kripos*, as the criminal policemen were called, sidled up to *Time* correspondent Dennis Fodor and me. One, wearing a checked, mustard-colored sport jacket, flashed a brass badge with an embossed gold star in the center. "Now we go to the police station," he said curtly in German. We balked, demanding to be taken to a Russian officer in accordance with Berlin's four-power agreement. Instead, the three plainclothesmen led us to a barbershop and locked the door.

Outside, the protesters continued to stream by. Just six weeks earlier I had watched one million overalled workers, blue-shirted "Free German Youths," and black-booted People's Army battalions march smartly together in a well-orchestrated May Day demonstration of Communist loyalty. Today they were marching not so smartly behind a bright blue banner demanding a lowering of the same production quotas they had so proudly boasted of bettering back then.

150

Inside the barbershop the *Kripo* in the mustard-colored sport jacket picked up the phone and called police detachment "K." "This is Undercommissar Erich," he reported, and then in a long, guttural spiel explained how he had caught two "conspiratorial Americans" who refused arrest. "Would Herr Commissar send a police car to the barbershop?" Evidently, Herr Commissar couldn't make up his mind and would call back.

During this phone conversation the barber nervously kept on cutting the hair of his lone customer, pretending to ignore the little drama unfolding in his sparsely equipped shop. There were no chairs to sit in. Glowering down from the otherwise-bare walls was a portrait of *"Spitzbart"* (Pointed Beard), as his subjects called Walter Ulbricht, the goateed East German puppet.

As *Life*'s man in Germany I had learned a lot about Ulbricht. He was a tough dictator all right, intransigent as Tito, though totally subservient to his Soviet masters. Western journalists never got to interview him. But through my East Berlin contacts I was able to piece together a fairly full biography. There were still a few career gaps to fill, and Communist revisions to clarify, especially concerning his early plottings with the Nazis. Still, I had a pretty clear picture of how this son of a Leipzig tailor rose to power.

Ernst Paul Walter Ulbricht had been known by many aliases during his climb through the Communist hierarchy—Comrade Cell, Comrade Motor, Sorenson, Urvich, Leo, and, behind his back, *Spitzbart*. At fifteen he had joined a workers' youth organization, at seventeen the German Woodworkers Union, before becoming a charter member of the German Communist Party, for which he proved both an enthusiastic organizer and a well-crammed encyclopedia of the dictums of his idol, Vladimir Ilyich Lenin.

But as I also discovered, Ulbricht was best known for his treachery. A German reporter once told me, "He's the kind of man who wants to enter a house which is guarded by a policeman at the front door, then decides it is easier to go in by the back door. He first begs a slice of bread, then seduces the maid, cleans out the refrigerator, works his way into the master bedroom, steals the owner's clothes, and finally strides through the house to the front door and tells the policeman to go away."

During the war Ulbricht became a Soviet citizen and helped organize German prisoners into a shock corps that would go home and convert the *Vaterland* to communism. For those who didn't respond, he fashioned a tiny cell of granite blocks in which the prisoner could neither stand nor sit. It became known as Ulbricht's "stone coffin." And there were those who said that "with bricks and mortar made in Moscow he would someday build a stone coffin for all of East Germany."

That opportunity came in 1947 when the farce of Germany's four-power occupation was replaced by the reality of two separate states. Stalin promptly named Walter Ulbricht the party's secretary general, the same job on which he had built his own power in Russia. But Stalin recognized the difficulty of bolshevizing the Germans. "Communism," he once admitted to an American diplomat, "fits Germany the way a saddle fits a cow."

Undeterred, Ulbricht set out to milk the cow by collecting immense war reparations for Russia. In so doing, he made life an Orwellian nightmare for the East German worker. Wages were based on unattainable job quotas. Unpaid "peace shifts" were introduced and workers were forced to march in demonstrations that demanded still more work for themselves at no more pay. A tough Two-Year Plan, followed by the start of a Five-Year Plan, did raise electrical output fifty percent, chemical production thirty percent, and lifted steel smelting well beyond the prewar level. By the time Stalin died in March 1953, his boy Ulbricht seemed to have saddled the cow.

Now, just three months later, as we waited locked up in that dingy barbershop watching the protesters stream by, it occurred to me that old *Spitzbart* might have pulled the cinch on that saddle too tight. The East German cow looked like it was getting ready to buck.

After an hour's wait, Herr Commissar telephoned back to the barbershop and ordered Undercommissar Erich to take our names and let us go. We jotted them down on a blank page from my notebook, and after each *Kripo* carefully examined the two signatures, they unlocked the door and set us free. But the jeering mobs had either dispersed or moved on to another district.

That night I heard RIAS (Radio in the American Sector), the West's most powerful voice behind the Iron Curtain, taunting Ulbricht's East German regime. "Remember your party discipline, remember your party discipline," it faceteously repeated over the air to East Germany's so-called "under-the-blanket listeners," many of whom had surely taken part in the protest.

By dawn the next day the columns of marching workers had multiplied into angry armies. I hurried back to the East Sector. Along Stalinallee, the newly constructed apartment complex dedicated in December as a birthday gift to the dying Soviet leader, more than 10,000 workers were yelling in ragged cadence: "Freedom! Freedom! Freedom!"

The sight of Stallinallee's fifty new buildings, occupied mainly by the Communist brass, seemed to fan the protesters' fury. Consisting of some 2,500 apartments, 150 shops, and a gigantic sports palace, the ugly clifflike complex was considered the "cornerstone of socialism in Berlin," or so Boss Ulbricht had bragged at the groundbreaking. Thousands of workers had been chivied into giving their time and money in exchange for a chance to acquire one of the apartments. For 300 hours of donated labor a worker received a lottery ticket for the grand drawing of leases. The same chance was given for a "loan" of three percent of the worker's annual income. Many thousands of tickets went into the lottery barrel. But only a few apartments were put up as prizes. The rest went to the party apparatchiks. That incensed the workers.

Still, Red pride in the project was such that Gerhart Eisler, an American Marxist who fled the U.S. to become Ulbricht's propaganda minister, had invited *Life* photographer Ralph Crane and me to cover the opening. He then tried to cajole us into broadcasting over the East German radio network a glowing report of what we had seen, which we refused to do. But already I could see the slipshod construction was beginning to crumble. And because furnaces to heat the buildings weren't available, an old steam locomotive had been parked outside with pipes running into the complex. "Uncle Joe's Miracle Mile in Red Berlin" is how we had waggishly titled our article in *Life*.

As the angry mob now marched defiantly on past Uncle Joe's Miracle Mile, a cordon of dark green riot trucks appeared, blocking the street ahead. In front of the trucks stood a wall of *Volkspolizei* (People's Police), their gray raincoats agleam, their arms locked elbow to elbow. For a moment I thought the marchers had been stopped. But they plunged forward, disregarding the thudding truncheons. The wall of police broke, and with a roar the marchers poured on down the street.

The mob and the sounds swelled. Shopkeepers clanged down shutters of their stores and peered through the slits. From side streets additional thousands joined the march. In parks and vacant lots, still heaped with war rubble, more men and women flocked together, expanding the chanting, fist-waving army. "We want free elections!" they screamed. "Down with the People's Army!"

By midmorning the entire downtown section of Soviet Berlin was chockablock with demonstrators. An odd, almost festive air made it hard to believe what was happening. For eight years since the war, taciturn, cold-eyed Walter Ulbricht had been striving to remake East Germany in the Soviet image. His motto was: "Strict control and complete discipline." Suddenly on this rain-drenched morning his mighty effort was coming unstuck.

The carnival spirit was still cresting when a gang of rioters pounced with a whoop of recognition on a small gray automobile. I could see old Otto Nuschke, the deputy premier and one of Ulbricht's underlings cowering terrified in the driver's seat. The mob pushed the car across the border into the American Sector. "Good riddance," swore the pushers. "*Spitzbart* will be next." Nuschke was detained for two days before being repatriated to the East Sector.

When the first Russians rolled into sight in armored cars and infantry trucks, the marchers whistled and jeered. They didn't seem to fear them either. I saw a man perched on a concrete mixer yell to a tall Soviet soldier: "Hello, long one. Your pants are open."

It was almost noon before the first brick smashed a government office window, followed by a cascade of stones bouncing off Ulbricht's headquarters on Leipzigerstrasse. As the rocks flew, the crowd chanted the forbidden anthem, "Deutschland, Deutschland, uber alles. Uber alles in der Welt."

Bent on destruction, the army of demonstrators charged down Leipzigerstrasse to Potsdamer-Platz. That open square, where the Soviet, British, and U.S. sectors join, served as a huge picture window in the Iron Curtain for the residents of West Berlin. Before thousands of gawking American spectators the rioters uprooted Communist signs, tore down propaganda billboards and red flags, and set fire to everything that would burn in the rain, including an effigy of Walter Ulbricht. "Down with *Spitzbart*! Down with the Ulbricht regime!" they yelled.

Young boys raced happily to and fro, waving burning flags. I was shooting pictures of these youthful frolickers when a burst of machine-gun fire sent them scurrying panic-stricken over to the Western side of the square.

Suddenly over the din came a new sound—the clatter of metalic treads on the cobblestones. A woman shrieked, "The tanks! The tanks are coming." With that, I, too, raced back to the Western side of the square as a dozen T-34 Soviet tanks lumbered into view, their 86mm guns ominously traversing the mob. A shower of rocks bounced harmlessly off the tanks' heavy steel armor. I watched two brave young men rush out in front of the rumbling monsters to drag away a wounded friend before he was mashed into the pavement. Another group scooted up to a T-34 and jammed a log into its tracks, crippling the tank with its Russian crew inside.

From other streets came more tanks, about two hundred in all. For a while they wheeled and snarled through the crowds. But the frenzy continued to build until in half a dozen places at once I could hear machine guns chattering. The people dove into doorways or down subway stairwells to dodge the bullets. Not all of them made it. I saw one man crushed by a growling tank. Scores were hit by point-blank fire.

At Potsdamer-Platz sirens wailed as West Berlin ambulances began carting away the wounded who were being carried to the border.

At one P.M. the East Berlin radio announced the beginning of martial law. Any groups of more than three people caught loitering in the streets would be fired on. The crowds ignored the warning, torching a new office building on Marx-Engels Platz and pulling down overhead streetcar wires in a Fourth-of-July shower of sparks.

In front of Ulbricht's headquarters on Leipzigerstrasse, thousands of workers continued to stand their ground, staring down the cold green muzzles of four tanks. "Come out, come out, wherever you are," they chanted in German.

Just behind Potsdamer-Platz in West Berlin, Red Cross women set up an emergency aid station. After each burst of gunfire, another batch of bleeding men—and occasionally a bleeding woman—arrived, needing emergency treatment. But not all the wounded made it to the aid station. In spots where a demonstrator had died, crude wooden crosses were already being driven into the asphalt.

More Soviet troops arrived. And so did *Volkspolizei* reinforcements, until gradually the rebellion just sputtered out in the rain. By two-thirty most of the drenched crowds had melted away. A police sound truck circled the riot area, repeating its booming message: "The Soviet commander of troops has ordered a curfew."

Not for several days did Walter Ulbricht and his Communist deputies realize the scope or seriousness of the rebellion. In Leipzig, Brandenburg, Chemnitz, Halle, and several other East German centers, similar spontaneous, uncoordinated outbursts had also erupted. They, too, were finally put down only with Soviet steel.

Six months earlier, when photographer Crane and I were shooting the story on Stalinallee, we were told that the city of Magdeburg had voluntarily sent building materials to Berlin for the project. Now we learned that workers there had broken open a jail, freed all the political prisoners, and hanged one policeman. The casualty reports from everywhere were enormous: 500 people killed, 40 ringleaders executed, 1,800 civilians wounded, and 25,000 arrested. Repercussions reached all the way to the Kremlin. One week later, Lavrenti Beria, Russia's much-feared KGB chief, was executed, presumably because his spies hadn't foreseen this embarrassing anti-Communist outburst.

Obviously, the Russians couldn't execute or jail all eighteen million East Germans. As I reported to *Life*, "The Russians' best chance is to conciliate where they can, in hopes that the hatred and yearnings which still smolder will die out." The Kremlin ordered Ulbricht to rescind his work-speedup decree, discard his antichurch campaign, and ease the other policies that had brought the country to the brink of revolution.

A few weeks later I watched the hated sixty-year-old Communist boss stand before a sullen and restless crowd and utter an apology. "Measures to improve the living conditions of our people will be carried out," he promised. "We know we can do this only by better organization and by a permanent increase in productivity. But first," he added, "we must make up production lost by the unrest."

That was a humbling confession for the disciplinarian who dreamed of becoming Germany's Lenin, the triumphant father and leader of that Communist state. As he spoke, I could see the pointed goatee bobbing from his chin, and I was struck by how much this thick-bodied, balding man actually resembled Lenin—a comparison, it was said, he didn't discourage

Ulbricht's new promises, however, didn't slow the flow of refugees fleeing East Germany. Called *fluchtlings* (fleers), more than one thousand a day were now pouring across the border in Berlin, "the last unplugged hole in the Iron Curtain," as I referred to it in *Life* "There, a ride on the S-Bahn [subway], or a walk across the Potsdamer-Platz, or simply a stroll down some sixty streets connecting the East and West sectors could mean the start of a new life."

Ralph Crane and I had already shot a story on the *fluchtlings* before the rioting began. It would have been repetitious to shoot another, even though the flow had become a torrent. Instead, we concentrated on showing the new barbed-wire barricades and *Volkspolizei* guard towers suddenly being erected on Ulbricht's orders to slow this tidal wave. The infamous Berlin Wall that Ulbricht finally built in 1961 to stop the exodus entirely (and which would earn him yet another nickname, "Ogre of the Wall") had not yet even been conceived.

No barbed-wire barricades, Berlin Wall, or Iron Curtain could obliterate the memory of what took place in East Germany on June 17, 1953. The pictures in *Life*, and in hundreds of other publications around the world, of rocks being hurled by brave East German civilians at Russian tanks, smashed as nothing ever had before the Soviet propaganda that the area behind the Iron Curtain was a workers' paradise. The bloody outburst proved to be contagious. Workers in Poland, Hungary, and Czechoslovakia eventually demonstrated that they, too, no longer considered it hopeless to resist Soviet tyranny. Hope, they saw, was possible. And resist they finally did, though not until a few years later. Even in today's unified Germany, June 17 is still celebrated as the date European workers dared to strike their first blow against communism. But on that day in 1953 nobody knew if the Russians would retaliate with a reign of terror.

"What will happen now?" I asked a young rioter who lay in a West Berlin hospital with his left ankle almost shot off.

"I'm not sure," he said. "But the Russians can't keep their tanks in the streets forever. When they leave we will fight again until they purge old *Spitzbart* and change his government."

Walter Ulbricht, contrary to such predictions, proved to be a canny survivor. After the riots he moved cautiously from place to place in his bulletproof Zis, or holed up safely in his fortified ten-room stucco villa in the suburb of Pankow. Politically, too, he proceeded more warily. He avoided issuing any more harsh workers' decrees, or engaging in dangerous Stalin-like vendettas with rival Communists. As a result, this Lenin look-alike, who was considered a mere Soviet scarecrow and Stalin's errand boy when he was first installed by the Kremlin, ruled unscathed until 1971, when he finally resigned.

CHAPTER XVII

Faubus vs. the Feds

MOVING FROM GERMANY TO NEW YORK, and then on to Chicago in 1955 as *Life*'s midwestern bureau chief, I soon found myself swept up in a different kind of battle—the school desegregation fight between the federal government and the southern states. But my fascination with powerful leaders and how they gain and lose control of the arenas they operate in continued unabated. The journalistic terrain was new. And so were the types of characters to be covered. Yet the psychological forces at work, as well as the physical hazards encountered, were familiar.

In Clay, Kentucky, Clinton, Tennessee, and Birmingham, Alabama, we correspondents got used to being taunted as "nigger lovers." We became adept, too, at dodging rocks hurled by hecklers, or clubs wielded by local cops posted outside the schools, supposedly to keep the peace.

Of course, our reporting wasn't confined to racial violence. We also covered floods, fires, tornadoes, and other natural disasters as well as bloody labor disputes, gangster executions, and a couple of celebrated murders committed by the most unlikely killers: "Dr. Sam," the Cleveland society doctor, convicted (and later exonerated) of mercilessly beating his pregnant wife, Marilyn Sheppard, to death; and Eddie Gein, the Plainfield, Wisconsin, "mama's boy," whose fetish for beheading and skinning his women victims inspired two Oscar-winning movies, *Psycho* and *The Silence of the Lambs*.

But it was Little Rock, Arkansas, that became the main arena in the battle to desegregate southern schools, and the main focus of our coverage in 1957. There, the wily Orval Faubus was seeking an unprecedented third term as governor. Considered a moderate on racial issues, at least by southern standards, he had already said, "Everyone knows that state laws can't supersede federal laws." Yet, in September, he suddenly decided it would be political suicide to proceed with the plan to allow nine carefully selected Negroes to enroll at Little Rock's all-white Central High. Defying the Constitution, the Supreme Court, and the president of the United States, he ordered 150 National Guardsmen, armed with carbines and billy clubs, to block the black students' entry to the school.

That same day—which is when I first met him—Faubus was holed up in his salmon-pink governor's mansion with another protective cordon of militiamen outside. To be precise, this man, whose defiance was causing shock waves throughout the nation, was bent over double, clutching what he called his "sore stomach." He greeted *Life* correspondent Paul Welch and me perfunctorily, then collapsed into a contour chair. *Life* photographer Grey Villet snapped his picture as he groaned in the agony of "two much corn and sweet potatoes" the night before.

His wife entered anxiously, carrying a bowl of stewed chicken and rice. Faubus peered distastefully at the chicken. "Put that rice in a bowl so I can pour some milk on it," barked the governor.

"But this is what the doctor ordered," protested Alta Faubus. "I don't care," he cried, and obediently she returned with the requested rice and milk. Faubus wolfed it, the milk dribbling down his chin. Then he turned to Welch, who was jotting notes about this testy husband-and-wife exchange, and belched gustily.

Listening to Orval, we had the feeling that the thirty-sixth governor of Arkansas would have preferred being back in his native Ozark hills. "I'm just a country boy," he said, diverting the conversation away from the school crisis. "I was born and raised in the woods. The nearest neighbor was a mile away."

He then told us about "rocking squirrels" as a boy. "It was sacrilegious to fire a gun on Sunday," he said. "If we saw a squirrel in a tree, we'd knock it down with rocks. Hill men can throw better than most men can shoot."

The governor explained that he sometimes used a "bean flip" to hunt with. He stood up to demonstrate, holding up two fingers in a "V" and drawing back an imaginary rubber band for Villet, who continued shooting pictures. "It's like a slingshot. But it's different than the kind David used to slay Goliath."

As he struck that pose, it occurred to me that Faubus had intentionally put himself in the position of David battling the Goliath of *Brown*

v. *the Board of Education*, the Supreme Court decision requiring public schools to integrate "with all deliberate speed." Although there had been some grumbling back in May when the Little Rock school superintendent's plan was approved to integrate Central High, most people in the community, as well as the governor and both daily newspapers, seemed ready to accept the inevitable.

Then at ten P.M. on the eve of school's opening, Faubus marched into station KTHV for an unscheduled television appearance. "The evidence of discord, anger, and resentment," he broadcast to the local citizenry, "has come to me from so many sources as to become a deluge."

To hear Faubus tell it on TV, Little Rock was indeed on the brink of riot. Outraged white mothers were prepared to march on the school. Caravans of indignant white citizens were converging on Little Rock from all over Arkansas. And Little Rock stores were selling out of knives and pistols—"mostly to Negro youths," declared the governor.

It was then that he announced: "Units of the National Guard are now being mobilized with the mission to maintain or restore the peace and good order of this community," which he added would be impossible "if forcible integration is carried out."

Mayor Woodrow Wilson Mann angrily contradicted him. "The governor's excuse is simply a hoax," bristled the mayor. "He has called out the National Guard to put down trouble when none existed." Police chief Marvin Potts also stated that his men had found no evidence of any planned violence.

The next morning the scene outside Central High was anything but violent. As usual, the high school boys stood around ogling the high school girls. The nine previously selected black students did not show up, having been asked by the stunned school board to stay home until the Faubus-created crisis could be straightened out.

After our interview in the governor's mansion, I decided to head for Madison County in the Ozark hills, from where Faubus hailed. Since the Central High confrontation had been temporarily put on hold, I wanted to learn more about the governor's humble origins—in the hope of discovering why he was taking this dangerous course.

To reach the remote and still-virgin country along Greasy Creek where Orval was raised, you need detailed directions and a sturdily springed car. At least that's what *Life* photographer Francis Miller and I found when we arrived in the little town of Combs.

First we stopped in at the town's only place of business, the Alfred and Jewel General Store and Gas Station. "Which is the road to Greasy Creek?" I asked.

"You better have Uncle Sam lead you there," advised store-owner Alfred Hawkins, who was married to a cousin of the governor's wife. Uncle Sam, it turned out, was J. Sam Faubus, the governor's seventy-year-old father. Briefly educated but widely read, he had been a "mountain radical" most of his life. He had even chosen Orval's middle name, Eugene, in honor of his hero, Socialist leader Eugene Debs.

"The papers are sure givin' Orval hell," said the governor's father with a big grin. "But Orval's smart. He was never full of mischief like I was."

Uncle Sam told us that his son didn't graduate from high school until he was twenty-three. But up in Madison County he explained that wasn't unusual for boys, who attended high school to teach grammar school during alternate semesters. "I made him his letters and learned him to read, and after that he was always readin'," Uncle Sam said. "Why, he passed into third grade the first three months of school."

"But he was a good worker too," added the old man. "When he hoed corn, it was hoed. He didn't leave a weed."

Uncle Sam, however, was not sure that his son hadn't gone too far in calling out the National Guard. "I think desegregation will eventually win," he surprised us by saying. "Of course the South hates to be pushed on it, but there's a big part of the nation where everybody's goin' to school together." He then told us a story about the governor's niece, who now lives in the state of Washington. The little girl had often heard Uncle Sam say, "Sweatin' like a nigger on election day," and one time in school she happened to use this expression in a conversation with a black classmate. "You know that little nigger girl punched her right in the nose," exclaimed the old man.

Uncle Sam apologized that his legs weren't steady enough to go over to Greasy Creek with us, but he enumerated a whole series of forks and turns that we should take. We drove back to Combs and stopped to check our complicated directions.

"Seems like everybody in Combs is writin' to Orval," said Clyde Blevins, the postmaster, a job Faubus once held. "Practically wore my arm out canceling stamps."

We drove on past the school, long deserted, and came to the home of Aunt Carrie Thornberry, widow of the governor's great-uncle. "I half raised Orval," she said. "There's nothing wrong with that boy, though when he had measles I had a terrible time keeping him in bed. Ain't nobody going to keep him quiet up in Little Rock today."

Continuing along a rutted road and over two "low-water bridges" described by the postmaster and consisting only of a bunch of rocks piled on the river bottom, we stopped at a house surrounded by yelping hounds. A woman came out of the house. She was Mrs. Ruby Keys, she said. "Why, I used to go to school to Orval. He was a fine, good teacher and very kind. She then proceeded to tell us stories about Orval's gentlemanly classroom manner.

"I went to him in the second grade and again in the fourth grade," explained Mrs. Keys. "One time I started talking about Ihio in class and all the kids got to giggling. Well, Orval just rapped on the blackboard and said, 'That's not funny. We all make mistakes. Ruby means Ohio.' He didn't believe in thrashing like some of the teachers, just in law and order, like he's proving in Little Rock today." After reflecting a moment, Mrs. Keys added: "But if he had to, he'd reach out for a hickory limb and hit us where the Lord best provided. Only now he's using soldiers instead of a stick."

One person after another recounted stories that helped explain the governor's current behavior. In Huntsville, the seat of Madison County, we were informed that Faubus really had no racial prejudice. "He's just being political," claimed county treasurer, J. O. Fowler. "We didn't have a single Negro citizen here when he was growing up."

In fact, Orval had admitted during our interview with him in the governor's mansion that he'd never met a colored person until he left the county. "We know Orval real well," continued Fowler. "We understand why he changed his spots on integration. He told us many times, 'When you run, run to win.' And he ain't about to stop winnin' because some colored kids want to get in that school."

Orval, we also discovered, had been a hero of long standing in Huntsville. Back in 1949, as a member of the State Highway Commission, he succeeded in getting Route 68 paved. It was the first highway in the county to be paved and Huntsville marked the opening with the biggest celebration in its history. Six thousand people attended a great picnic and the Madison County Fox and Coon Hunter Association paraded with dogs and floats. Governor Sid McMath, then a Faubus admirer and his political mentor, was on hand for the celebration.

When I returned to Little Rock I met McMath, whom I found violently opposed to Faubus on the segregation issue. "The biggest mistake I ever made," he cracked, "was to pave that highway and let Orval out."

McMath described Faubus's metamorphosis since he first got into politics. "He came down here to the Highway Commission," said the former governor, "in a ten-dollar suit that ended somewhere north of his socks, chewing on a match stick. But he was real smart and learned fast. Eventually, when he moved into the governor's mansion himself, he was considered an Arkansas-style progressive, raising more and more tax money for schools and highways. He won strong support from the Negroes for his moderation. Now he's biting the hand that fed him."

Several other Arkansas leaders besides McMath said they tried to persuade Faubus to back down and let the "Little Rock Nine," as the black students selected to attend Central High were known, enter the school. Winthrop Rockefeller, the state's future governor, for one, described coming down from his mountaintop ranch (he was the only mountaineer, his neighbors cracked, who owns his own mountain) to plead with the governor to stop interfering with the admission of the black children. "I told Faubus he was giving the state a bad name with industry," recounted Rockefeller, who at that time headed the Arkansas Industrial Development Commission.

"I'm sorry," Faubus replied, "but I'm already committed. I'm going to run for a third term, and if I don't do this, my opponents will tear me to shreds."

Faubus's intransigence finally drew a strong federal response. U.S. District Judge Ronald Davies issued a summons ordering the governor to appear in court and show cause why an injunction should not be issued forcing him to remove the National Guard. At the same time, Little Rock's highly respected congressman Brooks Hays checked with the city's leading citizens and found them shocked and ashamed of their governor. Hays then persuaded Faubus to go see President Eisenhower. As the congressman later explained: "It wasn't simply Faubus's integration stance that worried Ike. Faubus was setting a dangerous example for other governors who might want to thwart the national government."

A marine helicopter landed Faubus on the lawn of Ike's vacation headquarters at Newport, Rhode Island. First the president and the governor talked alone for twenty minutes. Then they met with Attorney General Herbert Brownell, Jr., White House Chief of Staff Sherman Adams, and Congressman Hays.

Faubus emphasized the progress that had already been made in integrating the University of Arkansas and the state's public transit system. He didn't specifically promise Eisenhower that he would remove the Guard from Central High. But he issued a statement after their meeting that sounded like a retreat: "The people of Little Rock are law-abiding, and I know they expect to obey valid court orders. In this they shall have my support."

Nevertheless, Faubus failed even to answer Judge Davies's summons. Instead, he challenged the District Court's jurisdiction. Davies then issued the injunction anyway, ordering immediate removal of the Guard.

"Now begins the crucifiixion," railed the governor, denouncing Davies's "unwarranted action." But he began removing his soldiers anyway, pending what he promised would be "the court order's certain reversal on appeal."

Finally, on September 23, with the Guard gone, the nine black students were free to enter Central High. Faubus had promised violence. When the class bell rang at eight forty-five A.M. his paid goons were there to make sure it came. And, as midwestern bureau chief, I had seventeen *Time* and *Life* reporters and photographers in Little Rock to cover this climactic moment.

Photographer Grey Villet teamed up with reporter Paul Welch, and photographer Francis Miller, working with me, were at the opposite ends of Park Avenue, waiting for the Negro students to arrive. From behind the barbed-wire barricade put up to keep the crowds off the street, a couple of middle-aged women agitators, spotting Miller's cameras, began screaming: "Nigger-lover! Nigger-lover!" Miller's nickname happened to be "Nig," though for reasons I never knew. But I had been scrupulously careful to call him Francis ever since we arrived in town.

We ignored the screaming women, which only made them madder. One finally signaled to a couple of beefy men standing nearby. Without warning, a fist landed on Miller's mouth, knocking him down. I grabbed the guy to keep him from kicking Miller. A couple of other guys grabbed me. Miller managed to get up. He stumbled a few feet toward the cordon of cops, who made no move to help him.

Instead, the police threw Miller, who was still gushing blood from his mouth, into a paddy wagon parked at the school entrance. Next, they shoved in his attacker. The man lunged at Miller again inside the paddy wagon before finally quieting down. At the police station, Miller was booked for "inciting a disturbance." Or, as he said to the judge: "For hitting a guy in the fist with my face."

Meanwhile Villet and Welch had been cornered by more oafs at the other end of Park Avenue. Every time they tried to break away, one big bruiser or another would step squarely in front of them. Finally, edging their way over to police line, the two *Life* men were ordered to get off the sidewalk by the cops, who shoved them back into the arms of the mob. The jeering crowd acted. A couple of men threw punches. Villet took mostly body blows. Welch got hit in the face, neck, and back of the head.

At this moment, *Time* correspondent Burt Meyers found himself in the ignominious position of chasing Welch and Villet. He had started over to help Villet, who was holding his long lens aloft, out of reach of his attackers, when a stocky boy asked Meyers, "What's goin' on?" Another fellow yelled, "It's one of them nigger-lovin' *Life* photographers."

"I've got a knife for him. Let's get him," yelled the boy pulling Meyers along with him.

So while Welch and Villet were trying to escape, Meyers was in pursuit. He stood beside the green police van into which the *Life* team was finally being pushed, with the mob howling obscenities after them. Said Meyers: "I looked Welch straight in the eye and pretended I'd never seen him before."

I was at the jail bailing out Miller when Villet and Welch were ushered in. A local lawyer, recommended by the editor of the *Arkansas Gazette,* succeeded in getting the police chief to drop the charges against Welch and Villet. And for a $200 fine we got Miller back too. All that took about three hours.

During this interval, the nine Negro students had gotten out of cars and walked calmly into the building. "The niggers are in the school," bellowed one man belatedly. "They're in! They're in!" echoed the crowd, which had been distracted by all the scuffling with the press on Park Avenue and missed the black students' arrival. But by the time Welch, Villet, Miller, and I returned to the school, Mayor Mann had already sent word to the mob that the "Negro students have been withdrawn." They had been escorted unnoticed out through a side door by the police, and driven home in patrol cars.

The removal of the students drew a fiery complaint from Daisy Bates, state president of the National Association for the Advancement of Colored People. That night a rock crashed through a window of her home. "Stone this time. Dynamite next time," warned a note attached to the rock.

Faubus was conveniently attending the Southern Governors Conference in Sea Island, Georgia, when this action was taking place. "The trouble in Little Rock vindicates my good judgment," he told newsmen covering the conference. But as *Time* pointed out: "By manufacturing the myth of violence, he had in fact whipped up the reality."

Eisenhower was still vacationing in Newport. His patience finally exhausted, he signed the historic document that for the first time ever ordered the Secretary of Defense to use the armed forces of the U.S. to uphold the law of the land in a school crisis. That night fifty-two planeloads carrying battle-tested units of the 101st Airborne Division landed in Little Rock. The Arkansas National Guard was also placed in federal service. "We are now an occupied territory," cried Faubus. Several sympathetic southern senators took up his cry and blasted Ike. "The South is threatened by the president of the U.S. using tanks and troops in the streets of Little Rock," shouted Georgia's Herman Talmadge on the Senate floor. "I wish I could cast one vote for impeachment right now."

By morning pup tents had blossomed in back of Central High's tennis courts. Jeeps lined the football field, parked neatly between the yard markers. Telephone lines hung from from the trees, and the combat-ready paratroopers known as the "Screaming Eagles" cordoned off two blocks of Park Avenue in front of the school. A walkie-talkie crackled: "Hello, Defiance, this is Crossroads Six."

I watched a crowd begin to gather at Roadblock Alpha, set up at an intersection just east of the school. A sound truck blared, "Please return to your homes or it will be necessary for us to disperse you."

Nobody moved. "Nigger-lovers," a man stepping out of the crowd, shouted at the soldiers. "They're just bluffing." A dozen paratroopers, their rifle butts on their hips, moved in front of him. The man held his ground for a moment against the advancing soldiers, then scurried away.

A few minutes later, a swiftly executed military maneuver put the nine Negro children safely into the school. The crowd was silent. But not for long. Trouble was developing again at Roadblock Alpha. I saw a man there grab for a rifle, pulling the paratrooper to the ground with him. Another trooper smashed his rifle butt against the man's head. Blood streamed from a scalp wound as the man scurried away. A sergeant yelled, "Keep those bayonets high, men. Right at the base of their necks."

The Screaming Eagles put an abrupt end to violence at Roadblock Alpha—and everywhere else around Central High. Orval Faubus, meanwhile, had flown back from the conference at Sea Island. "I feel like MacArthur," he joked feebly to the press. "I've been relieved of my job." But he had no intention of fading away politically, and was reelected governor four more times, an Arkansas record that has never been matched. Sensibly, he abandoned the race-baiting tactics during the latter years of his long tenure.

In 1981, a national school survey cited Central High as a shining example of racial balance. "Sixty-five percent of its students go to college," claimed the report, "and fifty-seven percent of its student body is black—solid proof that racial harmony and academic excellence are not mutually exclusive."

In 1986, in one of Faubus's hapless, intermittent comeback bids, he challenged Arkansas's only other governor to serve more than two two-year terms: Bill Clinton. During that campaign, Faubus claimed his actions in the Central High crisis were misunderstood. Again, in an interview shortly before he died in 1994, old Orval danced around the issue of what his motives really were, only to conclude: "It's true in politics as it is in life, that survival is the first law."

CHAPTER XVIII

Travels with Jimmy

"POWER," JIMMY HOFFA USED TO SAY, "is bad only when it's used bad." The implication was that he used it well. But that left a lot open to interpretation and depended on your perspective.

At the peak of his power in 1959, he was demonstrating what he meant by using it well. As general president of the International Brotherhood of Teamsters, he relentlessly put the squeeze on employers and threatening strikes that could choke the economy. "We are the transportation of America," he liked to say. "We are in control because raw materials must be transported in and finished products must be transported out." His 1.6 million union members roared their approval of that iron-fisted view, and then patted their fattened pocketbooks appreciatively.

There was at this same time a much darker view of Hoffa's power. A two-year Senate investigation into union corruption had just labeled him and his rank-and-file followers a "national menace." Studded with grafters, gangsters, and extortionists, the Teamsters had already been kicked out of the parent A.F.L.-C.I.O. and Hoffa himself faced two criminal indictments. But being harder than one of his trucker's tire irons, the furor served only to consolidate his strength. "I'm boss of an outfit that wins," he boasted.

Because of his power and threatened stranglehold on the economy, *Life* asked me to pursue Hoffa for what my editors called an "intimate profile of the man," and an "inside look at his union." But how do you get close to a labor leader who reviles reporters and whose image of invincibility seems to shine ever brighter with a bad press?

Based in Chicago, as I still was then, it occurred to me that racketeer and jukebox king Joey Glimco, who was also boss of Taxi Drivers Local 777, might help me get to Jimmy. Glimco, "Greasy Thumb" Guzik, a former Capone gang machine-gunner, and a group of other well-known mobsters used to show up regularly for Saturday lunch at Fritzels. Reporters could chat informally with them over a beer and sandwich. Glimco listened to me, but that was all. "Hoffa don't need no help from *Life* magazine," he assured me.

Next I turned to Robin Harris, or "Curly," as everybody called the former Hearst-reporter-turned-PR-man, best known for his attempt to refurbish the reputation of Mafia boss Frank Costello. Curly had a connection with Hoffa. My pitch to Curly was that anybody who could survive the televised grilling that Senator John McClellan's committee was subjecting Hoffa to couldn't be hurt by a mere magazine. By playing on the forty-six-year-old Teamster boss's invulnerability, I hoped he might relent.

That approach worked. Hoffa, although grudgingly at first, agreed to let me and *Life* photographer Hank Walker cover him and his union "without restraint," or that at least was the promise exacted by Curly. Remarkably, Jimmy more than made good on his promise.

For three weeks Hank and I virtually lived with Hoffa. We accompanied him to every meeting. We ate breakfast, lunch, and dinner with him. All over the country we were permitted to sit in on his closed-door huddles with conference chiefs, organizers, business agents, and shop stewards. In effect we became temporary members of this burly, broad-backed brotherhood, in which the fraternal symbols of identification were star sapphire rings, monogrammed shirts, king-sized cuff links, and Cadillac sedans.

In Washington, Walker and I had free run of the gleaming white Italian marble Teamsters headquarters. Often when we arrived, the door that sealed off Hoffa's office from the anterooms occupied by Yuki Kato, his Nisei assistant, and Jody Sullivan, his secretary who was a former Miss Washington, D.C., was closed to his associates. But we had only to push it open and walk in.

Sitting shirt-sleeved in a high-backed swivel chair, James Riddle Hoffa commanded a clear view of the Capitol, where his archenemy, Senator John L. McClellan was carrying on his searching investigation of the Teamsters. On the surface Hoffa seemed unconcerned by the charges of mob infiltration of his union. "Twenty years ago," he said, "the employers had all the hoodlums working for them as strike-breakers. Now we've got a few and everybody's screaming."

At his elbow was a forty-eight button intercom system and a control panel that operated electrically drawn drapes, a built-in television set, a muted hi-fi, and a concealed bar that teetotaler Hoffa could make slide out of the wall at the flick of a switch. Such elegant executive trappings would have brought hoots of derision from Hoffa in his early picket-line days. No longer, though. "Nothing's too good for the Teamsters," he joked, "and very little's good enough."

We had the same free access to his suite B-1250 in the Woodner Hotel. This was a luxurious three-room ten-telephone suite that Hoffa shared in Washington with his executive vice president, Harold Gibbons. No two close associates could have had less in common. Hoffa, squat and muscular with porcupine hair, was as blunt in conversation as he was in looks. Gibbons, tall and taciturn, was a keenly observant aide, known as the "Teamsters' intellectual." "Gib is my longhair," explained Hoffa.

Starting his working day in the Woodner suite around seven A.M., Hoffa bustled about the kitchen half-dressed, cooking breakfast for Gibbons, his personal assistant, Larry Steinberg, and any one of the three hundred Teamster lawyers who dropped in for a cup of coffee and quick legal conference. Several mornings he even made scrambled eggs for me.

The fact that Hoffa had a corps of attorneys huffing after him everywhere he went didn't mean that he had high regard for them, or even leaned on them for advice. "I keep tellin' them to quit yakin' and passin' papers around and get to work," he told me after one of the lawyers dumped a briefcase full of documents on the breakfast table. "Ed Williams is the only one I really depend on," he added, referring to Edward Bennett Williams, the Teamsters' chief counsel. "He's the only one that's got some original thought and imagination. To hell with all that book law."

I could appreciate Hoffa's reliance on Williams. Two years prior to our travels with Jimmy, the FBI had caught him passing twenty $100 bills to a lawyer he hired to steal secret testimony from the McClellan Committee. Brought to trial on charges of wiretapping and illegal possession of documents, Hoffa seemed a cinch to be convicted. He probably would have been except for a ploy by counsel Williams, who managed to persuade former heavyweight boxing champion Joe Louis to saunter into the courtroom in full view of the mostly black jury and warmly shake Hoffa's hand. The trial ended with a hung jury. Another case, charging Hoffa with using the mails to defraud union members, had also been dropped because Williams pounced on irregularities in the selection of the grand jury.

Leaving the breakfast dishes in a pile, Hoffa would move briskly about the suite as he finished dressing. As he hurried from bedroom to living room, he would shift from telephone to telephone, checking on Teamsters operations in Puerto Rico, Florida, California, and other parts of the U.S. Finally, at about eight-thirty A.M. he and his associates would climb into a black Cadillac and drive to the Teamsters headquarters. Hoffa always did the driving, just as he cooked the breakfast. "That," said Larry Steinberg, "is what he considers collective leadership."

At work, Jimmy Hoffa was no "desk bird," a term he mockingly applied to office-bound union officials. He spent about half his time hopping hurriedly about the U.S. hacking away at the problems of his vast Teamsters domain. Following him for three weeks, Walker and I found ourselves in New York, Harrisburg, Detroit, St. Louis, Los Angeles, Las Vegas, Chicago, and numerous smaller cities and towns in between.

Everywhere we went we saw Hoffa's underlings striving to emulate the boss. Hoffa neither drank nor smoked, and it was fun watching many of his local chiefs struggle to discard those habits too. But more than anything else, every Teamsters official in the U.S. seemed to be trying to copy Hoffa's breakneck pace. When Jimmy walked, he went at a jog. He skipped upstairs. Even his gestures were made in quick thrusts.

Traveling for Jimmy involved a merry-go-round of airplanes, speeches, banquets, and hotel rooms, punctuated by an onslaught of long distance telephone calls. Hoffa called any conversation, no matter how casual, a "meeting." On many days those "meetings" ran from breakfast to bedtime, a span of eighteen hours. One evening in Los Angeles, Hoffa had so many meetings scheduled that there were clumps of Teamsters cooling their heels around every palm tree in the motel patio. "I don't like to keep nothing dangling," said Hoffa, explaining his executive style. "I like to clean everything up every day."

Hoffa never seemed to let anything dangle for even five minutes. In Las Vegas I watched him idly pump a dollar's worth of nickels into a slot machine while making up his mind whether to invest $1 million of Teamsters pension fund money in a new Las Vegas hospital. But weighty decisions seemed to cause him little worry. "Don't worry about nothing," he frequently remarked. "Ninety percent of what you worry about never happens and the other ten percent you can always straighten out."

Hoffa lived by what he claimed was the Teamsters' cardinal rule: "Don't arbitrate grievances. Strike the bastards instead." As he himself admitted, Hoffa literally strangled his victim by degrees. "First," he said, "we close down the guy's outfit where the trouble is. Then if he won't settle, we prevent him from doing business in the surrounding states. If he still won't settle, we close him down across the whole goddamn country."

In Winston-Salem, North Carolina, for example, truck operator Malcolm McLean objected to the stiff terms of his new contract. Hoffa never even dispatched a picket to McLean's backyard. But all over the East, McLean suddenly found that yards wouldn't admit his trucks and they couldn't be unloaded. McLean held out for thirteen weeks, then one day, while Hank and I were still hanging around Hoffa's office, he came in and said: "How can we straighten this out?" Hoffa replied: "Just sign the damn contract." McLean signed.

Hoffa always emphasized to his rank and file the need for a tough bargaining line. He reminded them that the men who run the freight companies came right off the trucks and loading docks. "They know how to fight too," he'd say. Then, if his audience showed any apathy, he had one proven method for bringing them around. "You have to judge by your own paychecks if this union is being run right for you or whether you'd rather have some namby-pamby running it who hasn't got the guts to stand up for you." He never failed to remind his followers: "Without the word *Teamster* after your name, you're just another gear-buster."

I noticed that he enjoyed ribbing fat union bosses for being too prosperous. Once he pointed to the paunchy president of a Kansas City local and quipped: "Have charter, will steal." But usually it was the employers who were the butt of his jokes. When he heard that a new freight terminal manager in Detroit had restricted his cargo loaders to one toilet, Hoffa said: "Okay, guys, drive over to the union hall when you have to take a leak." He didn't care that it was a thirty-six-mile round trip. "I'm not trying to win any popularity contest," he crowed.

Several of Hoffa's associates confessed to me that the heat from the McClellan Committee investigation was making him edgy. While about a third of his time was taken up combatting the committee, he made light of this in his pep talks to the locals. "Senator McClellan," he'd say, "has the imagination of a mouse," and when he referred to the committee's chief counsel, Robert Kennedy, he'd always call him the "Little Nut." "I understand Bobby likes to play touch football," Hoffa once remarked when we were driving by a high school gridiron. "I sure would like to play with him sometime."

Actually, Jimmy and Bobby shared certain traits—singlemindedness, self-assurance, cockiness, and ruthlessness—similarities that I pointed out in the second installment of the *Life* three-part series. When the article appeared, Kennedy became so incensed by the comparison that he summoned me for lunch and a tongue-lashing at the Carroll Arms Hotel near the Capitol. Also infuriating to Kennedy was my description of the way Hoffa had eluded him and the other government pursuers.

In the middle of the lunch, a sudden, searingly painful toothache forced me to leave the table. Bobby telephoned his dentist, and half an hour later the infected tooth was being pulled. So Bobby never got to finish his tongue-lashing. However, *Life*'s editors agreed to let him have his say in a long rebuttal tacked on to my third and final installment. Wrote the exasperated young Kennedy: "In two and a half years the McClellan Committee has employed one hundred investigators, interrogated 1,366 witnesses, and disclosed a truly scandalous corruption in the Teamsters." But he concluded: "Racket-ridden and irresponsible, the union is stronger than ever."

There were obviously many questionable characters in the Teamsters' hierarchy—like New York City gangster Johnny Dio—whom Hoffa backed to the hilt, but always with excuses about all Dio did for the Teamsters. "And look at Joey Glimco in Chicago," Hoffa told me. "Just because he's Italian and gets bad writeups, everybody says he's a racketeer. That's no easy job of his running a bunch of cabdrivers. They'll climb all over you if you don't watch out."

If anything, the Senate hearings enhanced Jimmy's popularity among his membership. In every speech I heard him give during our three weeks together, he never failed to describe in dramatic detail the indignities of the hearings—the glare of the TV lights, the battery of lawyers, the gawking spectators. "We have no friends in Congress we can depend on," he declared at the end of these little tirades. "The only thing we can depend on is our own solidarity."

Hoffa didn't need histrionics of this sort; he had the whole membership behind him. The rank-and-file Teamsters I met spoke about "our Jimmy" as "a tireless worker," "a hard bargainer," and "a smart leader." Nobody referred to him as the foul-mouthed ruffian portrayed by Jack Nicholson in the 1993 Hollywood version of *Hoffa*. Many truck line operators as well regarded Hoffa as one union boss who abided by his contract. "We don't bargain easy," admitted Hoffa. "But if we make a bad deal, we live with it."

But more than anything else, what secured Hoffa's position as the unchallenged boss of the Teamsters was the union's phenomenal growth into 1,026 locals, grouped into four semi-autonomous regional conferences. At the time Walker and I were covering this octopus of an organization, some ninety percent of all intercity trucks were driven by Teamsters. Determined to expand his power base still further, Hoffa had begun to organize other groups—clerical help, supply handlers, and oil workers. Usually, he would show up personally to launch the organizing drive.

We flew to Baton Rouge, Louisiana, with him when the Teamsters targeted the Esso (now Exxon) refinery. "What a ruckus I found going on," Hoffa complained. "All the housewives are telephoning their friends saying we've got to keep the Teamsters out of town. They're saying we have too much power. Now, tell me, what the hell kind of a union does a guy want? If it hasn't got money and power, what can it do for him?"

Because his own clout depended on organizing, he was determined to get strong, persuasive men for the job—ex–truck drivers, loaders, and warehousemen, or, as Jimmy called them, "members of the craft." "I don't want any college boys in their slimmed-down Ivy League suits doing my organizing," he said.

Hoffa was also trying to extend further his control through pacts with other transport unions, like the National Maritime Union, the Seafarers' International Union, and the International Longshoremen's Association. "Some people tell me I shouldn't have anything to do with Harry Bridges," said Hoffa after we went with him to a meeting with the Communist-leaning leader of the West Coast Longshoremen. "Harry Bridges has a strong union, hasn't he? I'll tell you, the Teamsters and the Longshoremen are a natural together."

Expanding in all directions, with the wealth and membership of his Teamsters at an all-time high, I asked Hoffa, "What is it that you still want?"

"I want this to be the greatest international union that was ever dreamed of," he said. And how did he hope to make this happen? "We may eventually have to do what labor unions do in Europe," he replied, "and call general strikes. We are organizing in all transportation fields. We are trying to create a conference of transportation unions. If Congress is stupid enough to pass a bill banning secondary boycotts, we'll fix it so all our contracts expire on the same day."

Scare talk like that hastened Jimmy Hoffa's downfall. When Bobby Kennedy became attorney general in 1960, he made convicting the Teamsters president his priority, and assembled a task force to do it. Several Justice Department prosecutions failed, but in 1964 Hoffa was found guilty of jury tampering. Five months later he was convicted of defrauding the Teamsters pension fund of some $2 million. Although his lawyers tried repeatedly to have the convictions overturned, Hoffa entered the federal penitentiary in Lewisburg, Pennsylvania, in 1967 to begin serving thirteen years.

But he kept his title of Teamsters president while in prison, which he called "hell on earth, only worse." Only operational control was turned over to his trusted deputy Frank Fitzsimmons. In 1971, after he'd served four and a half years, President Nixon commuted his sentence with the proviso that he not participate in union activities until 1980. A former Justice Department official said the commutation was "part of a deal made during the 1968 presidential campaign," when the Teamsters threw a lot of money and the full weight of their membership behind Nixon. Hoffa was forced to officially retire from the union and was paid a lump-sun pension of $1.7 million.

As might be expected, his thirst for power was not slaked. In 1975, while waiting out an appeal to lift the restriction imposed by Nixon, Hoffa decided to run for the Teamster presidency. He accused caretaker boss Fitzsimmons of conspiring to block his return. "No one has ever been disloyal like this rat Fitz," he growled. "All stool pigeons are rats. They scratch and bite you."

Hoffa quickly rekindled rank-and-file support. Although he had been convicted of looting their pension fund, many truckers remembered Jimmy for gaining them the highest blue-collar pay in the land. "We don't care if he's getting his, as long as he gets us ours," went the pro-Hoffa refrain. Nevertheless, Hoffa was warned by Fitzsimmons's followers to quit campaigning or face the consequences. Cocky as always, he took no precautions. "I never had bodyguards, and I always drive myself," he had told me during our travels. "If anybody wants to get me, they know where I am." Another time, on the way to the St. Louis airport, we passed a funeral procesion of only a dozen cars. "Poor sonafabitch!" remarked Hoffa. "The guy didn't have many friends. I'll tell you, when I die, I'll have the biggest funeral in the world. Everybody'll come just to make sure I'm dead."

Hoffa was wrong about the funeral. He never had one. But he was right about not lacking friends who wanted him dead. On July 30, 1975, he climbed into his green Pontiac at his summer home in Lake Orion, Michigan, and headed for the Machus Red Fox Restaurant on the outskirts of Detroit. He told his wife, Josephine, that he was going to meet "a couple of the guys." He never returned. Since then there has been endless speculation about what happened to him. An FBI memo alleged that union cronies kidnapped and killed him, then handed his body over to a mob-owned sanitation service that disposed of it "by means of a shredder, compactor, and/or incinerator." One rumor had Jimmy's remains buried under the goal posts in Giant Stadium in the Meadowlands of New Jersey.

High on the FBI suspect list was Anthony "Tony Pro" Provenzano, former Teamster boss of northern New Jersey. In 1959, when Hank Walker and I visited Tony Pro's headquarters in Union City with Jimmy, they arm-wrestled and horsed around in front of Hank Walker's cameras. That same year, Jimmy helped Tony Pro win the presidency of Joint Council 73. But in the Lewisburg Penitentiary, where they later were inmates together, bad blood developed.

"I'll tear your heart out," Provenzano once yelled at Hoffa during a violent prison-yard quarrel. When they ran into each other at an airport after their release, the two men went at each other with their fists, and Hoffa broke a bottle over Provenzano's head. According to the FBI, it was probably on the pretext of making peace with Provenzano that Hoffa was lured to the Machus Red Fox Restaurant by his kidnappers.

Another key suspect was Chuckie O'Brien, a Hoffa protégé who was often with us during our travels with Jimmy. A combination goon and gofer, Chuckie was like an adopted son to the Teamster boss. In fact that's the way Hoffa referred to the burly young O'Brien until they had a falling-out some years later. Chuckie was allegedly seen driving the 1975 Mercury the FBI believes was used in Hoffa's abduction. Police dogs apparently also detected Hoffa's scent in the car.

The mystery of James R. Hoffa, Missing Person #75-3425, has never been solved. His son, who in 1995 launched a campaign to become president of the Teamsters, and daughter—both lawyers—believe their father was killed to keep him from reclaiming the union's leadership. Jimmy vowed he would run the Teamsters again. "What do they think I'm gonna do? Sit around and play the stock market," he said. "Money is just a commodity. Power is what lets you eat and sleep in peace." But it was his obsession with power that eventually destroyed him.

Power can be a lot of things. In Hoffa's hands it was dangerous. He used it so ruthlessly that laws have been enacted and procedures established to curb the strong-arming tactics of not only the Teamsters, but of unions in general. It's not that today's labor leaders are more docile. It's the mood of the country that has changed. Exorbitant wages and wildcat strikes now stir public wrath as never before. Sympathy has swung to management's side, as was proven when President Reagan fired all the air traffic controllers for calling a strike in 1981. The popularity of that move could be considered part of Hoffa's legacy.

When I learned of Hoffa's disappearance, I was reminded of our last meeting. As soon as the *Life* installment with my profile of him came off the press, I flew down to Washington with a copy and sat across his desk, watching as he silently mouthed every one of the four thousand words. It wasn't an unflattering piece, though Hoffa's ruthless determination emerged undisguised. Finally the cold blue-green eyes looked up and said: "You know, just because I've got a gun in my desk drawer doesn't mean I'm going to use it."

To this day I'm not sure what Hoffa meant, unless it was just another way of his saying, "Power is bad only when it's used bad."

CHAPTER XIX

The Man Who Shot JFK Being Shot

A DOZEN OF US WERE SEATED around the long boardroom table with Harry Luce when the maître d' poked his head in the door and interrupted our usual Friday editorial lunch. "The president is on his way out," he announced sonorously. Then he disappeared.

What president does he mean? I wondered. And on his way out of where? Having moved from Chicago to New York as *Life*'s assistant managing editor, I often attended Luce's Friday lunches. Never before had this polite headwaiter barged in and stopped the editor in chief in midsentence.

A moment later the phone rang. Otto Fuerbringer, *Time*'s managing editor, picked it up. "My God!" he exclaimed. "Kennedy's been shot."

I was sitting directly across the table from Luce. He stared down at his half-empty plate in silence. A staunch Republican, he nevertheless was an admitted admirer of the vigorous young president. The day after Kennedy's nomination we editors were amazed to learn from Hank Luce that his father had sat up half the night in his Waldorf Towers apartment watching the Democratic convention with old Joe Kennedy.

For a minute, nobody around the table spoke. Finally Luce looked up and in his twangy, nasal voice said: "Well, we better get to work."

Just a week earlier I had taken over the editing of *Life*'s news pages, or "front-of-the-book," as we called it. That was always the last part of the magazine to close, normally going to press about four A.M. every Thursday. I knew that by this time—two P.M. on Friday—at least a million copies with navy quarterback Roger Staubach on the cover, had already been printed, with another six million copies ready to roll.

By four P.M. I was on a plane headed for my old stomping grounds, Chicago. With me was the assistant art director, a layout man, a text-block and caption writer, and a researcher. The presses at Donnelley's, our big Chicago printing plant, had been stopped. And it had already been determined that the Staubach cover along with thirty-two pages inside the magazine would be scrapped. But we had no idea how we were going to fill them.

Life photographer Art Rickerby had gone to Dallas with the president, but was several cars behind him in the motorcade when Kennedy was shot. We didn't know what pictures Art had been able to make. Two Dallas-based *Life* reporters also were covering the president's visit. Neither did we know what they had seen or what information or pictures they'd been able to obtain.

Now, as my little editorial task force winged toward Chicago, a flock of other *Life* people, including Miami bureau chief Dick Billings and Los Angeles bureau chief Dick Stolley, were airborne for Dallas. Together, we had only thirty-six hours to rip up the issue and then get the magazine back on press with the best coverage we could assemble of this historic event.

By the time my group reached the printing plant, Stolley had set up a command post for *Life* in Dallas's Adolphus Hotel. He was there manning the phones when Patsy Swank, our Dallas stringer, called from the police station where Lee Harvey Oswald had just been brought in. Patsy's muffled voice was barely audible above the background frenzy of reporters shouting questions at the cops.

"I heard a rumor," she whispered into the phone, "that a business-man was shooting movies of the motorcade at the moment Kennedy was shot." Slowly she enunciated the businessman's name. "Zap-ROO-der is what is sounds like," she explained.

Quickly combing the Dallas phone book, Dick found a home listing for an Abraham Zapruder. He dialed the number. No answer. So he continued calling every fifteen minutes until eleven P.M., when a tired voice finally answered.

"Mr. Zapruder?" inquired Dick.

"Yes," came the weary reply.

"Is it true that you filmed the assassination?"

"Yes."

"From beginning to end?"

"Yes."

"Did you have the film processed?"

"Yes."

"Can I come out and see it?

"No."

"Has any other reporter contacted you?" inquired Dick, worried now that this exhausted man might have already sold the film rights and was ready to hang up.

"No," he replied. "Come to my office at nine tomorrow morning."

Dick got there at eight A.M. just as a covey of grim-faced Secret Service men in dark suits was filing into Jennifer Juniors, Inc., Abraham Zapruder's dress manufacturing company. They had come to see the replay of their catastrophic failure to protect the president.

"I said nine o'clock, didn't I, Mr. Stolley?" growled Zapruder. But he let Dick accompany the agents into the cubicle where a projector and screen had been set up.

"We watched in horror," said Dick. "Everybody in that little room gasped aloud when the president's head exploded in a pink halo of flesh, blood, and brains."

By nine A.M. reporters for the Associated Press, *Saturday Evening Post,* and Fox Movietone News had picked up Zapruder's trail and were camped outside his office door. It was a strange situation. An unknown dress manufacturer, of all people, was being pursued by the media giants of the nation. But Dick was already inside negotiating for exclusive print rights to the film. Unprepared as Zapruder was for his sudden celebrity, he understood the historic importance of the film as well as its value to his family's financial future. Yet, he was worried about its "exploitation," a word he repeated several times.

"Would you accept $15,000?" Dick asked.

The dress manufacturer frowned. "I had a nightmare last night," he said. "I was walking past a sleazy Times Square movie theater in New York and a barker on the sidewalk was shouting, 'See the president get killed!' " It was Zapruder's way of saying he wanted his accidental artifact handled with care.

Stolley vowed that *Life* would treat the film with respect and not permit its exploitation. At the same time, he kept raising his bid until he reached $50,000. "That's as high as I can go without further authorization," he said.

Zapruder nodded "Okay," and Stolley pecked out a five-line contract right there on the secretary's typewriter. Zapruder handed over the original film and one copy.

The three reporters outside were now banging on Zapruder's office door, shouting to him not to make any deal before he talked to them.

"Is there a back door to this place?" asked Stolley. There was, and Dick escaped through it, clutching his prize.

That afternoon a courier arrived at the printing plant in Chicago with the original film. We had set up a hand-cranked moviola machine to run it in slow motion, or to stop it precisely where we wanted a closer look. Cranking the film backward and forward countless times and watching the animated young president happily waving to the crowds just before his life was suddenly extinguished brought back vivid memories of the few times I had been with him.

In 1956, when he was campaigning to become Adlai Stevenson's running mate, I accompanied the Massachussets senator to the Nebraska State Fair. Jackie had already developed an intense dislike for going out on the hustings with her husband. A bull-judging contest had delayed Jack's speech and Jackie was impatient to leave. But back then politicking for Kennedy meant putting in time in a cattlemen's feed lot, not Camelot. "Shut up and sit down!" I overheard Jack whisper.

I also visited Kennedy at his Senate office the evening before he announced his candidacy for president. He made me feel as if I were the only one who had been let in on this not-so-big secret. I remembered his precise words. He didn't say, "I'm going to announce my candidacy," or "I'm going to run for president." Using the first person present tense, he said, "I *run* for the presidency because . . ." and ticked off a succession of reasons why he was seeking his country's highest office.

Then, after he became president, I called on him at the White House. It was a relaxed visit. The Cuban Missile Crisis had just ended, Russia having been forced to recall its missile-laden ships bound for Havana. Kennedy sat in his Oval Office rocking chair chatting informally, all the while looking at me with an expression that combined interest, amusement, and mischief.

That memory of our country's boyish chief executive, who had just outwitted the tough old Communist curmudgeon Nikita Khrushchev, haunted me as I tried to determine from the Zapruder film the precise moments Kennedy had been struck by bullets. Before the fatal shot that blew away the right side of his head, he could be seen clutching at his throat with both fists clenched. Clearly, he'd already been hit once by that time and was in great pain.

Many more viewings of the whole horrifying sequence didn't make it any easier to look at. Even worse were the reverse runnings of the film. Watching the dying president suddenly spring back to life and start waving again was eerie.

There wasn't time for more ruminations, or, for that matter, to make color separations of the shooting sequence and still meet our extended press deadline just twelve hours away. I realized we'd have to settle for black and white. But with the moviola machine I was able to pick the key frames from which to make the eight-by-ten black and white blow-ups.

Before the night was over we had one hundred or so pictures spread out on the printing plant floor. In choosing the final twenty-seven, some tough decisions and hasty assumptions had to be made. We knew that Texas governor John Connally, sitting in the limo's jump seat in front of the president, had suffered back, chest, wrist, and leg wounds. An almost pristine bullet was reported to have been found on his stretcher at Parkland Hospital. But had any other bullets hit him? And if so, from which direction had they come?

We decided not to even raise those questions in our captions and accompanying text. They could be dealt with later in a special memorial edition of *Life*, which was already being planned and which would reuse the Zapruder pictures in color.

Our worst dilemma that night in the printing plant was whether or not to publish the picture of the president's head exploding. I decided not to. Even in black and white it was just too gruesome. At some much-later date the American public might be able to stomach that one.

Then there was the mystery of why, as Jack lay dying, Jackie could be seen in the film scrambling out of the backseat and crawling on her hands and knees atop the trunk of the limo. Was she instinctively trying to flee? *Life*'s readers, I thought, might consider that a cowardly act, unbecoming so gallant a First Lady. I decided to fudge the question and say in the caption that she was reaching out to help a Secret Service man who at that moment could also be seen leaping onto the limo's back bumper.

In the months and years that followed, this twenty-two-second scrap of movie film would raise many more questions, and then be scrutinized again and again for the answers. But that Saturday night, as we worked feverishly to remake the magazine, we were forced to rely on our own interpretations of what we were seeing.

On Monday morning *Life* hit the newsstands just as thousands of grieving citizens were filing past Kennedy's coffin in the Capitol rotunda. That same day I showed the film to a group of Time Inc. executives in New York. *Life*'s publisher, C. D. Jackson, was so upset by the sight of the president's head exploding that he suggested the company also obtain television and movie rights to the film and with-hold it from public view.

Still in Dallas, Dick Stolley reopened the negotiations with Zapruder. The meeting took place in the office of the dress manufacturer's lawyer, Sam Passman. But this time Stolley discovered he was competing against Dan Rather and CBS.

"I started at $25,000," he recalled. "We exchanged pleasantries as I escalated. The dress manufacturer seemed relieved to be dealing with a familiar face."

A few times when a higher bid became necessary, Stolley excused himself, supposedly to check with us in New York. "Actually, I went into the adjoining room and called the Dallas operator for a time check," he said. "I knew precisely how much I had been authorized to spend, but figured a little suspense might not hurt."

Finally, a deal was struck—$150,000 for all rights to be paid in six annual payments of $25,000. The amount became the subject of considerable speculation, since Zapruder insisted that it not be made public. In fact, he was so concerned about being accused of profiting from the president's death that he took his lawyer's advice and donated the first installment to the family of police officer J. D. Tippit, whom Oswald had shot and killed in his effort to escape.

We at *Life* were less sensitive about the criticism the magazine might incur for acquiring control over so crucial a piece of evidence. But we didn't know then that this Russian-born dress manufacturer's home movie was destined to become the cornerstone of all investigations into the assassination. Twenty-two other camera buffs in Dealey Plaza were discovered later to have shot movies or still pictures of the presidential motorcade. But their film turned out to be fuzzy or taken from bad angles. Only Zapruder's provided the clear, unimpeachable record needed for reconstructing the timing and sequence of the rifle shots—the evidence that would eventually determine whether Oswald acted alone or was part of a conspiracy.

It was just a fluke that propelled Abraham Zapruder into such promi-nence. But then, fate sometimes catapults the least suspecting individu-als into a position of importance and power. He hadn't planned to take movies of the motorcade. What with his work and the morning rains, he thought, I wouldn't have a chance even to see the president. So he left his new Bell & Howell movie camera with its zoom telephoto lens at home.

When he arrived at the office, his secretary, Lillian Rogers, persuaded him to drive back and get it. "Mr. Z., it isn't every day the president comes through our neighborhood," she said. By the time her boss returned from the fourteen-mile round trip, crowds were already forming at Dealey Plaza to watch the motorcade.

Zapruder tried several vantage points for an unobstructed view. He finally perched precariously on a four-foot-high concrete abutment, and asked his receptionist, Marilyn Sitzman, who had gone with him, to steady his legs so he wouldn't fall.

Eight months later the Warren Commission sought him out as a key witness. In sworn testimony given to assistant counsel Wesley J. Liebeler, Zapruder described what he saw and did. The following transcript appears in the full twenty-six-volume version of the Warren Commission Report:

MR. LIEBELER: As you stood there on this abutment with your camera, the motorcade came down Houston Street and turned left on Elm Street, did it not?

MR. ZAPRUDER: That's correct. I started shooting—when the motorcade started coming in, I believe I started and wanted to get it coming in from Houston Street.

MR. LIEBELER: Tell us what happened as you took these pictures.

MR. ZAPRUDER: Well, as the car came in line, I was standing up here shooting through a telephoto lens, and as it reached about here, I heard the first shot and I saw the president lean over and grab himself like this.

MR. LIEBELER: Grab himself on the front of his chest?

MR. ZAPRUDER: Right—something like that. In other words, he was sitting like this and waving and then after the shot he just went like that.

MR. LIEBELER: He was sitting upright in the car and you heard the shot and you saw the president slump over?

MR. ZAPRUDER: Leaning—leaning toward the side of Jacqueline. For a moment I thought it was, you know, like you say, "Oh, he got me," when you hear a shot—you've heard these expressions and then I thought, I don't believe the president is going to make jokes like this, but before I had a chance to organize my mind, I heard a second shot and then I saw his head opened up and the blood and everything came out and I started .. [the witness crying]

MR. LIEBELER: That's all right, Mr. Zapruder, would you like a glass of water?

MR. ZAPRUDER: I'm sorry—I'm ashamed of myself really, but I couldn't help it.

MR. LIEBELER: Nobody should ever be ashamed of feeling that way, Mr. Zapruder. I feel the same way myself. It was a terrible thing. Let me go back now and for just a moment and ask you how many shots you heard altogether.

MR. ZAPRUDER: I thought I heard two, it could be three, because to my estimation I thought he was hit on the second—I really don't know. The whole thing that has been transpiring—it was very upsetting and as you see—I got a little better all the time and this came up again and it to me looked like the second shot, but I don't know. I never heard a third shot.

MR. LIEBELER: You didn't hear any shot after you saw him hit?

MR. ZAPRUDER: I heard the second—after the first shot I saw him leaning over, and after the second shot . . . then I started yelling, "They killed him, they killed him," and I just felt that somebody had ganged up on him and I was still shooting the pictures until he got under the underpass—I don't even know how I did it.

Zapruder then described how he stumbled back to his office in a state of shock. That afternoon he contacted the Dallas police. But by then they had Oswald in custody and considered the movie of marginal importance. Initially, so did the Secret Service and FBI. They told Zapruder the film was his property to dispose of as he saw fit, though they'd like a copy whenever it was processed.

That turned out to be no easy task. A local TV station explained it couldn't develop 8mm film, thus missing an epic news beat. In the end, Zapruder simply took the film to the local Kodak plant himself and asked for a rush job. By evening he had the original and three copies in hand. Astutely, he obtained sworn statements from the film processors that they had not bootlegged any extra copies. Besides the original and one copy given to *Life*, he gave the FBI and Secret Service the other two. He didn't keep one for himself.

Examination of Zapruder's camera by the FBI established that 18.3 movie frames were taken each second. Tests of Oswald's Mannlicher-Carcano rifle disclosed that at least 2.3 seconds were required between shots. Based on these calculations, the FBI was able to accurately reenact the assassination in slow motion, guided by Zapruder's film.

This was done early one morning in the spring of 1964. Elm Street was sealed off. Agents were selected as stand-ins for JFK, Jackie, John and Nellie Connally, and Oswald. Zapruder, the star of the show, played himself, climbing once again atop the concrete abutment from where he filmed the motorcade. With everybody in place, a Lincoln similar to the presidential limousine was pushed slowly down Elm

Street, stopping at every point that matched a frame of the film. The sequence began with the frame marked number one by the FBI, where the motorcycles leading the motorcade first came into view.

Up in the sixth-floor window of the School Book Depository, where Oswald's rifle and three spent shell casings had been found, an agent sighted through the scope of the assassination weapon. A camera was now attached to the scope, and every time the car stopped, the agent snapped a picture. The result was another sequence of photographs that matched every Zapruder frame, but taken from Oswald's presumed point of view.

The reenactment revealed that Oswald's view of Kennedy was partially blocked by the foliage of an oak tree beginning with frame 166. Oswald had a fleeting glimpse of the president again in frame 186. But if he fired then, he missed. It wasn't until frame 210 that he had a clear view of Kennedy's back.

However, Zapruder's view of the president was blocked by a highway sign beginning with frame 206, at which point Kennedy was still unharmed and waving to the crowd. By the time JFK emerged from behind the sign in frame 225, he was already clutching at his throat, reacting to his neck wound. It wasn't until 5.3 seconds later that another bullet penetrated Kennedy's skull, which, according to the Warren Commission Report, "was evident from the explosion of the President's brain tissues from the right side of his head" in frame 313. The fatal shot, however, didn't figure in the commission's debate on whether or not Oswald was the lone gunman. (Conspiracy buffs, however, claim the way Kennedy's head jerked backward, proves the shot came from in front.)

Most of the controversy centered around the bullet that passed through the president's neck. According to the agent aiming Oswald's rifle during the reenactment, that bullet then either struck the limo or someone else in it. Since it didn't hit the limo, the agent testified to the Warren Commission that it probably struck Governor Connally, who was seated directly in front of Kennedy. But after numerous screenings of the Zapruder movie, three of the seven commission members disagreed. And so did Connally.

Yet the commission's ultimate conclusion that Oswald was the lone gunman hinged entirely on this so-called "single-bullet theory," or "magic bullet theory," as skeptics dubbed it. It was determined during the reenactment that there wasn't time for Oswald to reload between the moment Kennedy was stuck in the neck and when Connally showed signs in Zapruder's movie of being wounded. So if the governor and president were struck by separate bullets, a second gunman must have been involved. To dismiss this possibility, the Warren Commission had to fudge the final wording of its report. "The alignment of the Governor and President was only indicative and *not conclusive* that one bullet hit both men," it stated.

This ambiguity left the door open for the proliferation of conspiracy theories that followed. Having studied the Zapruder film so many times myself, I was never fully convinced that Oswald acted alone. So for two years I pursued John Connally, hoping to persuade him to break his silence about the commission's findings.

In the fall of 1966, armed with more than a hundred eight-by-ten-inch color transparencies made from the individual frames of the Zapruder film, I finally connected with the governor and his wife. We met secretly in a hotel room in Memphis. I brought along a light box and magnifying glasses so the Connallys could examine the enlarged and illuminated movie frames in detail.

The Warren Commission had given the governor only a quick screening of the film, after which he testified as follows: "I heard this noise which I immediately took to be a rifle shot. I instinctively turned to my right, but I did not catch the president in the corner of my eye. . . . Failing to see him, I was turning to look back over my left shoulder . . . then I felt like someone had hit me in the back."

Nellie Connally had been even more specific in her official testimony. "I heard a frightening noise. . . . I turned over my right shoulder . . . and saw the president as he had both hands at his neck. He made no utterance, no cry. Then, very soon, there was a second shot that hit John."

As the governor and I scrutinized blow-ups of the individual frames together, he was able to see a number of significant details that he'd missed during the commission screening. These confirmed in his mind what he had testified—that he had been hit by a second bullet.

Pointing to frame 222, where he is just emerging from behind the road sign, Connally said, "See, I'm turning to my right. I'd just heard the first shot."

In frame 225 the president emerges from behind the sign. "It's very clear," continued Connally. "He's already been hit. His face is distorted."

By frame 230 Kennedy's shoulders are hunched and both hands are at his throat. "But I still look unperturbed," Connally pointed out. "You can see the grimace in the president's face. You can't see it in mine." The commission had tried to dispose of this discrepancy by claiming the governor experienced a delayed reaction to his wounds. Connally vehemently disagreed. "There's no question," he insisted, "I haven't been hit yet."

As clearly as Connally could judge from the blow-ups, it was frame 234 when the bullet struck him. "I might have been hit a frame or two earlier," he told me. "But I can begin to see myself slump in 234. The slump is very pronounced in 235," he added. "In that frame my mouth is open wide as I let out a howl."

A few weeks later, I sent a *Life* team to the Connallys' Picosa ranch near San Antonio to give them a second viewing, and also to photograph the governor poring over the enlarged color transparencies. Following these two revealing sessions, we ran a cover and fourteen-page lead story headlined A MATTER OF REASONABLE DOUBT. It contained pictures of the governor examining the blown-up movie frames, accompanied by detailed captions describing what he and Nellie saw, heard, and felt during the shooting. Neither Connally came right out and criticized the blue-ribbon commission chaired by Chief Justice Earl Warren. But *Life*'s own tightly reasoned text urged that a new investigative body be appointed and the case reopened because there was "reasonable and disturbing doubt" that Oswald acted alone.

Our story set off a firestorm of editorial challenges to the commission, including a wild claim that the FBI had altered its copy of the Zapruder film to make it conform to the official findings. Zapruder, though he never questioned those findings himself, was besieged once again by strangers who recognized his name and wanted to try out their conspiracy theories on him. The dress manufacturer had become the idol of the conspiracy buffs. But for him fame was a liability. He had no experience for handling it and tried to shun all the attention.

"Abe couldn't convince them," his wife said. "It amazed him that people couldn't comprehend how one crackpot could do this terrible thing." Privately, though, Zapruder suspected Oswald was shooting at Connally, not at Kennedy.

One of the most publicized attempts to prove the existence of a conspiracy was led by the flamboyant New Orleans district attorney, Jim Garrison. In 1969 he subpoenaed the Zapruder film from *Life* for his turbulent trial of New Orleans Trade Mart director Clay Shaw, the alleged conspirator. There was no reluctance on the magazine's part to surrender the film, as actor Kevin Costner as Jim Garrison suggested in the movie *JFK*. In fact, before the trial I had invited Garrison up to New York to examine Zapruder's blown-up frames and to explain his bizarre conspiracy theory.

For some reason Garrison didn't want to be seen in the Time &

Life Building. So we arranged an all-day editorial meeting with him at a nearby hotel. But after hearing his convoluted accusations against the New Orleans Trade Mart director, most of us felt he lacked any hard evidence. Certainly the Zapruder movie wasn't going to help prove his case. Nevertheless, the prosecution called Zapruder as its star witness. Once again the dress manufacturer found himself in the limelight. According to Garrison's scenario, several gunmen had taken part in the assassination. He claimed the movie, which he screened ten times for the jury, showed the "triangulation of their crossfire." Researchers digging into the case records recently proved that Garrison, who is now dead, used his prosecutorial power to frame an innocent man. The jury took forty-five minutes to return a not guilty verdict.

Unfortunately for Zapruder, the lax security and circus atmosphere at Shaw's trial apparently enabled lab technicians there to copy the film, duplicates of which were then sold to assassination buffs all around the country. Eventually, one of those bootlegged copies was aired nationally on ABC and given just the kind of sensational treatment Zapruder always feared it might.

In 1970 Zapruder died of cancer. Although his obituary appeared the world over, the public still knew almost nothing about him. He had steadfastly spurned all interviews and let thousands of telephone inquiries and sacks of mail go unanswered. Even close friends of the Dallas dress manufacturer claimed his life was a mystery.

He was born, he told a former business partner, in a small town in Russia on the "Prude River," hence the family name Zapruder. During the Bolshevik Revolution his father emigrated to New York City, where he made enough money to send for his wife and children. But police came through their train looking for Jews. They hauled away his dark-haired older brother and killed him. But the prepubescent Abraham still had blond hair and the police passed him by. That was how he escaped to the United States, he said.

Five years after his death, *Life* gave the original and all rights to the film back to the Zapruder family for one dollar. Son Henry Zapruder, a Washington, D.C., tax lawyer, still does a brisk business renting copies for one-time use, and at stiff prices. Movie producer Oliver Stone said he paid $40,000 to use a few snippets in *JFK*.

A suit filed in 1988 in Federal District Court in Washington raised serious questions about charging for the film. Should the law allow such a crucial piece of Americana to be copyrighted? Are some photographs so much a part of history that the First Amendment protects the right to use them? What constitutes "fair use" for which compensation need not be paid? These questions were never fully resolved.

The original 480 Kodachrome frames that I first ran through that moviola machine in Chicago now reside in the United States Archives in Washington alongside Eva Braun's home movies of Hitler. But the question of who should own the rights to Zapruder's priceless film, like the question of what it reveals about the assassination, is still being debated. Whatever is eventually decided, I'm certain that the grainy footage shot by this Russian refugee will flicker in America's memory forever. And the name Abraham Zapruder will remain a footnote in our history, proving that fame and power occasionally come to those who seek it the least.

CHAPTER XX

Lyndon's Coonskin Declaration

ONE OF HARRY LUCE'S FAVORITE WAYS of whiling away an evening was to enter into an intellectual jousting match with an important political leader. On the "proprietor's" visit to any of *Time*'s foreign outposts, the bureau chief was expected to produce the prime minister for dinner. Or if the chief of state happened to be otherwise engaged, then at least the chancellor of the exchequer or foreign minister. Always famished for more information, Luce relished these mental workouts. But he could be painfully blunt, giving no quarter to the invited dignitary if the two of them happened to disagree. Sometimes, however, it was just the language barrier that triggered a breakdown in their exchange.

I had heard about one such communication failure during a Luce visit to France. Paris bureau chief Frank White had gone to great lengths to arrange a tête-à-tête for him with Prime Minister Edgar Faure. But Luce insisted on using his Yale French while the P.M. stuck to his equally rudimentary Sorbonne English. Their conversing difficulties were compounded by Faure's cleft palate. "Neither man," reported White, "had a clue about what the other was saying."

In the New York office Luce's editors were also expected to lasso a governor, senator, or cabinet member from time to time, to break bread and hobnob with the boss for an evening. Soon after the 1964 election, which the Johnson-Humphrey ticket had won in a landslide, I invited the vice president–elect to come for dinner. I thought Humphrey would give Luce a good conversational workout. Talking, I knew from a couple of dusk-till-dawn sessions with Humphrey at a mutual friend's house in Washington, is what he liked to do best. However, I worried that he might not let the editor in chief get a word in.

Dinner was set for seven P.M. Frank McCulloch, *Life*'s Washington bureau chief, agreed to escort Humphrey from the capital. I also had invited a couple of the writers from my "newsfront" department to join us in the private dining room in the Time & Life Building. By eight P.M. Humphrey hadn't arrived. Luce had downed a stiff bourbon and was showing his impatience, while the rest of us, having polished off a stand-up martini or two, were trying to keep the conversation rolling without our guest of honor.

At eight-thirty, still no sign of the vice president–elect, but plenty of signs of the editor in chief's agitation. Harry never was one to suffer delays easily. One of the best-known Luce stories circulating the Time & Life Building involved a flight of his to Europe in which his plane, after sitting on the runway for more than an hour, was brought back to the gate for repairs. Exasperated, Luce called Corinne Thrasher, his secretary, and told her to get on the horn to his old friend Juan Trippe, Pan Am's president, to say that was no way to run an airline. Ten minutes later she called back. "Mr. Luce," she said, "Mr. Trippe says you're on TWA."

Of course, there were jokes, too, about the "Happy Warrior," as Humphrey was known, having a blind spot where most people have a clock. His unquenchable loquaciousness had kept him running late from one end of the campaign trail to the other. But his delay now had gone beyond the humorous stage.

"Is this man always so atrociously behind schedule?" asked Luce, who I suspected was further rankled by the way our missing guest had helped bury his friend and Arizona neighbor, Barry Goldwater, at the polls in November. No Republican candidate for president had ever been given a worse trouncing.

"Let's start without him," snapped Luce. But the minute we all sat down at the long oval table, in strode Humphrey, spewing apologies a mile a minute. The dinner was a bust. Harry let Hubert do all the talking, and as soon as the meal was finished, Luce, still smarting, said good night and departed.

I had seen him in such bad humor only once before. When I was Chicago bureau chief, he had come out on one of his periodic visits. A dinner discussion with the bureau reporters and photographers about midwestern politics had disintegrated, mainly because of Luce's pronounced Republican leanings. Besides, one of the photographers drank too much brandy and accidentally bit into his glass snifter, spurting blood over the white tablecloth. By that time Luce was impatient to end the evening. But suddenly his mood brightened. "What do you people do for fun?" he asked.

Just a few days earlier we had all chipped in and bought a $2,000 racehorse named Stepping Stone II. Luce was intrigued, instantly peppering us with questions about the horse's breeding, trainer, past record, and future prospects. All we knew about the critter was that he hailed from Nassau in the West Indies, where he'd won a few small purses. But there he'd always raced clockwise, as was the custom in the Bahamas.

"Harry, we haven't any idea how he'll do running in the opposite direction on American tracks," I explained. Luce didn't care. He insisted on buying a hundred-dollar share, and finally left the dinner table in good humor. Eventually, Stepping Stone II won two races at Waterford Park in West Virginia, and Luce got back $46 on his investment.

There was no such surprise, upbeat ending to the Humphrey dinner. Luce's hasty departure left McCulloch and me with the vice president–elect to entertain for the rest of the evening. We grabbed an unopened bottle of Scotch from the bar and accompanied our guest to his suite at the Hilton. Then, for the next four hours, we sipped Scotch and grilled him on what Lyndon Johnson planned to do about Vietnam, the most nettlesome question facing the U.S. at that moment.

The war there hadn't yet escalated. It was still sputtering along pretty much as it was in 1962, when Kennedy created the U.S. Military Assistance Command in Vietnam—or MACV as it was known. However, the number of U.S. troops assigned to MACV had been creeping up slowly, from an initial cadre of 3,200 to 22,000 by Election Day in 1964. But throughout the campaign Johnson had repeatedly pledged not to send over any more American boys. "The U.S. must neither retreat nor expand the war," he declared.

Frank and I hammered away at Humphrey for the truth. Was Johnson really determined to hold U.S. troops strength at that level? Or was his campaign promise just so much political palaver? Humphrey swore Johnson meant what he said.

I reminded the man about to become vice president that when Johnson had his job, Kennedy sent him on a fact-finding mission to Vietnam. "Remember how Johnson drove his translators crazy with his folksy hill-country talk?" I asked Humphrey. " 'The Communist fox is loose,' he told South Vietnam's president. 'He's after the chickens. And you live in the chicken coop!' " Humphrey smiled. He remembered all right.

But on that trip, Johnson hadn't minced words about whipping the

Viet Cong, "We're goin' to nail the coonskin to the wall," he promised the press corps in Saigon.

"Are you sure," I asked Humphrey, "that Johnson isn't still trying to nail that coonskin to the wall? And remember, back then he also predicted, 'If we throw in the towel in Vietnam, the vast Pacific becomes a Red Sea.' "

"Forget all that stuff about coonskins and a red Pacific," replied Humphrey. "The president has a chastened view of Vietnam."

The memory of that long, not entirely sober night with Humphrey kept coming back to me as our troop buildup swelled to 500,000 and the annual bill for the war ballooned to $33 billion. Either Johnson had changed his mind, I decided, or he'd lied to the voters in 1964—and to his vice president–elect.

As the news editor of *Life*, Vietnam had become my main preoccupation. We kept several reporters and photographers there at all times, and I made periodic visits myself. But just monitoring the news from Vietnam in the New York office had become disheartening. The huge U.S. buildup hadn't stopped Viet Cong sappers from blowing a hole in our Saigon embassy wall, and firing wildly at everything inside until nineteen of them and five American military guards lay dead on the embassy lawn. Although simply a symbolic strike, it marked the start of the Communists' countrywide 1968 TET (lunar New Year) offensive that killed 14,000 South Vietnamese civilians and left more than 600,000 homeless. It seemed to have broken the will of many Americans, who were watching all this happen on television.

I was substituting for *Life*'s managing editor when the TET attack occurred, and unfortunately had to stay put and run the magazine instead of flying off to Vietnam for an on-the-scene assessment. A few weeks later, however, Hedley Donovan, Luce's hand-picked successor, sent me to Saigon. Luce had died the year before. Although he was determined that the Communists should not be allowed to overrun Southeast Asia as they had China, he regarded the situation in Vietnam as "somewhat messy." Donovan, on the other hand, was an out-and-out hawk who had personally written a long editorial in *Life* titled "The War Is Worth Winning." Now suddenly he was having second thoughts. He wanted an entire issue of *Life*, he said, "devoted to the pros and cons of America's continued involvement."

As his own contribution to this special issue, Donovan handed me a list of crucial questions that he hoped *Life* would answer for its readers: "Can we still win, and if so what does winning mean?" "Should we add more troops, escalate the fighting, and invade North Vietnam?" "Conversely, should we withdraw to defensive enclaves or pull out entirely?" "Could a coalition government be established, with a substantial place in it for the Communists?"

Providing answers to those crucial questions I knew would involve helicoptering hither and yon, talking to company commanders, pacification team leaders, CIA spooks, relief workers, missionaries, and even village chiefs. Vietnam was familiar territory to me, having covered the war there on and off since 1948, when the French were still doing the fighting. So I figured interviewing those individuals out in the boonies wouldn't be so difficult. The hard half of my assignment would be getting close to our gun-shy Foreign Service, intelligence, and military decision-makers in Saigon. In fact, getting honest appraisals from them might not be possible.

The jet airplane doesn't allow modern-day travelers time to make the necessary physical and psychological adjustments to being flipped from one side of the globe to the other. Soon I found myself sitting in the old Continental Palace Hotel's street café—a raised veranda dubbed the "Continental Shelf"—trying to gather my wits together and figure out how to get all of this interviewing done in four or five weeks.

On the sidewalk next to my table, Saigon's nightly carnival was beginning. A boy acrobat cartwheeled down the street. A flower girl rushed up with chains of sweet-smelling jasmine. A young man stopped to demonstrate a hand-carved billiard cue that collapses into a cane. An old man held up an armful of elephant-hide money belts. Then, limping over toward my table, came an armless Vietnamese war veteran with frayed American magazines that he hoped to sell tucked under both stumps. Finally the waiter arrived.

"One bottle of '33'," I said, and the waiter shuffled off to get the beer as the carnival resumed: money changers, fortune-tellers, portrait painters, newspaper boys, shine boys, whores, pimps—the identical passing parade that I had watched entertaining red-bereted French Foreign Legionnaires in this same café twenty years before. Removing a notebook and pen from my safari jacket pocket, I plotted a schedule for obtaining a thoughtful assessment of the war during the next thirty or forty days.

My first interview was with Ambassador Ellsworth Bunker. He graciously laid on an informal lunch for my benefit with some of his staff. When I arrived, the entire street was blocked off. The official residence itself was guarded by a flock of security men brandishing revolvers and barking orders into walkie-talkies. And parked by the side entrance was a tank, part of the tightened security following the Viet Cong attack on the embassy. The ambassador told me how he'd been awakened by marines before dawn that day, and hauled away to safety, still wearing his pajamas, in an armored personnel carrier.

Bunker struck me as a spry codger for his seventy-three years. The Vietnamese called him "Mr. Refrigerator" because of his glacially cold Yankee demeanor. But a glass of wine quickly changed that. Pink cheeks suddenly glowed beneath the snowy hair. Except for occasional lapses in the luncheon conversation, when I wasn't certain whether he was listening or napping, the ambassador seemed very alert.

He had just come from a meeting with President Nguyen Van Thieu, who he said was finally regaining confidence after the tremendous losses suffered during TET. Evidently, the Vietnamese president had promised to recruit 125,000 additional soldiers if the U.S. would equip them. But Bunker predicted Johnson would surely reject the offer, especially after the strong antiwar campaign being run against him by Senator Eugene McCarthy in the New Hampshire primary. "Increased troop strength isn't a vote-getting proposition these days," admitted Bunker.

From his other comments, I surmised he held little hope for any outcome that might be considered a U.S. victory in Vietnam. Then, in a lighter vein, and with a sparkle in his blue eyes, the old ambassador described his weekend hops to Katmandu for "conjugal visits," as he called them, with his new bride, Carol Laise, the U.S. ambassador to Nepal. Being able to make those visits perhaps explained why he cast such a benevolently blind eye on the Vietnamese mistresses being kept by U.S. officials in Saigon. "There's a lot of plain and fancy screwing going on around here," Bunker was reported to have said. "But I suppose it's all in the interest of the war effort."

My next visit was with "Westy," as William Childs Westmoreland, as the fifty-four-year-old commander of U.S. forces in Vietnam was known to his troops. Having attended both West Point and the Harvard Business School, he was considered the very model of a modern soldier-administrator, combining personal bravery with management skills. But the general was already being criticized for "cooking the books," by inflating the enemy body count to show progress in his "war of attrition." The only trouble was the enemy forces weren't attritting fast enough.

Westmoreland appeared tan and trim when Life's Saigon bureau chief Don Moser and I walked in. For two hours he strode back and forth majestically across his large MACV headquarters office, delivering what he called "a monologue on the objectives of the war."

"No doubt about it," he said, "the Communists won a psychological victory with their TET offensive. They decided they weren't getting what they expected out of a protracted war—no major victory. So they struck one big blow and it cost them dearly."

The longer his monologue continued, the more defensive he sounded. "My objective," said the man whom *Life* sometimes referred to as the "Four-Star Eagle Scout," "is to grind the enemy down and raise the cost of aggression even more. But it's like trying to kill termites with a screwdriver," he admitted. "Finally, after they've weakened the beams, you decide to use a crowbar and the whole house falls down."

Before Westy let us go, he was singing the blues. "I'm a professional soldier. I don't make policy," he protested, although his latest request for 200,000 more American troops was forcing Johnson and his kitchen cabinet—the so-called "wise men"—to reevaluate the whole war effort.

"This is the first time a soldier has been blamed for making political decisions," grumbled Westy. "It didn't even happen to MacArthur," he added, apparently forgetting that Truman sacked his five-star commander in Korea for trying single-handedly to start a war against China.

Johnson didn't fire Westy. But a week after our session with him, he was kicked upstairs—and out of Vietnam—to be Army Chief of Staff. As one political commentator put it: "Westmoreland had brought about the kind of catastrophe MacArthur had perpetrated when he sent an American Army into the mountains of North Korea in the winter of 1950, but on a scale magnified many times by the extravagance of the failure in Vietnam."

Westmoreland passed me on to retired Air Force Major General Edward Lansdale. This CIA man, once hailed as the "attending physician at the birth of South Vietnam," was now relegated to a subsidiary role that he liked to call "professor emeritus of counterinsurgency."

I was eager to interview Lansdale mainly because of his previous role. When the French pulled out in 1954, it was Lansdale, then at the height of his undercover career, who had prevented a victory by Communist leader Ho Chi Minh. He installed the wealthy Catholic Jean-Baptiste Ngo Dinh Diem as president. But without Lansdale at Diem's side, the American venture in Vietnam would have foundered at the beginning. Lansdale didn't realize a revolution was brewing and that by putting Diem in charge of the remnants of the French colonial system, the U.S. had joined the wrong side.

Lansdale looked worn but offered a warm welcome anyway. "Of course you'll stay for dinner," he said, introducing me to his "upstairs brain trust." As the evening wore on, it was evident that he and his coterie of young advisers believed the "dark ideology of communism in

Vietnam" could be defeated only by instilling American ideals. "We need long-range political policies, not short-term power plays," explained the legendary CIA operative and inspiration for the fictional "Colonel Hillandale," one of the few good guys in *The Ugly American*, the classic novel about U.S. imperialism in Asia.

But I sensed how frustrated the real-life Lansdale now felt. He admitted that both Bunker and Westmoreland had become impatient with his preachments. I obviously represented a fresh ear, and it was late that night before he let me return to my hotel.

"The Vietnamese attitude is pox on both your houses," he kept repeating. "The people are fed to the teeth with the Viet Cong's hit-and-run tactics, just as they are horrified by the mass destruction of American weapons."

"So how do we prove our good intentions?" I interjected.

"By making it clear that what the U.S. really stands for is not brute force, but the constitutional process. A constitutional process adapted to Asians," he added. "But Westy just doesn't understand that. He wants to bomb these people back to the Stone Age."

Not all the American officials I met sounded so discouraged. One exception was CORDS chief Robert Komer. CORDS was the acronym for Civil Operations and Revolutionary Development Support—the grass roots aid program referred to simply as "pacification." Komer held the rank equivalent of a four-star general, as was indicated by the license plate on his car. But he was no bureaucratic administrator. Nicknamed "Blowtorch Bob" for the heat he generated in getting things done, he had a reputation for outrageous optimism. "The war is entering a critical stage," he told me. "Pacification programs have been reinstated since TET as fast as possible. And they seem to be working." Komer claimed he really did see light at the end of Vietnam's tunnel.

One of my most rewarding visits was with John Paul Vann, Komer's deputy at CORDS, and the regional pacification director in Bien Hoa. This fearless, feisty little Virginian with a reputation for invulnerability had retired from the army as a lieutenant colonel in 1963, following a dispute with senior officials over U.S. policy in Vietnam. Two years later he was back, driving the same dangerous roads and helicoptering into the same remote Viet Cong–infested centers. Only now he was incurring those risks as a civilian adviser out to win support of the peasantry with an ambitious aid program. "The big problem of pacification," he explained, "is security. Where security is precarious, the people withdraw into a shell. Where security is good, they cooperate."

After the TET attacks, of which Vann had forewarned Westmoreland, he proposed a plan for a phased reduction of U.S. forces. "Right now," said Vann with his usual abrasiveness, "I would send 100,000 troops home and turn some of the American base camps into refugee centers. We're fighting too comfortable a war." He also publicly advocated integrating the ARVN (Army of the Republic of Vietnam) forces with American fighting units. "That way," he said, "we can reduce American participation in the war to a residual force of advisers, technical personnel, and pilots." Doing these things, he believed, would also help mollify criticism of the war back home.

"Once again Vann is bucking the brass in Vietnam," I jotted in my notebook. "He won't get away with it this time either."

For two days Vann drove and flew me all over III Corps. "Things aren't much different here than they were before TET," he explained. "It's just that the people in Saigon suddenly experienced what people in the country have been up against for years."

During our travels I was struck by how this unyielding, dedicated man was willing to risk his life every day—"to redeem the unredeemable, to lay hold of victory in this doomed enterprise" as author Neil Sheehan stated so eloquently in A Bright Shining Lie, his Pulitzer Prize–winning biography of Vann.

Four years after I toured III Corps with Vann, he was killed when his helicopter crashed and burned in the mountains of Vietnam's central highlands. My only surprise was that it didn't happen sooner.

Vann wasn't the only dedicated civilian adviser I met during my month-long survey. In Ben Tre, a fire-blackened commercial hub in the delta, the Viet Cong had recently shot their way into town and then stood around gawking, wondering what to do next. Finally American troops returned and drove them out.

When I arrived, Dick Burnham, the senior Foreign Service officer, was trying to reestablish security. A big sign hanging on his office wall proclaimed DON'T FEEL DISCOURAGED IF YOU LOSE, DON'T BE TOO PROUD WHEN YOU WIN. The quotation, he claimed, came from some ancient military leader whose name he couldn't recall. But he said it summed up his mixed emotions about the loss and recapture of the city.

"The VC came in," Burnham reported, "beautifully armed with AK-47 automatic rifles and B-40 rockets. They also hauled with them old American pack Howitzers displaying their original World War II Rock Island Arsenal stencils. These, he claimed, were the same howitzers we gave Chiang, Chiang lost to Mao, Mao gave to Ho, and Ho gave to the VC. "So there we were," said Burnham, "being clobbered by our own hand-me-down weapons. Sometimes," he added wistfully, "our best intentions turn out to be costly blunders."

I already knew the name Ben Tre because it symbolized an even worse American blunder. Right after the VC had finally been driven out again under a hail of artillery and mortar shells, an American major remarked to Associated Press correspondent Peter Arnett: "It became necessary to destroy the town to save it." That mad logic, flashed around the world by the AP, helped savage the little sympathy left in the U.S. for what had become known as "Lyndon Johnson's war."

Will we destroy the whole country trying to save it? I wondered. Is that the price of nailing the coonskin to the wall?

In the late forties and early fifties I had watched the French attempt to subdue Indochina, as the country was then called, with their dilapidated captured German bombers. Now we were doing the same thing, only with much more deadly napalm and Agent Orange. There was no longer any question in my mind about the editorial thrust of *Life*'s special issue.

It was Sunday, March 31, when I finally returned to the U.S. loaded with ideas and stories. That night Lyndon Johnson was scheduled to deliver a televised address to the nation. Badly jet-lagged from the long flight home, I could barely stay awake while the president announced a pause in the bombing. Then, as I was about to switch off the set and fall into bed, Johnson dropped the bombshell he'd been saving for the end: "I shall not seek, and I will not accept, the nomination of my party for another term as your president."

That stunning announcement killed our plans for a special issue, though we did run a few of the stories. The war was no longer Lyndon Johnson's. He had in effect passed it on to his successor to resolve— perhaps to my friend Hubert Horatio Humphrey, the most logical candidate to oppose Richard Nixon in the fall election.

When the Democratic Convention opened in Chicago that August, the bitter debate about American policy in Vietnam erupted in a bloody pitched battle between 5,000 hippie protesters and phalanxes of blue-helmeted police, augmented by companies of National Guardsmen wearing gas masks and brandishing bayonets. "No more war! No more war!" roared the hippies blocking Michigan Avenue in front of candidate Humphrey's headquarters in the Hilton Hotel. First the Guardsmen fired tear gas. Then the cops attacked. Clubbing madly at their tormentors, they beat them to the pavement, and then dragged them, by the dozen, to waiting paddy wagons. It was a pitiful sight.

I was interviewing Humphrey in his hotel suite at the time. Seeing his anguish as he peered down from his fifteenth-floor window at the mayhem below, I was again reminded of how certain he'd been four years before that Johnson would not escalate the war. I could still hear

Humphrey admonishing me to forget all that stuff about Johnson wanting to nail the coonskin to the wall.

He turned sadly away from the window. All the usually loquacious Humphrey had to say was "What a terrible mark on what could have been a beautiful picture. I know they feel their hopes are dashed." Although I agreed with him, it struck me that this man was probably too sensitive, too thin-skinned to wield the raw power sometimes required of a president.

He knew how the demonstrators felt because his own hopes for peace had been dashed. Quietly during his four years as vice president he had opposed each escalation in the fighting, while Johnson loudly dismissed the antiwar protesters as "nervous Nellies," "knee-jerk liberals," and "half-brights."

Before the Chicago convention ended, Humphrey and his supporters made a halfhearted attempt to insert a liberal plank in the Democratic platform, promising a phased withdrawal of U.S. forces if he became president. It failed to pass, leaving one more scar on Humphrey's crippled campaign.

As Election Day approached, the fumes of battle from both Vietnam and Chicago choked his candidacy, while the coonskin had become a long-forgotten symbol of victory. In the end it was Humphrey's political skin that got nailed to the wall.

CHAPTER XXI

The Premier and the Princess

THE MASSIVE STAIRWAY SWEPT UPWARD, a white marble glacier with a river of red carpet cascading down its middle. Cumulus clouds of crystal glittered in the chandeliers overhead. Step by step we ascended those unending stairs in Beijing's Great Hall of the People. But the summit seemed to keep on receding.

"Old man Mao should have put in an escalator," whispered correspondent Arnaud de Borchgrave, my competitor from *Newsweek*.

Moving up the marble stairway ahead of us was the entire Ethiopian delegation led by Emperor Haile Selassie's granddaughter, Her Imperial Highness Princess Ida Desta. They had recently come from Addis Ababa on Ethiopian Airlines' inaugural flight to China. Following us up the stairway came a swarm of official Chinese welcomers, assorted interpreters, guides and security men, plus a full complement of foreign ambassadors, who felt obliged to forsake their steam-heated chancelleries on this freezing February evening in 1973 to attend the reception.

We finally gained the summit at the top of the stairs. Princess Ida and her royal entourage were herded onto a three-tiered wooden bleachers erected especially for photographing visiting delegations. Immediately, in strode Zhou Enlai, brisk and businesslike, and very trim in a plain gray tunic and matching gray trousers. A miniature red Chairman Mao button pinned to his tunic gave the only dash of color to his outfit.

The Ethiopians applauded the premier. And Zhou, still unsmiling, clapped in return as he assumed his front-and-center position in the

bleachers for the official photograph. Floodlights snapped on. The photographer cranked off three shots, then everybody trailed after the premier, heading for the main banquet hall.

"About as cozy a spot for cocktails and dinner as Madison Square
Garden," wisecracked de Borchgrave when our interpreter informed us
that the cavernous hall could comfortably seat six thousand diners. But
it was obvious that nobody was going to sit down. There weren't any
chairs, although the array of delicacies was lavish fare for a stand-up
supper—shrimp balls, baby ribs, and spring rolls all steaming away in
silver chafing dishes. In addition, there were cold platters piled high
with sliced goose liver, strips of beef, dried fish, duck, chicken, ham,
and mutton. A decorative red border was formed around each table by
packs of Flying Horse filter-tip cigarettes.

No sooner had we entered the banquet hall when a ballet of white-
jacketed waiters began orbiting around the tables. Each waiter was
weighted down with a tremendous silver trayload of tea, beer, orange
juice, red wine, and, as was customary at all Chinese parties, tiny
goblets of that white lightning, *Mao Tai*.

This was my first trip to China since Mao came to power in 1949,
and it took some fancy finagling and marathon flying to get there. I
had recently rejoined the Luce empire after spending two entrepreneurial years in New York City launching a couple of magazines for seafront
dwellers on the East Coast. Rehired as *Time*'s Hong Kong bureau chief
in November 1972, I had been trying unsuccessfully ever since to obtain a visa for Communist China. Although Nixon's much-heralded
meeting with Mao that same year had supposedly opened the way for
"journalistic exchanges," American reporters still weren't welcome.
Then, from a travel agent in Hong Kong, I learned about Ethiopian
Airlines' inaugural flight to Shanghai and Beijing.

"No harm trying to hitch a ride," I decided. I had once interviewed
Haile Selassie in Addis Ababa. In fact, the "King of Kings, Conquering
Lion of Judah," as the wily old five-foot-four-inch emperor was known,
had invited me to lunch at his palace. At first I wasn't sure if it was
I who was going to be the lunch for the pair of hungry-looking lions
flanking the palace gate. But escorted safely inside past those two
beasts, I was surprised how smoothly the luncheon interview went,
especially after being told that His Imperial Highness harbored deep
suspicions of the foreign press.

But that was several years ago. Now challenged by a Marxist revolt,
the Lion of Judah was eager to change his image from that of a feudal
despot. It seemed entirely possible that he might be taking a more
enlightened view of the press. So I wired him from Hong Kong for

permission to cover his granddaughter's junket that would open a new commercial air link between Addis Ababa and Beijing. "Please be informed that a seat has been reserved for your magazine on our inaugural flight," the emperor's secretary wired back.

The logistics proved more complicated than I expected. First I had to fly to Bombay via Bangkok and pick up a loosely connecting flight to Addis, where a special Chinese visa was issued, then backtrack to Bombay on the new Ethiopian Airlines jet, which finally flew nonstop to Shanghai—or would have if bad weather hadn't diverted the plane to Guangzhou. So after sixty-three hours and 11,565 miles of flying, I finally landed in China, exactly 111 miles from my starting point in Hong Kong. A few hours later the weather cleared and we took off again for an overnight rest stop in Shanghai.

What a disappointment! After a twenty-four-year absence, landing in Shanghai was like revisiting a roaring old reprobate who had survived a stroke. The physiognomy of the place was the same. But drained of its color and slaked of its ardor, the once wildest city in the world was barely staggering along under communism.

We checked into the old Cathay Hotel, a block up the Bund from where the Time-Life office had been. Sadly, the once-plush Cathay had metamorphosed into the decrepit Peace Hotel. The two cheery doormen who used to whisk the suitcases of arriving guests into the lobby with such speed had been replaced by a pair of stone-faced sentries armed with automatic rifles. The reception desk, formerly staffed with British-accented Chinese concierges in cutaways and striped pants, was manned by men and women of the Hotel Revolutionary Committee, all dressed in black padded jackets and baggy pants. A few blocks away I could hear the Big Ben clock atop the old Customs House sounding the hour. At last something familiar, I thought. But no, Red Guards had changed the chimes to play "The East Is Red," Communist China's national anthem.

I could hardly wait to get out of this half-dead commercial capital that had been my favorite haunt and first post as a foreign correspondent. The neon-splashed shops and nightspots were all gone. The teeming Huangpo River port appeared devoid of ships, and the clanging street traffic was reduced to a torrent of quietly whirring bicycles. Mercifully, Princess Ida's entourage took off for Beijing the following day before all my well-preserved memories of Shanghai were erased.

Flying north in our Boeing 707, there again was the vast beauty of old China—misty purple peaks marching off to meet the snowy Himalayas, the mighty Yellow and Yangtze rivers slithering like two dusty snakes across the dun-colored central plain, which finally turned a pale

green as we swooped low over fields of winter cabbage growing right
up to the edge of the runway at Beijing's airport.

Inside the terminal, beaming benevolently from the back wall, was
an oversized portrait of Chairman Mao accompanied by a few of his
favorite quotations: "Practice Marxism, Not Revisionism," "Be Open
and Above Board," "Do Not Intrigue or Conspire," "We Have Friends
All Over the World."

But Mao was too old and ailing to host his newfound friends from
Ethiopia. The official reception for Princess Ida was left to Premier
Zhou Enlai, the shrewd negotiator who single-handedly was reestablishing diplomatic and trade relations with the rest of the world while
anti-Western outbursts continued at home.

We "China watchers" in Hong Kong had been following his behind-
the-scenes maneuverings with considerable awe. When extremists
burned down the British embassy during the Great Proletarian Cultural
Revolution, it was Zhou who delivered an unofficial apology to Britain's
chargé d'affaires. But then the suave premier, it was said, "could put a
cosmopolitan face on Chinese communism," which he was now doing
with great aplomb for Princess Ida and her Ethiopian entourage.

As soon as everybody in the Great Hall had grabbed a beverage from
a passing silver tray, the blazing chandeliers dimmed. An announcement amplified by about a hundred loudspeakers suddenly boomed—
first in Mandarin, then in English for the benefit of the British-educated
guests of honor.

"Now I will propose a toast," echoed the voice, translating Zhou
Enlai's welcoming greeting. "To the great people of Ethiopia."

In the distance I could see the premier graciously holding his glass
aloft.

"And to the great unity of the peoples of the world," continued
the translator.

"And to their fight against imperialism, revisionism, and hegemony."
Zhou was known as a pragmatist, much more interested in economic
development than Communist ideology. Yet he always paid lip service
to the Great Leap Forward and Mao's other utopian lunges with the
ideological jargon he was now spouting.

I could see the premier's glass was still held high. The toasting wasn't
finished and the translator's voice droned on.

"To the health of the diplomatic missions present. To the health of
all comrades and friends gathered here. To the health and long life of
Emperor Haile Selassie. To the health and long life of Chairman Mao
Zedong, and to the health and long life of the people of the People's
Republic of China: GANBEI!"

"Skoal," said the Swedish ambassador, who was standing next to me and explaining that this reception, like so many others in the Great Hall of the People, was considered a command performance by Beijing's diplomatic corps. "The Chinese claim that *Mao Tai* tastes just like akvavit," he added, clinking his glass against mine. "But they have never tasted akvavit."

"Tastes like turpentine to me," said de Borchgrave, choking down his tiny goblet of the fiery, colorless liquid.

Zhou began his rounds of socializing with the Ethiopian dignitaries: first chatting animatedly with Princess Ida, then talking to His Highness Ras Mengesha Seyoum, governor general of the Ethiopian state of Tigre, followed by conversations with a couple of crown councillors, and finally His Excellency Zewde Gebre Selassie, the emperor's permanent representative to the United Nations.

For the next two hours Zhou table-hopped, shaking hands and toasting. From his carefree manner it was impossible to tell that this shrewd, sophisticated man had come under renewed attack from the so-called "Shanghai Mafia," the radicals threatening to plunge China into another Cultural Revolution. However, in typical Chinese fashion, their attack on him was being leveled obliquely by references in the press to the "Duke of Zhou," the power-hungry and deceptive Confucian villain.

As he moved through the assembled throng, Zhou alternately fielded and ducked the questions thrown at him, usually with a quip that evoked ripples of laughter from his guests.

"Are you coming to the United States?" one guest asked the premier through his attractive female interpreter.

"I don't know which airline to take," said Zhou.

"Sir, are you planning any trips abroad?"

"I have too many debts," he answered. "I'm going to let the foreign ministers do my traveling."

Each time Zhou moved to another table, he shook everyone's hand. His winsome but steely smile reminded me of the title of the Communist opera we had suffered through the night before: *Taking Tiger Mountain by Strategy.* The premier's social strategy was aimed at winning the hearts of the Ethiopians, and everyone else at the reception.

After each round of handshakes a waiter gave the premier a moist washrag to wipe his hands. His right hand, I knew, had been injured during the Long March, the epic 6,000-mile trek across China back in the 1930s, and was still sensitive. But the washrag routine didn't slow the flow of questions.

"When do you think the U.S. and People's Republic of China will establish full diplomatic relations?" asked *Newsweek* correspondent de Borchgrave as soon as Zhou reached our table.

The premier tossed back his head and laughed, but I noticed his piercing black eyes didn't give off the same gaiety. "You have Chiang Kai-shek's representatives in the U.S.," he said. "Once you realize that Taiwan is a province of China, that will solve everything. Then we'll shake hands."

"Is Henry Kissinger a good negotiator?" continued de Borchgrave, pressing on with his questions. It was Kissinger's secret meeting with Zhou that had paved the way for Nixon's visit to China and the rapprochement between our two countries that followed.

"I think so," said the premier. Although he didn't elaborate, it was well known how impressed he'd been by Kissinger's astute bargaining sense. And Kissinger, likewise, was reported to have been struck by Zhou's ability to dominate a meeting with his "air of controlled tension." But my thoughts about the high-level horse-trading between these two wheeler-dealers were quickly interrupted.

Suddenly there he was, the double-barreled boss of China's domestic and foreign policy, extending his hand to me.

"Your Excellency," I heard myself say. "I have something here for your archives." Then I handed Zhou the gift-wrapped photo album I had brought with me from Hong Kong. It contained some fifty enlargements of photographs I had taken in 1947 while convoying UNRRA supplies to Communist-held towns along the Yellow River.

I had debated whether or not to bring the album to Beijing. The chance of meeting the premier seemed slight. Not even Princess Ida knew in advance if she would be afforded that honor. It was only after her entourage had been treated to one exhausting round of sightseeing after another: to the Great Wall, Ming tombs, Dowager Empress Tzu-hsi's marble boat, sitting in Kunming Lake next to the Summer Palace, and all the other pagodas, pavilions, and palaces inside the Forbidden City ("Like jewel boxes within jewel boxes!" exclaimed Princess Ida) were we told about the premier's reception.

Zhou looked perplexed, reluctant to take my gift. The Communists, I knew, still had reservations about accepting anything that smacked of cumshaw. That became apparent when we were checking out of the Peace Hotel in Shanghai and the room boy chased me all the way down to the lobby with a worn-out razor blade I had discarded in the bathroom and that he mistook as an intended gift.

Finally Zhou's interpreter reached over and took the package for him. I explained what was in it and added that the premier's and my paths had crossed briefly in Henan Province. Zhou, I knew, had visited some of the same towns, perhaps even while I was there delivering food and clothing, though for security reasons his presence was always kept a secret. Once he had even breakfasted at our UNRRA headquarters in Kaifeng.

"That was years ago during War of Liberation," I said, using the Communists' term for China's civil war.

Zhou nodded. He seemed to understand what was being said even before it was translated. Then he raised his glass of *Mao Tai* and touched it to mine. *"Ganbei,"* he said before drifting away to the next table.

Evidently my gift to the premier was a faux pas of the first order. A few minutes later Qiao Guanhua, the deputy foreign minister, rushed over to our table and asked for an explanation of my bad behavior. No breach of protocol was intended, I assured him. My only purpose in presenting the album was the hope that the old pictures in it might elicit an invitation from the premier for me to revisit Henan.

"That's not possible," said the deputy foreign minister. "Perhaps some other time," he added, his scowl slowly changing into a smile. As things turned out, an invitation to go back to Henan and report on the changes there was extended to me eight years later. But I never found out if it was the old photos that did the trick.

Before the party for the Ethiopians was over, Zhou had clinked glasses with every person in the Great Hall. It was a remarkable performance for the seventy-five-year-old premier, rumored to have stomach cancer, heart trouble, and high blood pressure.

More threatening, however, were his political ailments, though for us in Hong Kong these were only hearsay. We had no firsthand information. But by listening to provincial radio broadcasts and reading *People's Daily*, we discovered that his speeches were being attacked as "poisonous weeds," and that he was charged with being a "capitalist roader" for putting so much emphasis on industry, defense, mechanized agriculture, and scientific development—"The Four Modernizations," as he called them.

Finally it was time for Princess Ida and her followers to bid goodbye to Zhou. We filed out of the Great Hall of the People into Tiananmen Square. Darkness had already enveloped the enormous parade grounds where just a few years earlier, during the Cultural Revolution, a million militant Red Guards had passed in review. The square was still dominated by monster billboards of Mao and Lenin, now glowering eerily in the moonlight.

As we climbed into the waiting *Hong Qi* (Red Flag) limousines lined up in the square, it occurred to me that politically, at least, the old premier and young princess were in somewhat similar predicaments. Ida's power was inherited from her grandfather, the stubborn monarch whom she had cajoled into establishing more links with the modern world.

Zhou's power stemmed from serving the headstrong chairman the way Chinese prime ministers traditionally served their mercurial emperors. "How shall we govern China without the premier," Mao once remarked. "It is quite impossible. He is the country's housekeeper." And Mao was right. Zhou had restored internal stability and revived economic progress following two decades of disastrous social engineering.

Zhou's and Ida's positions were also similarly threatened by radical elements within their respective countries: hers by a gang of Marxist rebels in the military seeking to overthrow the royal family; his by the so-called "Gang of Four," led by Mao's power-hungry third wife, Jiang Qing, who threatened to turn the country topsy-turvy once again as the aged chairman's strength began to ebb from Lou Gehrig's disease.

My premonition about the dangers faced by the princess and premier proved to be well founded. The very next year Ida's royal title was revoked after her grandfather became a prisoner in his own palace. She fled Ethiopia in 1975 following his assassination. Rumors flew at first that the emperor's pet lions had been starved for a week before being fed their master. But documents recently uncovered revealed that Haile Selassie was not eaten by his pets. He was murdered in his bed, suffocated by pillows pressed against his face by one of the Marxist rebels. (In 1995 his coffin was discovered in a closet of the Bhata Church in Addis Ababa.)

Not long after Zhou's reception for Ida, he, too, feared that he might become an assassination target and took a six-month hiatus in a well-guarded military hospital suite. The generals had always been his allies and he could count on their protection. There he could also continue to receive foreign dignitaries and engage in the classic Chinese ploy of making his political moves while appearing to be inactive.

In 1976 Zhou died of cancer, just eight months ahead of Mao. The chairman never visited him, nor did he issue any personal statement on Zhou's achievements and contributions. If it hadn't been for Zhou's skillful mediation and the unobtrusive use of his power, the revolution in China might have petered out as it did in Russia. Making Mao's revolution last was his great legacy.

Zhou himself sought no recognition. He simply willed that his ashes be scattered across the rivers and hills of his beloved land rather than hoping that his body would be enshrined in some mausoleum as he knew Mao's would soon be. Nevertheless, it is the former premier whom his countrymen still revere most for recognizing that economic incentive is more effective than ideological exhortation. And for the goal he single-mindedly pursued of making China, as he promised, "a technologically advanced Socialist state that will put it in the front ranks of the world by the end of the twentieth century." In an unusual display of sympathy and respect, even the American consulate in Hong Kong flew its flag at half staff to mark the passing of this progressive Communist leader.

CHAPTER XXII

Travels with Jerry

SECRET SERVICE MEN ALWAYS STRUCK ME as being very awkward at trying to blend in with their surroundings. It isn't just their dark suits, gold lapel pins, and the shoulder-holster bulges in their jackets that make these agents easy to spot. Their sideways glances and skyward squints are a dead giveaway that they're on the lookout for another Oswald, Sirhan, or Hinckley. So when my wife and I drove up to the house in Georgetown where we had been invited for dinner on August 2, 1974, and saw P street crawling with these furtive, black-suited fellows, we knew the vice president and his wife had already arrived.

We had good reason to think the Fords wouldn't show. For several weeks, while recovering from cancer surgery at New York Hospital, I had sat propped up in bed watching the Watergate hearings as Nixon's presidency unraveled. His impeachment now appeared imminent, the House Judiciary Committee having already voted to try to remove him from office through a Senate trial.

That's why when photographer David Hume Kennerly telephoned that he wanted to throw a little dinner party to celebrate my release from the hospital, and was going to invite "Jerry and Betty," as he called them, I assumed he was simply trying to cheer me up. Cancer has such a bad sound. He probably figured I was a goner, even though the doctors called my operation a success and promised I could soon return to Hong Kong.

Kennerly and I had spent a lot of time in Vietnam covering the war together before he came back to Washington. Early in 1973, we were

211

among a handful of correspondents and photographers picked to fly to Hanoi to inspect the American prisoners. The first 115 of the 562 POWs were about to be released, and their North Vietnamese captors foolishly hoped to convince the world that the horror stories of Americans being tortured, starved, and publicly displayed in tiger cages were made up by the Pentagon to infuriate the public and perpetuate the war.

Our one-day whirlwind visit to Hanoi was surreal. There we were in the enemy capital, surrounded by bomb craters blasted by our own B-52s, being given a Cook's tour of the city. Next we were treated to beer and lunch at the once-plush French-owned Metropole Hotel. Finally, we were escorted to the infamous "Hanoi Hilton." When we walked in, the prisoners were standing at attention in front of neatly made up bunks, as if undergoing a spit-and-polish boot-camp inspection back home. I spotted Air Force ace Robbie Risner and Navy Captain Jim Stockdale (who became Ross Perot's running mate in 1992), though some of the men were so thin they were barely recognizable. None was allowed to speak. A few winks and smirks, nevertheless, got their message across that this was all a sham.

Seeing all the Secret Service agents skulking around Kennerly's small white Georgetown house seemed just as incongruous. Could the vice president of the United States, about to be catapulted into the real White House, afford to while away an evening here? Yet, when my wife Helen and I walked in, there he sat, relaxed as could be, sipping the first of four martinis he would consume that evening.

Remarkably, the husky, former Michigan University football star never got a buzz on, as much as he might have wanted to. Just the previous day, as is now known, White House Chief of Staff Alexander Haig had secretly informed him that Nixon planned to resign.

"Mr. Vice President, I think you should prepare yourself for changes in your life" is the way Haig said in his memoir *Inner Circles* he told Ford that very likely he would soon be president. "I can't predict what will happen or when, but I think you should hold yourself in readiness."

Making this news even more onerous to Ford was the suggestion Haig passed on to the vice president, that Nixon's resignation could be contingent upon Ford's willingness to pardon him once he became president. "The whole thing reeks of a deal," Ford's closest advisers warned him just hours before he left for Kennerly's. According to Ford's own biography, he then telephoned Haig that he had "no intention of getting involved in Nixon's decision-making process." Although Ford certainly gave no hint of the momentous secrets he carried with him to Kennerly's party, this social gathering was probably the only one in Washington that night where Nixon's name was never mentioned.

For most of the cocktail hour, I sat with Ford discussing the fact-finding tour of Southeast Asia he was still scheduled to take as vice president. We both knew the trip would almost certainly be scrubbed. Yet we carried on this little charade of Ford asking questions about the region's political leaders and my offering a personal assessment of their strengths, weaknesses, and idiosyncracies.

A few more close friends of Kennerly's arrived—John Durniak, the picture editor of *Time*; Dirck Halstead, the magazine's White House photographer (who remarked as he entered, "Nothing in the president's in basket, nothing in his out basket," indicating that things in the Oval Office were at a standstill); and freelance photographer David Burnett.

We all assumed that we were dining at Kennerly's home, until he suddenly announced it was time take off for the Old Angler's Inn in Maryland, where he'd booked a private dining room. So sandwiched in between a pair of Secret Service fuel-injected Chevy four-by-fours crammed with submachineguns and communication equipment, our little convoy of well-lubricated passengers sped off to the Maryland countryside.

At the inn, we settled down congenially around one large table. I was seated next to Betty Ford, my wife, a fellow-Michigander, next to Jerry. This clearly was a not a night for serious conversation. David Burnett, known for both his sensitive photography and madcap mimicry, started things off by acting out an argument he'd recently witnessed on a train in India. With nary a stammer or stutter, he switched back and forth, imitating the two heavily accented, head-knocking Hindis as they hurled epithets at each other, all the while munching on their chicken tandoori and tossing the bones out the train window.

For the next three hours the jokes and stories never slowed, as if a pause might provoke somebody to stupidly ask Ford, "What the hell's going on at the White House?"

That same night, as Haig also revealed in his memoir, the mercurial president was reversing his decision to resign. "Let them impeach me," Haig reported Nixon had shouted to him over the phone. "We'll fight it to the end." But that turned out to be just a temporary change of heart. The next day Nixon reversed himself again, and on August 9, 1974, Gerald Rudolph Ford, Jr.—the same seemingly carefree Jerry who appeared to be having such a rollicking good time at the Old Angler's Inn just a week earlier—solemnly took the oath as the thirty-eighth president of the United States.

Three months later, on his first overseas foray as president, Ford came to Asia. Almost the entire Washington press corps, some 150 strong, tagged along. And as *Time*'s senior correspondent in the Far East, I flew from Hong Kong to Tokyo to join them. Soon, much to my surprise, a summons came from Akasaka Palace, the lavish three-hundred-room replica of Versailles, where Ford and Henry Kissinger were staying. Ford was still in his bedroom when I arrived, dressing for the formal banquet he was hosting downstairs that night for Emperor Hirohito and Empress Nagako.

It was amusing to see this man from Grand Rapids, famous for the utilitarian furniture it produces, ensconced in such regal surroundings. The enormous canopied bed, with twin bolsters and a gold damask bedspread, wasn't king-sized. It was emperor-sized. But Ford had given his ornate three-room suite a few personal touches. A presidential electronic call button with the White House seal affixed to it rested on the Empire table next to the bed. On a gold-encrusted desk was a pile of White House stationery, Ford's pipe, a package of Cavendish No. 79 tobacco, and a silver lighter, although his imperial hosts had provided fancy matchboxes with *Akasaka* embossed in gold—souvenirs for the palace guests to snitch. There was also a makeshift bar with the mixings for a good martini to get his blood circulating before dinner. I noted all these details for my file to *Time*.

"It's too bad Betty couldn't come," said the president as he greeted me. Gradually the reason for my visit emerged. It wasn't to brief him on Kakuei Tanaka's scandal-ridden government, or on any of the other leaders he was slated to meet in Asia. He simply wanted to say thanks for an article I'd recently sent to the First Lady when it was discovered she had breast cancer.

During dinner at the Old Angler's Inn, Betty Ford had lectured me on how all too often cancer patients she knew seemed to surrender to the disease. "Don't worry," I said. "I've been working on an article about the importance of an upbeat attitude to bolster the immune system. Writing the piece was part of my therapy," I explained.

The article, which later appeared in both the *Atlantic* and *Reader's Digest*, hadn't yet been published. "You lectured me. Now it's my turn to lecture you," I wrote to the First Lady in my note accompanying a copy of the manuscript.

"Your article helped a lot," said the president. "It gave her a lift just when she needed it." Then we chatted for a while about South Korea, where the president would go next before flying on to Vladivostok for his meeting with Soviet leader Leonid Brezhnev. From our conversation I gathered that Ford was counting heavily on Secretary of State Henry

Kissinger to steer him safely through his first summit. He still hadn't gained the confidence required of his newfound high office.

Suddenly the president realized it was time for the emperor and empress to arrive. The entrance to the palace was bathed in floodlights. "How'm I doing," he shouted back to me as he bolted out of the room and bounded down the red-carpeted stairway. His slicked-backed, blond hair was still wet from the shower. And his striped pants, I noticed, were too short, displaying a couple of inches of sock—a sartorial slip the Tokyo newspapers pounced on with merriment the next morning.

The local press, nevertheless, appreciated Ford's common man's touch. *Yomiuri Shimbun* reported that when he jumped out of his limousine to shake hands with the crowd, a housewife exclaimed: "Ford-san's hand was big, warm, and soft. I'm going home to wrap mine with a bandage to keep the honor he bestowed on me as long as I can."

Flying on to Seoul, where Ford conferred with Korean dictator Park Chung Hee, the president was greeted by much bigger, though well-orchestrated crowds. A million schoolchildren waving miniature American flags lined the road from the airport as we drove by. As our motorcade sped across the Han River bridge, I was reminded of the night in 1950, when we correspondents retreated across the temporary pontoon bridge spanning the Han in this same spot, chased by the Chinese and North Koreans who had just recaptured Seoul.

This visit, Ford had told me in Akasaka Palace, was one that his political advisers wished he could skip because of Park's increasingly repressive rule. But it didn't really matter. The stopover in Korea turned out to be mainly protocol. Ford respectfully laid a wreath on the black marble tombstone of First Lady Yook Young Soo, who was killed by an assassin's bullet intended for her husband. Then he helicoptered off to greet the 38,000 U.S. troops stationed just below the demilitarized zone. Again, it was an eerie feeling for me being back on this same frozen ground over which we had fled in panic and confusion exactly twenty-four years earlier.

My next contact with Ford came in May 1975 following a controversial sequence of events that ended up improving the image of U.S. power in Asia and, at the same time, enhancing his stature as president. It began in a welter of confusing reports. A radio operator down in Indonesia had picked up a mayday message from an American merchant ship in the Gulf of Thailand that it had been fired on and seized by a Cambodian patrol boat. The initial reports we got in Hong Kong were so sketchy, we weren't sure whether the story was worth covering. The ship, named *Mayaguez*, was a derelict cargo vessel scarcely worth risking a war for. Yet when the alarm sounded in Washington, Ford responded as if it were an American battleship of the first rank. He called out the marines, the air force, and the navy. He ordered assault troops, supported by warships, fighter-bombers, and helicopters, to invade the tiny island where the forty crew members were thought to be held. To prevent a counterstrike, he also ordered two bombing raids on the Cambodian mainland.

At first it appeared that the president had overreacted. "Why did the U.S. use a cannon to shoot a chicken?" editorialized a newspaper in Japan, recalling the devastation inflicted upon it during World War II. A few Democratic congressmen and senators echoed that thought. But most of them applauded. "Without Ford's fast action," replied Barry Goldwater, "every little half-assed nation would be taking a shot at us."

Politically, I realized, this hijacking at sea was not an entirely unwelcome provocation for Ford. It occurred just thirteen days after the whole world had witnessed the humiliation of Americans being forced to flee Saigon in helicopters from the roof of the U.S. Embassy. Having taken part in that evacuation, a kaleidoscope of disheartening images still churned in my mind: U.S. Marines with rifle butts pounding the fingers of Vietnamese trying to claw their way into the embassy compound to escape their homeland; looters ransacking the PX for caseloads of such nonessentials as maraschino cherries, or racing around the city in abandoned embassy cars until they ran out of gas. And out on the China Sea, millions of dollars worth of helicopters being tossed overboard like so many pop-top beer cans to make room on the U.S. Navy rescue ships for later-arriving choppers. But worst of all, the plaintive expressions of those silent thousands stuck in Saigon still haunted me. *You're leaving us*, their eyes said.

Ford felt the same way. "Sitting in the Oval Office and watching the last Americans being kicked out of the embassy compound was not a happy day for a U.S. president," he said.

After Saigon's fall, he confessed: "We were never sure if we were going to have trouble with the people left behind." He also predicted "some new Communist probe in the wake of Vietnam." But he was caught completely by surprise, he said, that it was the Cambodians who struck.

While his many years in Congress did not prepare him for exercising presidential power, they gave him a fingertip feel for what Americans would and would not support. Just before Saigon fell, we correspondents there heard that Kissinger was urging him to resume the bombing of North Vietnam. Ford refused. But under no circumstances, he announced, would he allow Cambodia to hold the crew of the *Mayaguez* hostage the way North Korea had held the crew of the U.S. Navy intelligence ship *Pueblo* in 1968. It was his first bold action.

I flew down to Bangkok, hoping to join the rescue mission, only to find that correspondents weren't being allowed to cover the marine assault of the Cambodian island where it was believed the *Mayaguez* crew was being held. It turned out to be a costly and futile attack. Eighteen marines were killed, three helicopters were shot down, and two others damaged. Another twenty-three air force security troops, preparing to back up the operation, were also killed when their helicopter crashed in Thailand. But the *Mayaguez* crew was not on the island.

Stuck in Bangkok, the press could only monitor reports of the fighting. Meanwhile, a second marine unit boarded the abandoned *Mayaguez*, but only after navy attack planes from the aircraft carrier *Coral Sea* had sunk five Cambodian gunboats and destroyed seventeen planes on the mainland. Still, there was no sign of the crew which, as it turned out, had been taken to the mainland. Fearing further attacks, the Cambodians then herded their American captives onto a fishing boat and were ferrying them back to their ship when they were finally intercepted by an American destroyer.

When the *Mayaguez* finally limped into Singapore, I was there to interview the captain and crew. That was on a Saturday afternoon, twelve hours before *Time* was scheduled to go to press—barely enough time to file some 8,000 words for the cover story headlined FORD DRAWS THE LINE. On the plane flying home to Hong Kong, it occurred to me that a full account of this unusual four-day miniwar might make a dramatic book. But to sop up enough detail would probably take a week or so of living aboard the *Mayaguez*, and then sufficient time in the White House to get Ford's firsthand account.

I telephoned the chairman of Sea-Land Services, Inc., the New Jersey company that owned the ship. He wasn't optimistic. "Captain Charlie Miller," he said, "is still too upset by all the marines killed in the rescue operation to allow a reporter on board." Next I called Kennerly, who had quit *Time* to become the official White House photographer. At that moment he happened to be breakfasting with the president at Camp David. "Just a minute," he said, "I'll ask him."

The president agreed to cooperate. So I called the Sea-Land chairman again and asked if the president's participation didn't change things. "Yes," he said, "Captain Miller will cooperate provided you donate half the money from the book to the families of the dead marines"—a stipulation I readily agreed to.

For the next week I rode Sea-Land's unsleek old container ship from

Hong Kong to Manila and back, until I came to know her colorful history just as well as I did the stories of her veteran skipper and crew. After all, she had become famous. So I also treated her as a character in the book, describing how a fresh coat of black had painted out the big starboard dimple where some overzealous tug had shoved her hard against the dock. I explained how through shipyard surgery she had been broadened in the beam, even cut in two and stretched out to carry more cargo, and then welded back together again. And I found out, even unbeknownst to her skipper, that she had borne three earlier names—none of them memorable—*White Falcon, Santa Eliana,* and *Sea*—before being christened *Mayaguez,* a name now identifying one brief moment in America's maritime history.

After taping Charlie Miller and his thirty-nine crew members, I flew to Washington to tape the president. Only two other people were present during my three-hour session with him in the Oval Office: Dave Kennerly and Brent Scowcroft, then the president's deputy national security adviser. Noticeably absent was Secretary of State Henry Kissinger. Ford made it clear that the *Mayaguez* rescue was *his* show, that he had followed his own basic instincts to use force rather than relying on Kissinger's diplomatic designs. He did mention that the secretary of state had made an unsuccessful attempt to get the Chinese to intervene, before he called in the marines. "The American people," said Ford, "expect their president to act, particularly during crises, to restore matters to normal and protect U.S. interests." He gave the impression of being very pleased with having flexed his presidential muscles for the first time.

Kissinger, however, was very much in evidence the next time I was with Ford, during his 1975 visit to the People's Republic of China. Politically, it was an important trip for the president. The U.S. election was just a year away, and Ford was considered weak in foreign affairs. But Mao Zedong was failing and Kissinger had to lean hard on his contacts in Beijing to arrange the visit.

I could feel the cool reception being given Ford right from the start of the state banquet at the Great Hall of the People. Substituting for Zhou Enlai, the gracious host at Princess Ida's welcoming party, was the Lilliputian, four-foot-eleven-inch first vice premier Deng Xiaoping. Deng was well known to us China watchers in Hong Kong for his lack of charm and manners. Even Kissinger referred to him as "that nasty little man." Aside from his blunt talk, Deng had a habit, at affairs like this, of expectorating noisily into a handy spittoon. "You must forgive me," he'd say. "I'm just a country boy."

As we in Hong Kong knew, that really wasn't the case. Crude as he often was, Deng's tastes were quite sophisticated. During the Cultural Revolution he had been charged with being "a high-living potentate who used his office to indulge his gluttonous tastes and his bourgeous devotion to Mah-Jongg and bridge." And for those sins Red Guards had paraded him through the streets with a dunce cap pulled down over his ears.

From off in the distance where the press was seated, I could barely see the diminutive Deng. Even when he stood up to give the usual toasts, all I could make out was his upraised glass. But the edge in his voice was clearly discernible.

"The Soviet Union," railed the first vice premier, "is the country which most zealously preaches peace and is the most dangerous source of war." That crack was obviously directed at Henry Kissinger, who had worked hard for detente with Russia and was seated at the head table. Deng followed that dig with another about the president's "futile disarmament negotiations" with Brezhnev. The tension finally eased when the People's Liberation Army band broke into "The Yellow Rose of Texas."

After the banquet Ford mentioned how much he liked my book *The Four Days of Mayaguez* which had received good reviews but had faded as fast as the public's memory of the incident. He also remarked that his promised meeting with Mao was still uncertain. The chairman had sent his wife, Jiang Qing, to the dinner. But she had given no hint as to when the meeting might take place. "It doesn't matter," said a British reporter friend stationed in Beijing when I told him of Ford's concern. "Mao is gaga."

The audience with Mao finally did take place. But no reporters were allowed to attend. David Kennerly tried unsuccessfully to crash the meeting. Not even the Secret Service agents were allowed in, and no official communiqué was issued when the visit was over. The enfeebled chairman had apparently repeated Deng Xiaoping's warning that no one but the Russians benefited from detente. Ford, we were told, replied that the United States would persist anyway.

"Mao doesn't really care about detente," my cynical British reporter-friend explained. "Like all Chinese, he enjoys having your presidents come to Beijing to kiss the Dragon Throne. It's his idea of detente."

During the three-year interval since my visit with Princess Ida, it was obvious that bits and pieces of American technology had also come to Beijing. The biggest crowd-stopper in town was now the new foot-activated front door at the Beijing Hotel, which magically slid open and shut as each guest entered. Orange and blue motorized street sweepers had replaced the old women broom brigades. Electric hair dryers were on display in the windows of the *Qianmen* (Front Gate) and *Wanfujin* (Well of the Emperor's Mansion) department stores, while the "Day and Night Grocery Store" was offering a rough approximation of our frozen TV dinners.

Local residents were also being introduced to American sports. Mass basketball practice had replaced mass military drills in Tiananmen Square—at least while we there. "Your president was an expert olive ball player," a Chinese reporter remarked to me at the airport as we were about to leave. "You mean football," I replied. "No, olive ball," he insisted.

For the long flight back to Washington, Henry Kissinger invited a few reporters to join him aboard *Air Force Two*. We stopped briefly in Manila, where Ford met Ferdinand Marcos. The Filipino dictator and his wife, Imelda, threw a lavish late-night banquet in Malacañang Palace for the entire presidential entourage, and early the next morning insisted on dragging everybody over to Corregidor for ceremonies marking Japan's attack on the island fortress. After that I welcomed the thirteen-hour ride on the secretary of state's plane to catch up on my writing and sleep.

Midway across the Pacific, Kissinger summoned all of us to his forward cabin for champagne and canapes. The effervescent secretary of state loved to crow and preen in front of the press. And in the seclusion of *Air Force Two* he could be sure of our attention.

Kissinger said even he was surprised by Mao's grasp of world affairs. But the translation process from Mao's stuttering Hunanese into Mandarin, and finally into English, Kissinger admitted, was "painful." (According to a book by Mao's personal physician published in 1994, "It was as though the chairman had lost control of his tongue.")

Kissinger reported that part of the time Mao's two interpreters had to rely on lip-reading. When that failed, he said the chairman would grip a soft lead pencil with his shaky right hand and scribble a few characters. "But there was no question," added Kissinger, "that Mao's head was still clear."

So much for my friend's claim that China's venerable leader, or "Great Helmsman," as he was deferentially referred to, had gone "gaga" in his old age.

Except for the opportunity to observe the secretary of state up close, there really wasn't much point in my flying to Washington. I had to turn right around and go back to Hong Kong, where I was still stationed when Ford was defeated by Jimmy Carter the following year.

From afar, the lampooning Ford received in the 1976 campaign as a foot-tripping, head-bumping klutz who didn't realize that Poland and the other Eastern European countries were under Soviet domination seemed unfair. Physically, the former University of Michigan center was the best coordinated, most athletic man ever to occupy the White House, and a good student who finished in the top third of his class at Yale Law School, to boot. The Eastern Europe remark was simply a slip, his aides claimed. Ford meant to say in his second debate with Jimmy Carter that the U.S. did not *accept* Soviet control of those satellite countries.

From my personal contact with Ford, I felt that his simplicity, decency, and rocklike common sense were being deliberately mistaken for stupidity. Ford impressed me as being a secure, straightforward man with a fundamental faith in the American system. Yet his critics acted as if these virtues were nice to have, but not important enough to base a presidency on. Ford's biggest handicap was having been handed the country's top job rather than having won it. He proved that power that is passed on by one leader to another is hard to hold.

A year after his defeat, I accompanied Ford on a 5,000-mile teaching and banquet tour around the U.S. The university appearances had been arranged by the American Enterprise Institute, a Washington think tank for public policy, which had signed up the former president as one of its "distinguished fellows."

By this time I had moved back to New York and switched magazines within the company, joining *Fortune* as a senior writer. My first article, called "Professor Ford Speaks His Mind," involved sitting in on his lectures. Newspaper reporters were strictly barred from these classrooms, but Ford made an exception for *Fortune*. He also consented to spend our flying time between stops discussing the issues of the day as well as his own political future. The only taboo was talk about the Nixon pardon, though before the trip was over, we got into that too.

It was fascinating to see the president in his new role—a little too stylish in his gray pin-striped suit, a little too straight in his athlete's posture, to be the very model of a college professor. Yet, when he laid his gold wristwatch on the lectern, picked up a piece of chalk, and peered over his steel-rimmed spectacles at the students in front of him, he gave the impression of having been a teacher all his life. Then suddenly he would revert to the politician he'd been for twenty-eight years and drop a nugget that would have made big news outside the classroom. "Nelson Rockefeller might have added more strength to the ticket than Bob Dole," he confided, though publicly he had defended his choice of the Kansas senator as his running mate.

One of his favorite lecture topics was what he called "the encroachment of Congress on the perogatives of the chief executive," a matter that is still debated today. Ford admitted that when he first came to Congress in 1949, the president had too much power. "But that pendulum has swung way over to the other side," he said. "You can't have 535 House members negotiating with another country." He cited the crucial decision about the evacuation of Danang that he had to make during the Easter recess. "Not one of the bipartisan leaders was in town," he explained. "Most were on junkets to Europe, the Middle East, or Asia. Yet it was important to try to reach them. We finally located one congressman at his California beach house, but it had an unlisted number. We had to get the local police to leave a note on the door: 'Please call the White House.' "

The students were not intimated by a live ex-president in their midst and asked tough questions. Ford responded with a frankness and articulateness that might have caught the fancy of the American electorate in 1976.

"You must understand," he said, "if I had *not* pardoned Richard Nixon, his trial would have torn the country apart. But there was no deal. I was simply following the dictates of my own conscience." Then he added wistfully, "I'll admit it may have cost me the election." A tougher, more power-hungry president, I thought, would have let Nixon go to prison.

Aboard Ford's chartered jet, his White House reminiscences flowed easily. Sometimes they revealed regret at not having been better prepared to take over as president. "We came in on such short notice, under such adverse conditions," he said. "First we had to heal the nation, convincing the American people they could disagree without being disagreeable. At the same time, we had serious economic problems. We had to do everything overnight."

Ford interrupted his college tour for a day at his home base in Rancho Mirage, one of the mushrooming satellites of Palm Springs, California. His makeshift office sat beside the velvety thirteenth fairway of the Thunderbird Country Club. I watched a couple of hooked drives carom off the roof and plop into the pool, much to the dismay of the golf-jacketed Secret Service men posted around the converted ranch house.

Inside, a dozen aides and secretaries buzzed around in slacks and sport shirts, gathering research material, working on appointment schedules, and helping to answer 250 letters a day. It looked as if Ford had just moved in. The office stationery was stacked behind the living room bar and the old White House signature machine was propped in a sunken bathtub with California-Roman gold faucets. "It is clear," I jotted in my notebook, "an ex-president becomes the source of a whole cottage industry."

There was no question in my mind that Ford yearned to be president again. At a speech in Lubbock for a retiring congressman, I saw the glow spread over his face as the cheering crowd assured him if the 1976 election were rerun, Texas would go for him. And when we were about to land in Washington, he started to say, "When I fly back here and see the lights on the Capitol dome and, yes, the lights on the White House, I don't hesitate to admit that I get goose bumps." But tears shone in his eyes and, suddenly choked up, he couldn't finish describing how he felt.

CHAPTER XXIII

Flight of the Iron Butterfly

HER HEAD WAS BOWED REVERENTLY. Her fingers fondled a diamond rosary worth millions as she renewed her marriage vows to the man who
promised twenty-five years earlier to make her first lady of the land.
There, attending the silver anniversary ceremony, were two cardinals,
the entire diplomatic corps, the Manila Symphony Orchestra, and some
five hundred friends including two planeloads of European royalty,
ready to dine and dance until the fiery tropical sunrise the next day. It
was the kind of regal celebration that Imelda Romualdez Marcos loved.

This silver anniversary blowout at Manila's Malacañang Palace took
place in 1979, at the peak of the Marcoses power. Even though the
local press was barred, Imelda had invited me to fly from the U.S. to
cover the event for the two articles I was writing about her for *Fortune*
and *Life*.

I already knew her well, having covered her and her husband on
and off for *Time* ever since the country was first clamped under martial
law in 1972. Also, two years with the army on Leyte and Luzon during
World War II had left me with a warm feeling for the Filipino people.
The people, of course, were much better off now, though per capita
income was still only about $500—which is why none of the opulence
of the silver anniversary celebration could be shown on local TV, or
even reported in any detail by the carefully monitored press. It wasn't
that the 47 million Filipinos didn't know their First Lady and all about
her international reputation for extravagant clothes and jewels. Her
combination of personal and public spending is what made the "Iron

Butterfly," as she was known, so controversial throughout the 7,100-island archipelago.

She acquired that name by the way she fluttered from job to job, while exerting a will of steel. But she was also called the "Orchid," because her pet projects appeared to grow on air without visible financial support, and was sometimes referred to as "Superma'am," since her insomniac's schedule kept her working or partying until the wee hours every morning.

Abroad, however, the kings, commissars, sheikhs, and prime ministers who had received this peripatetic woman knew her as an ambassador plenipotentiary who was equally adept at wheedling favors, arranging loans, and spurring trade. And while the other women leaders of Asia—Prime Minister Indira Gandhi of India, Prime Minister Sirimavo Bandaranaike of Sri Lanka, and Madame Mao Zedong of China—had all been rudely deposed, Imelda kept gaining power. No longer merely First Lady, she also was de facto vice president, governor of Manila, and minister of Human Settlements, the national housekeeping agency responsible for improving food, water, and shelter. Even more remarkable was the whispered word that she would eventually assume the twin titles of her dictator husband, Ferdinand Marcos, and become prime minister and president. Not bad for a beautiful but supposedly penniless provincial lass once called the "Rose of Tacloban."

I first met Imelda right after she had been slashed on her arms and hands trying to ward off blows from a foot-long bolo knife. While most assassination attempts are acts of stealth committed with as few witnesses as possible, this bloody scuffle was watched by millions of people, live and in color. Television crews had been assigned to cover the First Lady presenting awards in a national beautification and cleanliness campaign, and they caught the entire action, including the shooting to death of her assailant.

Her injured right arm still hung limply in a red bandanna sling when she greeted me at the palace. Long, curving fingernails painted a shiny silver protruded from bandages on both hands and extended easily an inch beyond the ends of her fingers. "You see," she said, "my hands are not only healing, they are manicured." Then she added: "Your president Richard Nixon very thoughtfully sent a surgeon from California to assist our doctors."

That first meeting, while she was still recuperating, sealed our friendship. Afterward, whenever I flew over to the Philippines from Hong Kong on one *Time* story or another, an invitation would come from Malacañang Palace. Sometimes it was just for a chat alone with the president over dinner. The palace chef would attempt—although not successfully—an elaborate four- or five-course Western meal for me, while the president, a fitness buff, sat there facing a lonesome-looking banana on his plate. Our conversations ranged from the status of the U.S. military bases to the status of women in the Philippines.

"We put women on a pedestal," he once told me, obviously referring to the First Lady. "Women have good judgment on investments. The husband who does not consult with his wife on investments is a strong-hearted man." He was speaking from experience. Imelda even then was rumored to have an enormous rainy-day cache of stock certificates and jewelry salted away in Swiss safe deposit boxes. *Cosmopolitan* had already ranked her one of the ten richest women in the world.

On other trips to the Philippines I spent more time with her. But keeping up with Imelda was no easy task as she juggled her mandates as governor, cabinet minister, and First Lady. Whipping down Manila's waterfront boulevard with sounds of von Karajan booming out of her Cadillac stereo and several carloads of bodyguards sirening along fore and aft—or twisting over an outlying road in her custom-built bus, with its video player showing the tape of her historic 1974 meeting with Chairman Mao—she offered a running commentary on her myriad plans for a brighter Philippines.

"See that little village," she would say, pointing a now-red-lacquered fingernail at a cluster of houses that her Human Settlements Ministry had just completed for less than $3,000 apiece. "It is a fish farm in the wet season and a chicken farm in the dry season." Then the fingernail would point to the video screen suddenly zooming in on Imelda tenderly holding Mao's hand—a well-photographed gesture that helped pave the way for diplomatic relations between their two countries. "The Chinese have a saying that women hold up half the sky," she explained.

Rarely thinking small, the chic, darkly beautiful Mrs. Marcos plunged into all these projects with unbridled confidence. As metro Manila governor she reclaimed nineteen square miles of waterfront, built a huge international airport, and cut a fifty-five-mile highway to a newly developed harbor east of the capital. That was after she had already added fourteen glittering luxury hotels to the Manila skyline preparing for the International Monetary Fund conference in 1976. Her other monumental building projects included a Cultural Center, National Art Center, the magnificently equipped Philippine Heart Center, Kidney Center, and Nutrition Center. "I had nine brothers and sisters," she sometimes joked. "Of course, that was before my family planning headquarters was built."

"How do you keep Manila building at such a frantic pace?" I once asked her. "I'm like Robin Hood," she said. "I rob the rich to make these projects come alive . . . not really rob, because it's done with a smile." Actually, this dunning came in the form of a personal letter, a call, or dinner at the palace, and was for as much as $150,000. "She suffers from an edifice complex," her contributors used to complain.

Manila's mushrooming growth depended also on Imelda's inexhaustible energy. As I found out accompanying her on several late-night forays, it was not unusual for the black Cadillac bearing the familiar IM777 license plate to wheel up to a construction site at 1 A.M. The First Lady maintained that night-shift hard hats, like the rest of her constituents, needed to know how much she really cared. "I don't want to go down in history as a Croesus," she said. "I want to be remembered as somebody who has served."

Wherever we drove, it seemed that her ubiquitous, mellifluous name adorned countless Imelda Streets, Imelda Avenues, and Imelda Boulevards—as well as a cheap new fuel obtained from fermented banana leaves called "Imelda gas." Often when we were driving through Manila, she would roll down the window of her chauffeured limo and extend a graceful hand to be touched by a group of squealing women. "When a person touches somebody, or kisses somebody, or embraces somebody, why do you think they do it?" she once asked me. "They want to see if you're real."

This woman, who had followed a storybook path to riches and power, hardly did seem real. Daughter of a scholarly lawyer from Leyte, she had been named Miss Manila, and was working as a secretary in a bank in 1954 when she was introduced to the World War II guerrilla hero and then congressman, Ferdinand Marcos. "He stood next to me," she told me, "measuring his height against mine. 'Perfect,' he said (although at 5'7" she was two inches taller). Eleven days later we were married."

That story doesn't quite jibe with the official palace biography published later, which depicted her as a poor country girl "dressed in house clothes, wearing slippers, and crunching watermelon seeds" when she and Marcos first met. Imelda was so impressed by Eva Peron's climb from poverty to power in Argentina that she embellished her own humble beginnings, true or not.

It was often hard to distill fact from the stories she told—like the one about how as a teenager she used to watch Douglas MacArthur taking his morning constitutional on the beach in Leyte shortly after the American invasion. She claimed, "I once shouted, 'Victory Joe,' and the general tossed me a candy bar."

That was nothing compared to her tall tale about the multimillion-dollar diamond rosary she was fondling at her silver anniversary. The opening photograph selected by the editors for my *Life* article showed the First Lady, her head lowered and her eyes closed in prayer behind her wedding veil, holding up this long string of sparkling stones. Her devotion to expensive jewelry was well known. But these rosary beads were all four and five carats each, and there must have been a hundred of them. For some reason, I forgot to ask her during the celebration if they were a wedding anniversary present from the president.

I was back home in Connecticut finishing up the *Life* article when the phone rang. It was Imelda, who never doubted that she could influence anyone, especially a journalist, with a few soft words.

"How is the article coming?" she inquired demurely. It was after midnight, but she talked on and on, wanting to know if photographer Co Rentmeester's pictures turned out well, adding that "with your writing, Roy, I'm sure the article will be beautiful."

Remembering how she had once treated me to a four-hour monologue on the misunderstood charms of Libyan strongman Muammar Qaddafi, I finally interrupted her. "By the way," I asked, "were those diamond rosary beads a present from the president?"

"Oh, no, they were my mother's," replied the self-proclaimed poor girl from Leyte, hardly missing a beat.

After twenty more minutes I interrupted her again, stating that I really had to get off the phone and finish writing the article, because I, too, would be celebrating a wedding anniversary the following day. The next morning a truck from the Waldorf Astoria hotel florist in Manhattan rolled into our driveway in Connecticut. There were so many flowers, they smothered the dining room table.

Life's eight-page layout was striking. Imelda looked almost beatific praying with her diamond rosary beads in the opening picture. This was followed by another stunning full-page overhead shot of her entering the glittering main foyer of the newly renovated presidential palace on the arm of twenty-one-year-old son, Ferdinand, Jr., or "Bongbong," as he was nicknamed. Next came a close-up of the president and First Lady, gazing adoringly into each other's eyes as they solemnly renewed their marriage vows, a Philippine custom on silver anniversaries. And after that, a shot of them dancing alone on a floor strewn with rose petals in front of the applauding guests. But the most striking photograph of all was a double-truck of Imelda, clad in a tailored, pea-green jump suit with matching parasol in hand, wading shoes and all into the sea to greet a group of fishermen's children on her native island of Leyte. Together they were singing "Bagong Lipunan," saluting the "New Society," Ferdinand Marcos's martial-law regime. (In 1995, these same children and their friends, grown to voting age, would elect her their congresswoman from Leyte.)

The last page, almost all text, was devoted to the pearls of wisdom dropped by the First Lady during our week-long tour of the islands together. She didn't care if those pearls were genuine or not as long as they were quotable. And they usually were. To wit:

• "Power is ugly if it is used for self, but if it is used for the greater goal of your people and country, it is the ultimate art."

• "It's a hypocrite who says, 'I don't want to be beautiful.' Who is the girl in the world who does not like jewelry? Our people understand this. They say, 'Imelda's our representative, our mama. She cannot dress like a hobo.' Even on trips to the poor provinces, the important thing is to go as someone who has made a little success in life. You must serve as a symbol of prosperity."

• "To all Americans I keep saying, 'Hey, you're nice people, but why are you such masochists? You're always ashamed of being wealthy, white, tall, good-looking people.' What's wrong with that?"

• "You can love others, but you have to love yourself first. That's why I like Muhammad Ali."

• "They tell me, 'Mrs. Marcos, you're always jet-setting.' It so happens that the presidents, prime ministers, and kings I meet do not ride in rowboats."

• "I have no ambition to become First Lady of the world. I'm content to be First Lady of this island country, and have always given my best to our people—all my energy, all my ideas, all my love. I will be judged by them and by history as to what I have done."

At that time neither the Filipinos nor history had cast their final verdict on her. Life's colorful, uncontroversial photo essay, with those little gems printed in bold type at the end, naturally pleased Mrs. Marcos. She was furious, however, with my Fortune article, which told of the business community's fear of her personal extravagance and reckless public spending. Or, as one Filipino banker put it: "The way she confused cloud nine with the bottom line."

One of her most worrisome business innovations was her "big brother" plan for getting the three hundred largest Philippine corporations to adopt a town and provide it with modern managerial and technical know-how. But, as I pointed out in Fortune, many of those big brothers regarded this concept as another of the First Lady's hidden levies, just as they joked that the B.I.R. that took the biggest chunk of their profits was not the Bureau of International Revenue, but the Bureau of Imelda Romualdez (her maiden name). "It's the rich," she had bragged to me, "that you can terrorize, not the poor. The poor have nothing to lose."

That barb, my article pointed out, didn't apply to other members of the Romualdez clan, who were all very rich. One brother, "Bejo" (Alfredo Romualdez), controlled the enormously profitable gambling monopoly. Another brother, "Kokoy" (Benjamin Romualdez), the governor of Leyte, and later the ambassador to the U.S., controlled banks and the Manila light and power monopoly as well as one of the few newspapers permitted to publish under martial law. Imelda's sister, Alita Martel, had also become extremely wealthy, partly from ownership of a block-square shopping plaza built on city property previously designated for a zoo.

Imelda scoffed at those connections. She observed that in authoritarian regimes, the first family is usually accused of owning just about everything. As for her wealthy brothers, sister, cousins, and in-laws, she simply said: "Sometimes you have smart relatives who can make it." Then she added, "My dear, there are always people who are just a little faster, more brilliant, and more aggressive."

Her explanation gave rise to the title of the paperback bestseller published clandestinely by a group of businessmen about the extent of crony capitalism in the Philippines. Unfortunately for me, an asterisk appeared after the book's title—*Some Are Smarter Than Others*—referring to the source of the quotation. "From an article by Roy Rowan in *Fortune* magazine," it stated on the cover.

For the next four years I was persona non grata in the Philippines. But the crisis of confidence caused by the cronyism revealed in that book finally forced the Marcoses to try to calm the growing fears of American investors. *Fortune* was a good place to start. And so in November 1983 I was invited back to interview the president, although by then he was receiving few visitors. Appearing shrunken and drained of color, he was rumored to be seriously ill with a kidney disorder. He was also under siege for the assassination of his old political foe, Benigño Aquino, Jr. Three months earlier, Aquino had been shot dead stepping off a plane in the Manila airport. And rumors still swirled that Marcos had ordered his murder, since Aquino was being guarded by government security agents.

Even so, the old dictator talked tough as ever. His eyes glistened as if they were about to tear when he spoke of the "shameful tragedy of

Ninoy," as Aquino was affectionately known to his supporters. "Whoever the guilty parties are, they're going to be punished," promised Marcos, though everybody knew the commission he appointed to investigate the murder was rigged. Marcos also said he recognized the pressures for economic reform being brought on him by local business leaders. "But they're the ones," he claimed, "who are concealing and salting away dollars in Switzerland and the U.S." During our hour-long conversation he never hinted once that his wife's and her family's greed might be undermining his administration.

By the time I returned to Manila again in February 1986, anti-Marcos sentiment was boiling over. The vice chief of the Armed Forces, Lieutenant General Fidel Ramos (now president), and Defense Minister Juan Ponce Enrile, had defected, accusing their commander in chief of fraud in the special presidential election he had just called.

A full-scale rebellion seemed imminent. Government soldiers and tanks stood at the ready while women protesters, armed only with rosaries and flowers, massed in front of the tanks. Other candle-carrying demonstrators surged through the streets. "Cory! Cory!" they chanted, invoking the nickname of Aquino's slight, bespectacled widow, who had challenged Marcos and lost in an election disrupted by ballot-stealing and bloodshed.

Those unforgettable images of huge crowds snaking along Roxas Boulevard and storming the streets leading to the palace were labeled "people power" by the press, and were being published and televised all over the world. "Democracy," I noted, "is always more picturesque seizing government than in governing."

Ferdinand and Imelda Marcos had become virtual prisoners in their own palace when I received a mysterious telephone call from "Baby," the First Lady's secretary. "Be in the lobby of your hotel at seven-thirty tonight," she said, and then, without providing any further details, hung up.

The Manila Hotel during those tense days was packed with foreign correspondents, forcing everybody to double up. I was sharing a suite with Peter Jennings of ABC, though I'd never met him before. The hotel lobby, also overpopulated by the press, struck me as a strange place to receive a secret emissary from Malacañang Palace, if that's what was going to happen.

At the appointed hour I spotted the First Lady's beribboned military aid surreptitiously scanning the cavernous lobby. He knew me well from my various visits to the palace, and giving a slight nod of recognition, indicated that I was to follow him. We entered the hotel's elegant Italian restaurant which had been closed for several days because of all the commotion. There, at a long table, sandwiched between two more officers, sat Imelda herself, dressed to kill.

"Roy, I'm so happy you could join me," she gushed. The revolution brewing right outside the hotel might just as well have been happening in Zimbabwe. And my position high on the First Lady's enemies list no longer seemed to matter. "You remember, Roy, this is my favorite restaurant," she added, continuing to radiate good cheer as a covey of waiters began putting plates of prosciutto and melon, cold langouste, and other appetizers on the table. The Manila Hotel had always been part of Imelda's private domain, and she obviously had succeeded in cajoling the management into opening the restaurant specially for her.

Our conversation touched only briefly on the explosive political situation. The president, she explained, had called for a "snap election," as she called it, when she was away in Japan. "I said, 'Oh, no!' But it turned out to be an enriching and ennobling experience. I was the advance party and went to all the lions' dens where the opposition was strongest."

Imelda admitted to "some little imperfections" during the voting. "But how can you cheat in 93,000 precincts?" she asked innocently. I was suddenly reminded of California congressman Pete Stark's comment after Mrs. Marcos faced a group of House members probing her husband's human rights violations. "It was like talking to the tooth fairy," Stark declared. "She never heard the charges."

We were having this same kind of tooth fairy conversation, and the First Lady kept it percolating for several hours with few interruptions. Once, visiting PR specialist Charles Black, formerly a top aide to Senator Bob Dole, was escorted to the table to confer briefly with the First Lady. Black's Washington firm, I'd heard, was being paid $900,000 to smooth over the stolen election and make Marcos's victory look a little more credible.

Another time she requested the yellow legal pad her aide always kept handy for her—usually to sketch out for baffled listeners the confusing lines of authority connecting her various government posts. But this time she sketched a quick map of the Philippines. Then, with a bold stroke of her Magic Marker, she drew a longitudinal line through Manila.

"Roy, everything above this line," she explained, "is the president's sphere of influence. Everything below is mine." But lest I thought she was suddenly claiming jurisdiction over all her ailing husband's southern territory, she added, smiling angelically, "I mean as First Lady I'm going to spend my days down there being mother to the poor. It was the poor from that area who voted for Marcos. The only people who'll go hungry are the lazy ones."

Four days later the Iron Butterfly and her family flew off to exile in Hawaii as the exploding force of "people power" propelled Corazon Aquino into Malacañang Palace. Filipinos danced in the streets celebrating the deposed president's departure—"sort of a cash-and-carry exit," I called it, in which Imelda, her husband, and their eighty-eight-member entourage took along twenty-two boxes of freshly minted pesos and 278 crates of jewelry, artworks, gold, and real estate deeds. That cache became merely the first round in a long tug-of-war with the new government, which laid claim to the estimated $5 billion loot squirreled away by the Marcoses in U.S. and Swiss banks. (In 1995 the Swiss government agreed to return $475 million held by the Marcos family to the Philippines.)

Ferdinand Marcos died in Hawaii in 1989. Four years later Imelda finally obtained permission to bring his body back to the Philippines for burial in Batac, his hometown in northern Luzon. The newspaper picture of the former First Lady, her head bowed in prayer, peering sadly through her black mourning veil at the polished coffin, reminded me of *Life*'s portrait of this same woman taken fourteen years earlier at her glittering silver anniversary celebration. Only then her veil was white, and in her hand were those incredible diamond beads, which became a symbol of her own undoing after Filipino investigators traced them back to one of her wild shopping sprees in New York City.

In making a mental comparison of those two photographs, it struck me that the Marcos family's hunger for wealth was her obsession, not his. The Philippine president was more concerned about his place in history than he was in high living. He ate sparingly, dressed simply and exercised strenuously to keep physically fit. Sure, he loved power, but hated its ceremonial functions and fancy trappings.

Back in 1972, when Ferdinand Marcos first declared martial law, I reported: "He did it to save his country from anarchy." Looking back, I don't believe he did it to expropriate other people's businesses for his wife and her relatives. So how did such insidious corruption bring him to this ignominious end? Catching the Iron Butterfly had been easy. But trying to trim her wings was another matter.

CHAPTER XXIV

"Silver Thursday"

FOR A MAN OF SUCH ENORMOUS PERSONAL WEALTH, expansive physical
size, and expressive verbal flair—"a billion dollars ain't what it used to
be"—Nelson Bunker Hunt had succeeded in escaping public notice for
most of his career. Brother William Herbert Hunt, a little sleeker
shaped and smoother talking but no less rich, had remained equally
unobtrusive. But suddenly there they were in May 1980, cheek by jowl,
facing the television cameras with their right hands upraised, solemnly
swearing to tell the whole truth, and nothing but the truth, to one
congressional committee after another.

No, they swore, they weren't trying to corner the world's supply of
silver. They had simply lost faith in paper money. No, they weren't
shipping vast vaultloads of silver abroad, just exchanging U.S. warehouse receipts for those in Europe. No, they weren't the master manipu-
lators of America's commodity futures market, but its principal victims.
And the staggering $1.7 billion-dollar tab they ran up in the first three
months of 1980 seemed to bear out this contention. Mired in debt,
the afflicted pair indicated that they were considering suing all those
who had defrauded them by changing the rules of the futures game
when they were ahead.

This studiously posed picture of two wounded innocents was the
impression I had of the Hunts during the congressional investigation
into the collapse of the silver market on March 27, the day that had
become known as "silver Thursday." Prior to their rare public appearances, which I avidly covered for *Fortune* along with the rest of the

press, the brothers had evoked an entirely different image. They had been seen as the wealth-bloated sons of the legendary Texas oil baron H. L. Hunt—an odd couple of whippersnapper boys trying to stake out even wider claims than their multibillionaire father. The sums of what they gathered or dispensed hardly seemed to matter. Or as Bunker once said: "Money never meant anything to us. It was just sort of how we kept score."

Bunker, obviously, had been scoring well, amassing 3.5 million acres of real estate, including much of downtown Anchorage, 95,000 head of cattle, and 700 Thoroughbred racehorses, besides all the oil, gas, and coal properties that he and Herbert had added to their tremendous inheritance.

By my count, Bunker alone had become far richer than H.L. ever was. All his investments just seemed naturally to bloom and multiply. He had also become every bit as enthusiastic a John Bircher as his dad—a Texas-sized Christian, moreover, who pledged to help raise a cool billion dollars for evangelist Bill Bright's Campus Crusade by corralling one thousand tycoons to drop donations of a million each. His invitations to fund-raising prayer meetings that "could help determine the destiny of civilization" were amiably signed "Bunker."

As if the public glimpses of the Hunts needed more colorful daubing, a final bit of embellishment had been provided by their younger brother, Lamar. It was he who had indulged in the sport of buying up all those teams—the Kansas City Chiefs, the now-defunct Dallas Tornado soccer team, a piece of the Chicago Bulls, and the World Championship Tennis tour. This completed the family portrait until silver Thursday came along. Suddenly, all seemed blighted. Incredibly for H.L.'s scions, big chunks of the old family assets, plus all the newer acquisitions, had to be hocked so they could hang on to their $4 billion hoard of silver.

I had already turned out two articles for *Fortune* on the Hunt brothers' spectacular foray into the silver market, as the price of the metal spiraled up from $11 an ounce to $50 before crashing back down to $10.80 on silver Thursday. My first piece, titled "A Hunt Crony Tells All," was based on a fifty-one-page sworn deposition that one of the lawyers for the House Subcommittee on Commerce, Consumer, and Monetary Affairs had allowed me to look at. The signer of the deposition, one William Bledsoe, was a disgruntled former Hunt employee who charged Bunker and Herbert with acting in concert to try to corner the world silver market, despite their assertions that they were purchasing silver individually, and merely as an investment. According to Bledsoe, "their strategy was determined daily whether they would buy in their own names or in family or corporate names." The brothers, he claimed, even bought silver in the name of their pal, C. W. "Catfish" Smith, and Ted Curtain, Bunker's horse trainer in Ireland.

My second article, titled "Who Guards Whom at the Commodity Exchange," described how its chummy, self-regulated board of governors, who were also traders, had purposely sent the price of silver into a tumble to protect their own highly speculative short positions. The Hunts had cried foul, accusing the Comex governors of "manipulative action." Although Congress and the public managed to suppress any tiny quiver of compassion, my *Fortune* piece called the Hunts' accusations "pertinent and accurate." In my mind, there was no question that the Comex governors were trying to mask their roles as double agents—as officials and traders, as rulers and the ruled.

What I still wanted was to interview Bunker and Herbert Hunt, something they had never allowed. I had tried just about everything I could think of to win their confidence. At one of the congressional hearings I dashed up to the witness table where they were testifying and thrust a letter into Bunker's hands. "The public is entitled to hear your side of this lopsided story," my letter pleaded. No response. I followed up the letter by telephoning Marge Johnson, Herbert's secretary in Dallas. She gave me a ten-minute religious sermon, but no other encouragement.

Finally, I flew to Texas and persuaded Clint Murchison, Jr., owner of the Dallas Cowboys, to intercede with his friends the Hunts on my behalf. I had done a *Life* article on the Murchisons and had gotten to know Clint quite well. In fact, when our *Life* touch football team had played Bobby Kennedy's fleet-footed Justice Department team in Washington many years before, Clint produced former Cowboy quarterback Eddie LeBaron to play for us. With LeBaron's passing we squeaked out an 18-to-18 tie with Bobby's much faster players. But even Clint struck out with the Hunts.

Jimmy Cleaver, another Dallas friend of mine, had business dealings with the Hunts, and he offered to do what he could. Cleaver couldn't do anything either, but he had a suggestion. An acquaintance of his at the PR agency Hill & Knowlton had been hired by the Hunts to try to salvage their business reputations following the damaging congressional hearings.

The PR man made it clear that the two brothers had shunned the press, not just because they were instinctively private people, or had been counseled by their attorneys to keep quiet. They had shunned it, he explained, because, as Bunker said, according to his conspiracy theory, "the same Comex guys in New York that were able to break the market were also able to get the media to attack its victims—which happened to be us."

"Perhaps *you* can persuade Herbert to cooperate," the PR man told me. "Bunker's a harder case." He then arranged for me to go for a morning jog with Herbert around the track that circles Bachman Lake in Dallas. "You can make your own pitch along the way," he added.

It was six A.M. and the scorched sky over Dallas indicated the dawning of yet another 105-degree July day, when Herbert Hunt and I commenced our four-mile run around the lake. "The trouble with those congressional hearings," he started off telling me, "is they're no-win deals. You may not get convicted, but you sure as hell don't get acquitted either."

When the four miles were finished, Herbert, drenched in sweat, climbed into his eight-year-old green Mercedes. "I drive my wife's hand-me-downs," he explained, inviting me to ride home with him.

So far so good, I thought as we drove back to the manicured suburb of University Park, where he and his family lived. Herbert struck me as a gracious, unassuming man of fifty-one, whose most aggressive trait appeared to be a war against an appetite that could easily expand him into Bunker's more generous proportions. "I'm strictly a weight-control jogger," he explained. "I'm not out there for fun." Even though he said he'd been running since he was in his early thirties, he admitted to still being twenty pounds too heavy.

Back at his house, he invited me to come in, and I soon saw why the pounds didn't melt away from all his running. A quick dip in the pool was followed by a solo dash around the big kitchen in dripping trunks while he dished up a truck driver's breakfast—half a cantaloupe, half a Texas Ruby grapefruit, a tumbler full of orange juice, and two soft-boiled eggs served in a soup bowl with a couple of slices of crumbled toast thrown in. "Herbert is a much better cook than I am," said his wife, Nancy, who explained that since the family had only a part-time maid, he got lots of practice.

Bunker, she said, is an even more prodigious eater, though she recalled he once dropped fifty pounds, scaling down to Herbert's size. "That's when he was courting Caroline. As soon as they were married he returned to his old eating habits and poundage. 'The honeymoon's over,' Bunker announced."

As Herbert quickly added, the differences between him and his older brother went far beyond their physical size. "Bunker," he said, "is very far-sighted, very perceptive. He's not one to fool with details. He prefers to conceive something and then step back." Herbert, on the other hand, admitted that "I get more involved in the details."

On this particular Saturday morning, one detail that concerned Herbert was Bunker's whereabouts. Apparently, there were some contracts for Bunker to sign. Bunker had been in Europe for thirteen days. He and Herbert had talked on the trans-Atlantic telephone several times, but for the past couple of days Bunker had been out of touch. "He doesn't make hotel reservations," explained Herbert, "and he just shows up at the airport and waits in line to fly standby."

By now I realized that Herbert had decided to cooperate on an article about the role the brothers played in the climb and collapse of silver. He made it clear, however, that while he was willing to tell me his side of the scary silver drama, he couldn't promise that Bunker would also talk to me. "You'll have to ask him yourself," he said. "That is, if he ever comes home."

Another concern of Herbert's that day was the flood of mail they were receiving—much of it addressed simply: "Hunt Brothers, Dallas." Some letters were quite laudatory. "You may be taking a lot of flak," wrote an engineer, "but we in the mining industry consider you heroes." A Ph.D. in Bethesda, Maryland, wrote that he had asked the Franklin Mint to create a silver medal honoring the Hunt brothers as a scholarship-fund-raising device. "I hope your sense of humor will authorize me to have the medal struck," added the professor.

Many other letters were hostile. Some echoed the question posed by Congressman John Conyers of Michigan at one of the hearings. "How could the Hunt brothers have received a $1.1 billion bank bailout arranged by Federal Reserve chairman Paul Volker, while Chrysler was having so much difficulty obtaining one?" To Herbert the difference was perfectly clear. "Chrysler needed a government guarantee," he pointed out. "The Hunts didn't need any guarantee at all because we have the assets."

After he crisply uttered those last four words, Herbert went on to make an astonishing disclosure about the Hunts' riches. Their indebtedness at that time was notorious. Just about every income-producing asset owned by the two brothers, as well as other properties owned jointly with the rest of the Hunt clan, had been pledged as collateral against the $1.1 billion bank loan that saved Bunker and Herbert from dumping their remaining 63 million ounces of silver on a depressed market. What was not known was the extent to which the collateral exceeded the loan. In Herbert's words, "The terms of the loan were awful tough—the collateral is probably eight or nine times as large."

In a backhanded way, Herbert was saying those assets were worth a staggering $8 or $9 billion. Even if a sizable chunk had to be sold off to repay the bank loan, the Hunts would have still been $8 billion away from the poorhouse. That figure included the brothers' hoard of silver, which after a temporary rebound was worth enough to cover the loan all by itself. Even if a calamity drove silver prices through the floor—which eventually happened—the Hunt family would only be down to its last $7 billion.

Never in history, I thought, had a family gone so deeply in hock with so little hardship. Still, Herbert talked about that bank loan like any strapped homeowner who wants to get the finance company off his back. "We're going to work hard getting it paid off," he vowed. Some securities, he indicated, had already been liquidated. But no silver had been disposed of, and he expected it wouldn't have to be before the bullion regained the real value he and Bunker believed it had. "I personally think the price of silver is very cheap at this point," he said, though history proved him wrong. It's a lot cheaper today.

By mid-morning a major search was mounted for Bunker. His wife, Caroline, who was visiting friends in Houston, was called to see if she'd heard anything. Tom Whitaker, a former FBI man and the Hunt Energy Corporation vice president in Dallas, telephoned several hotels in London, as well as Bunker's horse trainer in Paris, all without success. Herbert had just about accepted the possibility that his peripatetic brother might not reappear until the yearling sale in Lexington, Kentucky, a week hence, when the doorbell rang. "Uncle Bunker's here," announced Herbert's son, David.

An effusive man in ballooning sports shirt and slacks sallied in, smiling. He did not resemble the dour, fat-cat figure that had stood before the House Subcommittee on Commerce, Consumer, and Monetary Affairs to face accusations that he tried to corner the world's supply of silver. Instead, he was a picture of jauntiness. Before Herbert could even ask his brother how he felt about having a *Fortune* writer around to record his thoughts, the Bunkerisms started seeping out: "When they give you a bill at the Ritz, you think you've bought the place." "No such thing as a bad meal in Paris—or a cheap one." "The disease of socialism is pretty far along over there."

The missing brother's return was a cause for celebration. With Uncle Bunker at the wheel of his mud-spattered maroon Cadillac DeVille, followed by a caravan of nephews, nieces, and spouses, the Hunt clan headed for a restaurant named Chiquita. Chiquita, as Bunker was quick to observe, was not one of Dallas's fancier Mexican eateries. The Hunts entered unnoticed by the other customers, which, I discovered during the next few days, seemed to be the case wherever they went. Yet the trust funds represented around that long, bare-board restaurant table comprised one of the greatest concentrations of wealth in the world.

Herbert had already explained how that massive family fortune, involving some two hundred separate entities, was administered. Once a month all the Hunts, down to the youngest grandchild, were invited to the Hunt Energy Corporation headquarters for what amounted to a general information session. A recap of the financial statements was presented. The amount spent purchasing new oil and gas leases was pointed out, and the various family members were then billed for their share of the overhead. In the case of the $1.1 billion loan agreement following the collapse of silver, every member of the family was asked by the banks to concur. "We're not a highly structured organization," said Herbert. "That's probably a weakness. The family members are free to pick and choose the businesses they want to get into."

Bunker, though hardly a finicky eater, was not an aficionado of hot Mexican food. "One of these Mexican meals a month is enough for me," he announced. In any case, he kept coating his tortillas and tacos with butter, either to slake the fire or to make them slide down more easily.

Horse racing, which he regarded as an "irresistible combination of business, sport, and genetics," was the main topic of the lunch conversation. Bunker owned such outstanding Thoroughbreds as Exceller, Emprey, and Dahlia, the 1973 and 1974 winner of the Diamond Stakes at Ascot.

Even if he wanted to abandon his expensive hobby, Bunker claimed he couldn't. "I've got seven hundred racehorses and they're all mortgaged," he explained. "But horse racing is a way of life for me, and I can still do whatever I want with my horses even while they're hocked."

Herbert admitted he didn't care for horses. As a boy he said he kept all kinds of animals around the house, including chickens, turkeys, pigs, and a pet deer. "But now," he added, "I don't want anything that can get sick and die on me. I'd rather have something that just rusts away, like an oil rig."

Herbert and Bunker Hunt lived only about a dozen blocks from each other. Nevertheless, the brothers were miles apart in taste, temperament, and style, as I found out in the next three days of interviewing—a sort of progressive journalistic feast that moved from their office, through their homes, clubs, and Bunker's Circle T ranch. Bunker, despite his colorful speech, was more sophisticated than Herbert. He spent more time jetting around the world—though always economy class—hobnobbing with royalty or the moguls of business. His house in Highland Park was grander and more elegantly furnished, displaying the artistic treasures of frequent foreign travel—an inlaid coromandel screen, a Waterford crystal chandelier, a portrait of Lord Lyttelton painted by the eighteenth-century British artist George Romney. Also predominantly displayed was a Frederic Remington bronze.

Herbert admitted his taste in art tended toward "photographic paintings with sharp, realistic images." He said he often bought pictures simply for their frames, and his favorite sport scene came from the Collector Covey in a shopping center within strolling distance from his house.

The brothers also differed in the way they expressed their opinions, which did not always coincide. Herbert, who usually served as the spokesman for the two, as he did during the congressional hearings, was much more restrained. Bunker was irrepressible in his scorn for such eastern establishment outfits as the *New York Times*, the Trilateral Commission, and especially for the short sellers on the Comex board of governors, who in his opinion caused silver prices to tumble. "All those commodity exchanges," fumed Bunker, "are run by the shorts, for the benefit of the shorts, and with the connivance of the shorts."

For all their differences, the brothers spoke of their father, the legendary H. L. (Haroldson Lafayette) Hunt, with equal reverence. "He was a phenomenon," claimed Bunker. "At his peak he was much the smartest fella I ever met, a mathematical wizard. He just always knew the best thing to do."

Would the old man have approved of his sons' foray into silver? "He would have liked the investment," mused Bunker, "but not the rules."

Herbert was not so sure H.L. would have agreed with their strategy in silver. "Dad said, 'Never borrow money unless you can get it paid back.' I guess I didn't listen well enough."

What Herbert remembered most fondly about his father was the unassertive way he let his children decide what they wanted to do in life. When Herbert informed him that he had decided to major in geology at Washington and Lee, H.L. cracked: "That's going to cost us millions. You'll end up drilling wells just to prove something rather than to find oil." Herbert said his father "never pushed any of us to do one thing or another. But since he worked eleven or twelve hours a day, *we* just kind of grew up working."

The office then shared by the brothers surveyed Dallas's blooming skyline from the twenty-fifth floor of the First National Bank Building. A hole in the ground directly below marked the spot where their fifty-story Placid Oil Building now stands. But until it was built, Bunker and Herbert continued to operate out of their aging quarters with Astroturflike carpeting that served as Hunt Energy's executive suite.

Nelson Bunker Hunt, chairman of the board, occupied the room on the right. Its walls were adorned with racehorse portraits and a painting of H.L. playing checkers with a country storekeeper. A sign outside of his door suggested: IF YOU MUST SMOKE, DO NOT EXHALE. William Herbert Hunt, vice president of Hunt Energy, occupied the room on the left. Its windowsill was laden with the trophies of an oil and gas career—drilling cores, rock samples, and little bottles filled with dark, viscous fluids from newly discovered wells. An 1879 silver dollar embedded in Lucite was a gift from the brokerage firm Bache Halsey Stuart Shields (now Prudential Securities), through which the Hunts bought a lot of their silver and whose margin calls they couldn't meet when the price skidded.

In the reception area separating the two offices sat the two secretaries who had faithfully guarded the Hunt brothers' doors for a grand total of forty-two years. White-coiffed Lois Snow served Bunker Hunt. Devoutly religious Marge Johnson, whom I had spoken with during my unsuccessful attempts to reach the Hunts, took care of Herbert. "Marge thinks it's her God-given duty to convert people to Christianity," he said. "You should have heard her work on a few of those New York silver traders over the phone when I put them on hold." Marge admired her boss's courage and tenacity, and would boast to any visitor in vivid detail how Herbert bravely rode out Hurricane Betsy in 1954 on an oil rig off New Orleans.

How both brothers rode out the storm in silver was the real story I wanted to write, and the story only they could tell. Taking turns, they provided an exciting blow-by-blow account of what had taken place.

The high drama, said Herbert, really began in the fall of 1979 when he walked unannounced into the New York office of Mocatta Metals Corporation, which had bet heavily against the steep price rise in silver and had a precariously large short position. The company's chairman, Henry Jarecki, a former Yale Medical School professor, was in turmoil. "He was getting eaten alive by margin calls," recounted Herbert. "Between us, Bunker and I had put up 10.7 million ounces of silver with Mocatta. But suddenly I discovered that Jarecki had hocked our silver for as much as the banks would lend him—about $185 million, I believe.

"As soon as I found out that Jarecki was having financial problems, I called Bunker and said, 'You better come up here and look after your own interests,' Bunker hustled up to New York. We spent most of the next seven days in the Mocatta office. We did everything but sleep there. They brought in dinner about ten or eleven each night. And each day we went out and bought another shirt."

Bunker chimed in with his own memories of the Mocatta episode. "When the price of silver is going up," he said, "Jarecki would give you almost a religious speech about how he's fully hedged." In other words, as Bunker told it, Jarecki claimed to have enough bullion on hand to cover his short position in case the price went up. "But let me tell you," continued Bunker, "I was concerned about getting our silver back before he blew it."

One day when the price of silver pushed up past $17, Herbert recalled, Jarecki rushed into his office and announced: "When it hits $22.90 I'm broke—Mocatta is insolvent."

"A few minutes later," added Herbert, "he came back in even more alarmed and said: 'I've miscalculated. The figure's a little lower.'"

Herbert and Bunker got their bullion back, but only through a convoluted deal with a Bermuda-based international company that the Hunt family owned jointly with a pair of Saudi partners. Jarecki disputed the Hunts' claims that he borrowed so heavily on their bullion, or that Mocatta's solvency was ever in question. His company had all the collateral and lines of credit it needed, he said.

Later, after the price of silver plunged, the Mocatta chairman admitted to me that "Bunker Hunt cost me a lot of sleep. But now for every hour he's cost *me* I'm going to make *him* lose ten."

The story amused Bunker. "I want you to know I'm a very good sleeper," he drawled. "I may lose money, but I don't lose sleep."

Jarecki, however, was one of the twenty-three Comex governors who changed the rules of the silver game. With the Hunts holding as much as 80 million ounces and the price spiraling to $50 an ounce, Comex issued an emergency edict that banned all futures trading except for the purposes of liquidating speculative positions. The sudden rule change, the Hunts and others claimed, helped bring about the collapse in silver prices. Once it was imposed, said Bunker, "there was no way to sell anything except at a distressed price. Jarecki and the other shorts were sitting on the Comex board, and we were sitting down here in Dallas long, trusting them."

After the crash on silver Thursday, the Hunt brothers stated that they were thinking of suing Comex on the grounds that the rule changes were anything but market neutral. Because they considered themselves the victims and not the villains, they wondered why the politicians and press kept picking on them. "I feel like the lady who had her purse snatched and then got arrested for indecent exposure because her clothes were ripped," said Herbert.

But for all the grief silver brought the Hunts, they still considered it an excellent investment. "I'll stick to my prediction of 5 to 1," said Bunker, meaning that's how he appraised the true gold-silver value ratio. By Bunker's reckoning, silver should really be selling at $125 an ounce instead of slightly more than $5, as it is today. "Practically all the gold mined since the days of the pharaohs," he reasoned, "remains stashed away in strongboxes, while the world's silver supply is constantly being used up." That just goes to prove how bad a miscalculation even a multibillionaire can make—an error in judgement that ended in a wildly expensive series of suits and countersuits.

In 1988, with the consortium of banks still impatiently trying to recover part of the huge $1.1 billion bailout loan arranged by Fed chairman Paul Volker, I continued to follow the brothers' legal skirmishing with great interest—occasionally getting an update from Herbert when I was in Dallas and called him for lunch.

He seemed chagrined that he and Bunker had finally been driven to file for personal bankruptcy. "They were the largest personal bankruptcies ever filed in the U.S.," announced one of the trustees responsible for liquidating the brothers' assets. But when the banks finally tried to sell the properties, they charged that large portions of Bunker and Herbert's wealth had been transferred into a tangle of Hunt family trusts, partnerships, and corporations belonging to some thirty-six children and grandchildren.

The brothers countered that the transfers were made for tax and estate planning, not to fend off creditors. And so back to court they all went. The trustees sued the brothers, and Bunker and Herbert retaliated by suing the banks for trying to force them out of business. As the battle raged, whole planeloads of lawyers were flying in and out of Dallas every week. "This is really a fight to make the world safe for capitalism," claimed one of the exasperated creditors. By 1994, when the legal bills for both sides reached $20 million, settlements were finally agreed upon—but for less than one fifth of the $1.1 billion loan.

Still, it was pointless speculating on how poor the two brothers might have become. Though after Herbert mentioned to me one day that he had taken to ordering his shirts and shorts from a Lands' End catalogue, I wondered if this was just bit of poor-mouthing for the press. I had also read that Bunker, who usually ate lunch at the Tower Club atop the downtown office building he and Herbert once owned, was reduced to a noontime meal of a can of chili poured over Fritos. Were they down to their last billion, as recent articles describing how they'd squandered their patrimony suggested? There was no way to tell. But then I remembered what Bunker had told me during one interview session when I bluntly asked what he was worth. "I have no idea," he answered. "But I do know that people who know how much they're worth generally aren't worth much."

CHAPTER XXV

Bunker's Big Sister

WHILE HER YOUNGER BROTHERS Bunker and Herbert were talking disastrous plunges in sugar, soybeans, and silver, big sister Caroline remained discreet. Although she has often been called "the richest woman in America," with a vast and wide variety of gas, oil, and property holdings, at first she seemed committed to a rather lowly commodity—pumpkins. But then, she always was dippy about pumpkins, having published a 275-page cookbook called *The Compleat Pumpkin Eater*. Together with her second husband, Hugo "Buddy" Schoellkopf, a pilot, she also started a charter plane service named Pumpkin Air that flew a flock of bright orange helicopters and Cessnas. Then, in 1981, she emerged as the owner of a brand-new pumpkin-colored hotel, The Mansion on Turtle Creek, which despite its Halloweenish exterior became the most elegant place to eat and sleep in Dallas, and still is. Soon it was evident that her power, wealth, and impeccable taste would be applied to creating more beautiful structures and providing other magnificent services for people who appreciated—and could pay for—those luxuries.

I first met Caroline Hunt while writing the *Fortune* series on the thrills and spills that her rotund brothers were taking in the commodity pits. She was attractive and smart, all right, and much more stylish. But I didn't pay any attention to her since she hadn't taken part in their wild and ruinous gamble to corner the silver market. "I never got interested in silver myself," she told me. "Perhaps because it wasn't pumpkin-colored." That, of course, wasn't the real reason. This polite, unassuming woman obviously took a much more conservative view of what to do with her rich inheritance. Besides, her personality and business perspective contrasted sharply with her brothers'.

Although Bunker and Herbert had been forced to hock her assets along with the rest of the family's following the collapse of silver prices, she had plenty of spare cash for a fling in the luxury hotel field—part of an initial $350 million investment she talked about making in eight or ten cities. But more impressive than all the money she was prepared to spend was the personal attention she paid to details of The Mansion on Turtle Creek. Her care and exquisite taste are what drew my attention to this unusual woman, and made me decide to write a separate article about her for *Fortune*.

She insisted on everything in the 144-room hotel being designed to please the eye and pamper the needs of the most critical guest. In the front foyer she saw to it that a great jardiniere was replenished every three days with thirty dozen gladiolus flown in from Holland. To the ninth-floor penthouse suites she added such touches as antique celadon porcelain bowls and Ming Dynasty dishes along with the mundane modern conveniences of microwave ovens and garbage compactors. Even the guests in single rooms found peonies, a Neiman-Marcus credit card, a hand-painted bottle of champagne with a souvenir glass to match, plus a tiny carafe of crème de cassis to mix with the champagne to produce a kir—all provided with a personal note of welcome from Caroline.

She also made sure that sumptuous service matched those lavish trappings. The hotel's staff-to-guest ratio was two to one. Included among its 290 original employees were two Somalian refugee brass polishers and a Texas college girl who spent all day going from room to room massaging the dust off the palm fronds so they would absorb more light. Guests dialing 173 for laundry would hear a British-accented voice answer: "This is Stewart in behalf of housekeeping." But the opulence Caroline insisted on providing her guests wasn't the kind of thing she relished herself. "I'm a little more stark," she said. "Exclusivity is not my thing."

Until she bought the Mansion, Caroline told me, "I never had much interest in business of any sort. My energy was focused on family life." Most of her time, she explained, was devoted to raising her five children. This zealous nest-tending, I suspected, was a reaction to her bigamist, oil-baron father, who sired eight daughters and seven sons with three wives, and whom she reportedly compared to King Ibn Saud of Saudi Arabia. Obviously, Caroline's view of her father differed sharply from the reverential one expressed by her brothers. "My father liked children just until they got to be six or seven," she once told a friend. "Then he wasn't interested anymore." By the time old H.L. died in 1974, he had seventy living direct descendants.

Daughter Caroline apparently became such a homebody that few people in Dallas knew she was a Hunt. Her hobby was cooking. The ad in her cookbook bragged that she was one of three American women elected to *Commanderie des Cordons Bleus de France.* "With four sons, one daughter, and no cook," she said, "there was ample opportunity to practice." But it was her frugality, not culinary skill, that she claimed prompted her to start collecting pumpkin recipes so she could utilize the leftover pulp of the jack-o'-lanterns.

While her children were growing up, she had little to do with the maze of corporations, partnerships, and trusts that made up the Hunt family fortune. "I did dabble in an investment club," she said. "Not to buy stocks but just because I loved hearing about all those companies." Her outside activities also revolved around family life. She taught Sunday school, became the first woman deacon of the suburban Highland Park Presbyterian Church, a board member of Planned Parenthood, and a trustee of her alma mater, Mary Baldwin College of Staunton, Virginia—quite different from her dad, an ultra-right-winger who began life as a riverboat gambler on the Mississippi, and later proudly admitted: "Everything I do, I do for profit."

During all her do-gooding, the vast Caroline Hunt Trust Estate, of which she was the sole beneficiary, kept on discovering more and more oil. "Drill, drill, drill!" she explained was the family slogan. "But the oil business," she added, "was too scientific for me. I had no idea where to sink a well. So I left all that up to Bunker and Herbert." Along with them, she became a multibillionaire with ample discretionary income for her to invest in building fancy hotels and converting old mansions into modern palaces.

Government investigations and lender threats against the two brothers after the collapse of silver prices finally prompted Caroline and her sister, Margaret, together with a mentally impaired older brother, to separate their assets. But there was no animosity involved in the split-up of the family fortune. "I'm proud of my brothers," Caroline said. "They're wonderful people, excellent citizens, and elders in our church. One is not embarrassed by honest mistakes." Bunker and Herbert, in turn, repeatedly declined to ask their sisters for help during their personal bankruptcy cases.

Caroline's trust came away with a $1 billion package of oil and gas properties, plus ranch and timber lands that generated healthy profits and weren't encumbered by debt. By then her children were grown and she started casting an eye on more entrepreneurial opportunities, the kind only an enormously wealthy woman might entertain. Nevertheless, she still viewed herself as a cautious investor, and preferred to linger over a business decision. "Nothing is black or white," she told me. "And most decisions tend to be emotional anyway."

The sudden detour into hotels was the idea of her eldest son, Stephen Sands (Caroline had all five children with her first husband, Lloyd "Boomer" Sands), who was smitten with the success an acquaintance was having renovating and running elegant small hotels in Washington and Chicago. Steve and his mother had their first site all picked out—an ornate Mediterranean-style mansion that looked out on the nearby skyscrapers of Dallas from the manicured park bordering Turtle Creek. This dilapidated, red-tile-roofed structure, painted green and topped with a white mosque-like minaret, was slated to be razed. "I hated to see anything bulldozed down that deserved to stay," said Caroline.

The old landmark had a colorful past. It had been built by cotton magnate Sheppard King II before he lost his fortune in the Great Depression. Converted to offices, its exotic interior was kept intact. Carved bacchanalian columns from Spain flanked the entrance to the main salon, whose ceiling consisted of 2,400 pieces of elaborately enameled and inlaid wood. Stained-glass windows depicted the English barons witnessing the signing of the Magna Carta at Runnymede, a touch added by the snooty Mrs. King, who liked to remind her "cow-town" (as she referred to Dallas) friends that she was descended from British royalty. But that was before her playboy son, Sheppard King III, embarrassed the family by changing his name to Abdulla and marrying the famous Egyptian belly dancer Samia Gamal.

Steve and Caroline, whose middle name is Rose, quickly formed Rosewood Hotels, Inc. The company bought the run-down King mansion for $1.6 million and spent another $19.4 million renovating the place and converting it into a hotel. "They didn't agree with the concept that less is more," said the interior designer hired to do the job. "They realized that less is less."

That realization explains why even the Mansion's smallest suites were equipped with six telephones, two TVs, a stereo system, and two marble-lined Roman bathrooms. The hotel's forty-man kitchen not only produced the sumptuous fare required of a five-star restaurant, but also served as a classroom for Cordon Bleu commander Caroline. I observed her several times amid the bubbling cauldrons, studying the spry moves of her imported young French *chef de cuisine*. "Now, why are you doing that?" she would ask, and he would patiently explain.

"At my request," she admitted, "a pumpkin cheesecake with a macadamia-nut topping was eventually perfected for our restaurant patrons."

Spurred on by her success in Dallas, Caroline and Rosewood's architects scoured Houston for another old mansion to recycle. But they finally gave up and started from scratch, building a palatial $50 million, 12-story marble structure among the sprouting skyscrapers in a new office park being developed by Tenneco. The 248-room Remington, so named, was geared to the high-flying international oil set. Included in its design was a cozy ballroom that could comfortably seat 250 diners, a rentable twenty-four-seat boardroom perfect for negotiating an oil merger, a business communication center with satellite facilities, a multilingual secretarial service, and a research library. Unfortunately, the Remington opened in 1982 just as oil prices were plummeting. It's low initial occupancy rate couldn't support the high $200,000-per-room construction cost, and Caroline sold the place two years later for an $8 million loss, although Rosewood continued to run the hotel for its new owners, and under its new name, the Houston Ritz-Carlton.

Undiscouraged, Caroline said she was determined to continue building or beautifying existing hotels located in unusual garden-like settings, thereby raising the value of both the structure and land. Expanding westward, her company picked up the picturesque but run-down Bel-Air nestled in a tree-shaded canyon away from Hollywood's throngs. She bought this hotel at auction for $22,737,000 in 1982, following a bidding war with New York arbitrager Ivan Boesky. The bids were sealed. And while Boesky, who already owned a controlling interest in the Beverly Hills Hotel, prematurely announced victory, Rosewood's offer turned out to be a smidgin ($8,161.42) higher. Caroline then poured $12.7 million more into renovations and expansion, although she was warned by old pros in the hotel business that her expensive gamble might never pay off. Seven years later Rosewood sold the Bel-Air to a Japanese company for $110 million—representing a record price of $1.2 million per room, or two-and-a-half times what Donald Trump paid per room for New York's Plaza. Ms. Hunt (who after divorcing a second time went back to using her maiden name) showed that she had not only impeccable taste, but an eye for turning a profit and an astute sense of timing. In 1995 Prince Jeffrey, the sultan of Brunei's brother, bought the Bel-Air for $50 million less than the Japanese company paid for it.

On Maui in Hawaii, Rosewood also bought a remote 4,700-acre ranch with a run-down hotel that was using an old army Quonset hut for its dining room. To convince local residents that gutting and rebuilding the Hana-Maui wouldn't destroy the pristine landscape, Caroline suggested hiring a Hawaiian historian to hold awareness workshops for the employees. "But then, her influence on management," said a Rosewood executive, "was always aimed at instilling a certain ethos among the local people in charge—an insistence on integrity and propriety noticeably absent from her brothers' affairs."

I was fascinated by the way this super-rich woman never flaunted her wealth and authority. While so many heiresses of her day were gadding about with gigolos and getting cheated in one investment scam after another, Caroline Hunt kept a sharp eye on business. Her energies always seemed to be directed at improving the appearance of her properties and the style in which they were being run.

The Hana-Maui was also sold after Rosewood decided to concentrate on the less risky hotel-management business. Today Caroline's company manages the Lanesborough, London's priciest hotel ($5,140 for the three-bedroom Royal Suite, which comes complete with a private security officer, personal butler, and chauffeured Bentley); Hotel Seiyo Ginza in Tokyo; Caneel Bay in St. John; La Samanna in St. Martin; Little Dix Bay in Virgin Gorda; as well as the Bel-Air. New luxury hotels are being added to the chain in Saudi Arabia and Indonesia, while twenty-three expensive condominiums are presently being appended to The Mansion on Turtle Creek.

In 1986, Caroline unveiled her grandest and most ambitious project yet: a thirteen-acre office, hotel, and shopping complex in Dallas that was intended to rival New York's Rockefeller Center. Designed by architects Philip Johnson and John Burgee, the mansard roofs, dormer windows, and miles of filigreed iron made the mammoth development named the Crescent look like it had been transplanted to Texas from the court of Napoleon Bonaparte, a fact that didn't escape the history-conscious Ms. Hunt.

By this time she considered herself more Rosewood's arbiter of taste and design than its chief executive. "Though I've learned that you can't design by committee," she admitted. "And you can't decorate by committee either. You've got to find the right people and then give them some rein." Then with a wink she added: "Not too much rein."

While no longer involved in Rosewood's day-to-day operations, she is nevertheless very proud of the Crescent—her monument to Dallas. This huge complex, she feels, has not only added a sense of rarified residential luxury to the city, but has redefined the northern border of the downtown area with 1.2 million square feet of choice office space in three eighteen-story towers; 750,000 square feet of retail space, mostly for small, chic boutiques; a spa; indoor tennis courts, and a 216-room super-luxury hotel called the Crescent Court, which was modeled after its British namesake in the ancient city of Bath. Hidden beneath the complex—its builders boasted it required more limestone than the Empire State Building—is a four-level 4,100-car parking garage that fills the biggest hole ever dug in Dallas. Superlatives such as those are often associated with her undertakings.

At the Crescent's opening party, 3,500 guests drank champagne, dined on duck tamales and baby boar, and danced to the music of Ramsey Lewis and Asleep at the Wheel, while tuxedo-clad maintenance workers scurried about squeegeeing up the water from a burst main. But this affair was soon overshadowed by a lavish weekend gala held there to raise half a million dollars to send talented Texas actors and musicians to play at the John F. Kennedy Center of the Performing Arts in Washington. Caroline, who had just been named to the center's board of trustees by President Reagan, made the gala a memorable event. Cab Calloway and his orchestra were flown in for the Friday-night black-tie dinner-dance. The next day, the world's top clothes designers staged a tea and champagne fashion show in the hotel's Fountain Courtyard, after which brother Bunker took all the celebrants out for a tour and barbecue supper at his Circle T Ranch.

For Caroline and her five children, who now all work for the company, Rosewood has served as the corporate umbrella for numerous other investments. Not all have been successful. In 1987 Rosewood made a $333 million bid to take over Phillips-Van Heusen, the New York–based apparel company. The bid failed. In 1990 Rosewood made another $400 million bid—which was also rejected—to acquire the First Executive Corporation, a debt-laden Los Angeles insurance company. And in 1992 Caroline's company even lost one of its own prize possessions, Premier Place, a twenty-story silver-glass office tower in suburban Dallas. Travelers Insurance company refused to renegotiate the mortgage and grabbed the building instead, after Rosewood defaulted on a $49 million note.

Most of the company's diversification attempts stemmed from Caroline Hunt's constant scanning of the business horizon. "Mother was always looking ahead for the next opportunity," said her son Stephen. She also insisted that her employees likewise "think long-range." Once she even challenged Rosewood's top executives to write their imaginary obituaries to define what they still hoped to accomplish. To imbue this same long-range perspective in her children, she reportedly has willed that her vast Caroline Hunt Trust Estate be divided equally among them—but not until twenty-one years after her death.

So far this whirlwind of a woman shows no signs of slowing down. "Evidently, all my brothers and my sister and I have very good genes,"

she said. (Her father used to brag that he was sowing "genius genes").
In 1995 the mandatory age limit at the Tandy Corporation forced
Caroline to resign her seat on the board of that electronics retailing
giant based in Fort Worth. But she remains on numerous other boards
and chairs countless committees. With a friend she also opened an
antiques and accessories shop at the Crescent bearing the elongated
name Lady Primrose's Shopping English Countryside. Twice a year she
flies off to Europe on buying expeditions to restock the store with the
luxury items that catch her eye. "That's nothing compared to Herbert,"
she explained. "He's made thirty-six trips to Russia, where he's drilled
a very successful oil well in a joint venture with Dresser Industries.

Still another company of Caroline's, Earthpreserv Products, packages
expensive all-natural soaps, shampoos, and lotions for sale in drug- and
department-store chains. Her only neglected endeavor is a novel—"an
Alaskan *Deliverance*," she calls it—begun fifteen years ago. "I haven't
had time to finish writing it," she says. "Guess I'll wait until I'm bedrid-
den." She has too many other projects vying for her attention, energy,
and vast resources, to sit home alone writing a book.

Although her attendance at Rosewood's executive committee meetings has become sporadic, Caroline still makes her presence felt through
a stream of handwritten notes. "But I've learned you don't get your
way on everything," she admitted.

That attitude further explains her way of exercising the power that
came with her enormous inheritance. Instinctively, she sensed when
to forge ahead and when to pull back. And unlike her headstrong
brothers, Bunker and Herbert, who figured with their money and clout
they could beat out all the other speculators and corner several commodity markets on their own, big sister Caroline wisely saw the importance of enlisting the cooperation of others. Besides, she never liked
wielding power so visibly. "Given my position," she added, "if I can't
persuade people and bring them around to my point of view, then I
figure I must be wrong."

CHAPTER XXVI

The Toughest Boss in America

THAT FRANCISCO ANTHONY LORENZO had once been a wide-bodied airline executive with a reputation for remoteness hardly seemed possible. When I first met him in 1983 he'd already slimmed forty-five pounds from his bulging corpus and become just plain Frank. And as this sleek, smooth-running 3-hour-38-minute marathoner, he was then striving to work the same metamorphosis on bloated, bankrupt Continental Airlines, although the medicine he was administering was far less palatable than his own diet of yogurt, raisins, and wheat germ. By slashing salaries, fares, and the route system in half, he was trying to lighten Continental's overhead and keep it in the air as a cut-rate carrier. However, flying right on through a thunderhead of bankruptcy meant defying the airline's powerful unions. And in so doing, Frank Lorenzo was already on his way to winning the unenviable title—one bestowed for several years by *Fortune*—of "America's Toughest Boss."

Toughness, of course, can be both good and bad. The good kind pushes people to the limits of their endurance and abilities for constructive purposes. The bad variety pushes them to their limits or beyond mainly for selfish reasons. Lorenzo's aggressive, confrontational management style seemed to involve a mixture of both. He was a visionary and a great deal-maker but also a union buster and a showboater. His harshest critics called him a "loose cannon who could wreak as much havoc among his own crew as among the competition."

Watching the drama unfold as this forty-three-year-old tried to bail out Continental, I was able to observe all these traits. At the bankruptcy hearing held in the Southern District Court in Houston that September, Continental's chairman was reported by the press as looking "tired and gaunt." Actually, he was in fine fettle, having just shed the final fifteen pounds training for the New York City Marathon. Besides, he was buoyed by business prospects. "We filed for protection from our creditors not because the company doesn't have a future," he confided to me, "but because we think it has a hell of a future."

Airline analysts watching from Wall Street were not so sanguine. Yet Frank's friends, who used words like "quiet," "introspective," and "cerebral" to describe him, also claimed he was "quite a crapshooter." They were right. Within three years he would parlay his control of then-foundering Continental into a flying conglomerate that included Frontier, People Express, New York Air, and Eastern—the largest U.S. passenger fleet aloft, accounting for about one fifth of all domestic air travel.

Lorenzo reached this pinnacle of power not by ascending a managerial hierarchy, but by being an imaginative entrepreneur. The son of a hairdresser who immigrated from Spain, he grew up in New York City in the borough of Queens within earshot of the planes taking off and landing at nearby LaGuardia Airport. He worked his way through Columbia University driving a Coca-Cola truck, and went on to Harvard Business School, where he received his MBA in 1963. But like so many self-propelled men, Lorenzo displayed an inherent restlessness that kept egging him on to seek broader challenges. It was his unceasing scramble to start something new that I thought made him an apt subject for a profile in *Fortune*.

After my series on the Hunt brothers and profile on Caroline, my editors began to think I was hooked on Texans. And there was some truth to that. I was intrigued by the way the Big Sky Country down there seemed to inspire risk-takers—or gamblers, if you will—who assessed the odds, and even if they looked a little long, still weren't frightened away by the fear of losing. Or as my friend and Connecticut neighbor David Nevin wrote in his book *The Texans*: "It's not that they have so much money, but rather that they have learned how to get money and how to use it, how to shove all the chips into the pot with a steady hand and a clear eye and go for a showdown in the toughest game left in America today."

The launching pad for Lorenzo's entrepreneurial eminence was what he now calls a "peapod firm" founded in 1966 with a Harvard Business School classmate, Robert Carney. Each invested $1,000. Called Lorenzo Carney ("Not Carney Lorenzo," emphasized Carney, who told me he was "shyer, more conservative, and less confrontational" than his partner), the financial advisory firm focused on airlines. In 1969 the pair formed Jet Capital Corporation, raising $1.5 million in a small public offering. Their announced goal was to get into aircraft leasing. But, as Carney explained, "basically we were selling ourselves."

In 1972 Jet Capital bought control of Texas International Airlines, a regional carrier wallowing in debt. Lorenzo and Carney restructured the debt, revamped the fleet, and won Civil Aeronautics Board approval to introduce half-price off-peak "peanut fares," as they were advertised. In 1978 Texas International earned $13 million, enough of a cushion to make the restless Lorenzo look acquisitively in other directions. He began by bidding aggressively for National Airlines. Pan American won out, but Texas International pocketed a $47 million profit from the sale of its National stock.

Flusher than ever, Lorenzo and Carney reorganized Texas International into a holding company called Texas Air Corporation, designed to branch out into other areas. It launched New York Air in 1980 as a low-fare but full-service nonunion carrier to challenge Eastern's monopoly in the Boston-Washington corridor. New York Air became profitable in the second quarter of 1983.

Texas Air's biggest gamble culminated in the takeover of Continental in June 1982. That wild west battle for control had raged on and off for three years and involved suit and countersuit, a desperation bid by Continental's pilots to buy their company, and finally the suicide of Continental's chief executive Alvin Feldman, who shot himself in the head in his office in Los Angeles International Airport.

When Lorenzo looked closely at what he had won, Continental hardly seemed much of a prize. "I discovered this wasn't going to be simply a matter of grabbing hold of a badly-run company and blowing out all the cobwebs," he told me. Added Carney, who had opposed the takeover; "Continental was in infinitely worse shape than even I expected."

High labor costs and what Lorenzo called "a crazy-quilt route system" put Continental in a poor position to survive the free-for-all brought on by government deregulation. Losses were staggering, continuing undiminished right through July, August, and September, the peak months for airlines. Fighting to stay alive and aloft, Continental sold $109 million in aircraft and other assets. It raised another $167 million from other sources. At the same time, parent Texas Air provided a capital infusion of $80 million.

"Competing just by cutting fares is not a rational, long-run strategy," Lorenzo told his staff. "Competitors can cut too. Deregulation means carving out your own niche." His view of Continental's niche was to provide all the frills of flying, but at discount fares. "Other airlines cut costs by cutting services," he explained. "They take the cherries off the desserts and the ticket agents off the counters." He believed that by focusing his full-service formula on high-density markets, Continental could win over many new passengers and become highly profitable—provided he could get costs down by breaking the stranglehold of the unions on his airline.

To achieve big reductions in costs, Continental had to cut pay scales. Pilots were averaging $73,000, flight attendants $28,000, and mechanics $33,000. Making matters worse, in August 1983 the mechanics demanded a $6,000 increase, and struck when they didn't get it. Continental kept on flying. But the cost of maintaining the planes by paying overtime and hiring nonunion mechanics further eroded the company's precarious cash position.

In September, Continental finally shut down and sought protection from creditors under Chapter 11. But just fifty-six hours later, like Lazarus, it was up and running again. It was able to do that because Lorenzo had deliberately filed for bankruptcy before the airline ran out of money. Continental, while overdue on paying many suppliers, still had $58 million in the kitty, enough to hire back 4,000 of its 12,000 employees at drastically reduced salaries. It thus became the first airline to defy the gravity of bankruptcy, so to speak, by staying in the sky. "We weren't going to let a great company with 106 airplanes go down the drain," vowed Lorenzo.

The embittered pilots and flight attendants went on strike, accusing the airline of feigning bankruptcy simply as a ploy to abrogate its labor contracts. "The unions are confusing the messenger with the message," replied Continental's feisty chairman. "It's the other side of the deregulation equation. You can't open the skies to free competition if labor, too, isn't subject to the law of supply and demand." The enemy isn't Frank Lorenzo, he was telling them, but the new competitive environment.

He launched a PR campaign to lure the strikers back, figuring if Continental could keep flying he would thus free up the wage structure of his entire industry. First, he dangled five percent of the company's stock as bait, giving so-called "founding employees" of the revived Continental 250 shares apiece with an option to buy 250 more. Two DC-10s were rechristened *Employee Owner Ship I* and *II* to further the pilots' and ground crews' feeling that they had a stake in the airline. Then, hopping back and forth to Houston Intercontinental Airport in his Volkswagen Rabbit, he delivered almost daily pep talks to the "rehires" and "new hires." But the pay was poor. The flight attendants, dubbed "scabettes" by the strikers, had their pay reduced to $15,000, and the pilots' to $43,000, the same salary Lorenzo volunteered to pay himself until Continental became profitable. "I wanted to personally feel the economic change we were asking our employees to make," he said when I asked if he could support his wife, Sharon, and their four children on one seventh of his former salary.

Since returning captains were earning less than the strike benefits they would get by staying home, their decision to fly wasn't easy. They also faced harassment from the strikers. One pilot reported that a phony VD test report was sent to his home to upset his wife. When another pilot mistakenly landed a Continental DC-9 on a snow-covered taxiway instead of a runway at Denver's Stapleton International Airport—and it so happened with Lorenzo aboard—the Air Line Pilots Association bought a full-page ad in USA Today to publicize the error. Surviving that kind of publicity was bad enough. But harder yet was the problem of beating back the attempt of the three unions to void Lorenzo's bankruptcy petition, even though their counterattack had a kamikaze aspect. If the bankruptcy judge sided with the unions, Continental would then be forced into immediate liquidation.

When Lorenzo returned to Houston's bankruptcy court in December 1983 to resolve this matter, a battery of lawyers representing the Air Line Pilots Association, the International Association of Machinists and Aerospace Workers, and the Union of Flight Attendants were attempting to prove that Continental filed for bankruptcy in bad faith.

"We view Chapter 11 as the end of the line, the last resort," I heard Lorenzo testify in a voice barely audible to the strikers seated in the back rows. "The company would have run out of cash in a few days."

The bankruptcy judge was persuaded by Lorenzo's strategy for making Continental profitable. Over the unions' and creditors' objections, the judge agreed to release $40 million in cash and substitute the company's new receivables for collateral. That kind of financial juggling act, which was required to keep even half of Continental's fleet in the air, was considered a specialty of Lorenzo's, who after all his years in the airlines business was still regarded as a "money man."

Actually, he was much broader-gauged than that. As I noted in my Fortune profile: He was a "complex man of opposites." Simultaneously philosophic and pragmatic, instinctive and analytical, aloof and warm, he viewed the well-being of his passengers as a big part of the airline equation. "We're more consumer-responsive than any carrier," he liked to brag. At the same time, he never did lose sight of profit. "What fascinates me about this business," he told me, "are the various forms of leverage that are possible—and not just financial leverage. There is the chance for enormous operating leverage as well. Once you operate at break-even, every additional passenger provides an incremental profit that is very great. All you pay for is the meal and a little more fuel."

As he turned Continental into a full-frill discount airline, he spied a wide spectrum of new markets still to be exploited. "I've always been amazed that only a fraction of the American public flies," he said. And he was convinced that Continental's new bargain fares would lure many of these fly-hards off the buses and trains and into the air.

Since no major airline had attempted before to fly on through bankruptcy, Lorenzo and his aides didn't know what to expect. Would enough pilots be willing to cross the picket lines? Would suppliers keep servicing Continental's planes? Would travel agents continue to write tickets on a bankrupt carrier? But the biggest imponderable of all was whether passengers would risk flying with a struck airline?

An eye-catching $49 fare for any nonstop flight on Continental's domestic route system answered that question. "You can buy the back page of the newspaper anytime you want," said Continental's vice president for marketing. "But $49 for a ticket from Denver to New York will get you on the front page for free." He was right. Even though the offer was good for only the first four days after the airline resumed its flights, the packed planes and pandemonium at the counters proved Lorenzo's contention that even some of those heretofore earthbound folks could be coaxed into the air with the proper inducement.

The $49 fare was not designed to propel Continental into the black. Even the escalated $75 fare put into effect on all flights during the following three weeks was too cheap to do that. "These super-bargain prices will simply help convince the public that we're back in business to stay," Lorenzo said.

Most of his decisions about fares and flight schedules were made during brainstorming sessions, which Lorenzo let me attend. I was fascinated by the switch in his management style. This formerly aloof policymaker was suddenly burrowing deep into operating problems. His spartan 12-by-15-foot office in Houston's America Tower, once a secluded corporate aerie visited mainly by bankers and lawyers, became a busy command post. Trooping in and out were ticketers, pilots, flight attendants, dispatchers—everybody down to a manufacturer's rep come to peddle a newly designed airplane seat with improved lumbar support.

When the traffic got too heavy upstairs, Lorenzo would slip downstairs and go for a run of five or six miles on the mulched jogging track that passed right by the building. Often he was joined by Continental's No. 2 man, executive vice president Philip Bakes, Jr., an avid proponent of deregulation who had formerly served as general counsel of the Civil Aeronautics Board.

Jogging with them one time, I discovered that their strategic planning didn't stop during these runs. Lorenzo's biggest fear was the possibility of triggering a fare war. "Always remember the other guy's got to make a buck too," he warned Bakes as they glided along in step together, maintaining a smooth seven-minute-mile gait. "If you don't leave him a profitable option, you'll hit his hot button." For this reason, Lorenzo considered fare-setting an airline's highest art form. "I'm surprised," he told me after the run, "how many people think you can throw a hand grenade at a competitor and expect he'll stand there and enjoy it."

Yet, in the years ahead the outspoken Lorenzo failed to heed his own advice and threw a few grenades. In 1985, because of his antiunion reputation he lost out to Carl Icahn in a battle for foundering TWA, though Lorenzo could point to a remarkable turn-around at Continental and a profit of $65 million that year—even after he agreed to a $30 million settlement on severance pay for striking pilots who opted not to return to work. TWA's employees tipped the balance in favor of Icahn in spite of the man's history as a cut-throat corporate raider.

Next, Lorenzo zeroed in on Eastern, whose chairman, former astronaut Frank Borman, couldn't gain enough givebacks from his employees to keep the big airline from slipping into bankruptcy. Eastern's unions fought hard to block Lorenzo. "We will show how evil and how wrong Lorenzo is," said Charles Bryan, head of the machinists' local, which also represented the baggage handlers, fuelers, cabin cleaners, and other ground workers. "By the time we're through, nobody will want to be associated with him."

Nevertheless, Texas Air bought control of Eastern for $650 million in 1986. "Obviously, Wall Street perceives how well these two pieces fit together," glowed Lorenzo as Eastern's stock rose fifty percent and Texas Air's stock more than doubled after the merger was announced.

When I flew back to Texas to write another episode for *Fortune* on the perils of Frank Lorenzo, he was alive with plans for reviving Eastern. "It's like adding eight or nine companies to ours," he exclaimed, promising Eastern passengers "straightforward low fares," "less overbooking," and "hassle-free, full-service flights." Once again he reminded me: "Most people still think of me as a financial guy. But I'm not. I have very little to do with that. I'm the guy who'll determine the marketing equation, and figure out how to make this company work."

One of Eastern's biggest marketing advantages was its computerized

SODA (System One Direct Access) reservation system linked to travel agents all over the world. Lorenzo saw the chance to plug in Continental. Additionally, he also spotted an opportunity to sell packaged tours to the Caribbean and South America through Eastern's extensive contacts there. "We're in an environment where the consumer is king," he said. "He wants to fly with an airline that goes to a lot of places. So when you operate sixty percent of the flights out of a city like Miami, you should be able to also get a large portion of the tour business as well. That's what I call marketing mass."

Looking back today, Lorenzo admits that he failed to perceive the problems of an airline that derives eighty percent of its revenues exclusively from the north-south leisure market. "Eastern's business," he says, "was primarily based on unprofitable bargain fares to Florida. But for some reason we missed seeing the danger lurking there."

That same year, 1986, Lorenzo seized another chance to expand. Donald Burr, a close friend who learned the business working for Texas Air, got in trouble with People Express by growing too fast. Lorenzo agreed to buy it together with the planes of bankrupt Frontier for $300 million in cash and stock. He merged Frontier into Continental and continued running People as a separate operation. But by this time Texas Air's balance sheet was being stretched pretty thin and Lorenzo's soaring career was about to hit some high-altitude turbulence.

The first big bump came at Eastern in March 1989 when the machinists struck. Nearly all of the airline's 3,600 pilots walked out in sympathy, forcing the carrier to cancel ninety percent of its flights. Even Columbia University, Lorenzo's alma mater, bowed to the pressure of the pickets and canceled its John Jay awards dinner at which he was to be honored as a prominent alumnus.

Lorenzo refused to back down and gradually got two thirds of the flights back in the air using union defectors. But the fractious labor relations generated so much heat—as well as some dubious safety questions—that in 1990 a bankruptcy judge pronounced Lorenzo "unfit" to run the airline and appointed a trustee to oversee operations. "It's time to change the captain of the ship," the trustee claimed, and appointed himself president. The following year Eastern shut down, throwing 30,000 employees out of work. "The unions killed Eastern," Lorenzo still angrily insists. And he was mostly right.

He now believes he might have saved the airline by taking an even tougher divide-and-conquer stance with the unions. "The machinists were the culprits," he says. "All they cared about was establishing precedents that would improve their negotiating position with other airlines. It wouldn't have been as forthright," he adds. "But what we should have done is patted the pilots on the back and said, 'Look, you guys gave at the office and made nice concessions. The real problem is the machinists because they didn't give at the office.' That way we wouldn't have had both unions pulling so strongly together."

His wings clipped, Lorenzo eventually sold his stake in Continental to the Scandinavian Airlines System in 1990 for $30.5 million. Later that year, when Continental filed its second bankruptcy petition, the unsecured creditors claimed Lorenzo knew the carrier was insolvent when he sold out and they demanded retribution. He denied the charge though he settled with them for $5 million. "Bankruptcies," he says, "are surrounded by lawyers who feast on hourly fees. So they'll go ahead and litigate something that has only one chance in ten of prevailing. In the meantime I was off doing other things. I wanted to put it all behind me."

One of his "other things" was helping financially stressed airlines like Iberia, the Spanish carrier, obtain fresh capital. Former competitors who admired Lorenzo's success in holding costs below those of any other major carrier also flocked to him for advice. But he was wary of giving it. "Maybe the more you see, the more you don't know," he admitted with uncharacteristic humility. "I've earned a lot of scars learning about this business."

Those scars, however, didn't keep him from trying to take to the skies again in 1993 with a new company called ATX. But as soon as Lorenzo revealed plans for ATX to launch Friendship Airlines, a non-union low-cost carrier serving the East Coast, he set off a firestorm of opposition. Randolph Babbitt, president of the Air Line Pilots Association, castigated Lorenzo: "He is not just a symbol of evil in the workplace. He is the very embodiment of it." ALPA then placed full-page advertisements in the Congressional newspaper, *Roll Call*, claiming that "to allow Frank Lorenzo back in the business was akin to letting jailed junk bond traders Michael Milken and Ivan Boesky return to the scenes of their crimes."

Some 120 members of Congress responded by writing letters urging the Department of Transportation to reject Lorenzo's bid to license Friendship even though the big carriers like American, United, and Delta had already begun laying off thousands of employees and new airline jobs were at a premium. Congressman Michael "Mac" Collins, a Republican from Georgia, went so far as to introduce what he named the "Two-Time-Loser Bill." Had it passed, this blatantly discriminatory legislation would have barred licensing any carrier controlled by an investor involved in two bankruptcies: specifically Frank Lorenzo.

The anti-Lorenzo furor presented a conflict for President Clinton because of his desire to stimulate employment and at the same time support organized labor. His Department of Transportation finally bucked Lorenzo's application over to an administrative law judge, who used some fancy semantics to duck this political hot potato. He ruled that while ATX had the capital and expertise to run a scheduled carrier, it "lacked the proper compliance disposition."

True, Francisco Anthony Lorenzo never was disposed simply to comply. He was too rugged an individual, too much of an innovator, too intelligent to accept the status quo. His concept of a low-cost carrier that could lure travelers off the buses and trains was being copied successfully by Southwest Airlines. But Lorenzo had a problem articulating his idea without sounding abrasive and confrontational. "I'm an airline builder, not a union buster," he still insists today. Yet he continues to be vilified as a hard-nosed manager who perverted the bankruptcy laws to beat down organized labor. Perhaps he overestimated the operational freedom bestowed by airline deregulation. Possibly he was too emboldened by President Reagan's firing of the striking air traffic controllers in 1981, an action which the public applauded. Whatever the reason, the tough tactics employed by Lorenzo to get four failing airlines back in the skies are still being misconstrued as the work of a mean-spirited boss.

He's mellower and more philosophic today. "The irony of it is," he now says, "if I had been charged with a crime and found guilty, I would have been sentenced and that would have been the end of it. But nobody ever accused me of doing anything illegal. At what point is a man entitled to go on with his life?" he asks plaintively, though he is quick to supply the answer himself.

"All the major carriers are now playing my austerity game," he claims. From his perspective, he and the hard-pressed airline industry have finally reached the point in America's deregulated skies where their flight paths are converging. As he points out, you can fly from New York to Los Angeles for little more than it cost twenty-five years ago. U.S. airlines are also much cheaper than European carriers. "Friendship Airlines may be dead," he admits. "But our company, ATX, has the money and the know-how to wing it in the highly competitive environment that presently exists. And with Republicans in control of Congress, we entrepreneurs should get a better break."

It's obvious that long-distance runner Lorenzo doesn't intend to quit the race.

CHAPTER XXVII

Reagan's Other Nancy

DISCONNECTED FROM THE POWER CENTER for four years, the business brass surged into Washington in January 1981 for more than an inaugural ball. This time ruffles and flourishes heralded their kind of man—a pragmatic Republican president whose administration they hoped would heed their ideas. And for this reason, *Fortune*, a magazine that didn't ordinarily devote many pages to the pomp and circumstance of politics, sent me to the capital to record in colorful detail the swearing-in of this sportscaster-turned-movie-star-turned-politician, Ronald Reagan.

In 1960 and 1964 I had covered the inaugurations of Kennedy and Johnson for *Life*, with all the hoopla and pageantry staged by their Democratic supporters. But this time, from the moment my plane touched down at National Airport, it was obvious that the backers of Reagan were of a much richer hue. An armada of four hundred corporate jets snarled the runways. Downtown streets were bumper-to-bumper with stretch limos, some even imported from Baltimore, Philadelphia, and New York because there weren't enough in D.C. to go around. The cloakrooms in every restaurant were chockablock with mink.

California companies, especially, were vying to make a splash for their adopted son. It didn't matter what business they were in. They all wanted to be part of the show. The Shaklee Corporation of Emeryville, a manufacturer of nutritional supplements called Vita-Lea Chewables, paid for the National Symphony Orchestra's inaugural concert. And Occidental Petroleum, headquartered in Los Angeles, threw a huge cocktail party at the Corcoran Gallery, at which chairman Armand Hammer used a display of his $5 million private collection of Leonardo da Vinci's technical notes and drawings to lure the capital's movers and shakers.

Caught up in a whirl of company-sponsored lunches, dinners, and balls, even the blasé business leaders seemed impressed. "This had become the gloomiest capital in the world," commented Robert Anderson, chairman of Atlantic Richfield, picking at his poached steelhead salmon at PepsiCo's brunch. "Jimmy Carter covered this city with a coat of gray paint."

Anderson, like many of the other invading executives, were among eight hundred "Republican eagles" who had written personal checks of $10,000 to the National Committee during the campaign. One noticeable no-show, however, was Bendix chief executive William Agee, chairman of the Businessmen for Reagan-Bush Committee. But then, as I soon discovered, Bendix had a powerful Washington voice that could catch the president's ear whenever needed. Her name was Nancy Reynolds and her role was so special that a few months after the inauguration, *Fortune* sent me back to Washington to write a profile on her.

The Reagans called her "the other Nancy." The Washington press corps referred to her as "First Friend." Bendix, which had the good fortune to hire her as its chief lobbyist long before her pals from California swept to power, bestowed on her the title Vice President, National Affairs. No matter how she was identified, Nancy Clark Reynolds was an important private link to the White House, as the people who worked there readily confirmed.

"She has always been willing to help in any way that is suitable for her," Ronald Reagan wrote to me in his own hand while convalescing from the bullet wound inflicted by would-be assassin John Hinckley, Jr. Apparently the president had been informed that an article was being written about "the other Nancy," and insisted on weighing in with a personal testimonial before he was fully recovered. "She has sound judgment," his note concluded, "and can raise the morale of all around her just by saying hello."

As a presidential confidante, Nancy preferred anonymity, although she wasn't bashful about giving Reagan her views. "I was so pleased," she said, "to be around a person of his stature who had total faith in me, even when he knew I didn't always agree with him. But he never equated disagreement with disloyalty, which is why I found him so easy

to talk to." Nancy Reagan didn't always find her husband that willing
to listen. "Go ahead, you tell him," she sometimes goaded Nancy Reynolds. "You can talk to him. He won't listen to anybody else."

That power, even though few people in Washington were aware of
it, made "the other Nancy" wary of her own position. "You wouldn't
want to abuse that sort of relationship by being a harridan," she said,
"some shrew who's always complaining and disagreeing."

During the tense days in April 1981, right after the president was
shot, her closeness to the Reagans became more visible. TV cameras
had caught the two Nancys sitting together (the First Lady dressed in
red, "the other Nancy" dressed in blue) at the president's swearing-in.
But after that Reynolds stayed out of sight, preferring to operate quietly
behind the scenes as "a friendly persuader." However, suddenly seen
shuttling between George Washington University Hospital to visit the
wounded president, and the White House to comfort the distraught
First Lady, she could no longer duck the limelight. Kitty Kelley, in
her unauthorized biography of Nancy Reagan, told of Nancy Reynolds
breakfasting at the White House with son, Michael Reagan, and daughter, Maureen, cheerfully taking charge of things early in the morning
after the shooting. "Those were the hours," wrote Kelley, "in which
no one knew the president's fate."

Reynolds, however, minimizes her role as chief White House cheerer-
upper at that crucial time. Today she will admit only how shaken she
was at the sight of the stricken president lying ashen-faced in his hospital bed. "What sticks in my memory," she says, "is how small and dark
the room was. The windows were closed and the shades drawn. The
nurses were pounding him on the back and making him cough up
phlegm. They had to do that every few minutes to keep his lungs clear,
and he didn't like it at all. 'That hurts,' he grunted. The public never
knew it, but I think things were touch-and-go."

Nancy particularly remembers standing at the foot of his bed with
Secret Service agent Ed Hickey. "We were grinning like fools," she
says. "You know, not knowing what else to do, when the president
looked up and said: 'Well, if it isn't the other Nancy and Boston
Blackie,' I didn't know what to say. I couldn't say, 'How do you feel,
Mr. President?' He looked terrible."

Naturally, Nancy Reynolds was also there at the White House to
greet Reagan on his return from the hospital. "He was in his robe,
looking a little wan," she recalled, "but joking, joking, joking. On his
way from a nap in the Lincoln Bedroom he passed a couple of workmen
eating sandwiches in the corridor. 'I didn't know there were any good

take-out restaurants in the White House,' cracked the president. He was ebullient, thrilled to be alive and back home. He loved the sunlight streaming through the windows—'therapeutic light,' he called it."

With Reagan fully healed and back on the job, "the other Nancy" reverted to her regular behind-the-scenes kibitzing, though that gives the wrong connotation because she was not a meddler. Edwin Meese, the president's counselor and later his attorney general, elaborated: "She plays an important role by keeping us abreast of the feelings of business." It was a strange part for a strong-willed frontier lady to be playing, especially one who claimed she would rather be raising cattle in the Sawtooth Mountains of Idaho than jawboning her buddies at 1600 Pennsylvania Avenue. But then, fifty-three-year-old Nancy Reynolds was a new kind of White House crony, who spent half her time as an unpaid worker for the president's team.

More than anything, she regarded herself as an "early warning system" for the president and his staff. "Washington is a city where monsters grow out of little whispers," she explained. "Say a cabinet member thought he was being undercut by the White House, I didn't hesitate to call Mike Deaver, the president's rumor-squasher, right away." At the same time, if anxieties were brewing in the business community, she reported on them at the weekly meetings of an ad hoc corporate advisory group convened by the White House liaison office and attended by seven or eight people from the Business-Government Relations Council, that inner sanctum of lobbyists whose members all wielded lofty titles and bottomless expense accounts to make nice things happen for their companies. Or better yet, she conveyed her worries directly to the Reagans.

She also used her Washington contacts to suggest candidates to fill key slots at the Agency for International Development, Peace Corps, and numerous other government divisions. Her high-level head-hunting began right after the election. On leave from Bendix for five months following the Republican Convention, she worked in the campaign and then ran Nancy Reagan's transition team, finding the people to staff the First Lady's East Wing offices. As a westerner with Washington upbringing—her father, D. Worth Clark, was a Democratic congressman and senator from Idaho—Nancy was also just the person to introduce the president-elect to the capital's business and cultural leaders. The Reagans made their grand entry into Washington in November 1980 at a black-tie dinner at the F Street Club, arranged by Nancy Reynolds.

Back at work again for Bendix, her office still doubled as a message center for business leaders trying to catch the eye and ear of the president. Her office was a former corner grocery store, which Nancy bought and transformed into Bendix's sleek triangular two-story command post on Capitol Hill. Her desk there, I noticed, was always snowed under with résumés and inundated with ideas about everything from the most complex synfuel proposal to a simple request for Mr. and Mrs. Reagan to serve as International Horse Show sponsors.

By eight A.M. when she got to work, there were always a dozen or more pink callback slips awaiting her. Before she could escape to her private office upstairs, the buzzing, blinking telephone console signaled several more incoming calls. "How're yooo, Elizabeth," Nancy drawled with her raincoat still on when I walked in with her to witness a typical workday. It was Elizabeth Dole, then deputy assistant to the president for public liaison and wife of the Republican senator from Kansas. Mrs. Dole was foraging for White House advisers on women's affairs. "Guess I kinda got derailed," laughed Nancy, explaining why she hadn't been reachable the prior afternoon. The phone then got tucked in between Nancy's feather-cut blond head and her raincoat-clad shoulder, freeing both hands to flip through an appointment book. On went the gold-rimmed granny glasses, magnifying the piercing blue eyes. "That's super," said Nancy, signing off and scribbling in her appointment book.

Before the phone could be extricated from between the cocked head and shoulder, another caller was on the line. "Hey, Mark," she shouted. "When're yooo and Antoinette leaving?" Close friend Mark Hatfield, chairman of the Senate Appropriations Committee, was calling to say good-bye before flying off on a Middle Eastern junket.

Next it was Ann Sullivan of the Senate's Small Business Committee seeking Bendix's support for a pending bill. That particular request led Nancy to tell me about the blur between her Bendix and White House roles. "Some people don't realize I'm back working for the company," she said.

Three more calls, and Nancy finally made it upstairs to her office, where the cluttered desk sat beneath the glowering gaze of a Crow Indian woman in full parade regalia, painted by one of her favorite artists, Kevin Red Star. On the desk, symbolic of her double role, was a stack of letters extolling the Reagan economic program. She was mailing them to Bendix managers, who would rewrite them to fit local circumstances and styles and then fire them off to their congressmen. Whether the press could be counted on not to jump on her if Bendix landed a big Pentagon contract for its weapons system, she and her company still weren't sure. But in the euphoria of postinaugural Washington, her boss, Bill Agee, couldn't have been more pleased. "We never question how she allocates her time," he said when I interviewed him about Nancy. "She serves the corporation well at the same time she serves her country. What a beautiful combination."

Nancy herself I found pretty sensitive to the conflict-of-interest dangers lurking for Washington lobbyists. She admitted things got so bad during the warm honeymoon between the Reaganites and the business community that the corridor outside the House Ways and Means Committee became known as "Gucci gulch," after the expensive Italian shoes worn by the swarm of influence peddlers. "I wouldn't be caught dead with that bunch," she exclaimed. "I'm a low-key catalyst. My job was to mix the right Bendix people with the right government people. Not to twist arms."

Growing up in the capital, she learned firsthand the meaning of "power corrupts." Looking back, she now says, "In Washington you enter into an unreal world, where you're suddenly king or queen. Even the most junior congresswoman is bowed down to. It's very hard not to succumb to that. The press, the staff around you, they all adore you. They build you up to unrealistic heights. And then systematically they begin to tear you down. Washington is a seductive city, but it's not a place that wishes you well.

Watching her work, I saw how careful she was in wielding her own power and exercising her close White House connection. She never began a conversation with "I believe the president would like ..." or "The president mentioned to me ..." Nor did she ever wheedle or cajole or use her clout in a way that was offensive. "Throwing your weight around," she said, "can be a very negative thing in Washington, though government bureaucrats love to do it."

That may be why she was continually trying to escape from the capital. Even as the daughter of a senator best known as a poker-playing pal of Harry Truman's, Nancy yearned for the freedom and informality of the West. When the family got home to the ranch during congressional recesses, she herded cattle and rode in rodeos. Her family finally talked her into going to Goucher College in Baltimore by letting her take a horse along.

Shortly after graduation in 1949 she got married and produced three sons. But the housewife's life eventually palled and in 1958 the family moved to Idaho, where her marriage hit the rocks and Nancy landed a job hostessing a television interview show called *Periscope* for KTVB in Boise. This led to an offer from Westinghouse Broadcasting to co-anchor the six o'clock news on KPIX in San Francisco. She was covering California's 1966 gubernatorial campaign when she first met Ronald Reagan.

Lyn Nofziger, then Reagan's press secretary, hired Nancy as his assistant for radio and television. He didn't think much of her writing skills, he told me. "But if you could keep her away from a typewriter," he said, "she was one of the most competent people you'd ever find." From that job she graduated to "special assistant" to the governor, arranging such events as the California homecoming celebration for the Vietnam POWs, and accompanying the Reagans on their foreign travels. "He used his power as governor the same way he did as president," Nancy claimed. "You might not agree with what he did, but he always felt he was using it for the ultimate good of the people."

Shortly before going to work for Reagan, she married Frank Reynolds, the state's deputy director of consumer affairs. She had another son, but this marriage, like her first to William Wurzburger, a Baltimore manufacturer of wood fittings, ended in divorce. "Nancy eats husbands alive," blurted Nofziger during my interview with him. "But on second thought," he admitted, "the long hours she spent working for Reagan didn't leave her much time for family life."

Considered "family" by the Reagans, she became a regular at their ranch and once even went with them on a week-long pack trip high into the Sierra Nevada. Once on a trip to New York City with the Reagans, she received word that the barn on her own ranch in Idaho had burned down, killing three of her horses. "I was crushed," said Nancy. "When we arrived back in Los Angeles, there was the governor's chauffeur holding Reagan's favorite Italian jumping saddle. "I know you've lost a lot," Reagan commiserated, "and I know they can't be replaced. But I want you to have this."

When Reagan challenged Gerald Ford for the 1976 Republican nomination, Nancy Reynolds became "advance man" for the eastern and southern states. One day in Amarillo after she had herded two thousand Texans out to the airport to greet Reagan, a tornado struck nearby and his plane was diverted to Dallas. Nancy thought it was still circling overhead and made everybody stay. "The governor claimed I kept those folks handcuffed to the fence," she said. "But those were wonderful days," she recalled. "I made friends in places nobody ever heard of."

Reagan's loss to Ford at the 1976 convention finally forced Nancy to look for more secure work. Boise Cascade spotted her PR potential and signed her up as associate director of government affairs, the No. 2 job in its Washington office. "It was a very scary assignment," recalls Nancy. "I didn't even know what a trade association was." Eleven months later, Bill Agee took her by surprise with what he described as "an offer you can't refuse." He explained: "Most of the lawmakers still think of Bendix as a washing machine company. They don't know about our aerospace, automotive, or heavy equipment divisions. Your job is to tell them."

The capital had never before encountered a full-fledged lady lobbyist fluttering all over town spreading the word about a giant corporation. Nancy's appointment caused the most consternation at the august, all-male Business-Government Relations Council. Restricted to "policy spokesmen," it couldn't decide at first whether to let her in. By 1983 she had become president and was considered "a great door-opener" by its won-over male members.

"As head of the council," she said, "I had power in my own right. The position gave me access to information from other business lobby-ists. Even though I wasn't 'one of the boys,' a phrase that's almost obsolete now, I could also get to see anybody in the Cabinet or Capitol. They now decided I probably knew what I was talking about. It was a groundbreaking appointment. Today companies make an effort to hire women because they are persuasive and have other abilities and charac-teristics that make them good lobbyists."

Reagan's election finally forced her to decide whether to go to work full-time in the White House or to stay with Bendix and become what Agee called an "inside outsider." That role, she decided, really suited her best. "I thought I could be more effective looking at the administra-tion with a jaundiced eye," she told me. "I knew what the president liked to do and I knew what Nancy liked him to do. So they both could be sure I would never come up with some harebrained idea that wasn't natural for him."

Yet, that didn't mean she couldn't ever be a burr under his saddle. She cited the president's refusal to support the Equal Rights Amend-ment for women as a case in point, and described how one afternoon she slipped into the Oval Office to make her feelings felt. "I talked quietly to him about it," said Nancy, who claimed that her only real disagreement with Reagan during their long association involved her concern about the members of her own sex. "I didn't get argumentative. But I let him know that I thought he was wrong. But Reagan," she added, "wanted things done on the state level and not by constitutional amendment."

Nancy's strong convictions about women were given a much wider forum when United Nations representative Jeane Kirkpatrick picked her to become U.S. representative to the U.N. for the Status of Women, a post that has since been upgraded to the rank of ambassador. For almost four years she spent three or four days every month at the United Nations in New York, besides making periodic overseas trips, mainly to underdeveloped countries. "It was an eye-opening experience," she said, "one of the most fascinating jobs I've ever had. And it sparked my unquenchable interest in Africa that keeps me going back frequently today." But she also found international politics unsettling. At a world conference of women in Nairobi, she drew boos and hisses when the Reagan administration was blamed for bombing schools and hospitals in Nicaragua.

That conference was a forerunner of the one held in Beijing in 1995, which Hillary Clinton attended. "Her going was extremely important to women in the U.S. and throughout the world," Nancy claims. "In Beijing they got ten times the publicity we did because of the First Lady's powerful presence."

The U.N. assignment coincided with a Washington job switch that made Nancy freer to travel. In November 1982 she quit Bendix to join Anne Wexler, an ardent Democrat and former assistant to President Carter for public liaison. Despite their ideological differences, the duo became the most powerful lobbying and political strategy team in Washington. Their clients included General Motors, Aetna, the Motion Picture Association of America, and the National Football League. "No matter who occupies the Oval Office next year," boasted Wexler on the eve of the 1984 election, "we're administration-proof."

Said Nancy: "When Anne and I joined forces we were perceived as two females who really had a handle on business and knew how it was related to Washington. I think a lot of our success was based on reputation. Because everybody was watching us, we were very careful about not abusing our power. We also paid attention to the little things— how we dressed, how we talked, how we acted, where we went, who we were with—by which our effectiveness was also being judged." But she added: "I think the hardest thing is maintaining power because you know how fickle people are. It means maintaining a great reputation, and with it people's confidence and trust."

Reagan's landslide reelection allowed Nancy to keep her entree to the White House, though her visits during his second term became more social than political. She began bringing new books to the president's attention. Before Tom Clancy's first novel, *The Hunt for Red October*, became a best seller, she gave him a copy. In nonfiction books she sometimes even underlined pertinent passages. Unbeknownst to me, she also gave the president a marked copy of a book of mine, published in 1986, called *The Intuitive Manager*. Only a few paragraphs were devoted to Reagan, and not all of them were flattering. "That son of Eureka [Illinois] College," I wrote, "has tried to beguile America into believing he is just an actor, while actually he is one of the most intuitive politicians ever to occupy the White House—and one of the Eureka Factor's best salesmen."

The "Eureka Factor," as the book explained, is that sudden, illuminating "I've found it" flash that separates intuitive leaders from more analytical plodders. I quoted pollster Lou Harris, who told me "the amazing thing about Reagan is how unerring his instinct is in knowing when to duck and when to go for the jugular, and how to go for broke communicating about it." Concluded Harris: "He is the absolute opposite of Jimmy Carter, who immersed himself in details and never sensed his political options."

I also quoted John Sears, the president's former campaign adviser, who prophetically pointed out: "Reagan has given us one thing the people will cling to regardless of our future problems. He has presided over the restoration of our confidence. Blindly optimistic, fiercely patriotic, and unbending in his loyalty, he is the embodiment of a peculiar American virtue that says all things are possible if you will make them so—that reality is an illusion that can be overcome."

Several times during the televised Iran-Contra hearings, it occurred to me that Reagan perhaps considered the illegality of the so-called "arms-for-hostages" swap an illusion. That somehow it really didn't register in his mind that his two top national security advisers, Admiral John Poindexter and Lieutenant Colonel Oliver North, were defying the orders of congress.

Those brief passages quoting Harris and Sears must have pleased the president, because he picked up the phone and called Nancy. "Hi, this is the intuitive manager in the White House," he said, and asked her for my telephone number. Then he called me at the Time & Life Building in New York. But I was out to lunch. When I got back, our chief operator was having fits. "The president has been trying to reach you," she said, immediately connecting me to the White House. Before I had a chance to grab a pen and flip open a notebook, Reagan's unmistakable voice was saying, "I received your book and I want to thank you for your very kind words."

I was stunned. If you win the World Series or the Super Bowl, you could expect a call from the president, but not for writing a book. Also, I realized Reagan was scheduled to leave the next morning for a summit meeting in Japan, and must have been immersed in various briefings. "You're so nice to call," I said. "I know you're just about to embark for Tokyo, so I really appreciate it."

"With that long trip ahead of me, your book is going to be in my bag," Reagan responded.

"Take care of yourself with all those terrorists out there," I blurted out, still groping for the right words to thank the president.

The entire exchange lasted less than two minutes. But that didn't stop Little, Brown, my publisher, from buying a full page in the *New York Times* Sunday book review section to spread the word. The ad pictured *Air Force One*, the president's jet. THE INTUITIVE MAN-AGER IN THE WHITE HOUSE TAKES THIS BOOK IN HIS FLIGHT BAG, blared the headline, prompting the White House general council to write a letter ordering Little, Brown to "cease and desist using the name of the president of the United States for commercial purposes."

Of course, Reagan's surprise call would never have come but for "the other Nancy's" sleight-of-hand—and her Magic Marker. Typically, she pretended it was all the president's idea. But that was the way Nancy Reynolds got things done, by claiming it was another person's idea. "Power," she once confided to me, "is pulling the right levers that will make somebody else be your prime mover. That way your power re-mains hidden." No deviousness intended. That simply was her modus operandi. She was one political operative who knew enough not to flaunt the force she wielded.

After the Reagans left the White House and "the other Nancy" reverted to being just plain Nancy, she still retained considerable clout in the capital. She also kept her seat on numerous corporate and non-profit boards, including Sears, Norrell, the Smithsonian Museum of the American Indian, and the Central African Foundation. But the pull of the West was too strong. In 1993 she finally succumbed and returned to her pioneering roots, buying a house in Santa Fe and building what must be the world's fanciest log cabin in Crow Canyon, Colorado, in the wide-open land, where she says, "the desert meets the Mesa Verde, and politics is confined to campaigning in the school board election."

CHAPTER XXVIII

Running After Ross

AT FIVE FEET SIX, H. (for Henry) Ross Perot sits short in the saddle as Texans go. But when I first interviewed him in 1985, he had already become a hero of Sam Houston proportions. Exuding ego and energy in equal amounts, he was known in Dallas as an iconoclastic entrepreneur, an overgenerous philanthropist, and a superpatriot who wasn't shy about speaking out on what's wrong with America. He nevertheless insisted back then that running for president would be the one thing he'd be terrible at. "My mother used to say, 'Ross, a little bit of you goes a long way,'" he cackled, and then candidly added, "I guess quite a few people would agree. That's why I'd be no good at politics in this laid-back, cool world of television. I'd be too hot, too trigger-quick in offering opinions."

I had just resigned from *Fortune* to begin writing my book on intuition at the time of this encounter. Perot was still running Electronic Data Systems, the computer processing giant that he had built from scratch and just sold to General Motors for a princely $2.5 billion. The news of that sale caused quite a stir. However, a couple of derring-do exploits had already spread his fame well beyond business, which is why I wanted to pursue him for my book.

His first adventure to catch the public eye was a failed effort (some said grandstanding attempt) in 1969 to personally deliver two planeloads of Christmas dinners and medicines to the American POWs in Hanoi. When the North Vietnamese refused his planes permission to land, Perot made more headlines by flying on to Laos and standing bullhorn in hand before the North Vietnamese embassy, shouting: "Let us have our men."

"It was Henry Kissinger," Perot said, "who got me involved with the POWs, and my original contact was with an army colonel nobody ever heard of then, Alexander Haig." Furthermore, he said, "I never expected they'd let us land those planes in Vietnam." Then he surprised me by adding: "The purpose of the Christmas trip was not to take packages to the prisoners, but to create a pressure-cooker situation where the folks in Hanoi had to talk to us."

Ten years later, when two of his EDS employees were tossed into jail in Iran, Perot mounted a daring (and this time successful) commando raid to spring them. This hairy adventure was turned into the best seller *On Wings of Eagles* by author Ken Follett. The book also became a hit TV miniseries with actor Richard Crenna playing Perot, thus catapulting him from Dallas tycoon into a national celebrity.

"There were a few details in that show that weren't accurate," admitted Perot, who I discovered during this first meeting was a master of self-deprecating humor. "Probably the ultimate fiction," he said, "was casting Richard Crenna, who is much taller, as me. A few of the guys at EDS told me that for accuracy's sake, Mickey Rooney should have been given the part."

The thrust of my interview, however, didn't involve either of those two highly publicized exploits or, for that matter, his self-proclaimed aversion to politics. It concerned the intuitive powers of this Depression kid from Texarkana who earned his keep breaking horses and delivering newspapers to the black community; graduated from the U.S. Naval Academy as senior class president although he had never seen an ocean until he got there; became IBM's star salesman; and then launched his own company, EDS, which when it was eventually acquired by GM made him the largest stockholder of the world's largest corporation.

I wanted Ross Perot to tell in his own words how he had been guided by gut feelings through this highly successful series of career changes. After all, he claimed he started EDS after picking up a copy of an old *Reader's Digest* in a barbershop and spotting the Thoreau quote: "The mass of men lead lives of quiet desperation." He said, "I knew down to my toes that my idea for a data processing company would work, even though everybody at IBM thought it was a dumb idea."

The cocky, bantam-rooster-of-a-man didn't disappoint me. He described intuition as "knowing your business," drawling out the three words for emphasis. "It means being able to bring to bear on a situation everything you've seen, felt, tasted, and experienced," he said. He described how he ran a memoless company. "Like Napoleon," he explained, "who tossed out all written reports from his generals, figuring he'd already heard the important news, I prefer to conduct my business instinctively and by personal contact." He claimed written reports stifle creativity, "They discourage the recipient from responding intuitively." Perot plainly had a knack for coming up with pithy quotes. I put in my notes, "He makes life easy for an interviewer."

During our four-hour conversation, he cited a study done at Annapolis to find out what instinct made some midshipmen better leaders than others. The answer, he said, "was an intuitive feeling of being able to win," although he added that "in nearly every case it was not known how." He explained that when he organized the commando raid to free his imprisoned employees in Iran, he didn't know how their escape would be brought off. "But instinctively," he said, "I felt it would succeed, and remarkably, it did."

Perot, however, claimed he personally was no longer motivated by an overriding need to win. He said his biggest pleasure now came from watching his five children. "I don't have any unsatisfied power drives," he said. "I feel no urge to climb another mountain or do anything that would take the edge off their future."

My next encounter with Perot was not until the fall of 1987. With the billionaire superpatriot now lashing out more and more unabashedly on the ills of our country, *Life* asked me to spend some time with him, gathering conversational nuggets for a long profile titled "The World According to Ross Perot." But I wasn't sure how much time he could spare. He was busy, I'd heard, launching new ventures and looking for new investments. By then he was no longer running EDS for GM, and had sold eighty percent of his GM stock. What had been originally billed by the business press as a "marriage of EDS's entrepreneurial genius with GM's vast resources" was on the rocks. It turned out that once the wedding bliss evaporated, he had become, as the press subsequently reported, "such a burr under Chairman Roger Smith's saddle" that GM's board voted unanimously to pay Perot $700 million for the stock he still held—about double the market price—just to get rid of him.

Freed from his EDS and GM responsibilities, and having forgotten, or so it seemed, all that folderol about not needing to climb another mountain, he was out recruiting personnel for a new international data processing company called the Perot Systems Corporation and talking to inventors like Steven Jobs about possible electronic ventures, besides managing his own vast array of assets. He had also begun gadflying around the country, brashly expressing his impatience with the way the bureaucracy in Washington works, or "life inside the tent," as he called it. So when I called him in Texas I wasn't too optimistic about the likelihood of an extended series of interviews, essential for the kind of long, intimate close-up *Life* wanted.

"Come on down, Roy. We'll do some stuff" was all Perot drawled into the phone.

The next week we were bouncing together over the waves of an anonymous lake (he wouldn't let me name it in the *Life* article for fear of kidnappers) at seventy-five miles an hour in one of his two Cigarette boats, which he proceeded to demonstrate was also dandy for high-speed water skiing. After that he hopped into a miniature, fire-engine-red Hovercraft to show me how he could make it fly over tiny islands and sandbars. But his pride and joy was a long tubular-shaped craft powered by a pair of Pratt & Whitney airplane jet engines that he bragged would have gone much faster and been much more fun for us to ride than anything else in his flotilla. Thank goodness, it was laid up for repairs. He loved aquatic speed, he said, and acted as if he were capable of just about any physical feat that involved going fast on the water. So it wasn't surprising to hear that one of the participants at a roast honoring him just a few nights before I arrived had exclaimed: "Ross Perot was hit by a speedboat while walking on Lake Dallas."

Even on dry land, most of my interviews were conducted while Perot was in motion. For the next five days we tooled all over Dallas with the billionaire behind the wheel of his Chevy, jetted across Texas in one of his Gulfstreams, and helicoptered around the 20,000-acre "metroplex" northeast of Fort Worth that he and Ross Jr. were developing into an industrial park with an 8,000-foot runway now called Alliance Airport for giant cargo planes, surrounded by ample space for factories and warehouses. "When the city spreads north," announced Perot, "we'll be waiting." He called such profitable foresight "a kind of tunnel vision that can lock on to things." Then he added: "Successful people have the ability to lock on."

But Perot, I discovered, didn't let his enormous financial success interfere with his instinctive frugality. Although he had rained gifts totaling more than $100 million on universities, hospitals, and other nonprofit organizations, including a new symphony hall for Dallas, a 690-year-old copy of the Magna Carta for the National Archives in Philadelphia, even twenty prize Tennessee Walking Horses for New York City's mounted police, when we ate lunch near his office it was at Dickey's Barbecue, where he suggested we order the $3.50 chicken and okra special, which included a free ice cream cone for dessert.

Over lunch he once again renounced any interest in a political career. Yet, there was a restlessness, an urge to embark on a big new project of some kind, compressed in that little man. "The only reason I sold EDS to General Motors," he confessed, "was because I couldn't think of anything more interesting to do with the rest of my life than to help revitalize the biggest corporation in the world. I didn't need the money. I needed the challenge. But when I talked to GM's executives about meeting the competition head-on and beating them, and treating workers as human beings and not as a commodity, I might as well have been speaking Swahili."

When I pressed him more on the possibility of his running for office and mentioned that we'd both heard the battle cry "Run, Ross, run!" from an audience he was addressing at the University of Texas, again he dismissed the idea. "Just a bunch of students letting off steam," he insisted, and reminded me that he had already worked hard in his home state for public causes, first as head of the Texas War on Drugs Committee and then as chairman of the governor's Select Committee on Public Education.

"That last job made me pretty unpopular," he said. "I insisted on literacy tests for teachers and a 'no pass, no play' rule banning students from sports if they failed a course.

"But that wasn't the worst of it," he continued. "We had some school districts so rich they couldn't spend all their money, and others so poor they couldn't keep the lights on. I announced that we were going to redistribute the wealth. Well, you can imagine the enthusiasm for that in the legislature. Anyway, I took the gloves off and built the power structure to do it. I started making three or four speeches a day all over Texas. Ranchers would sit there with their hats pulled down and squintin' and listenin'. I'd tell them it costs more to keep a man in the penitentiary than it does to send him to Harvard. One old guy stands up, pushes his hat back, and says, 'Hell, Ross, the answer's simple. Send those jailbirds to Harvard.' "

Despite all his protestations, it was obvious Ross Perot loved being out on the hustings regaling his fellow Texans. Listening to him hold court in his seventeenth-floor office tower filled with Norman Rockwell originals, a Gilbert Stuart portrait of George Washington, Frederic Remington bronzes, carved wooden eagles, and myriad other patriotic artifacts, the man seemed a strange mixture—part Boy Scout, part business promoter, part college professor, part stand-up comedian, and part country bumpkin. During our conversations I could visualize him mounting the stump and giving the same spiel to the country that he was giving me for my magazine article.

"We've got to clean up the mess we've made," he'd say. "America's been on a nonstop party since the end of World War Two. It's been getting bigger, better, wilder, and crazier all the time, until now everybody's snorting cocaine. We've go to stop hallucinating and realize our best days are in the future and not in the past."

Although these conversations all took place a year prior to the 1988 presidential election, well before George Bush and Michael Dukakis got into what Perot called their "mud wrestling and dirty-tricks campaign," he was already privately lamenting: "My heart aches today that there are no presidential candidates out there shouting, 'This is blood, sweat, and tears time for our country.'"

So it didn't really surprise me when in February 1992 Perot first told talk show host Larry King, "No," he wouldn't run for president and then forty-five minutes later dropped the biggest bombshell of the campaign. Yes, he'd run, and run hard, if his supporters would put him on the ballot as an independent in all fifty states.

As we now know, that "if" was answered by one of the greatest outpourings of volunteer enthusiasm ever witnessed in the country. It eventually won for Perot nineteen percent of all the votes cast—siphoning off enough of them from George Bush to put Bill Clinton in the White House. But he's been coy ever since about whether he'd try again.

When another reporter asked him about 1996, he cracked: "I'd rather undergo major surgery without anesthesia than become a candidate again." But hopscotching around the country, strutting the stage of one cheer-filled rally after another, he's given the impression that he's running for something, though it isn't clear whether it's for the presidency or just for ego satisfaction.

Perot is one of those powerful people I could never resist running after and reporting on. In my fifty-year career in journalism, the compelling urge to stalk the leaders of our day, to discover the intangible chemistry that imbues a few men and women with the power to sway, control, or even subjugate their followers, remained undiminished. With no magazine article in mind, I nevertheless contacted Perot in July 1995 to find out exactly what had propelled him to invite President Clinton and all the Republican presidential candidates for a get-together in Dallas. It struck me, here was Perot, the noncandidate, in effect summoning these political luminaries to his home turf for what he called "a three-day educational session focusing on the key issues facing America"—the budget deficit, taxation, and possible changes in the campaigning laws.

It was typical Perot. The cocky little man who tried to deliver Christmas dinners to the POWs in Hanoi, who ran a commando raid to free his own company captives in Iran, and who challenged the management of General Motors until they paid him "hush money" to stop bombarding them with his ideas was trying single-handedly to shape the 1996 campaign. "What I'm doing is good shock therapy for the country," he told me. "If these problems continue to fester, America's middle class will be destroyed and, along with it, the opportunities for our children."

But once again he uttered his old refrain, "I have no interest in politics." And he promised, "There will be no partisan sniping at any time," at the conference, which he pretended was really being sponsored by his grass-roots organization, United We Stand America. "I merely want to educate the public so they will focus on the issues facing our country and not react to the emotional tricks and slings and arrows of the campaign."

His critics, however, saw this meeting as more of a self-promotional ploy. "Ross Perot says his audition for presidential candidates will be about 'issues, issues, issues,' " quipped a New York Times editorial lambasting the conference. "But of course it will be about Ross, Ross, Ross."

No doubt about it, Perot was once again portraying himself as the Texas outrider ready to help the little guy reclaim the country from the power brokers who run it. It's an appealing image, though some of his backers may remember that when the tough questions were thrown at him by the press during the 1992 campaign, he bridled and bolted.

When he read the polls in 1995 that showed more than fifty percent of Americans want a third party, it obviously made him antsy. "The message is clear," he said. "Democrats and Republicans have to get their houses in order. And they've got to start preparing our country for the twenty-first century. Whatever I have to do to keep that message alive, I'll do." For a while I wondered, What is the whatever?

The answer came in September. Back again on Larry King Live, Perot announced the formation of the Independence Party [renamed the Reform Party], a move that caught the Republican front-runners by surprise and seized some of the limelight away from General Colin Powell.

A month later I visited Perot in Dallas. The budget impasse between Clinton and Congress that would temporarily shut down the federal government, was already underway. "My new party," he said, "is interested in bringing the country together, not in tearing it apart as the politicians in Washington are now doing."

"Does that mean you're going to run?" I asked him. Perot just grinned. It was the same inscrutable smile he gave me ten years earlier while describing how he planned to take on General Motors and revitalize that corporate giant.

"He can be the king-maker and the king-breaker," opined his former pollster Frank Lutz. "But he will never be king." Lutz, however, is now working for Republican contender Phil Gramm.

One thing is certain. Whether he becomes king or not, or just opens his billionaire's pocketbook to try to block one nominee or another, Perot will be an important factor in the 1996 campaign. "My strength is being able to motivate others," he says—a strength he demonstrated by capturing more votes than any third-party candidate since Theodore Roosevelt split the Republican Party in 1912, running (and losing to Howard Taft) as a "Bull Moose" progressive.

Perot, the late-blooming politician that he is, shows a rare combination of cunning and charisma out on the stump. His caustic one-liners and twangy sound bites are perfect for television—that "laid-back, cool medium" he told me ten years ago he'd be "too hot for, too trigger-quick in offering opinions." In fact, it is those hot, trigger-quick barbs of his that the voters love.

Many political prognosticators predict Perot's power will fade as fast in 1996 as it bloomed in 1992. But he certainly doesn't see it that way. He likes to tell the story about a man named Hondo Crouch of Luckenback, Texas, who died dancing with a pretty girl in his arms at the age of ninety-four. Politically, at least, Henry Ross Perot plans to do a lot more dancing.

Conclusions

WHAT LESSONS ABOUT WINNING, wielding, and losing power can be learned from the people in the preceding pages? Do they exhibit common characteristics? Is there some special plumage, so to speak, by which we can identify these rare birds?

Raw ambition alone doesn't explain their ability to make important things happen. There are too many individuals who aspire to greatness who get nowhere.

A rich inheritance isn't the answer either, since practically all of the individuals included in this book were self-made—with a few notable exceptions. The nizam of Hyderabad, seventh in line of princely rulers, assumed wrongly that his unrivaled wealth would enable him to preserve the independence of his state and stem the tide of India's history. Bunker and Herbert Hunt thought the fortune willed to them by their oil-baron father was sufficient for them to beat out all other speculators in what turned out to be a disastrous attempt to corner the world silver market.

But then, power isn't easily passed down from father to son, although James P. Hoffa, Jimmy's son, is campaigning for the Teamsters' presidency, promising to "bring back the glory days" enjoyed by the union under his dad.

Passing power from one leader to another without a family connection is hard enough. Despite his many years in Congress, Jerry Ford didn't wear the presidential mantle he inherited comfortably. His pardon of Nixon, critics claimed, revealed a soft-hearted chief executive.

"I was simply following the dictates of my own conscience," he said, though conscience has never proved much of an impediment to the powerful. Ford also intimated to me that he didn't care for the head-to-head confrontations with Soviet Boss Leonid Brezhnev, or his encounters with the Chinese Communist leaders, whose idea of detente confused him. During the tough cold war negotiations he gladly deferred to Secretary of State Henry Kissinger, who built his reputation as a global chess player.

Education has been cited as a path to power. Yet the most erudite and scholarly are often too introspective to aggressively seek commanding positions. And those who do may go off in unpredictable directions despite identical educations. China's premier Zhou Enlai started out as Generalissimo Chiang Kai-shek's star student at Whampoa Military Academy, but became his archenemy in the battle for control of China. And how did Zhou then survive the succession of vicious attacks by rivals who had gone through the same Communist indoctrination, retaining power right up until he died? By keeping a firm but never a grasping hand on the tiller as he helped Mao, "the great helmsman," steer the ship of state. A skillful maneuverer, Zhou knew better than to overstep his bounds.

Certain common traits of the truly powerful do emerge. Presence is important. A cool, confident exterior usually separates leaders from their frailer rank-and-file followers. In just a few months time I saw the dominating appearance displayed by Chiang Kai-shek while presiding over the National Assembly dissolve into edginess and meddling impatience as he suffered one battlefield defeat after another. His power visibly evaporated. General MacArthur exhibited a stunning presence, though in the end he became a victim of his own hubris and suffered the humiliation of being fired for insubordination.

Stamina is also essential. Having the energy and persistence to keep soaring higher usually prevents powerful people from stalling in midflight. And when they do falter, a spirit of indomitability often helps them bounce back. Ross Perot, whether he was skipping across a lake on water skis or chasing after new customers, or out on the hustings haranguing voters, appeared to me to be in perpetual motion, as did insomniac Imelda Marcos at the peak of her power. And speaking of persistence—she, after being kicked out of her palace, came back to the Philippines to win seventy percent of the votes in 1995 as the congressional candidate from her native district in Leyte.

Jimmy Hoffa demonstrated boundless energy by working eighteen-hour days, or just by the way he sprinted upstairs two steps at a time. Not even prison drained that vigor or deadened his craving for authority. But he couldn't abide not being boss, and that's what got him killed—or, more precisely, made him the FBI's missing person #75-3425.

Sensing when to press ahead and when to pull back can make the timing of powerful people appear almost infallible. Mao Zedong's military strategy hinged on surrounding his objectives and then patiently waiting until they fell by their own weight. Continental Airlines chairman Frank Lorenzo, conversely, was shorn of his power and reputation by bad timing. He pushed too hard and too fast for employee givebacks. His pilots and ground crews didn't realize that those were not the demands of a mean-spirited boss, but were brought about by airline deregulation and the cutthroat competition that followed.

In the same way, President Clinton wounded himself politically soon after he took office by plunging ahead without first selling his program to Congress. Another former Arkansas governor, Orval Faubus, doomed himself by bad timing, trying to turn back the clock on school desegregation. That brought the wrath of a president, and then an occupation army, down on his state. Never a racist, Faubus also proved that the way a leader rises to power may not indicate how he will ultimately wield it.

Failing to act quickly or not issuing precise orders can undercut a leader's power. When Eisenhower conferred with Faubus in Newport a week before he sent the 101st Airborne into Little Rock, the president thought the governor got the message. Yet as Harry Ashmore, editor of the *Arkansas Gazette*, said: "Faubus came away from that meeting believing he could get away with keeping the nine black students out of Central High until after his next gubernatorial campaign." The dire consequences of his continued defiance hadn't been made clear.

Truman, too, in his meeting with MacArthur on Wake Island, didn't indicate that he might fire the general if he continued campaigning publicly to carry the Korean War to China. "MacArthur left me no choice," Truman wrote in his diary. "I could no longer tolerate his insubordination." Truman's comment implies that he was aware of having virtually invited the general's defiance by ignoring it earlier.

Willingness to fight for a cause is another attribute of the powerful. Stubborn, proud, and uncompromising, Marshal Tito stood ready to die for Yugoslav independence. Considering Yugoslavia today, his power appears even more remarkable. With solid grass-roots backing, he succeeded in building a consensus in a traditionally fragmented country. Yet this renegade Communist, who outfought the *Wehrmacht* and dared defy Stalin, had the compassion to lend his power to one of his partisan's widows caught in an international legal battle to regain her kidnapped son. Chiang Kai-shek, by contrast, ruled autonomously with no compassion, and never built a consensus. He tried to compensate for those deficiencies by being haughty and making himself feared.

Resiliency, the ability to bounce back from defeat, usually compliments power. Walter Ulbricht, the hated East German puppet leader nicknamed *Spitzbart* because of his pointed Lenin-like beard, survived the wrath of his Kremlin masters following a bloody uprising in 1953, and kept control until he retired eighteen years later. Ronald Reagan was defeated for the Republican presidential nomination in 1976. That didn't dent his determination. He remains the only two-term White House occupant from either party since Eisenhower vacated the premises in 1960. But then, as pollster Lou Harris explained: "Reagan had an unerring instinct in knowing when to duck and when to go for the jugular."

In 1990 I spent two weeks on the streets of New York City disguised as a homeless man for an article in *People*. I wanted to find out how in our affluent society an estimated two million Americans could completely lose their resiliency and succumb to such squalor. It wasn't the drunks, drug addicts, or other derelicts that interested me. It was the seemingly sane, reasonably well-dressed drifters who had once experienced success and a certain amount of power in their careers.

Wandering about—myself unshaven and dressed in ragged clothes— I came upon a former college professor, a TV actor, an opera singer, and a fashion model whose picture had appeared on the cover of several European magazines. How could four talented, intelligent, accomplished individuals lose their drive and sink so low? Their plight, I discovered, wasn't the hard surfaces they had to sleep on, or the soup-kitchen meals that left a sour aftertaste in their mouths. It was the dehumanizing loss of dignity that had destroyed the will required for them to climb back up. But there was still another power-depleting factor. "You can live without money," one of them told me. "But you can't live without plans."

For the truly powerful, the word *plans* doesn't adequately describe their long-range objectives. They have the ability to anticipate what will come to be. A leader must have a strongly defined purpose and a clear idea of what he or she wants to do. Being able to identify a need, predict an outcome, or understand an accomplishment in advance enables a few people to steer a course that brings stunning victories— and, when this vision dims, stunning defeats.

Vision means goals, and a sure sense of how to attain them. As hockey star Wayne Gretzky said: "It's not where the puck is that counts. It's where the puck will be." Premier U Nu, the mystic premier who led Burma through twelve of its first fifteen years of independence, admitted he was a dreamer: "Slow," he said, "to go from thought to deed." Yet he envisioned how Buddhism, socialism, and democracy might be combined to create the sense of national unity that has held his country together despite its many warring factions. U Nu also foresaw what he called "the power of nonalignment," helping to convince Indonesia, India, and several other newly emerged nations not to take sides in the cold war.

Some visions are realized by virtue of a leader's strong persona, as the power-hungry Lyndon Johnson demonstrated by hounding Congress until he got the legislation needed for his "Great Society." Others bring their picture of the future to fruition by repeating a clear, convincing message. "If we do not speak," said Mao to his minions, "who will speak? If we do not act, who will act?" A romantic poet with a strong ideology, Mao was able to move China's peasants with his words as well as with his armies. He unified China by creating the myth of an unending class struggle. Yet his ability to look ahead finally faltered. The social engineering he advocated in his older years sapped the people's efforts and ingenuity.

Ronald Reagan had a vision. He came to Washington promising to cut taxes and government, and as the "Great Communicator"—a skill that he honed in Hollywood—he got his message across. The fact that he didn't achieve either goal didn't seem to mar his reputation. But then, Reagan had a way of talking himself out of trouble, while his predecessor, Jimmy Carter, got mired down in his promises.

In building a company, if the employees are aligned behind a leader with a vivid conception and purpose, that combination can produce a powerful organization, as Henry Luce proved when he formed Time Incorporated. After its acquisition of Warner Communications and Turner Broadcasting, the fledgling firm he founded in 1923 has grown into the world's most powerful media and entertainment enterprise. Today the question is, do Luce's successors have the vision and power to hold his greatly expanded empire together?

There is a more nebulous, harder-to-define ingredient that imbues a special few men and women with the urge and audacity to grab the controls and drive headlong into the future. Robin Williams, as the ruggedly individual prep school teacher in the movie Dead Poets Society, kept urging his students to "seize the moment." Moment-seizing, I believe, is one of the key characteristics of powerful people.

But while burning ambition may prod them to keep both eyes open for the big chance, the moment must be right. MacArthur ignored several warning signals and seized the wrong moment in 1950 to chase the North Koreans up to the Manchurian border, just when Mao's Chinese forces were poised to enter the war.

Perot is a moment-seizer, for sure. In 1992 he decided the time was ripe (and the electorate ready) for an independent candidate to run for president, and proved he was right by winning a surprising nineteen percent of the vote. Recently he announced the formation of a third party, whether or not he himself becomes the candidate in 1996. Again he senses *his* time is at hand. But politicians don't always get to pick the most propitious moment to make their move. Hubert Humphrey's presidential campaign was spoiled before it got started—ironically by the Vietnam War protesters with whom he sympathized.

There are also more subtle characteristics of powerful people. Creativity is one—the eye that can spy beauty in the mundane, the way the deaf old Chinese painter Qi Baishi seized on a bottle full of shrimps, crab, and crickets as the inspiration for his now-priceless scrolls. Or the way Bunker Hunt's big sister, Caroline, took a decrepit Dallas landmark and turned it into a stunning hotel.

The ability to motivate, and to inspire loyalty, are also key qualities. General Li Mi, unlike most of China's Nationalist generals, built a strong allegiance among his troops. They followed him to Burma to continue fighting the Communists after Chiang's defeat and flight from the mainland. Perot claims his knack of convincing others is the key to his power. But his mastery of a new technology—another source of power today—certainly contributed to his success.

Courage, too, combined with the willingness to gamble and take risks, can be crucial. Ace pilot Bill Odom proved his mettle, first by setting a round-the-world speed record, and then flying ballpoint-pen tycoon Milton Reynolds on a mission to find a mountain higher than Everest. Luck, likewise, is often associated with power. Odom ran out of that competing in the Thompson Trophy air race and was killed. But then, powerful people don't usually retire gracefully. They tend to stay in the race too long, after they've lost the edge that made them so strong. Chiang Kai-shek and his warlords didn't sense that their power had ebbed until it was wrested from them.

Pope John Paul II, in a somber Easter message in 1995, assailed human callousness and selfishness. "The desire for power contradicts the truth of man," he declared. Perhaps. But the desire for power is deeply ingrained in people and is clearly what will spur their most important future pursuits.

Acknowledgments

THE WRITING OF THIS BOOK has been a long voyage back to the beginning of my career as a journalist. All during this journey I was deeply grateful for the cheerful support of my wife, Helen, who never complained about all the hours I spent secluded with my word processor instead of with her. I would also like to belatedly thank William P. Gray. He not only found me, a frustrated relief worker and would-be reporter in China in 1947, and recommended me to Life magazine, but also introduced me to Helen before he died.

Photographers Jack Birns, Carl Mydans, Hank Walker, John Dominis, David Hume Kennerly, Mark Godfrey, Dirck Halstead, Grey Villet, Co Rentmeester, and Ralph Crane—my close comrades-in-arms while covering the battles described on these pages—were great morale-boosters as well as great picture-takers.

Richard Stolley, my good friend and former associate, provided much of the information about Abraham Zapruder contained in chapter 19.

Henry Muller, Time Inc.'s editorial director, and a friend for many years, was very helpful by granting reprint rights for some of the reporting and pictures.

I appreciate Beth Zarcone letting me use the extensive card catalog in Time Inc.'s picture collection, containing clues for tracking down elusive bits of background information.

Barbara Baker Burrows, Life's picture editor, assisted by Melanie deForest, were particularly helpful in finding several of the old photographs used as illustrations.

Time's erstwhile China expert, Oscar Chiang, very kindly checked the Pinyin spelling of the Chinese names, places, and words in the early chapters.

Roger Donald, my former editor and occasional luncheon companion, provided enough favorable comment to propel me forward on this project. And my literary agent Carol Mann demonstrated great patience during the two years it took to complete it.

Aside from his friendship and general encouragement, my present editor Kent Carroll deserves special mention for his guiding hand and discerning eye, particularly in accenting the book's recurring theme in the final draft of the manuscript. His assistant, Jennifer Prior, worked hard to shape the picture inserts, while copy editor Johanna Tani did a nice job spotting my miscues.

Finally, I am immensely grateful to *Life*, *Time*, and *Fortune* magazines for sending me on the odysseys during which I encountered the main characters in this book—members of the power-elite who helped shape the last fifty years of our history.

Index

291